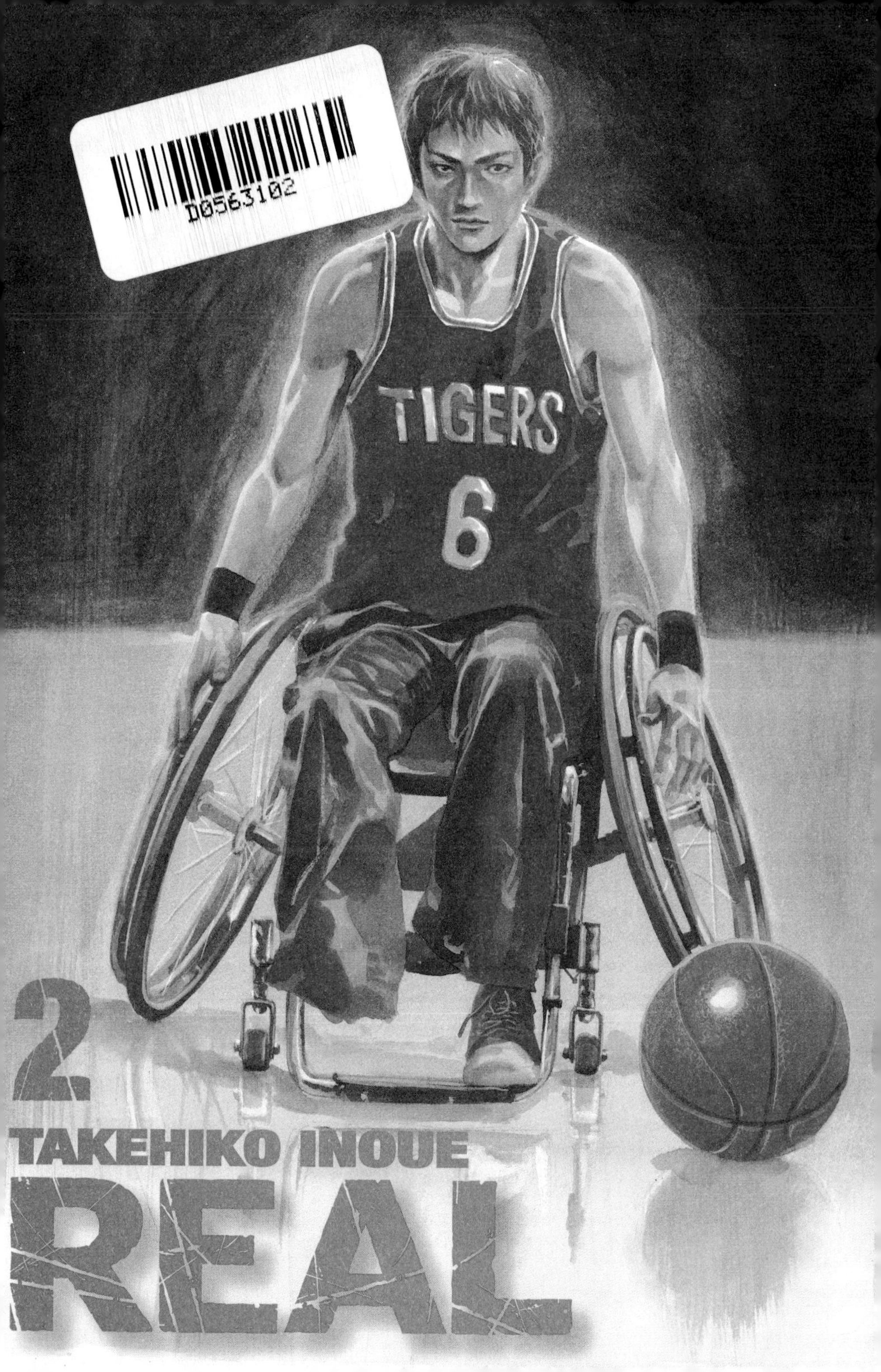
TIGERS
6
2
TAKEHIKO INOUE
REAL

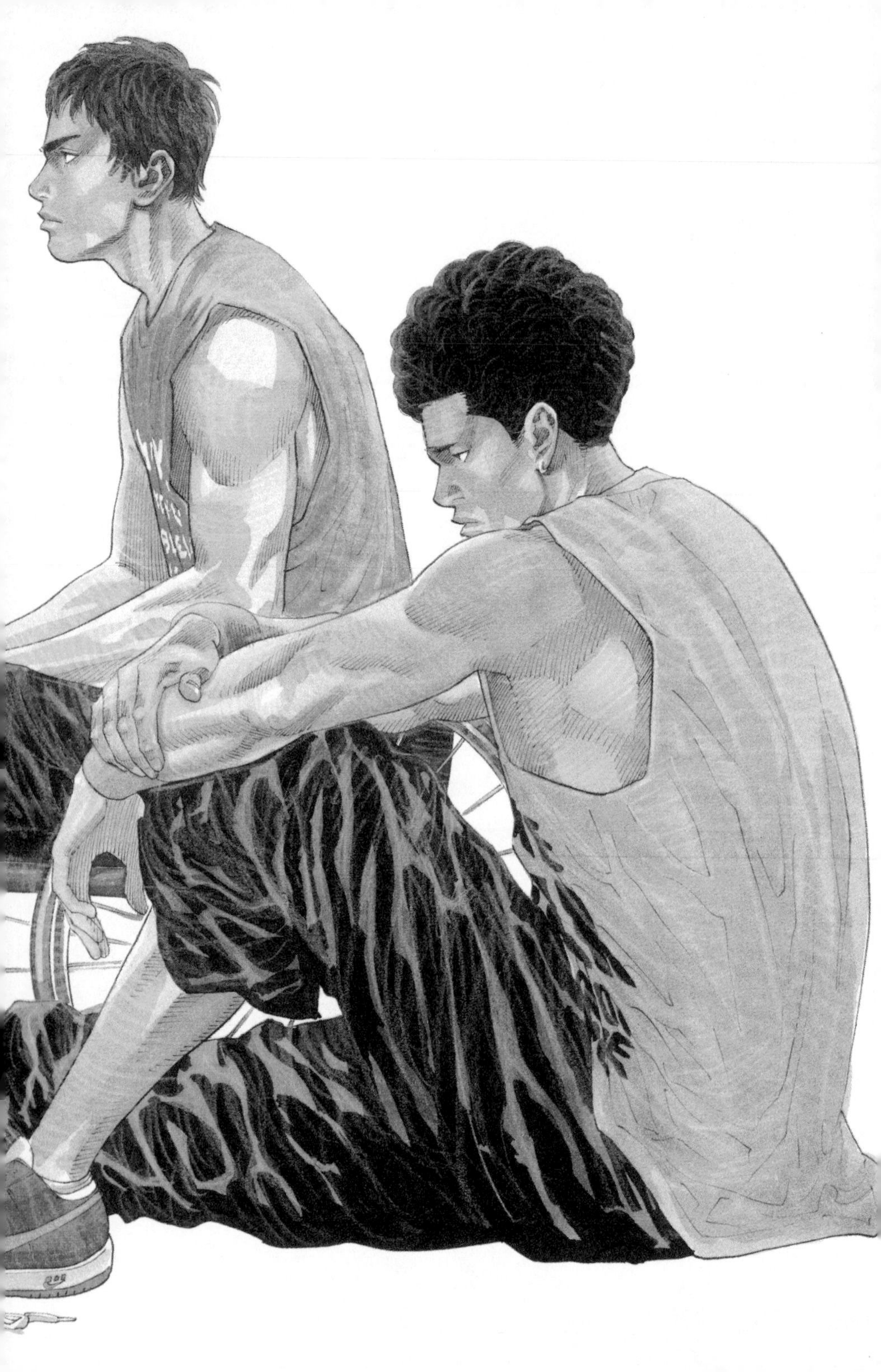

REAL

contents

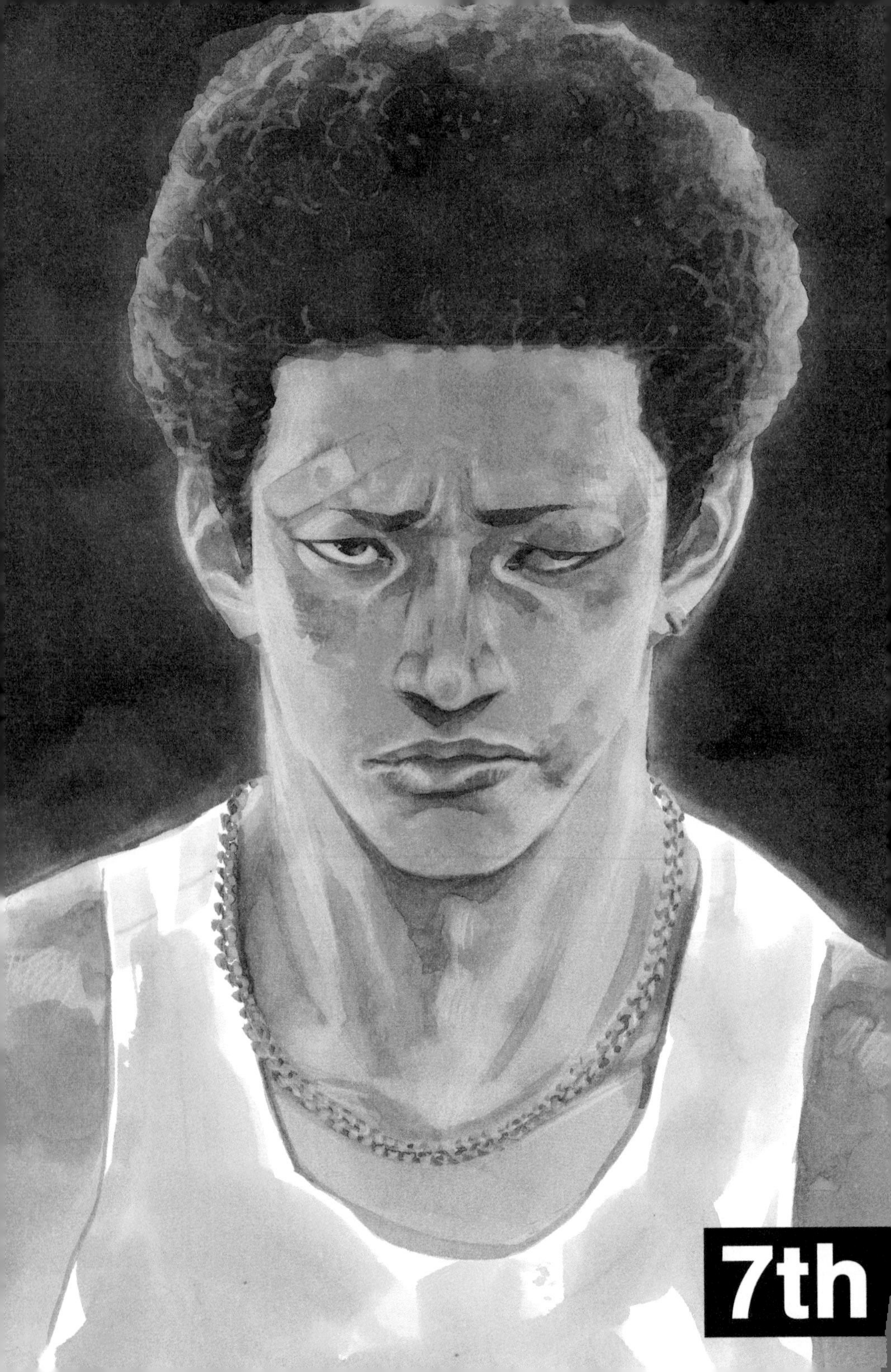
7th

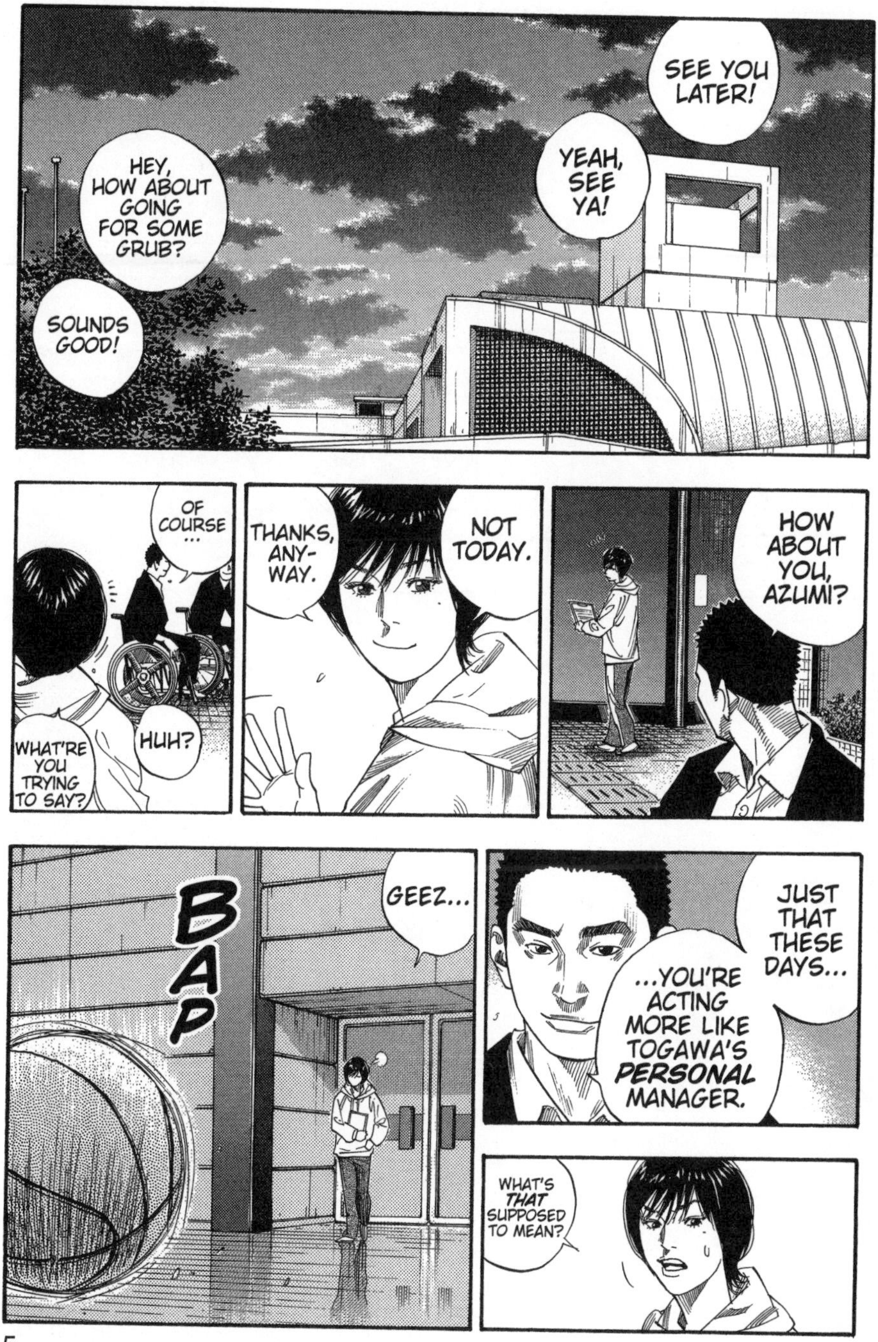
SEE YOU LATER!
YEAH, SEE YA!
HEY, HOW ABOUT GOING FOR SOME GRUB?
SOUNDS GOOD!
HOW ABOUT YOU, AZUMI?
NOT TODAY.
THANKS, ANY-WAY.
OF COURSE ...
HUH?
WHAT'RE YOU TRYING TO SAY?
JUST THAT THESE DAYS...
...YOU'RE ACTING MORE LIKE TOGAWA'S **PERSONAL** MANAGER.
WHAT'S ***THAT*** SUPPOSED TO MEAN?
GEEZ...
BAP

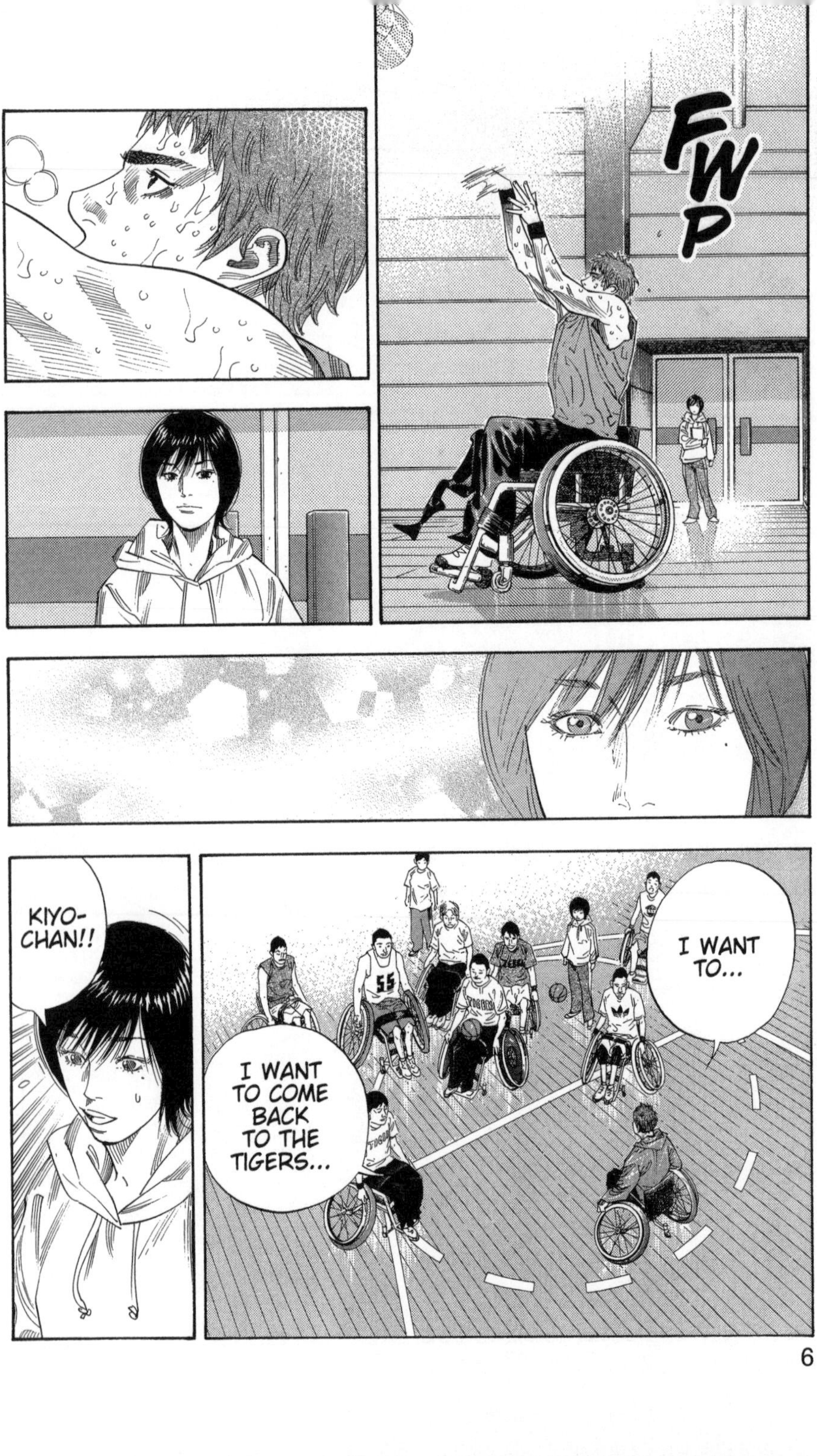
FWP
I WANT TO...
I WANT TO COME BACK TO THE TIGERS...
KIYO-CHAN!!

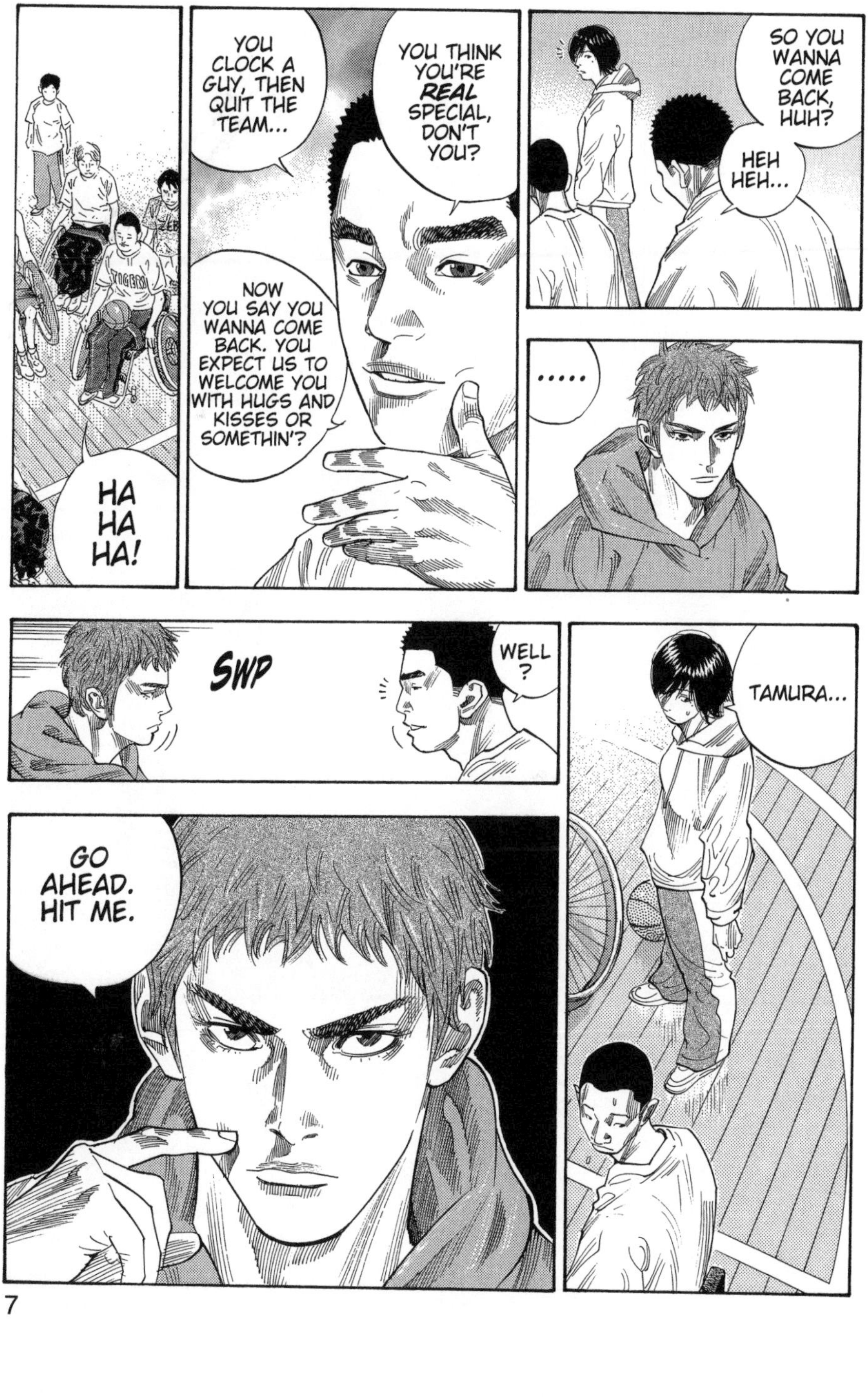
SO YOU WANNA COME BACK, HUH?
HEH HEH...
.....
YOU THINK YOU'RE **REAL** SPECIAL, DON'T YOU?
YOU CLOCK A GUY, THEN QUIT THE TEAM...
NOW YOU SAY YOU WANNA COME BACK. YOU EXPECT US TO WELCOME YOU WITH HUGS AND KISSES OR SOMETHIN'?
HA HA HA!
TAMURA...
WELL?
SWP
GO AHEAD. HIT ME.

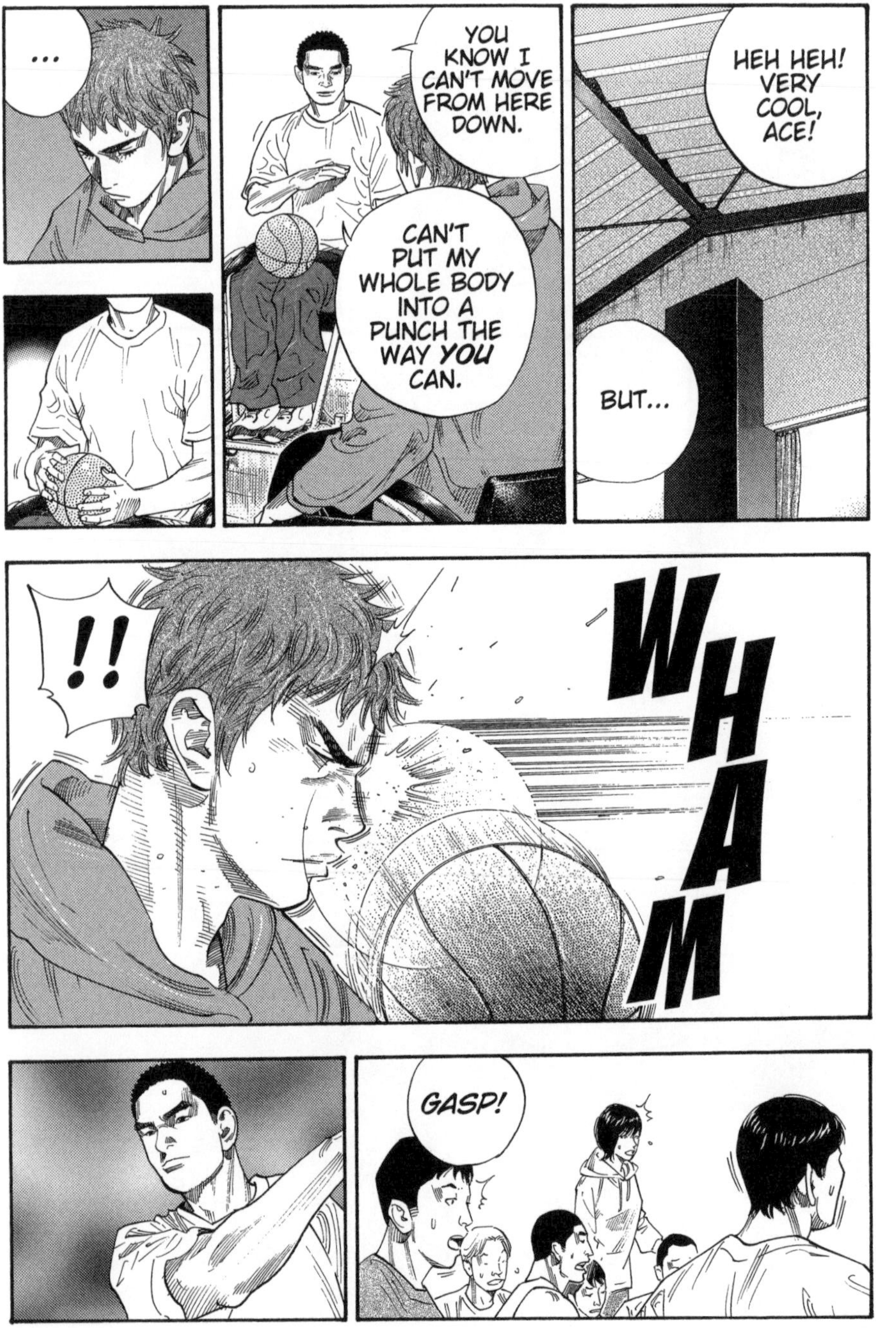
HEH HEH! VERY COOL, ACE!
BUT...
YOU KNOW I CAN'T MOVE FROM HERE DOWN.
CAN'T PUT MY WHOLE BODY INTO A PUNCH THE WAY *YOU* CAN.
...
WHAM
!!
GASP!

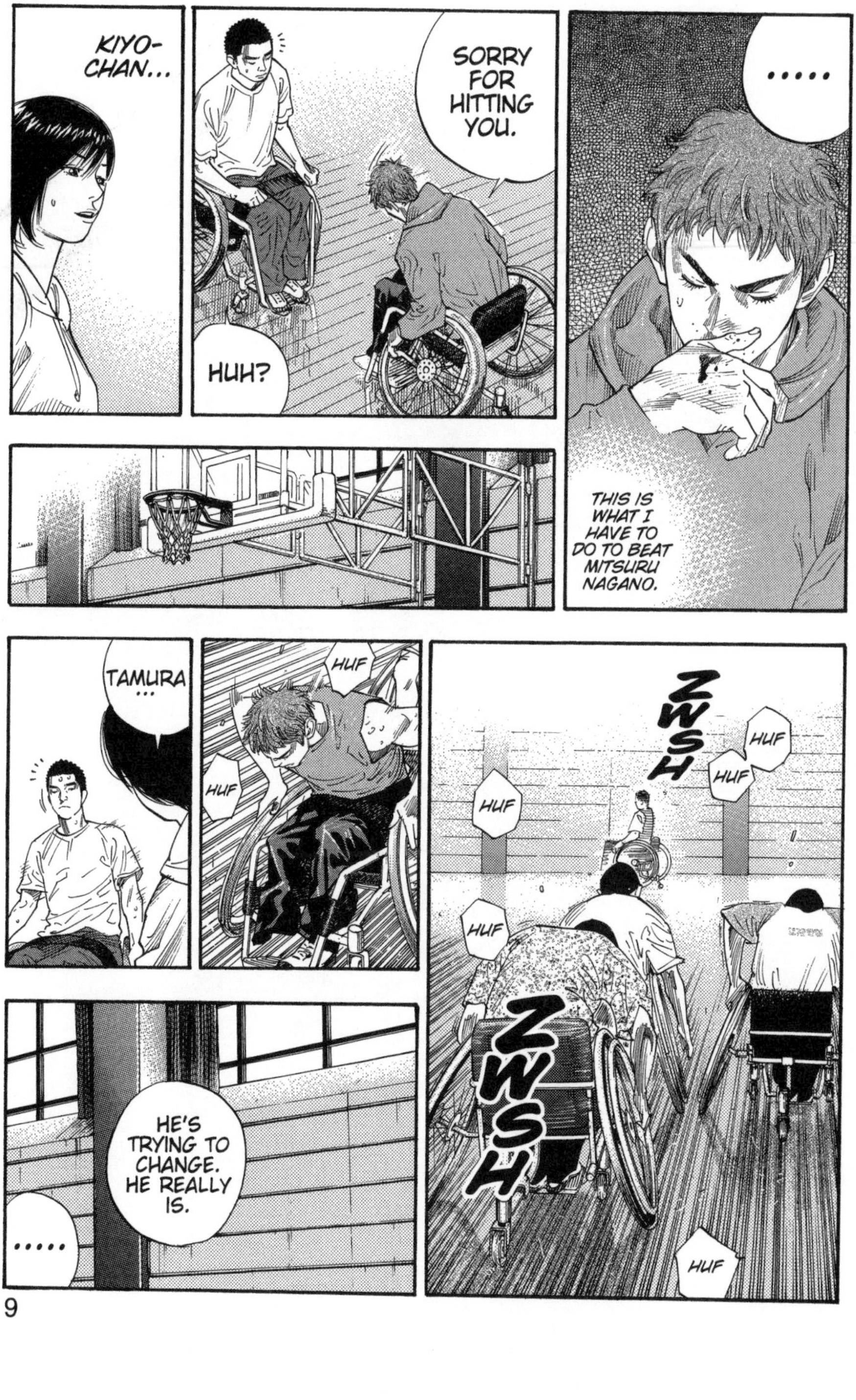
.....
THIS IS WHAT I HAVE TO DO TO BEAT MITSURU NAGANO.
SORRY FOR HITTING YOU.
HUH?
KIYO-CHAN...
ZWSH
HUF
HUF
HUF
HUF
ZWSH
HUF
HUF
HUF
TAMURA...
HE'S TRYING TO CHANGE. HE REALLY IS.
.....

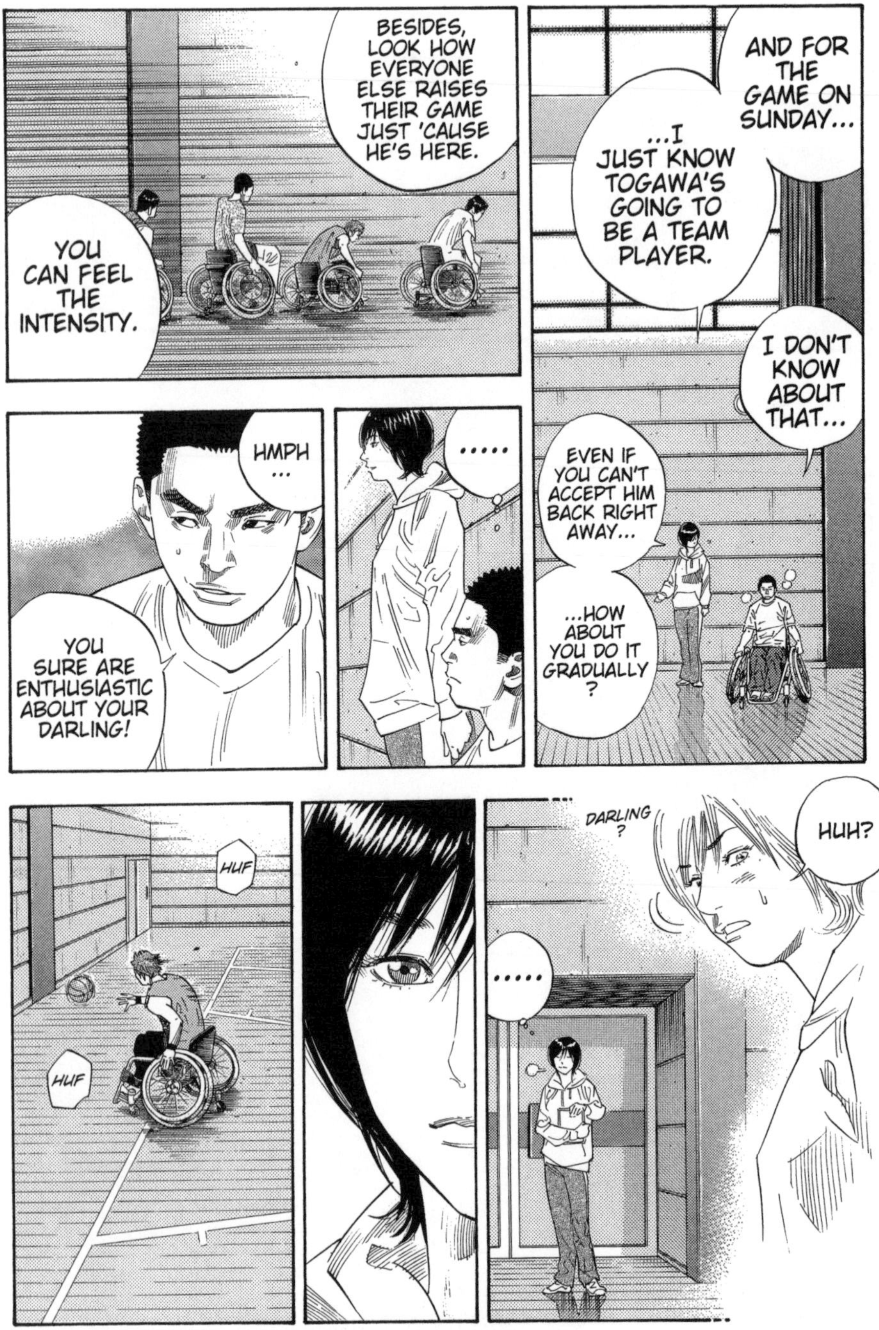
AND FOR THE GAME ON SUNDAY...
...I JUST KNOW TOGAWA'S GOING TO BE A TEAM PLAYER.
I DON'T KNOW ABOUT THAT...
EVEN IF YOU CAN'T ACCEPT HIM BACK RIGHT AWAY...
...HOW ABOUT YOU DO IT GRADUALLY?
BESIDES, LOOK HOW EVERYONE ELSE RAISES THEIR GAME JUST 'CAUSE HE'S HERE.
YOU CAN FEEL THE INTENSITY.
.....
HMPH ...
YOU SURE ARE ENTHUSIASTIC ABOUT YOUR DARLING!
HUH?
DARLING?
.....
HUF
HUF

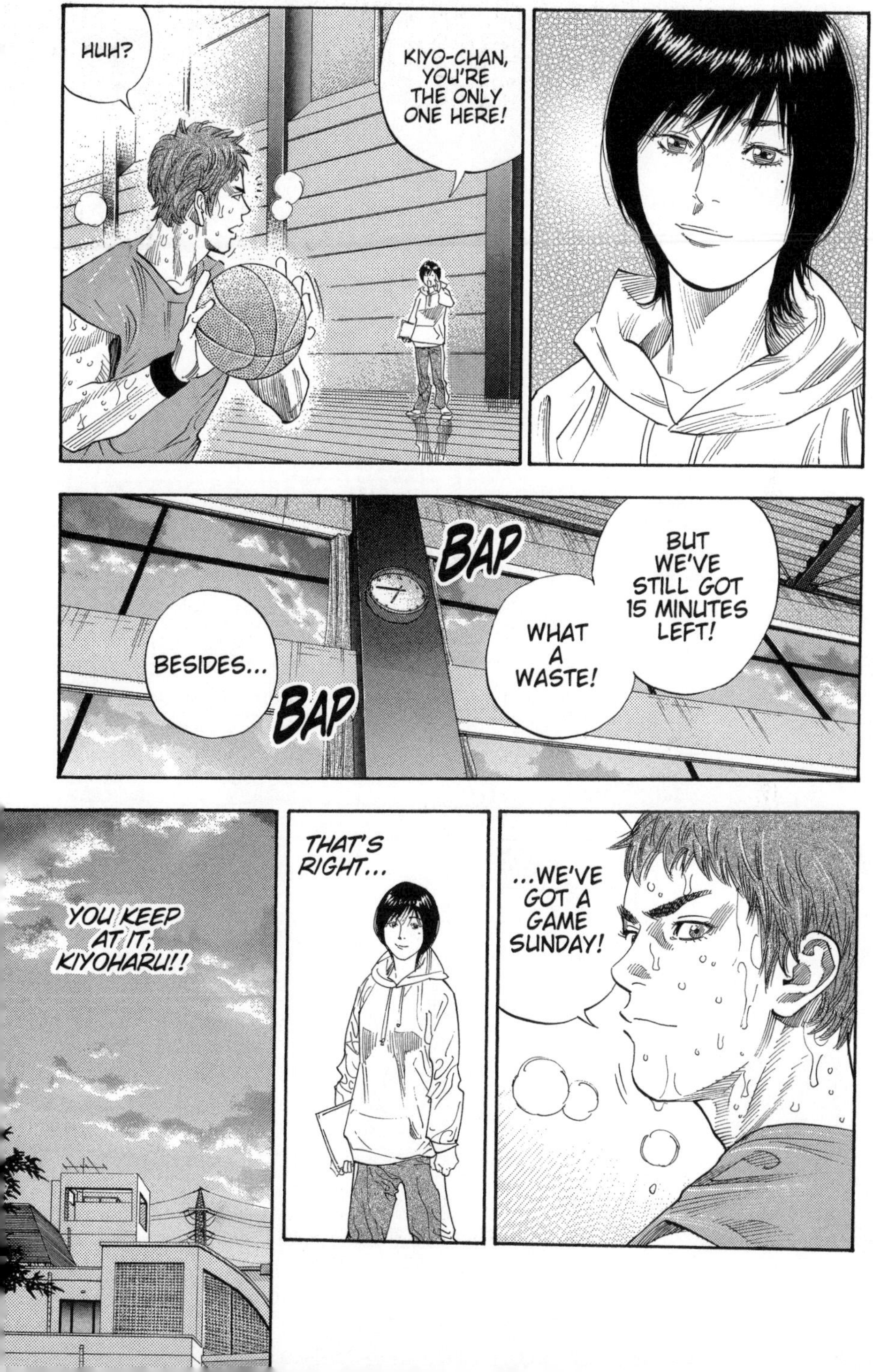
KIYO-CHAN, YOU'RE THE ONLY ONE HERE!
HUH?
BUT WE'VE STILL GOT 15 MINUTES LEFT!
WHAT A WASTE!
BAP
BESIDES...
BAP
...WE'VE GOT A GAME SUNDAY!
THAT'S RIGHT...
YOU KEEP AT IT, KIYOHARU!!

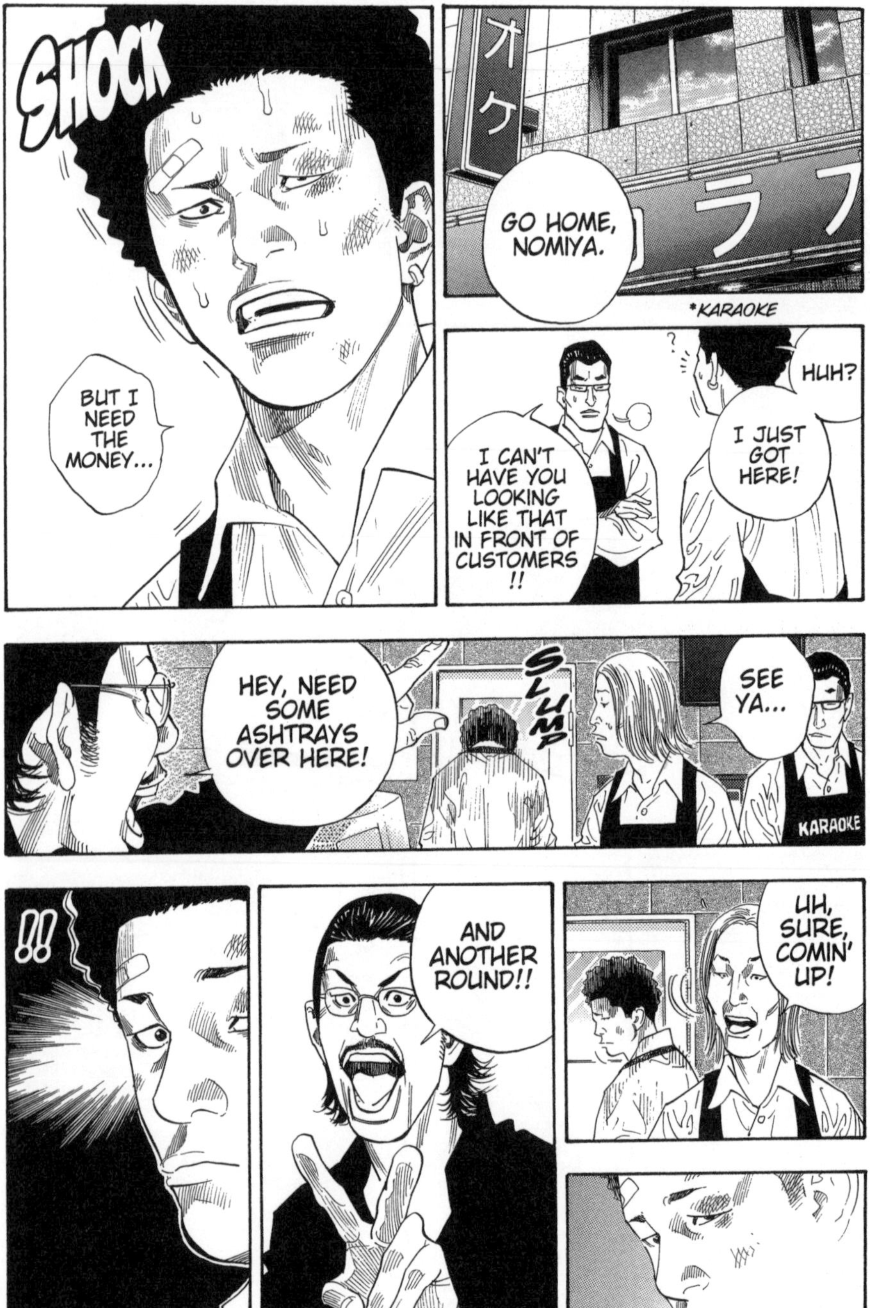
GO HOME, NOMIYA.
*KARAOKE
HUH?
I JUST GOT HERE!
I CAN'T HAVE YOU LOOKING LIKE THAT IN FRONT OF CUSTOMERS!!
SHOCK
BUT I NEED THE MONEY...
SEE YA...
KARAOKE
SLUMP
HEY, NEED SOME ASHTRAYS OVER HERE!
UH, SURE, COMIN' UP!
AND ANOTHER ROUND!!
!!

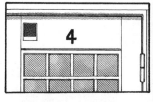

KNOCK
KNOCK

C'MON,
MAN!

PUNK
!!

...LIKE
A....

YOUR
ASH-
TRAYS.

?!

KONK

NNGH!

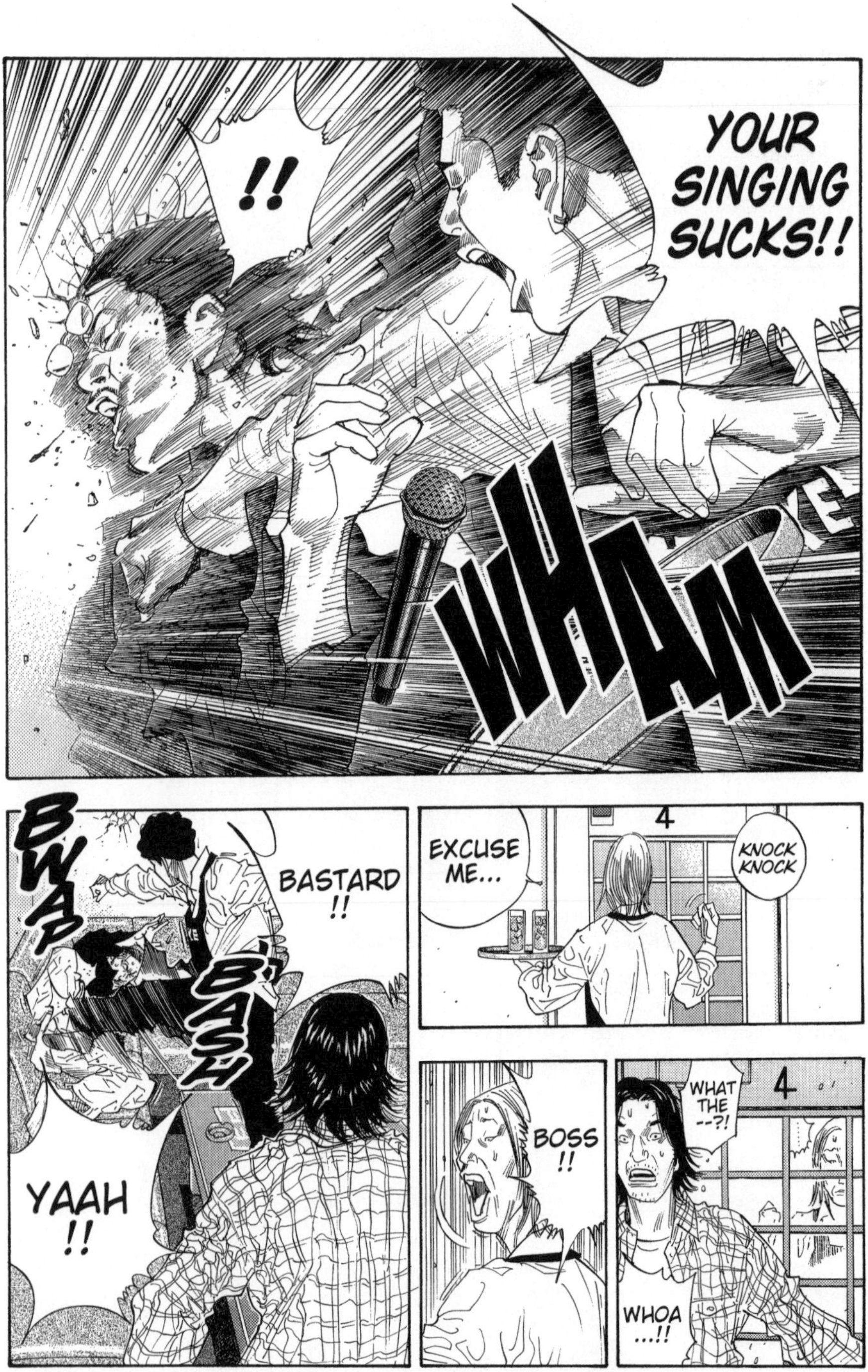
YOUR SINGING SUCKS!!
!!
WHAM
KNOCK KNOCK
EXCUSE ME...
WHAT THE --?!
WHOA ...!!
BOSS !!
BASTARD !!
BWAP
BASH
YAAH !!

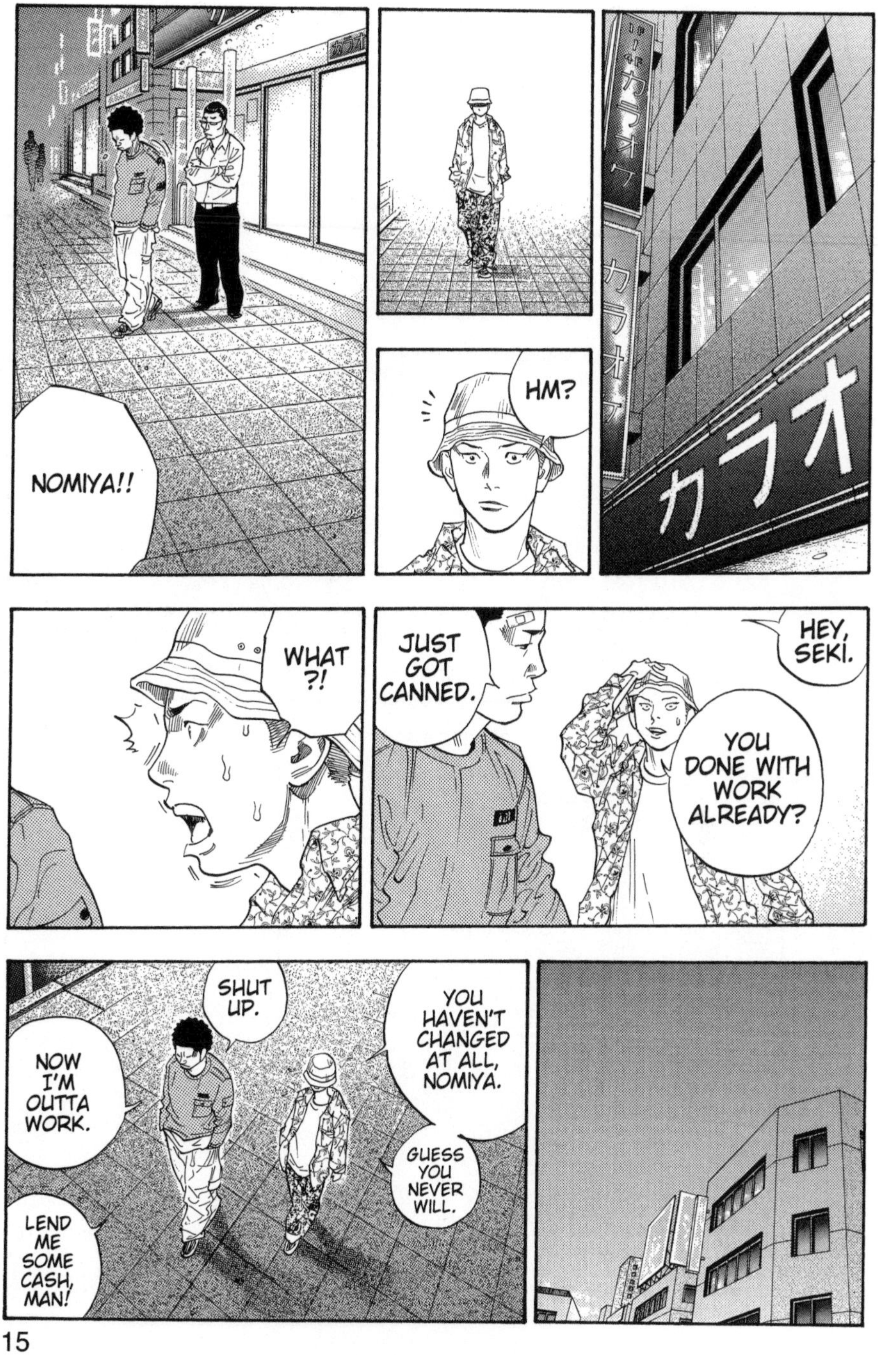
カラオケ
カラオ
HM?
NOMIYA!!
HEY, SEKI.
YOU DONE WITH WORK ALREADY?
JUST GOT CANNED.
WHAT?!
YOU HAVEN'T CHANGED AT ALL, NOMIYA.
SHUT UP.
GUESS YOU NEVER WILL.
NOW I'M OUTTA WORK.
LEND ME SOME CASH, MAN!

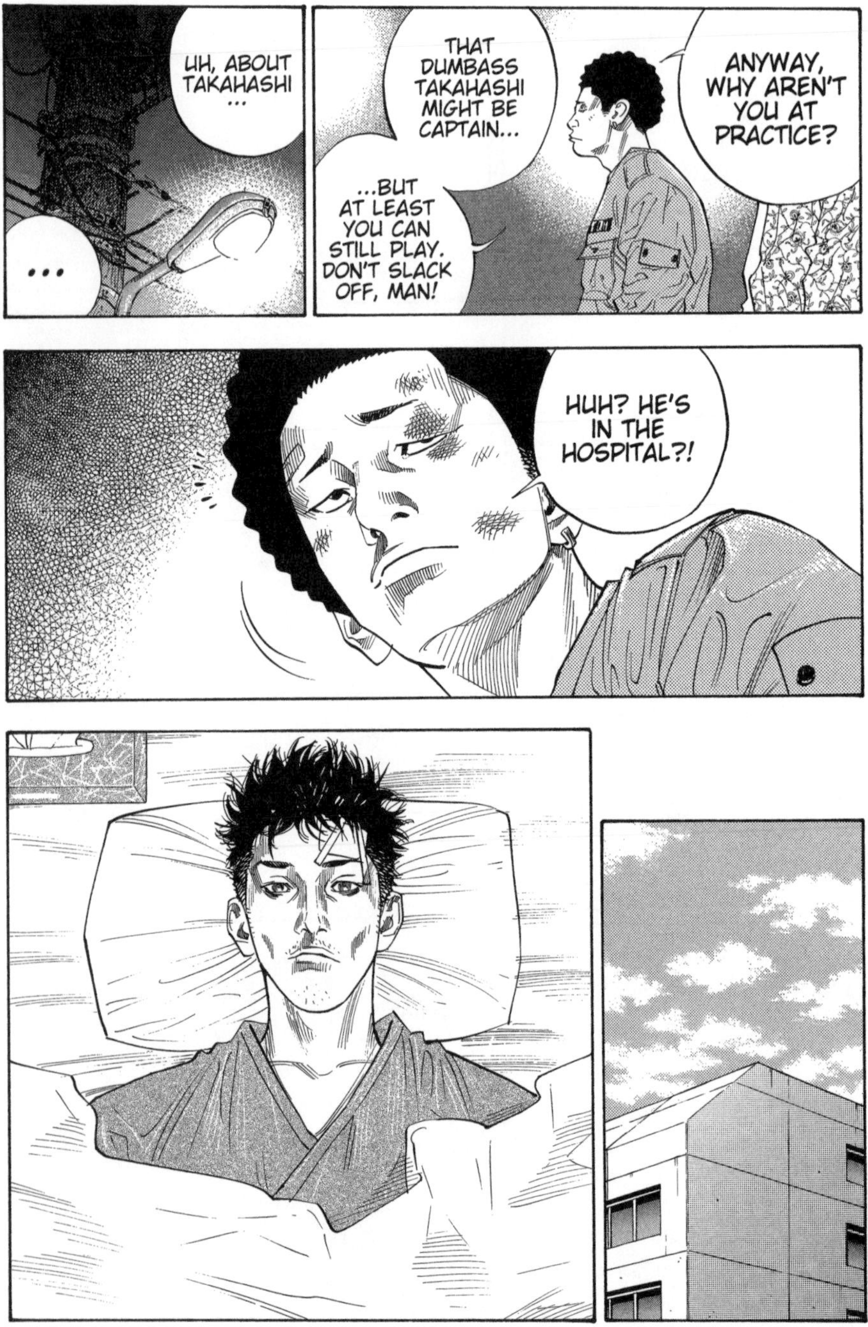
ANYWAY, WHY AREN'T YOU AT PRACTICE?
THAT DUMBASS TAKAHASHI MIGHT BE CAPTAIN...
...BUT AT LEAST YOU CAN STILL PLAY. DON'T SLACK OFF, MAN!
UH, ABOUT TAKAHASHI ...
...
HUH? HE'S IN THE HOSPITAL?!

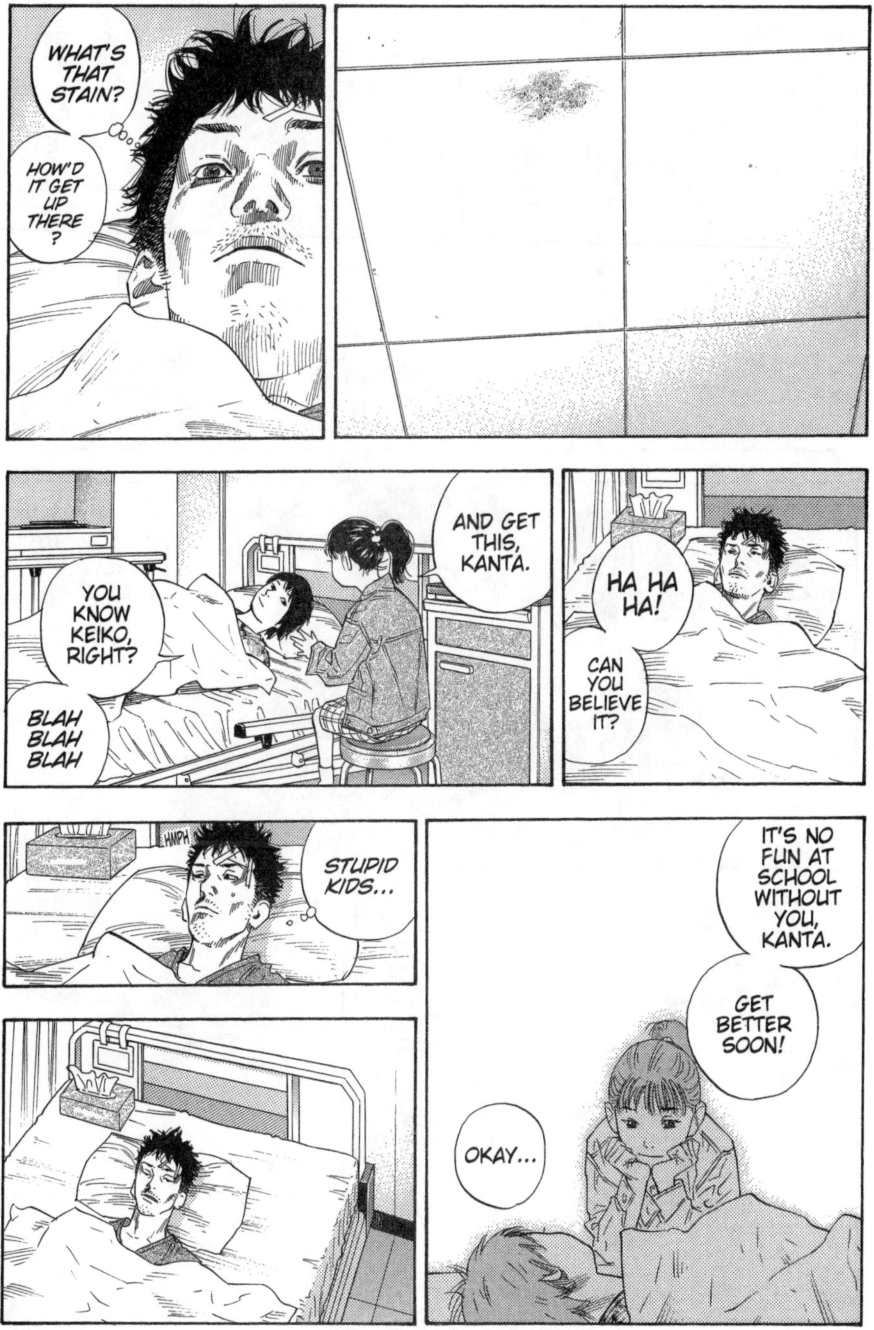
WHAT'S THAT STAIN?
HOW'D IT GET UP THERE?
HA HA HA!
CAN YOU BELIEVE IT?
AND GET THIS, KANTA.
YOU KNOW KEIKO, RIGHT?
BLAH BLAH BLAH
IT'S NO FUN AT SCHOOL WITHOUT YOU, KANTA.
GET BETTER SOON!
OKAY...
HMPH
STUPID KIDS...

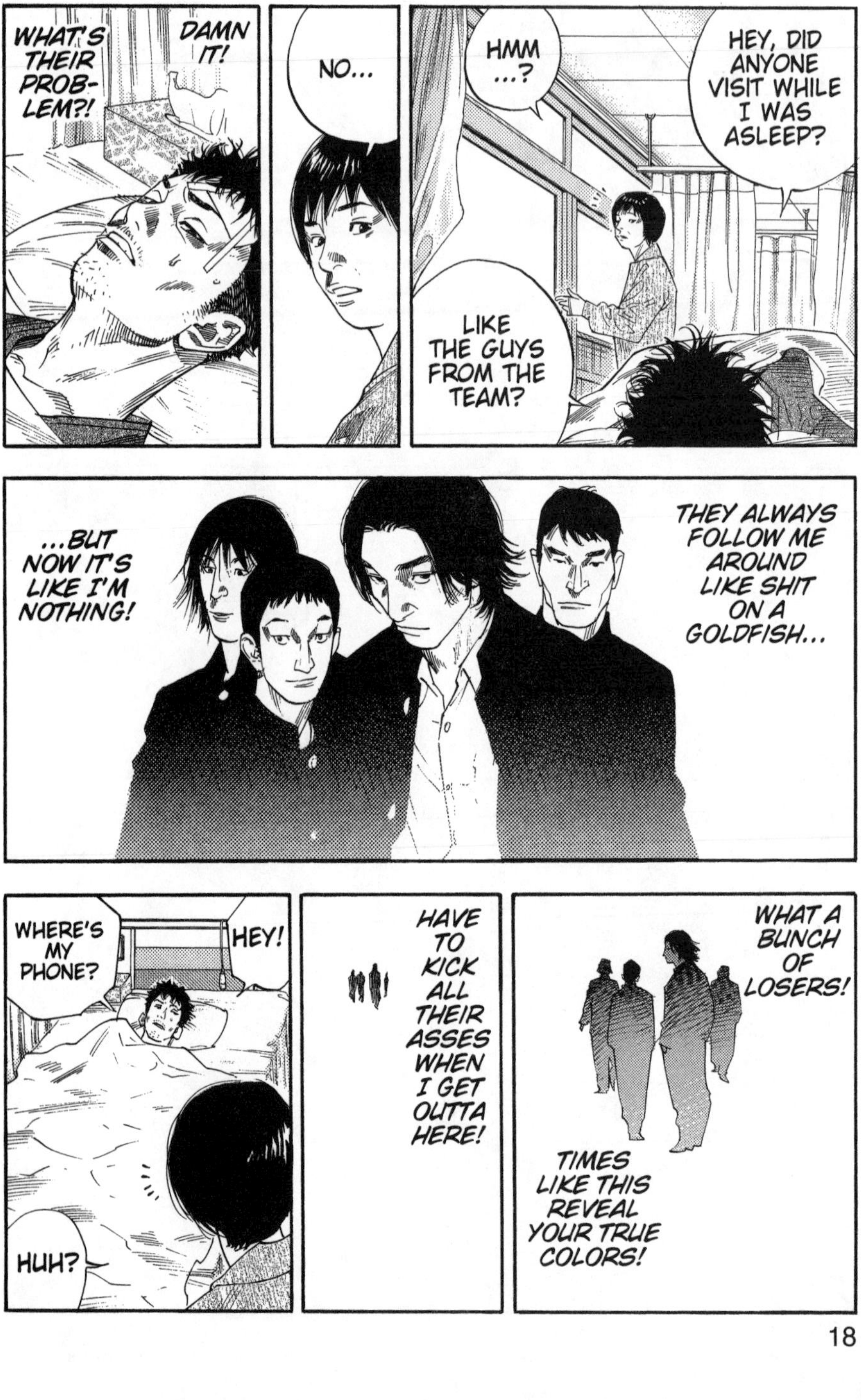
HEY, DID ANYONE VISIT WHILE I WAS ASLEEP?
HMM ...?
LIKE THE GUYS FROM THE TEAM?
NO...
DAMN IT!
WHAT'S THEIR PROB-LEM?!
THEY ALWAYS FOLLOW ME AROUND LIKE SHIT ON A GOLDFISH...
...BUT NOW IT'S LIKE I'M NOTHING!
WHAT A BUNCH OF LOSERS!
TIMES LIKE THIS REVEAL YOUR TRUE COLORS!
HAVE TO KICK ALL THEIR ASSES WHEN I GET OUTTA HERE!
HEY!
WHERE'S MY PHONE?
HUH?

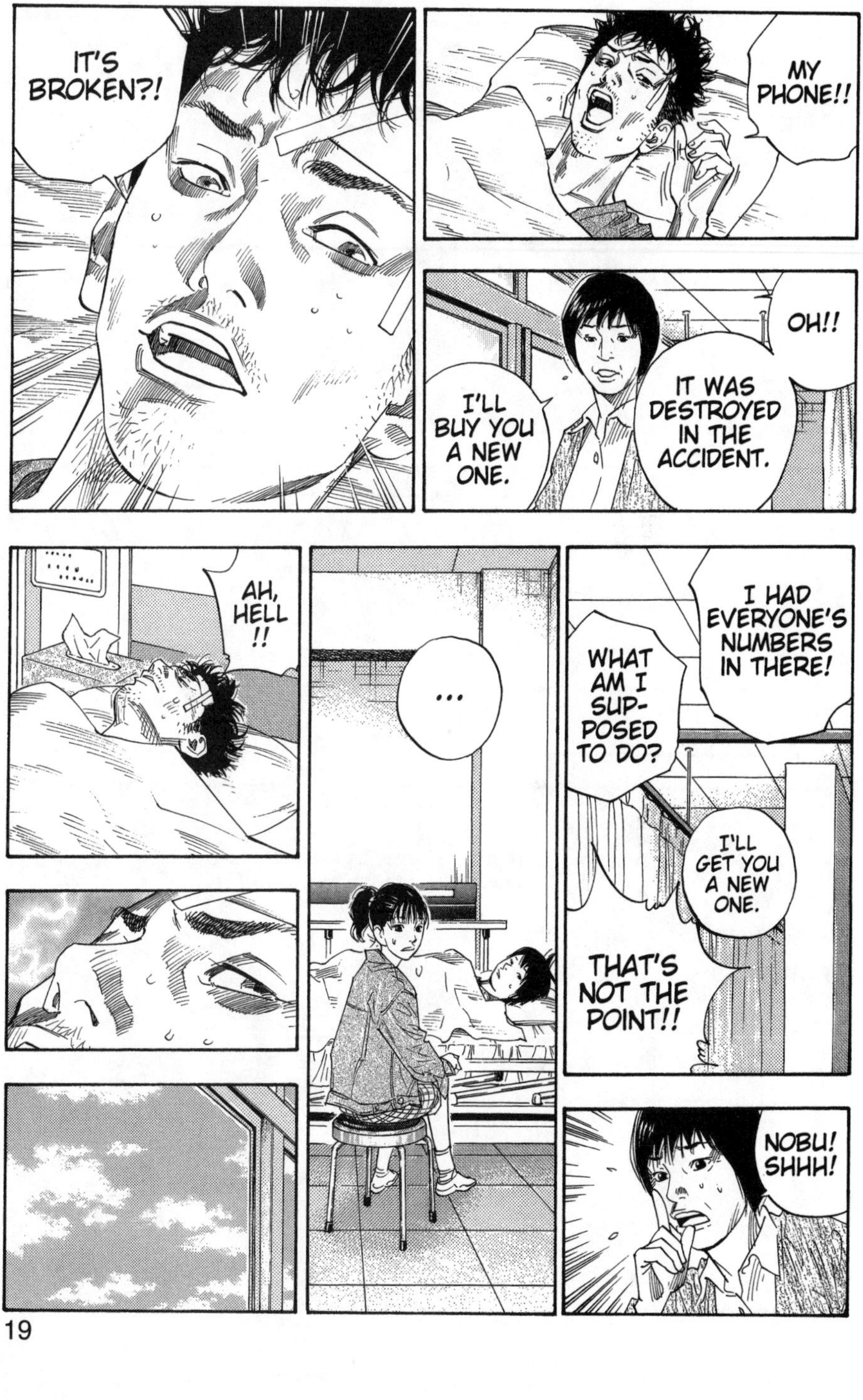
MY PHONE!!
OH!!
IT WAS DESTROYED IN THE ACCIDENT.
I'LL BUY YOU A NEW ONE.
IT'S BROKEN?!
I HAD EVERYONE'S NUMBERS IN THERE!
WHAT AM I SUP-POSED TO DO?
I'LL GET YOU A NEW ONE.
THAT'S NOT THE POINT!!
NOBU! SHHH!
...
AH, HELL!!

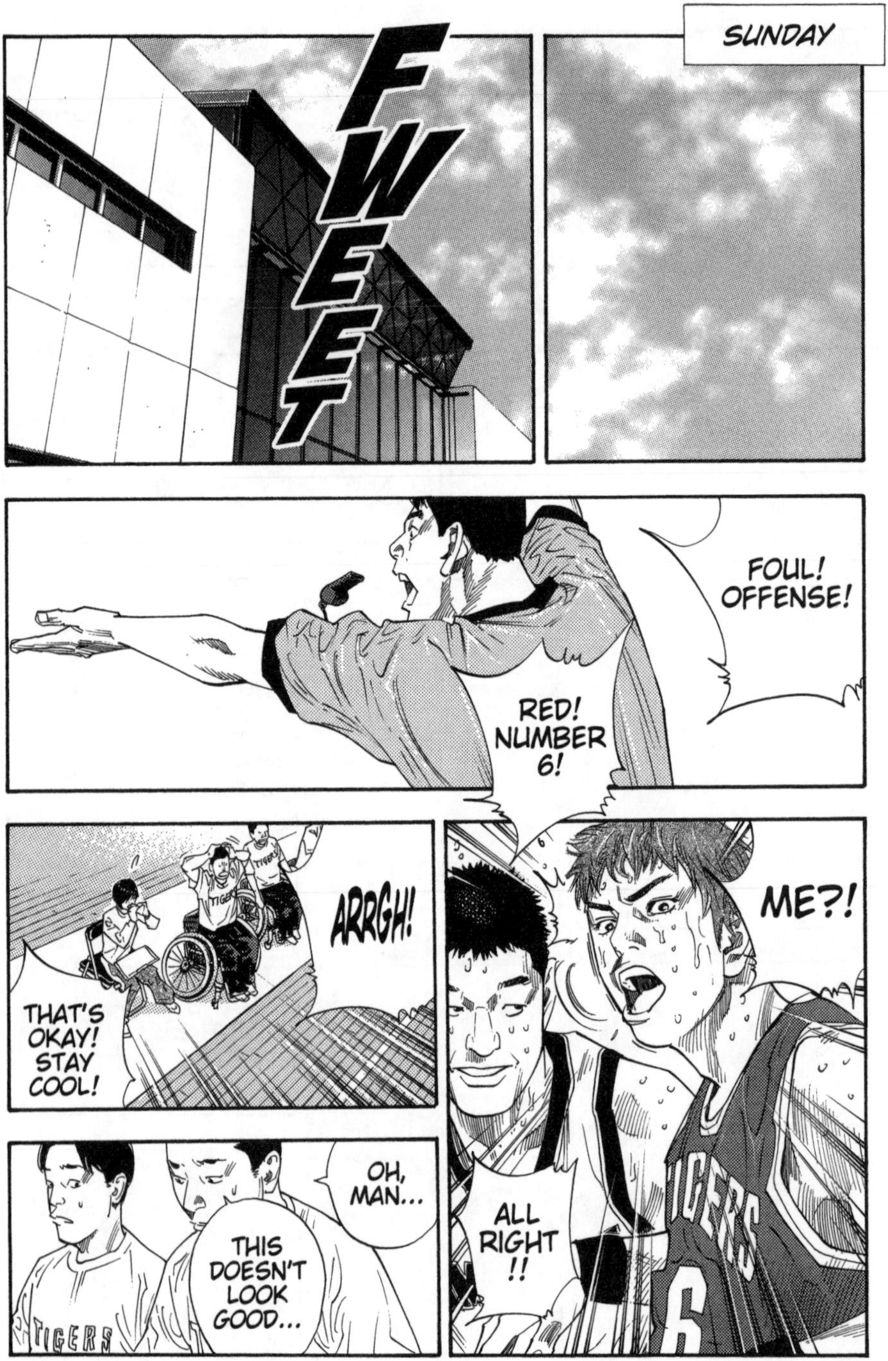
SUNDAY
FWEET
FOUL! OFFENSE!
RED! NUMBER 6!
ME?!
ALL RIGHT !!
ARRGH!
THAT'S OKAY! STAY COOL!
OH, MAN...
THIS DOESN'T LOOK GOOD...

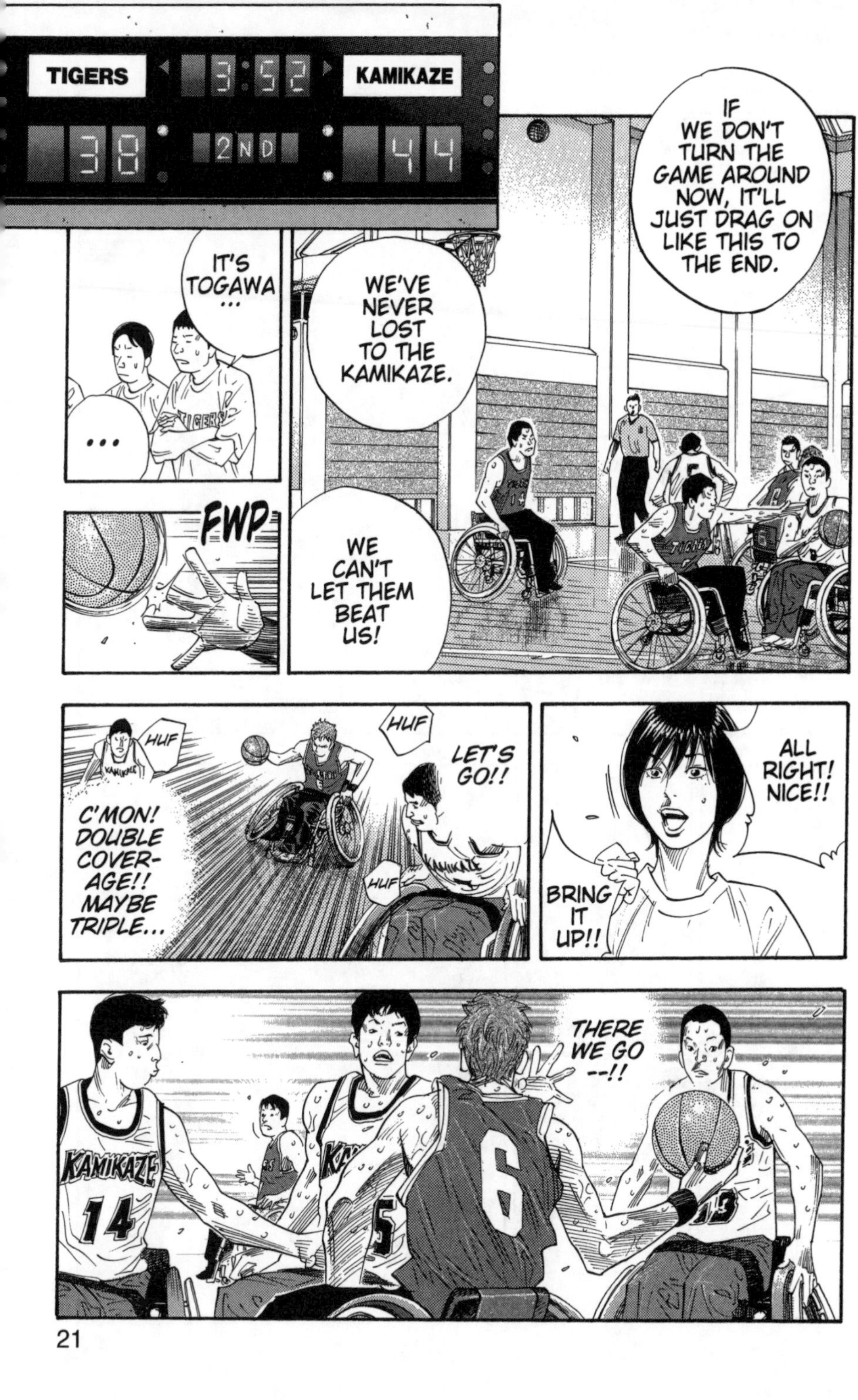
TIGERS
3:52
KAMIKAZE
38
2ND
44
IF WE DON'T TURN THE GAME AROUND NOW, IT'LL JUST DRAG ON LIKE THIS TO THE END.
WE'VE NEVER LOST TO THE KAMIKAZE.
WE CAN'T LET THEM BEAT US!
IT'S TOGAWA ...
...
FWP
ALL RIGHT! NICE!!
BRING IT UP!!
HUF
LET'S GO!!
HUF
HUF
C'MON! DOUBLE COVER-AGE!! MAYBE TRIPLE...
KAMIKAZE
THERE WE GO --!!
KAMIKAZE
14
6

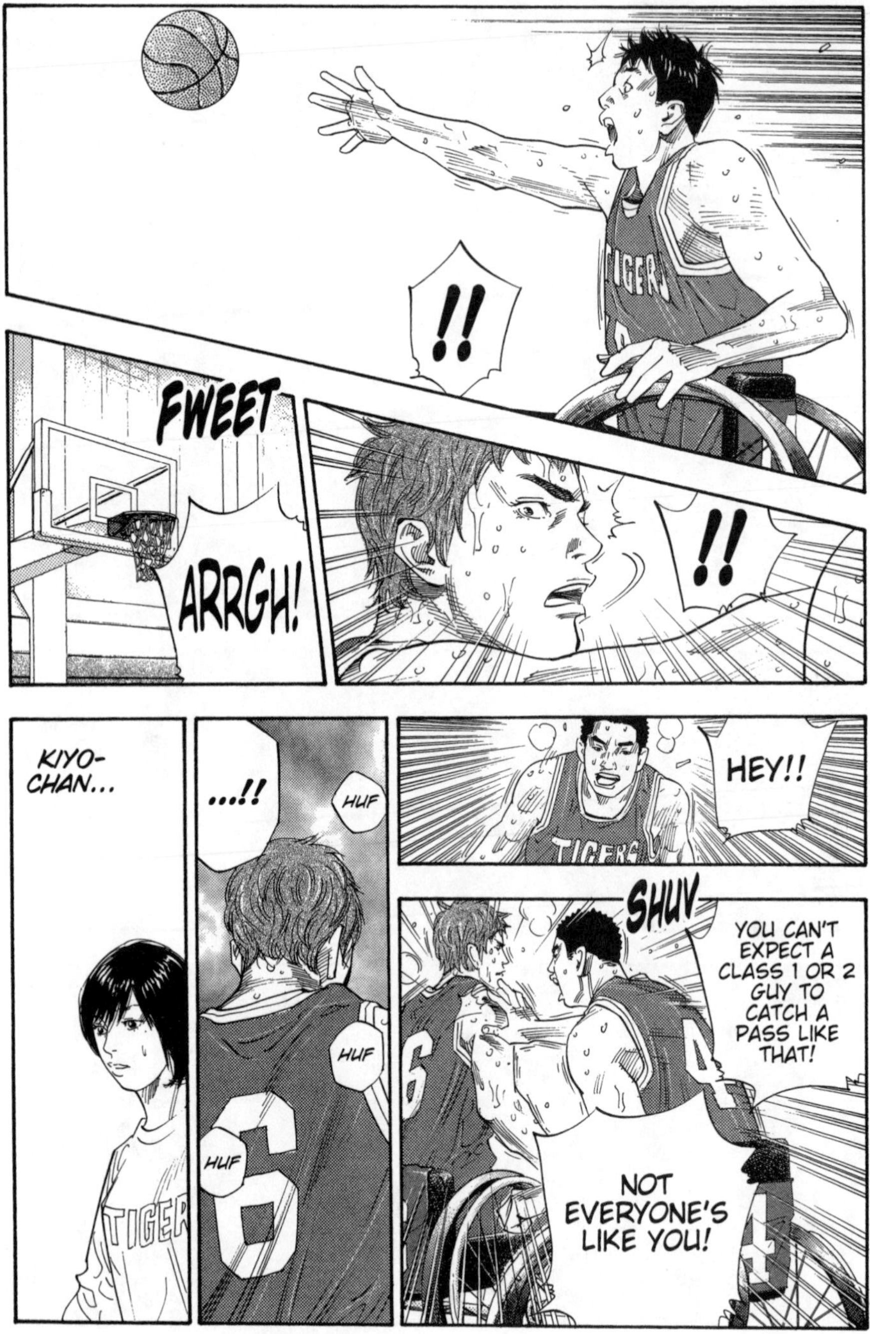
!!
!!
FWEET
ARRGH!
HEY!!
SHUV
YOU CAN'T EXPECT A CLASS 1 OR 2 GUY TO CATCH A PASS LIKE THAT!
NOT EVERYONE'S LIKE YOU!
...!!
HUF
HUF
HUF
KIYO-CHAN...

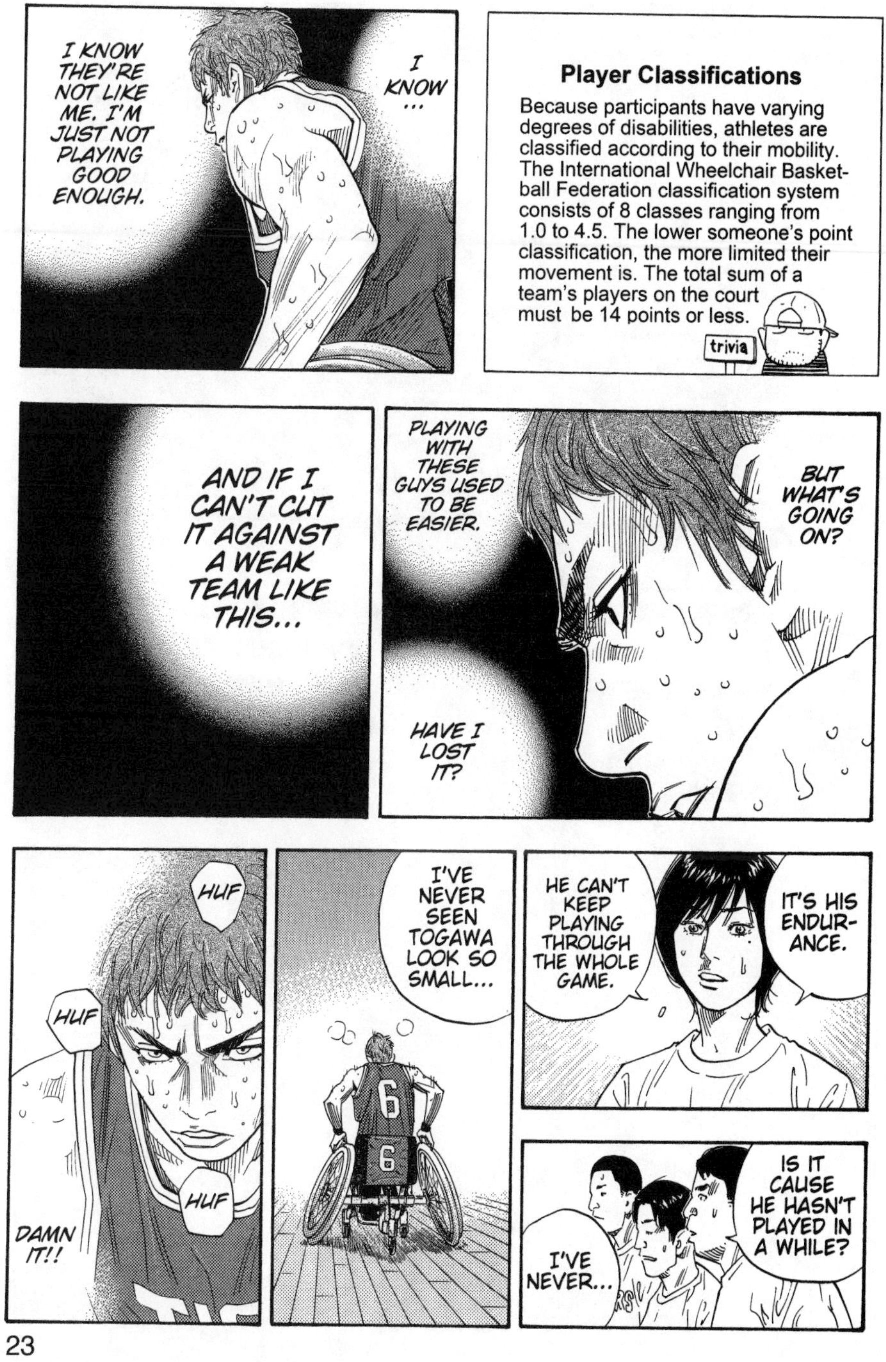
Player Classifications
Because participants have varying degrees of disabilities, athletes are classified according to their mobility. The International Wheelchair Basketball Federation classification system consists of 8 classes ranging from 1.0 to 4.5. The lower someone's point classification, the more limited their movement is. The total sum of a team's players on the court must be 14 points or less.
trivia
I KNOW...
I KNOW THEY'RE NOT LIKE ME. I'M JUST NOT PLAYING GOOD ENOUGH.
PLAYING WITH THESE GUYS USED TO BE EASIER.
BUT WHAT'S GOING ON?
HAVE I LOST IT?
AND IF I CAN'T CUT IT AGAINST A WEAK TEAM LIKE THIS...
IT'S HIS ENDURANCE.
HE CAN'T KEEP PLAYING THROUGH THE WHOLE GAME.
IS IT CAUSE HE HASN'T PLAYED IN A WHILE?
I'VE NEVER...
I'VE NEVER SEEN TOGAWA LOOK SO SMALL...
HUF
HUF
HUF
DAMN IT!!

MITSURU NAGANO IS SO FAR AHEAD OF ME...

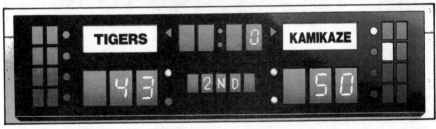

TIGERS 0 KAMIKAZE

43 2ND 50

WE SHOULDN'T HAVE LOST TO A WEAK TEAM LIKE THE KAMIKAZE.

IT'S ALL BECAUSE OF YOU, TOGAWA.

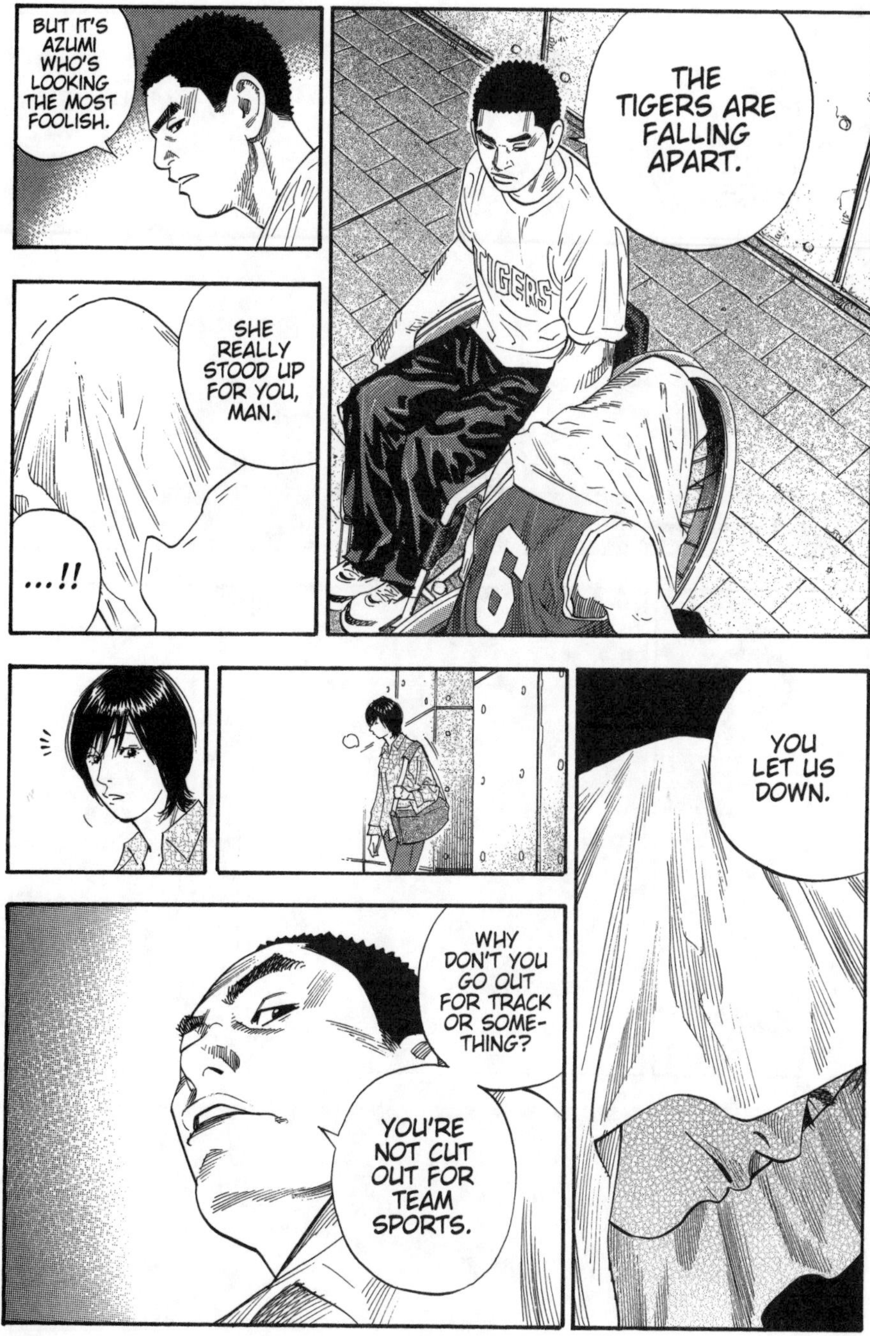
THE TIGERS ARE FALLING APART.
BUT IT'S AZUMI WHO'S LOOKING THE MOST FOOLISH.
SHE REALLY STOOD UP FOR YOU, MAN.
...!!
TIGERS
6
YOU LET US DOWN.
WHY DON'T YOU GO OUT FOR TRACK OR SOME-THING?
YOU'RE NOT CUT OUT FOR TEAM SPORTS.

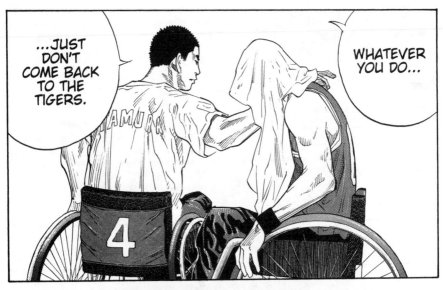

WHATEVER YOU DO...
...JUST DON'T COME BACK TO THE TIGERS.
...?

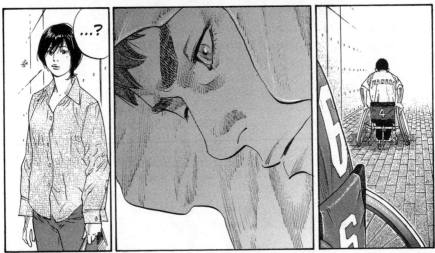

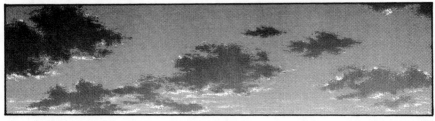

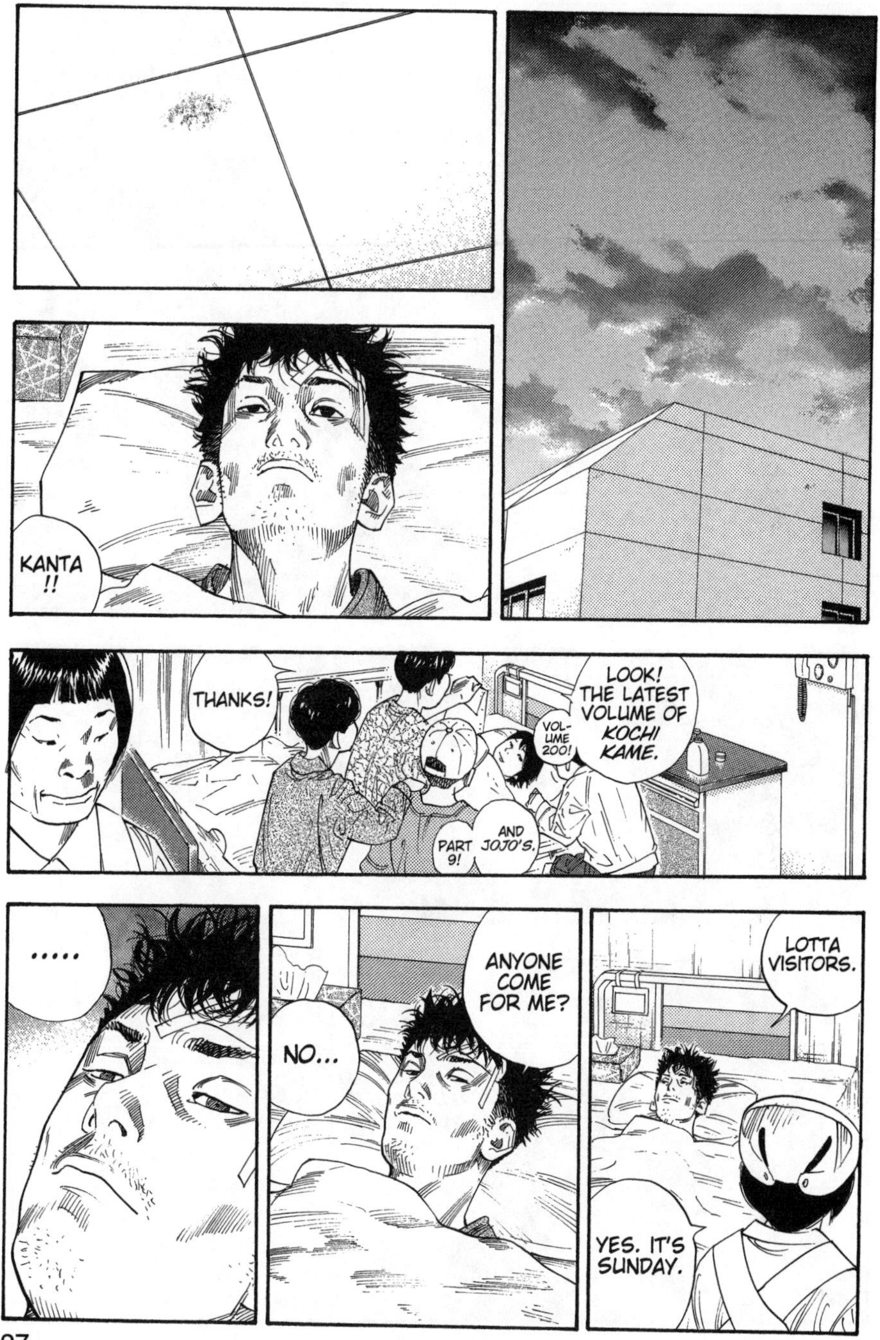
KANTA !!
LOOK! THE LATEST VOLUME OF KOCHI KAME.
VOL-UME 200!
THANKS!
AND JOJO'S.
PART 9!
LOTTA VISITORS.
YES. IT'S SUNDAY.
ANYONE COME FOR ME?
NO...
.....

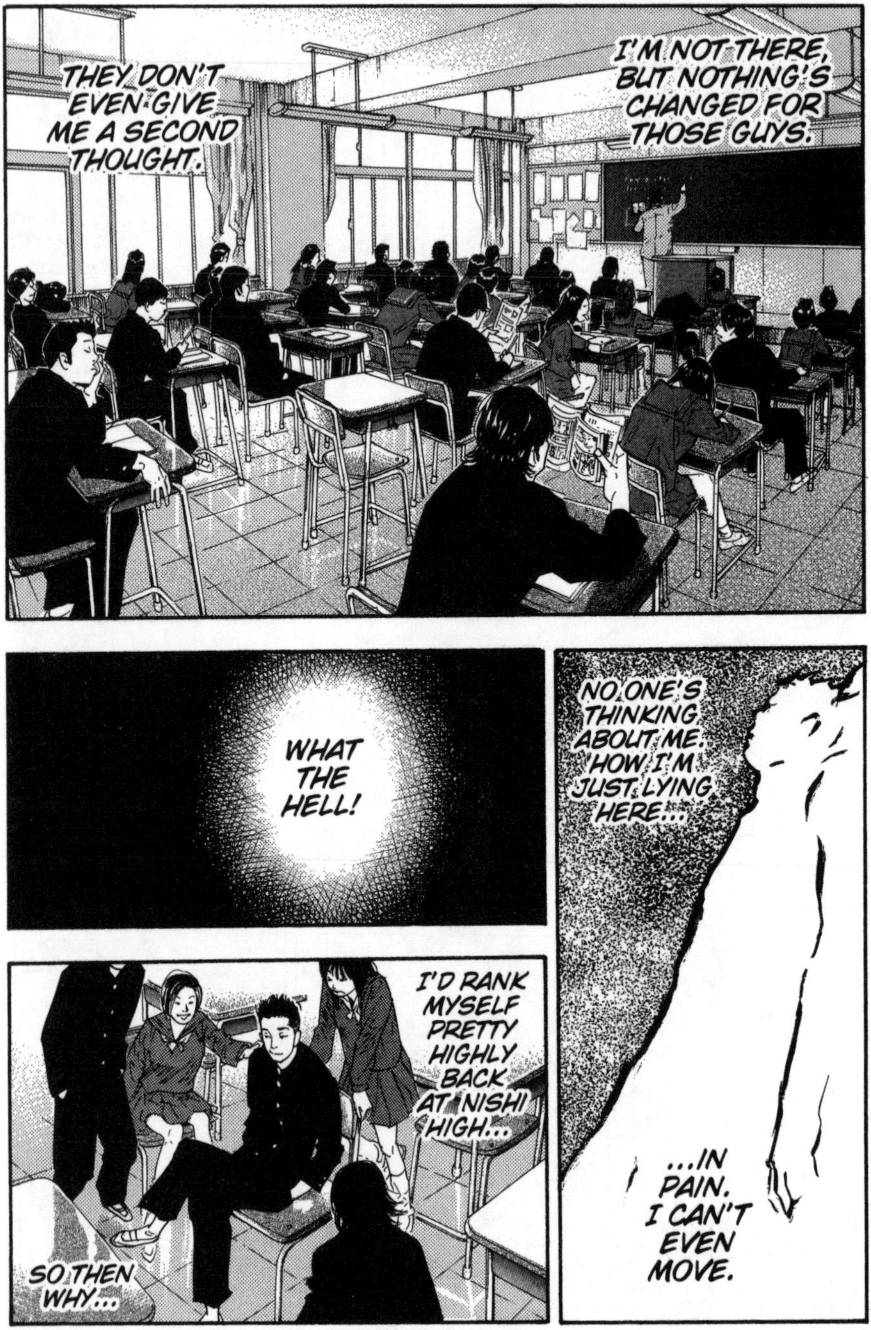
I'M NOT THERE, BUT NOTHING'S CHANGED FOR THOSE GUYS.
THEY DON'T EVEN GIVE ME A SECOND THOUGHT.
NO ONE'S THINKING ABOUT ME. HOW I'M JUST LYING HERE...
...IN PAIN. I CAN'T EVEN MOVE.
WHAT THE HELL!
I'D RANK MYSELF PRETTY HIGHLY BACK AT NISHI HIGH...
SO THEN WHY...

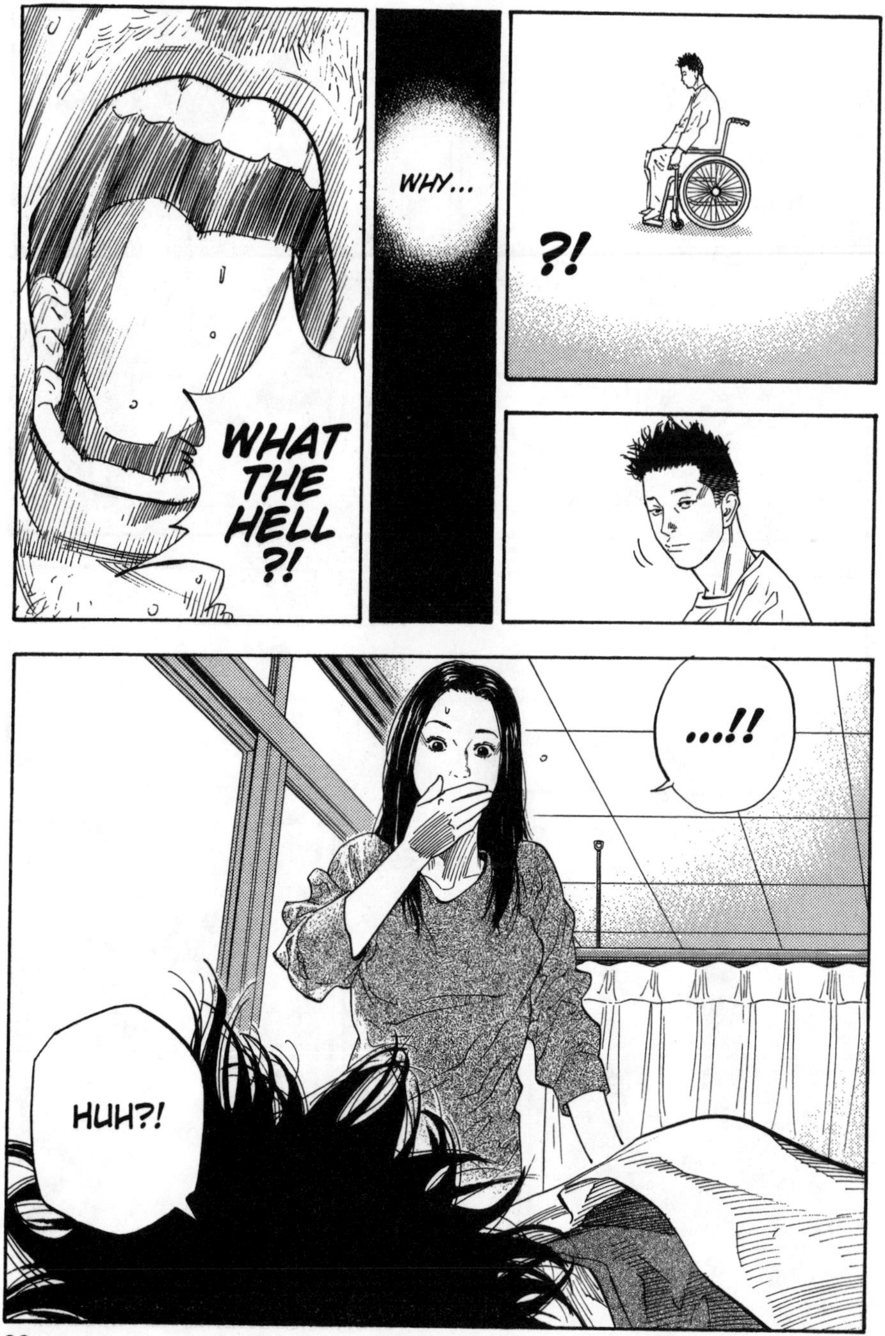
?!
WHY...
WHAT THE HELL ?!
...!!
HUH?!

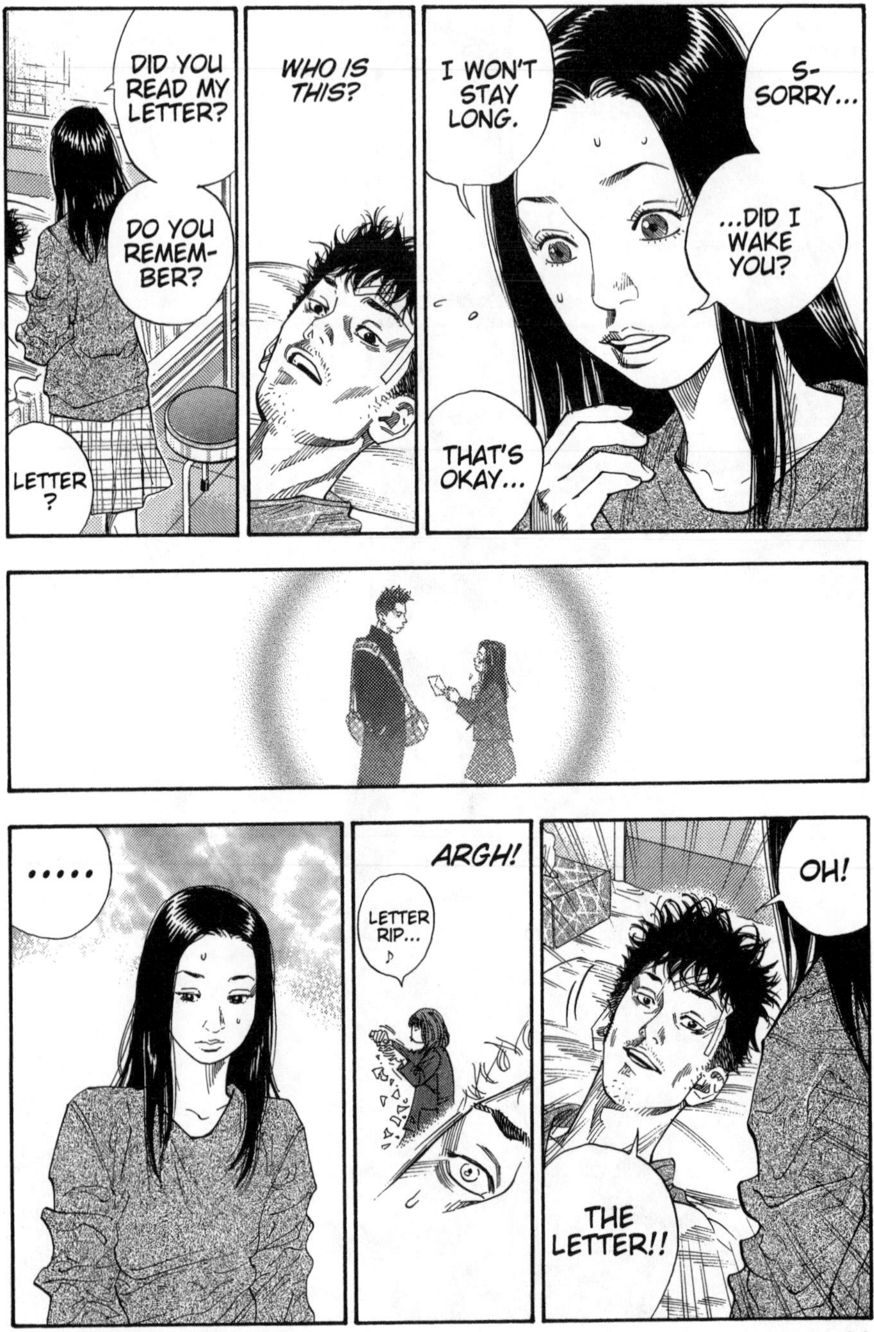
S-SORRY...
...DID I WAKE YOU?
I WON'T STAY LONG.
THAT'S OKAY...
WHO IS THIS?
DID YOU READ MY LETTER?
DO YOU REMEMBER?
LETTER?
OH!
THE LETTER!!
ARGH!
LETTER RIP... ♪
.....

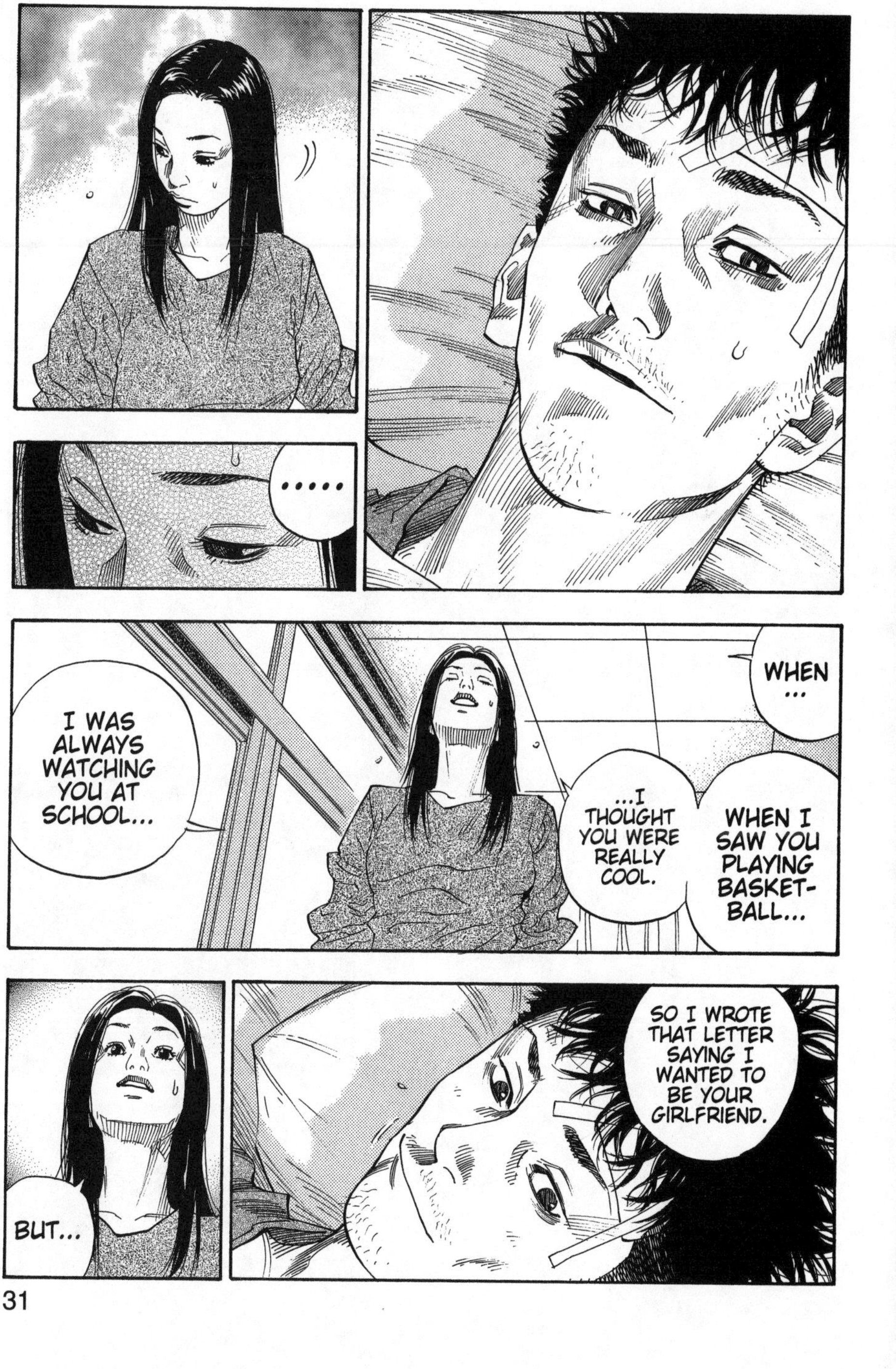
.....
WHEN ...
WHEN I SAW YOU PLAYING BASKET-BALL...
...I THOUGHT YOU WERE REALLY COOL.
I WAS ALWAYS WATCHING YOU AT SCHOOL...
SO I WROTE THAT LETTER SAYING I WANTED TO BE YOUR GIRLFRIEND.
BUT...

...IT WAS JUST A SILLY CRUSH. I'M SO IMMATURE.

I'M SORRY!!

?!

LET ME OUTTA HERE!

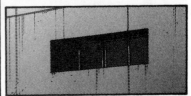

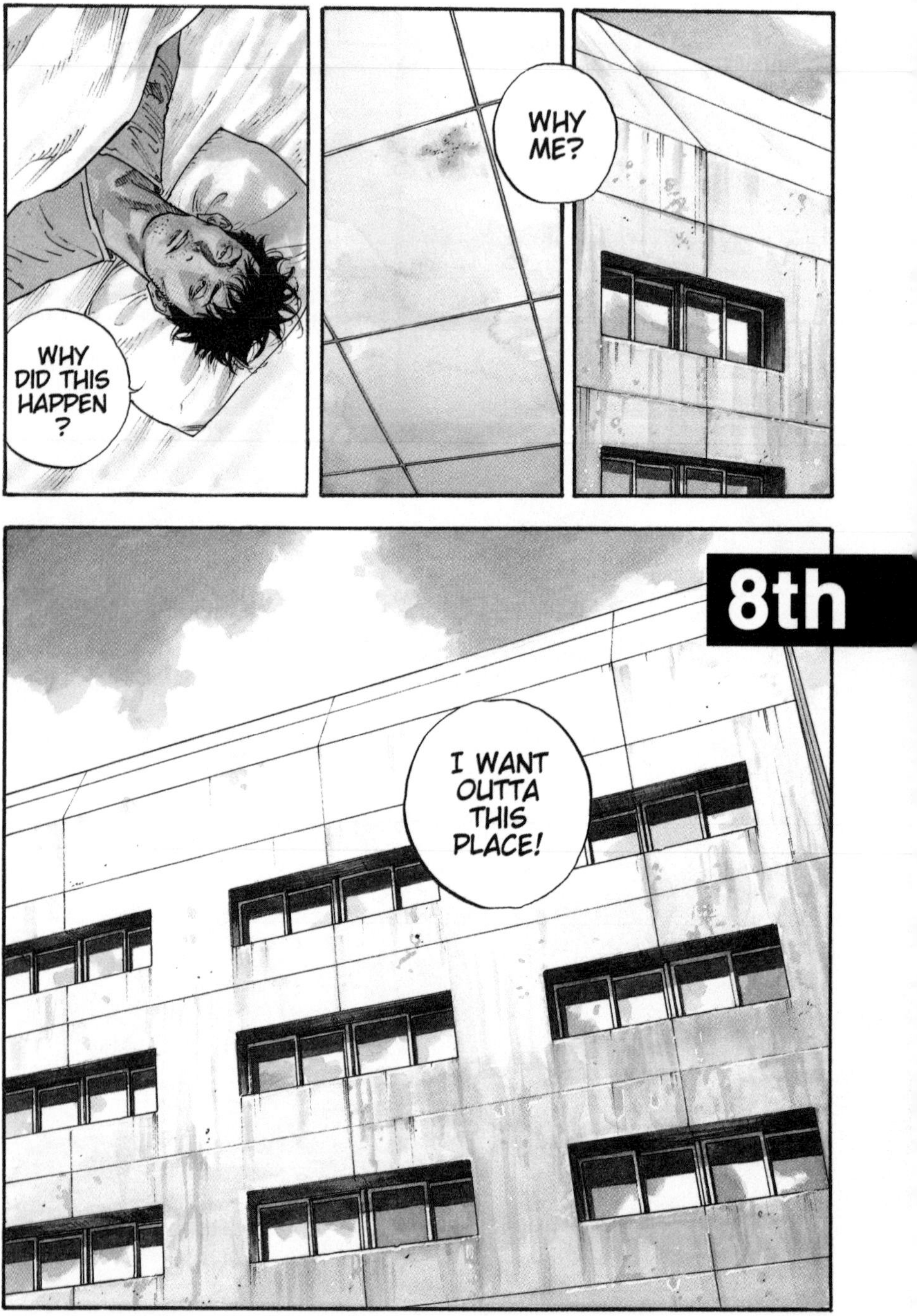
WHY ME?
WHY DID THIS HAPPEN ?
8th
I WANT OUTTA THIS PLACE!

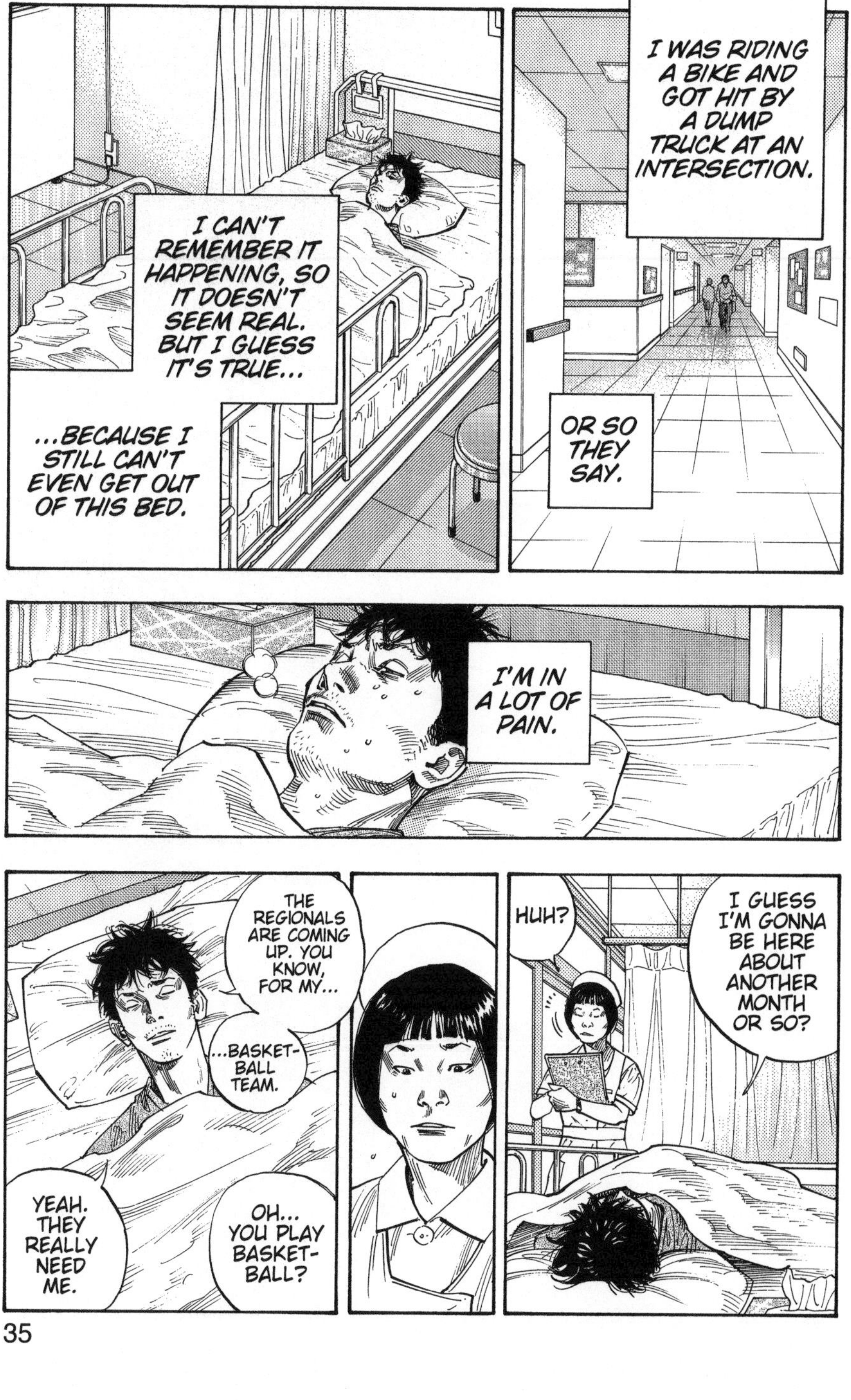
I WAS RIDING A BIKE AND GOT HIT BY A DUMP TRUCK AT AN INTERSECTION.
OR SO THEY SAY.
I CAN'T REMEMBER IT HAPPENING, SO IT DOESN'T SEEM REAL. BUT I GUESS IT'S TRUE...
...BECAUSE I STILL CAN'T EVEN GET OUT OF THIS BED.
I'M IN A LOT OF PAIN.
I GUESS I'M GONNA BE HERE ABOUT ANOTHER MONTH OR SO?
HUH?
THE REGIONALS ARE COMING UP. YOU KNOW, FOR MY...
...BASKET-BALL TEAM.
OH... YOU PLAY BASKET-BALL?
YEAH. THEY REALLY NEED ME.

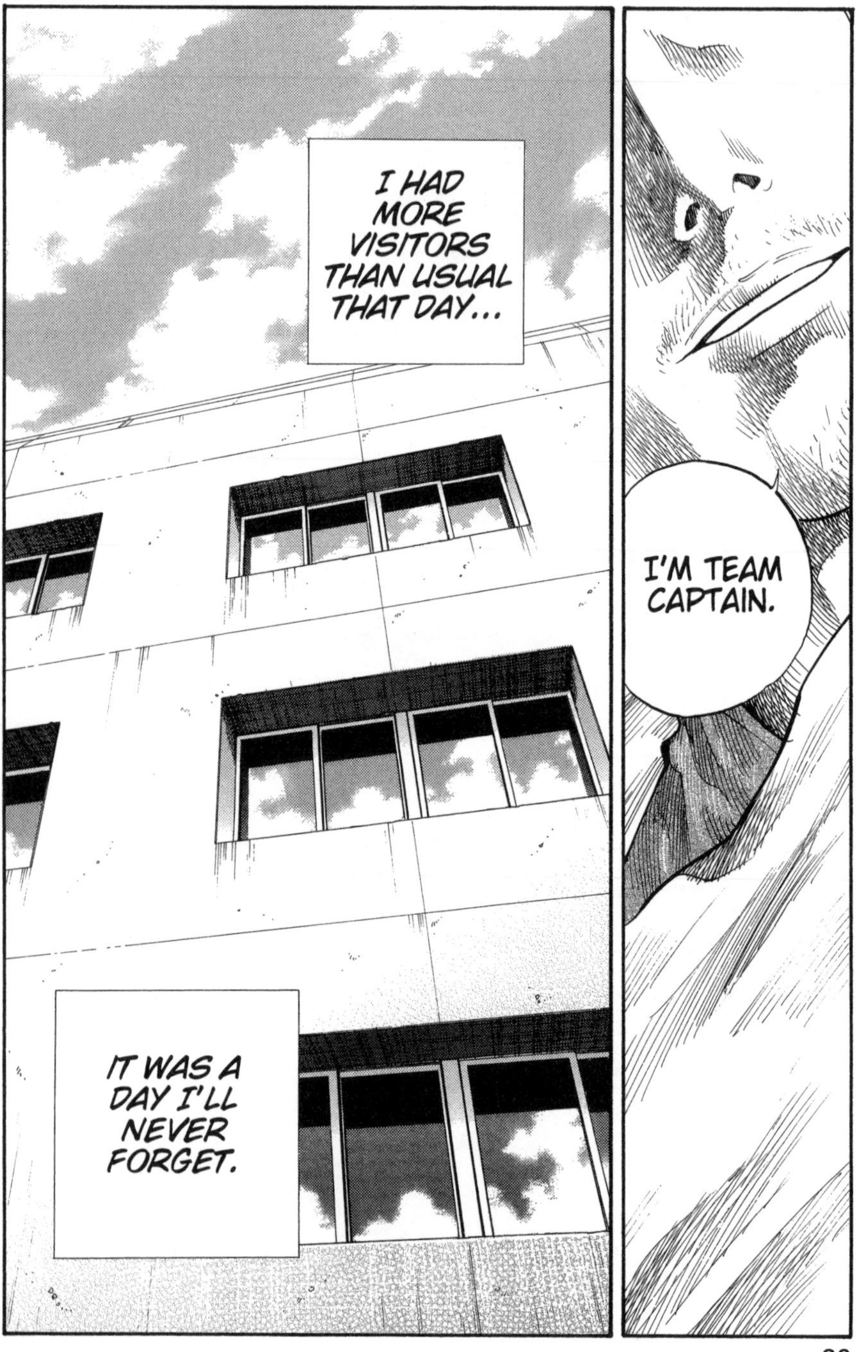
I'M TEAM CAPTAIN.
I HAD MORE VISITORS THAN USUAL THAT DAY...
IT WAS A DAY I'LL NEVER FORGET.

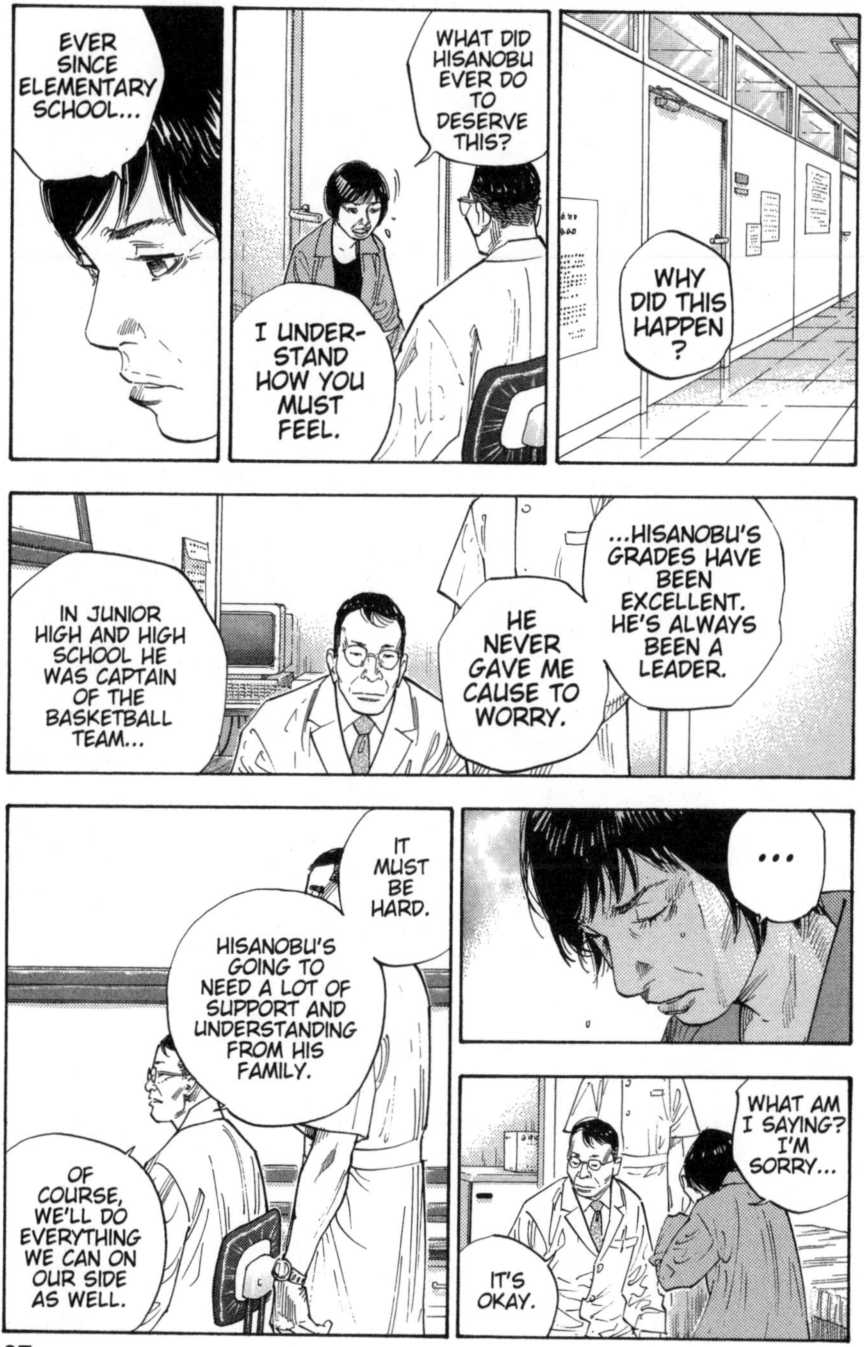
WHY DID THIS HAPPEN?
WHAT DID HISANOBU EVER DO TO DESERVE THIS?
I UNDER-STAND HOW YOU MUST FEEL.
EVER SINCE ELEMENTARY SCHOOL...
...HISANOBU'S GRADES HAVE BEEN EXCELLENT. HE'S ALWAYS BEEN A LEADER.
HE NEVER GAVE ME CAUSE TO WORRY.
IN JUNIOR HIGH AND HIGH SCHOOL HE WAS CAPTAIN OF THE BASKETBALL TEAM...
...
WHAT AM I SAYING? I'M SORRY...
IT'S OKAY.
IT MUST BE HARD.
HISANOBU'S GOING TO NEED A LOT OF SUPPORT AND UNDERSTANDING FROM HIS FAMILY.
OF COURSE, WE'LL DO EVERYTHING WE CAN ON OUR SIDE AS WELL.

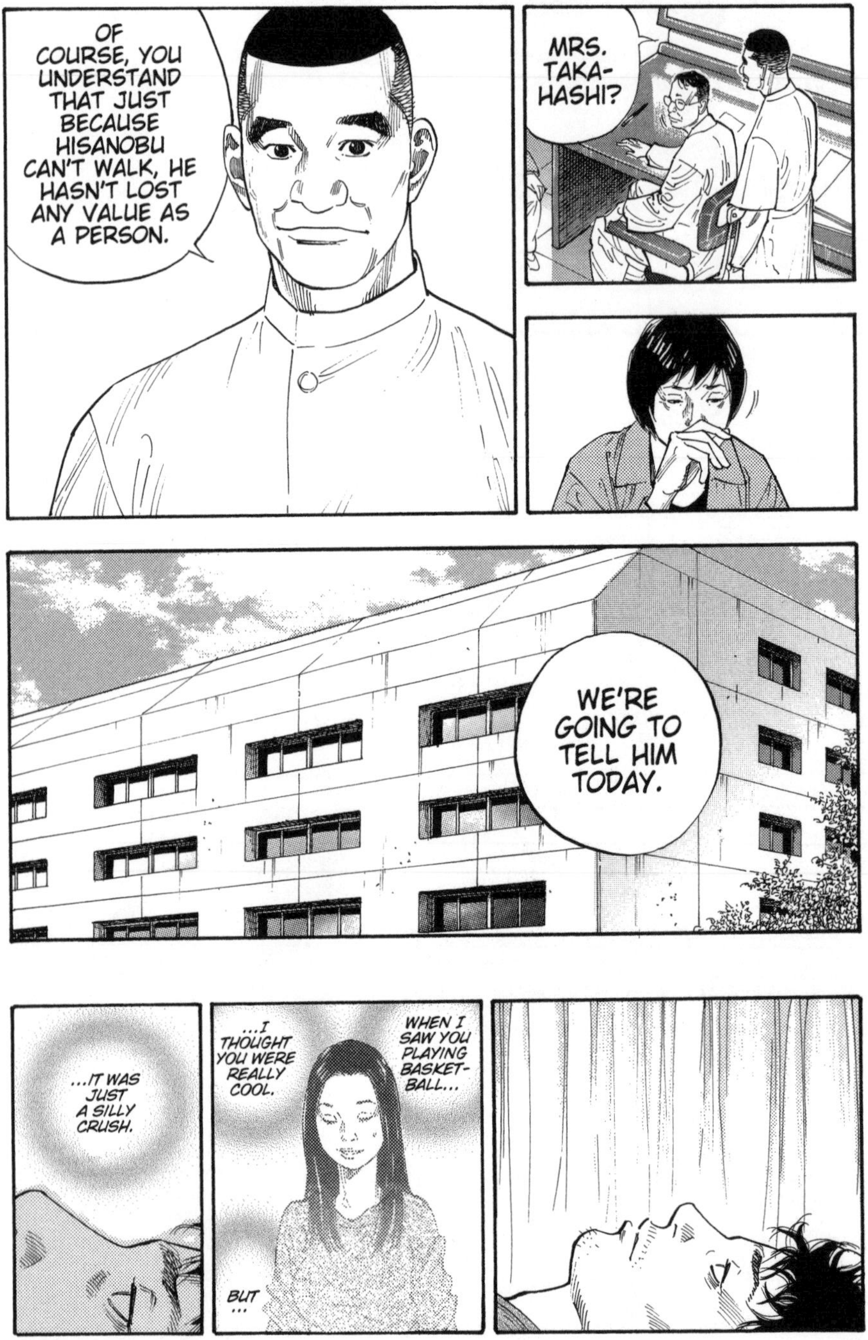
MRS. TAKA-HASHI?
OF COURSE, YOU UNDERSTAND THAT JUST BECAUSE HISANOBU CAN'T WALK, HE HASN'T LOST ANY VALUE AS A PERSON.
WE'RE GOING TO TELL HIM TODAY.
WHEN I SAW YOU PLAYING BASKET-BALL...
...I THOUGHT YOU WERE REALLY COOL.
BUT ...
...IT WAS JUST A SILLY CRUSH.

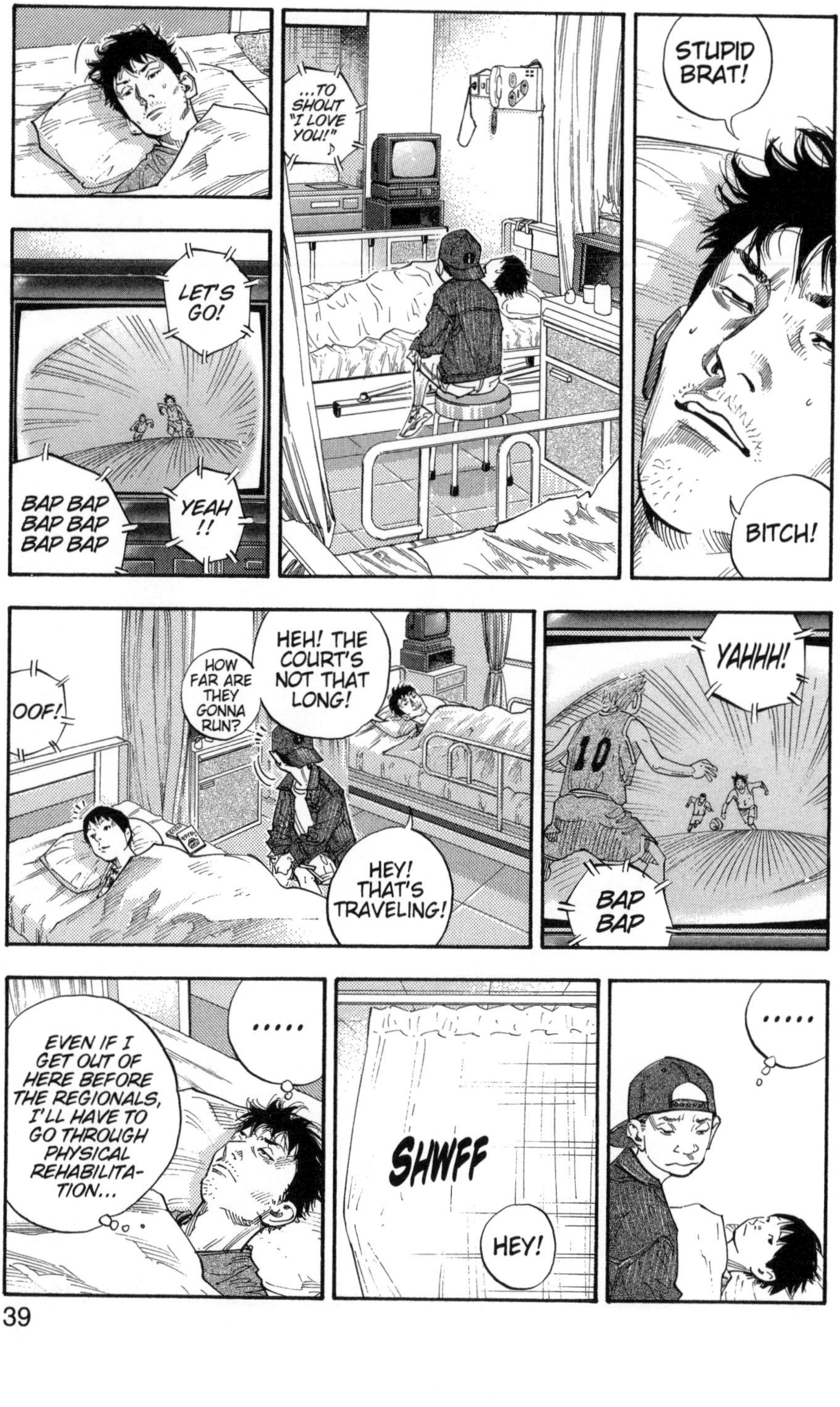
STUPID BRAT!
BITCH!
...TO SHOUT "I LOVE YOU!" ♪
LET'S GO!
YEAH!!
BAP BAP BAP BAP BAP BAP
YAHHH!
BAP BAP
HEH! THE COURT'S NOT THAT LONG!
HOW FAR ARE THEY GONNA RUN?
HEY! THAT'S TRAVELING!
OOF!
.....
SHWFF
HEY!
.....
EVEN IF I GET OUT OF HERE BEFORE THE REGIONALS, I'LL HAVE TO GO THROUGH PHYSICAL REHABILITA-TION...

. . . . .

I STILL CAN'T FEEL MY LEGS...

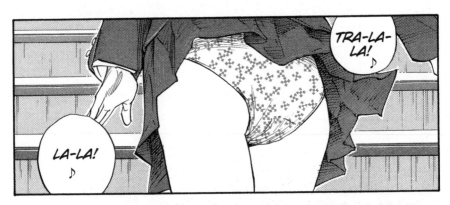

TRA-LA-LA! ♪

LA-LA! ♪

MR. NAKA-MURA, ARE YOU OKAY?

GRAAAAGH!

MR. NAKA-MURA?

SLP

BMP

CRASH

LA-LA-LA! ♪

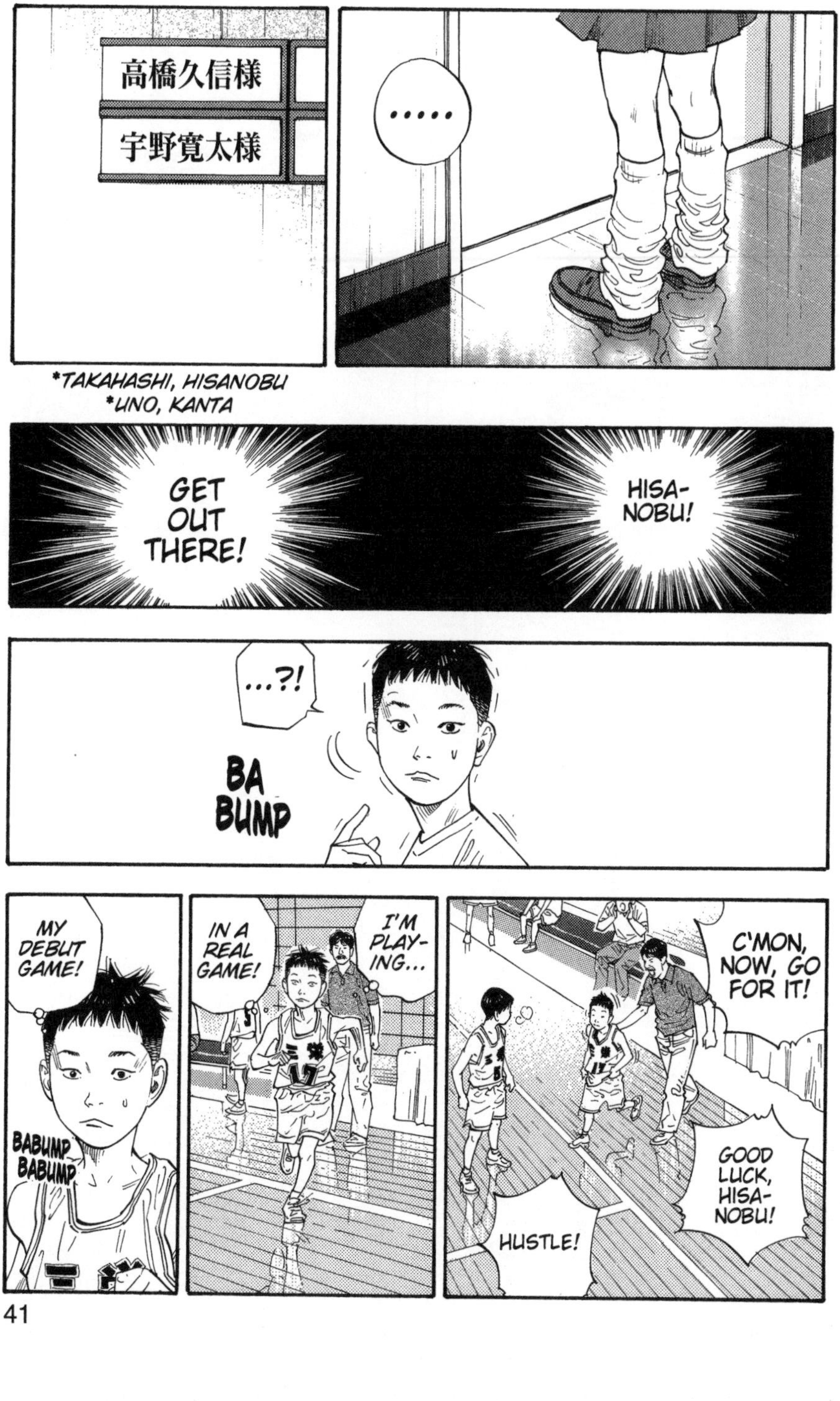

.....
高橋久信様
宇野寛太様
*TAKAHASHI, HISANOBU
*UNO, KANTA
HISA-NOBU!
GET OUT THERE!
...?!
BA BUMP
C'MON, NOW, GO FOR IT!
GOOD LUCK, HISA-NOBU!
HUSTLE!
I'M PLAYING...
IN A REAL GAME!
MY DEBUT GAME!
BABUMP BABUMP

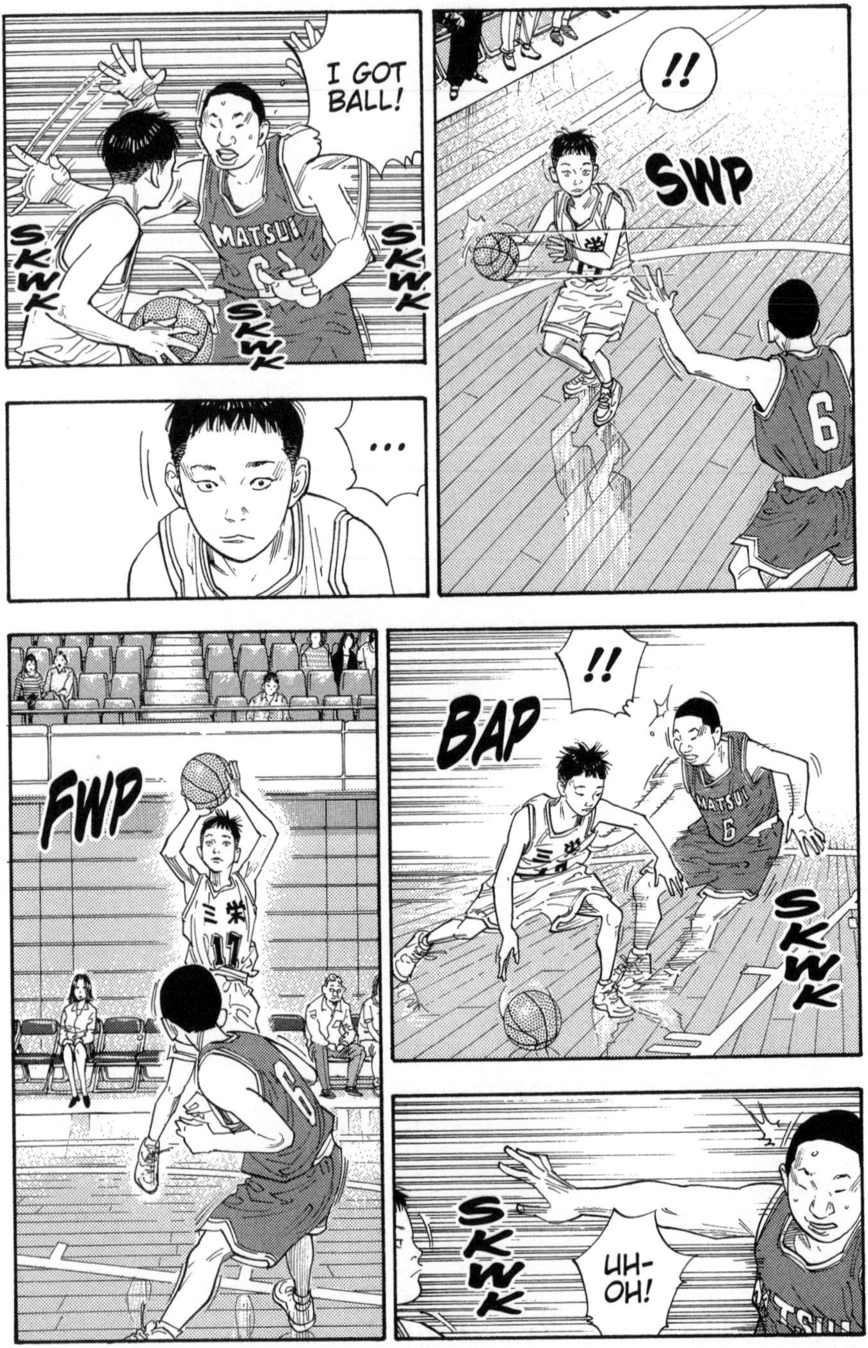
!!
SWP
I GOT BALL!
SKWK
SKWK
SKWK
...
!!
BAP
SKWK
SKWK
UH-OH!
FWP

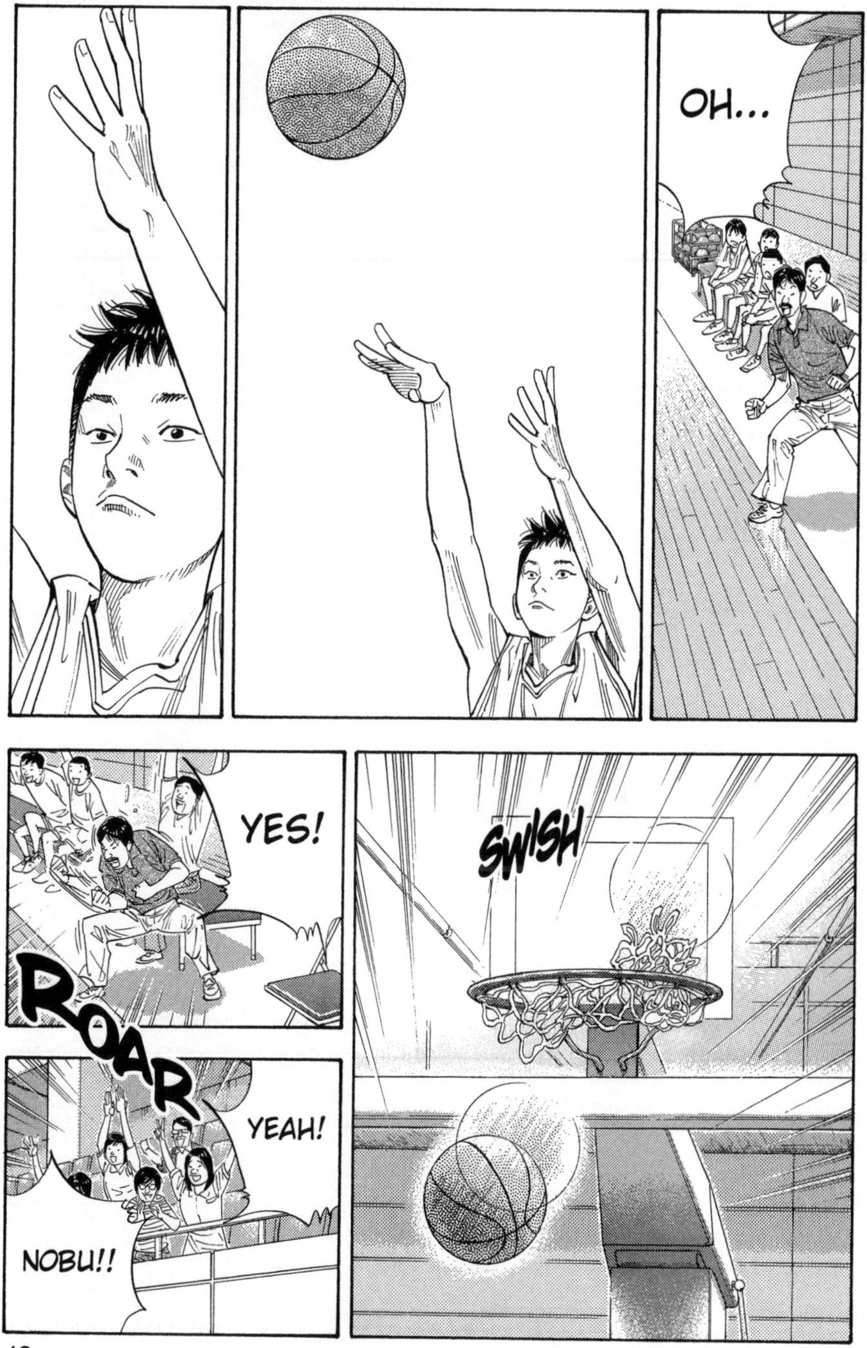
OH...
SWISH
YES!
ROAR
YEAH!
NOBU!!

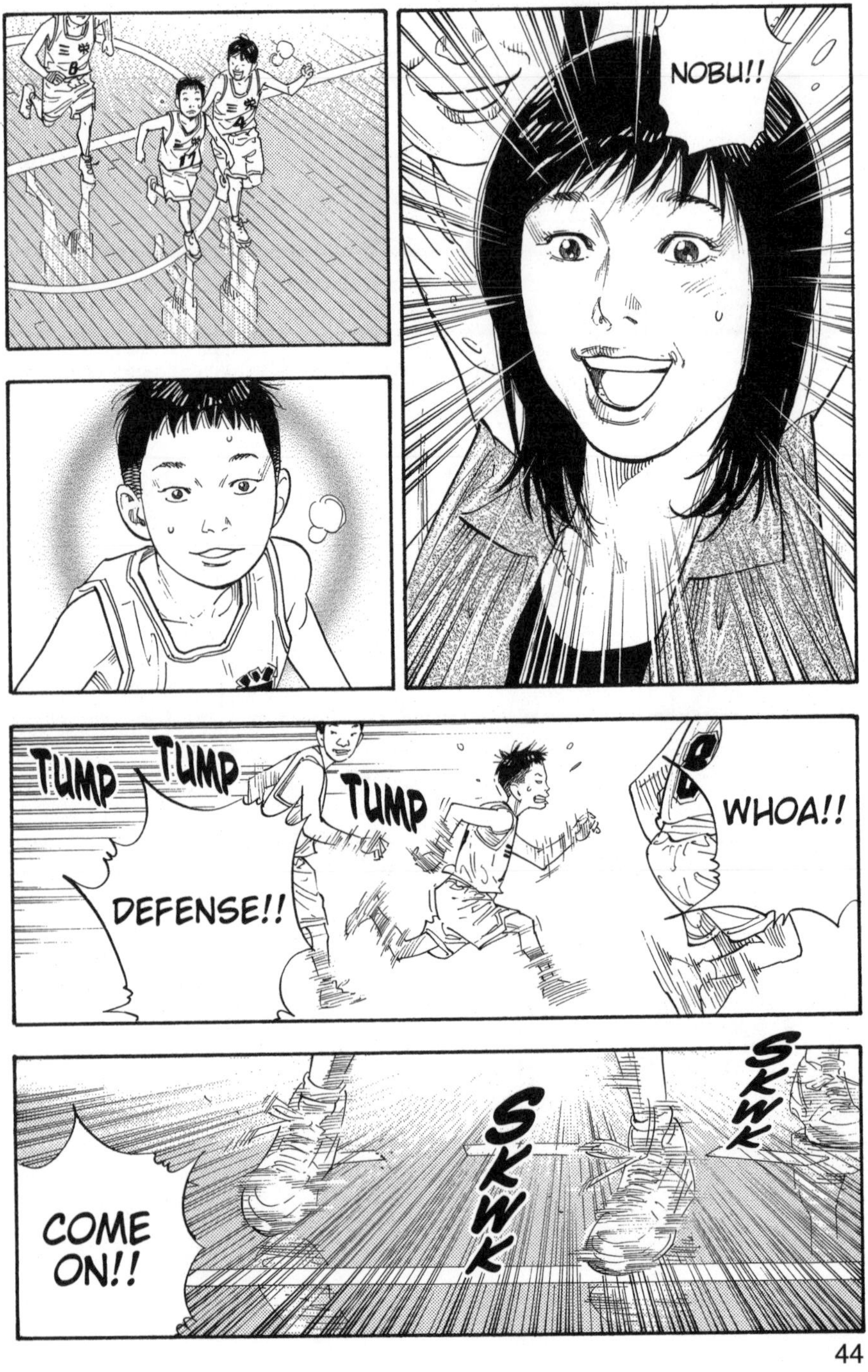
NOBU!!
WHOA!!
TUMP
TUMP
TUMP
DEFENSE!!
SKWK
SKWK
COME ON!!

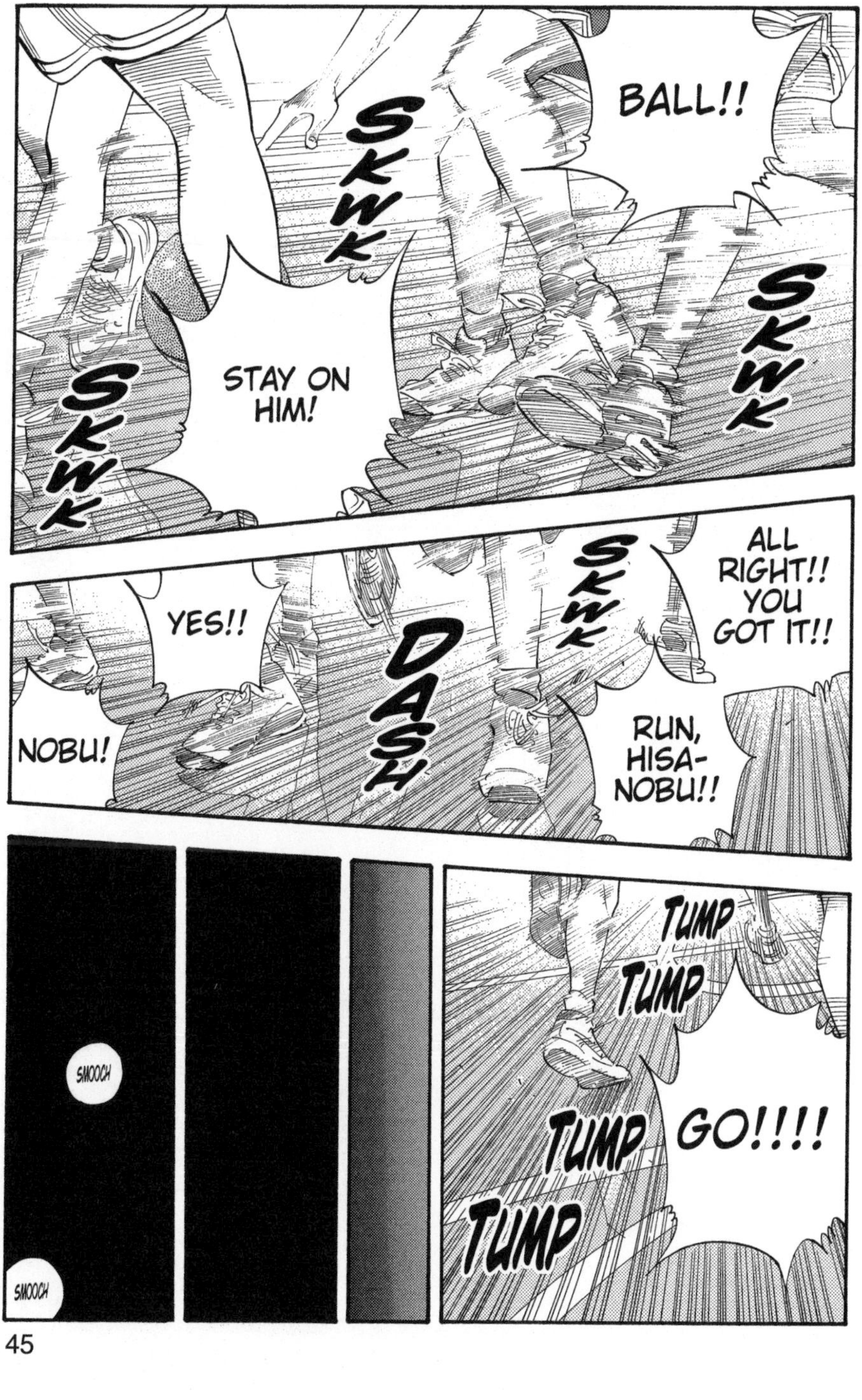
BALL!!
SKWK
SKWK
STAY ON HIM!
SKWK
ALL RIGHT!! YOU GOT IT!!
SKWK
RUN, HISA-NOBU!!
DASH
YES!!
NOBU!
TUMP
TUMP
GO!!!!
TUMP
TUMP
SMOOCH
SMOOCH

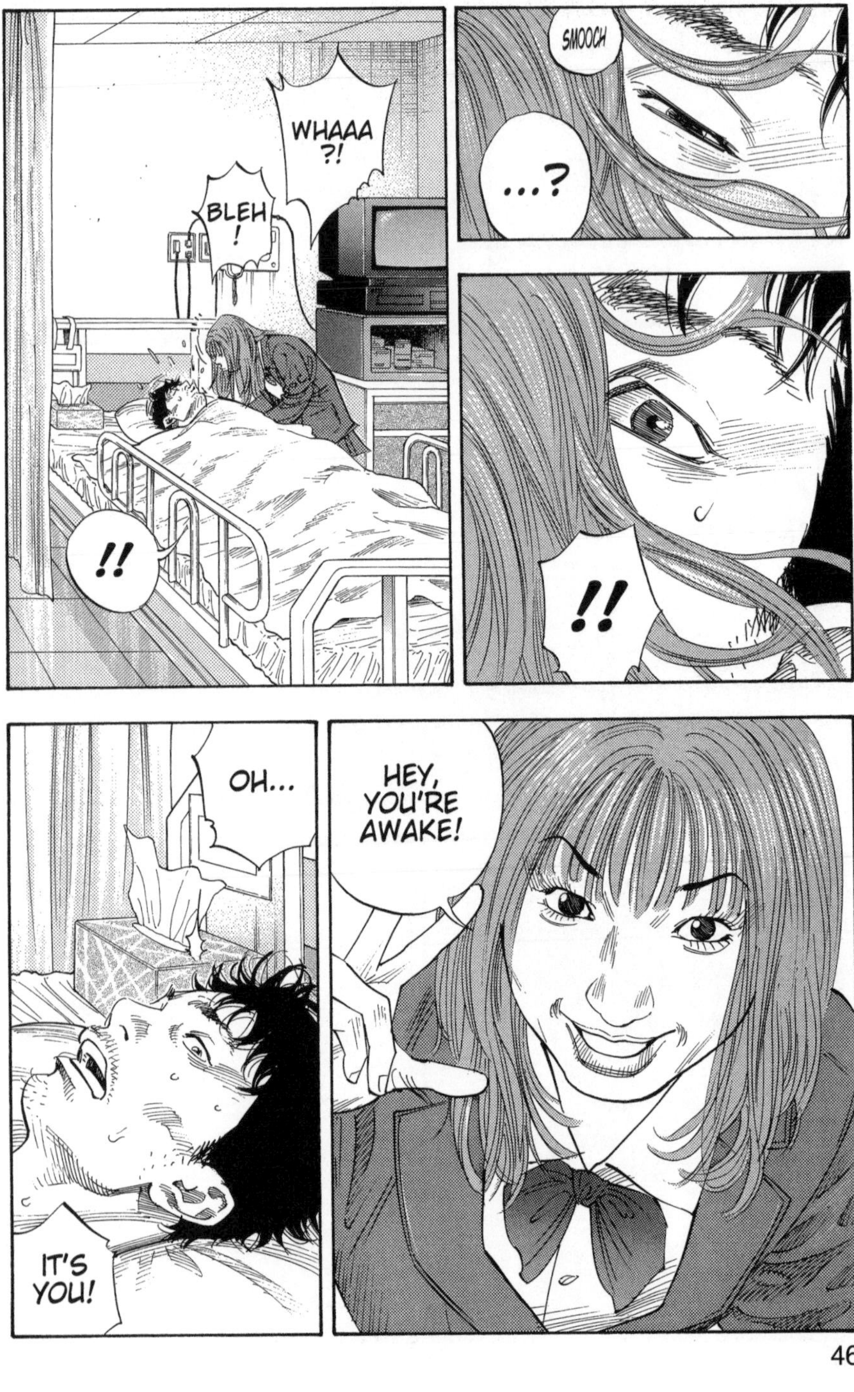
SMOOCH
...?
!!
WHAAA ?!
BLEH !
!!
HEY, YOU'RE AWAKE!
OH...
IT'S YOU!

UH...

BROUGHT YOU SOME-THING. ♡

ISN'T IT PRETTY ? ♡

YOU'VE LOST WEIGHT. MUST BE NICE.

MAYBE I SHOULD CHECK IN HERE TOO.

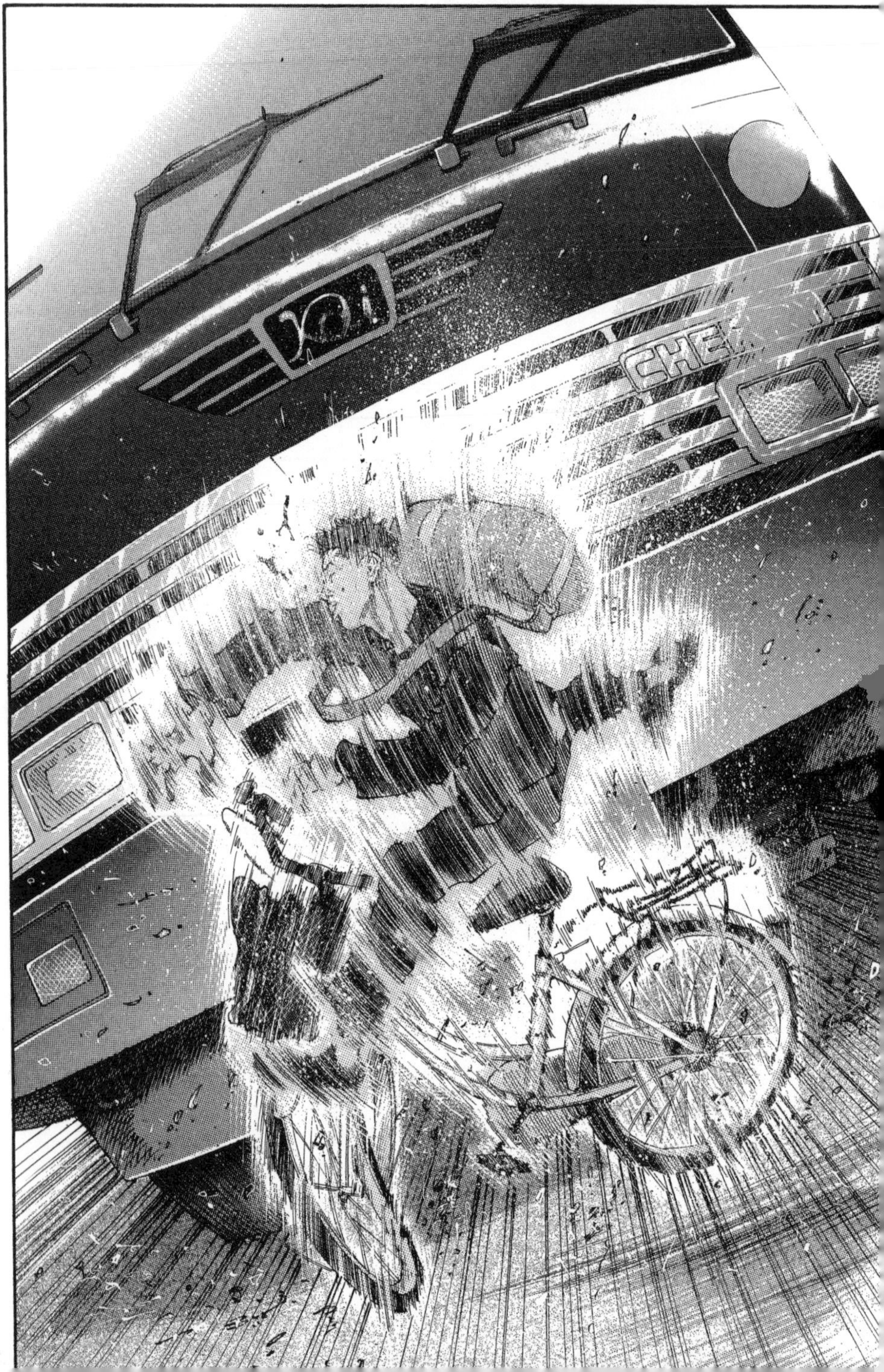
CHE

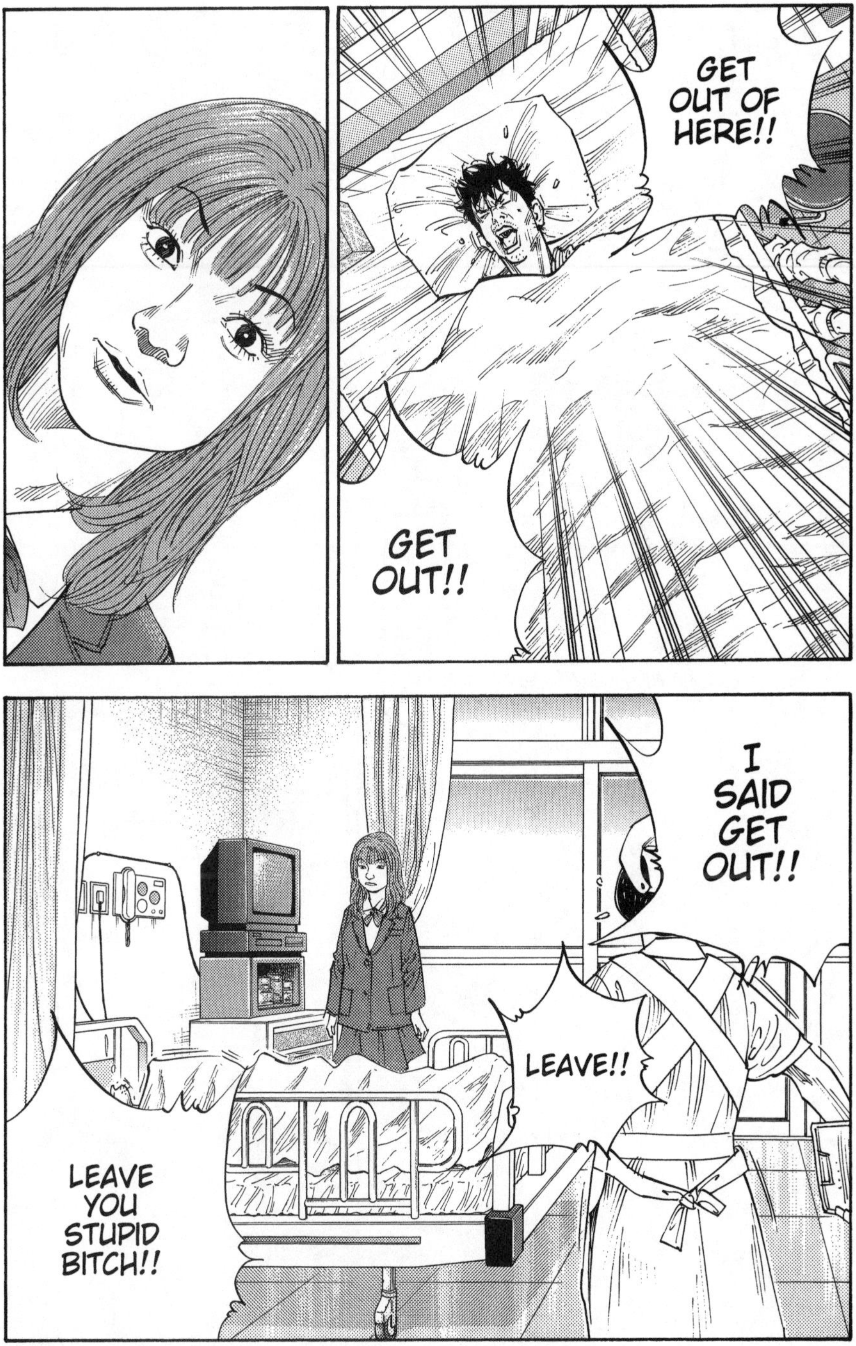
GET OUT OF HERE!!
GET OUT!!
I SAID GET OUT!!
LEAVE!!
LEAVE YOU STUPID BITCH!!

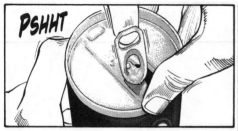

PSHHT

GET OUT!!

*TACHIZAWA GENERAL HOSPITAL

HM?

50

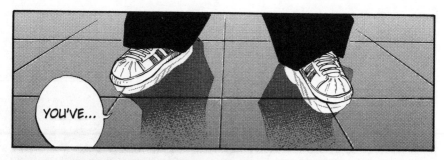

YOU'VE...

WHAT'RE *YOU* DOING HERE, SEKI?

YOU'VE LOST WEIGHT...

...TAKA-HASHI.

EVEN THOUGH NO ONE'LL PASS TO YOU?

...THOUGHT I'D VISIT YOU.

I JUST ...

I SKIPPED SCHOOL TODAY.

BUT I'LL STILL GO TO PRACTICE.

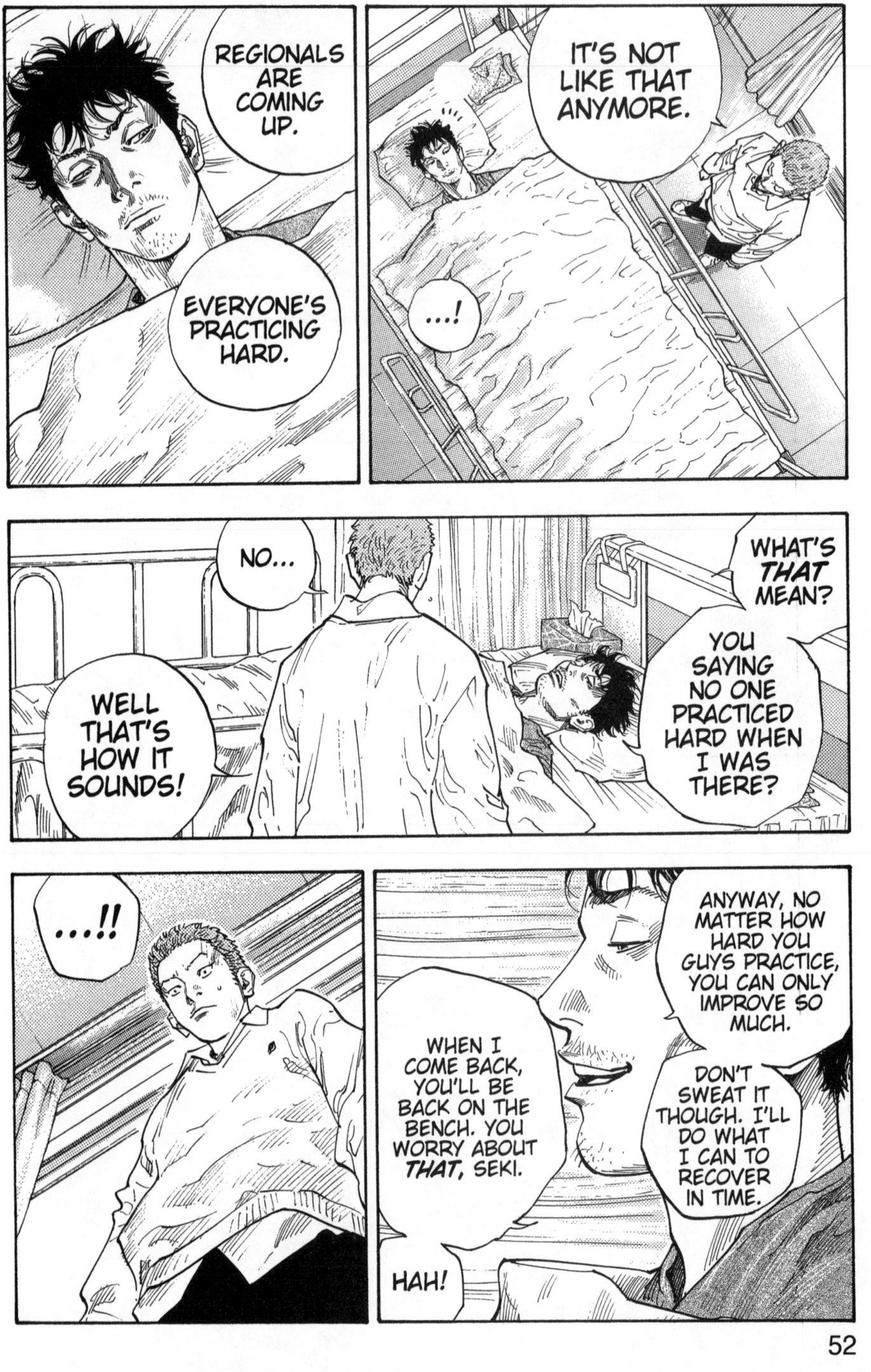
IT'S NOT LIKE THAT ANYMORE.
...!
REGIONALS ARE COMING UP.
EVERYONE'S PRACTICING HARD.
WHAT'S *THAT* MEAN?
YOU SAYING NO ONE PRACTICED HARD WHEN I WAS THERE?
NO...
WELL THAT'S HOW IT SOUNDS!
ANYWAY, NO MATTER HOW HARD YOU GUYS PRACTICE, YOU CAN ONLY IMPROVE SO MUCH.
DON'T SWEAT IT THOUGH. I'LL DO WHAT I CAN TO RECOVER IN TIME.
WHEN I COME BACK, YOU'LL BE BACK ON THE BENCH. YOU WORRY ABOUT *THAT*, SEKI.
HAH!
...!!

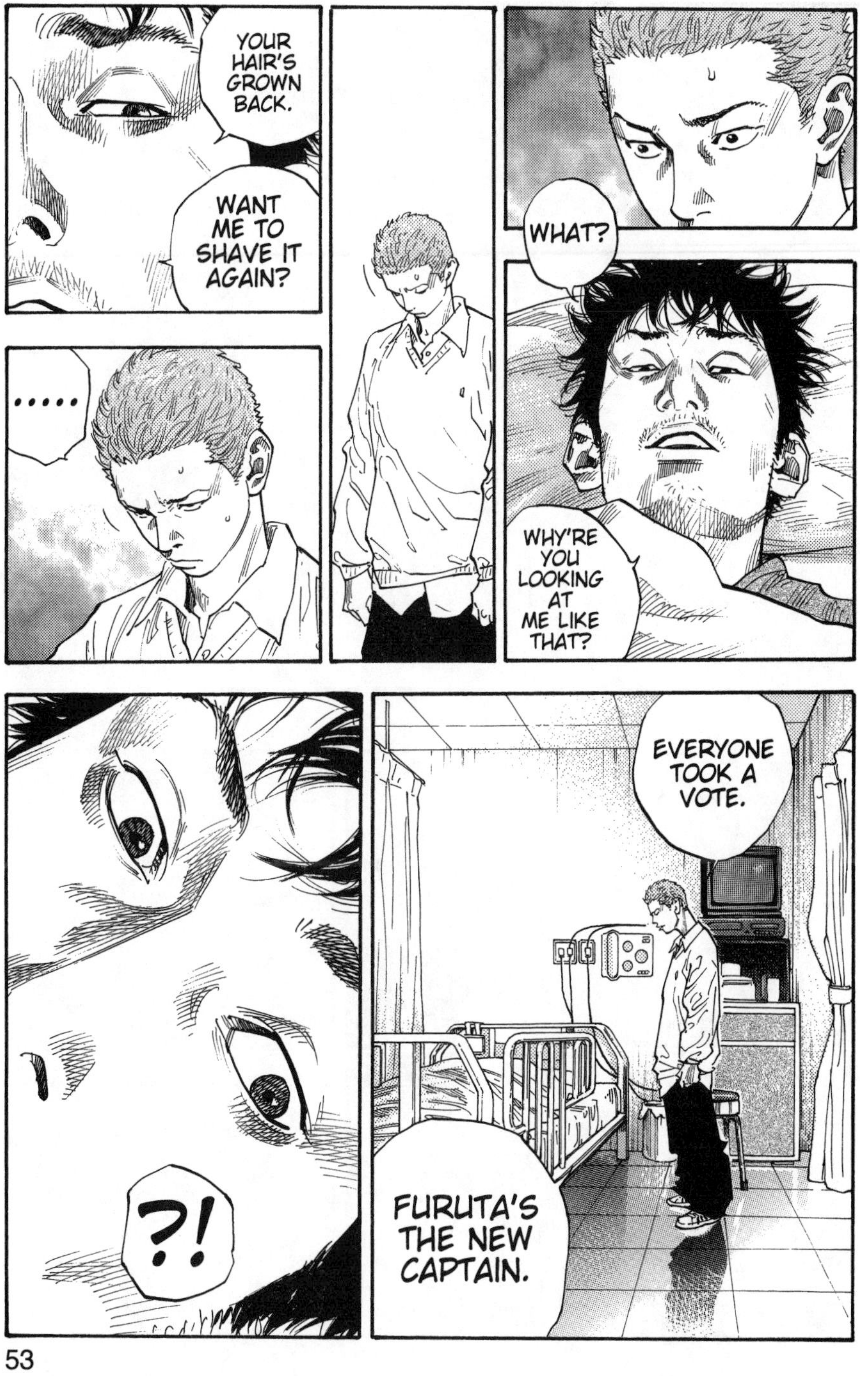
WHAT?
WHY'RE YOU LOOKING AT ME LIKE THAT?
YOUR HAIR'S GROWN BACK.
WANT ME TO SHAVE IT AGAIN?
.....
EVERYONE TOOK A VOTE.
FURUTA'S THE NEW CAPTAIN.
?!

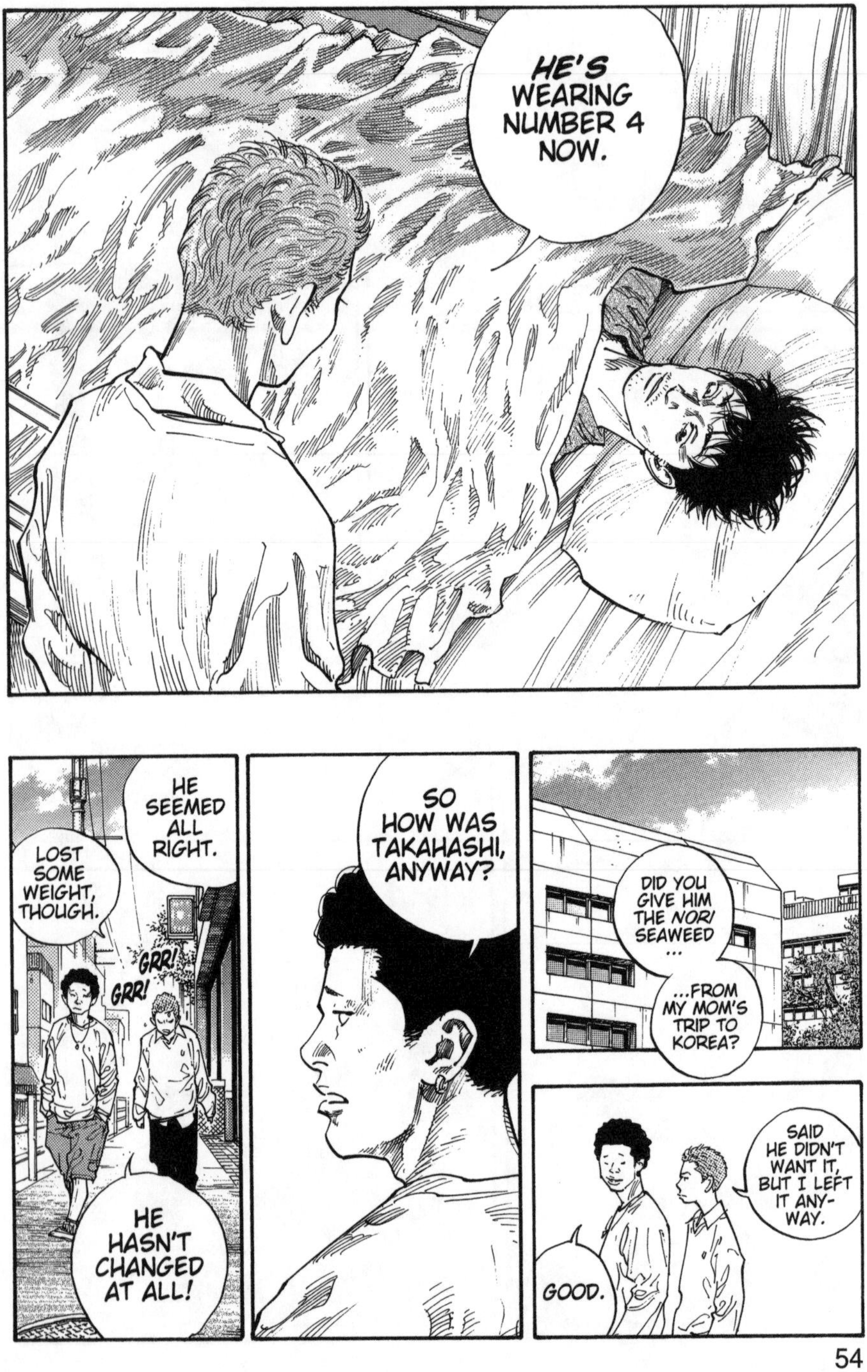
HE'S WEARING NUMBER 4 NOW.
DID YOU GIVE HIM THE NORI SEAWEED ...
...FROM MY MOM'S TRIP TO KOREA?
SAID HE DIDN'T WANT IT, BUT I LEFT IT ANY-WAY.
GOOD.
SO HOW WAS TAKAHASHI, ANYWAY?
HE SEEMED ALL RIGHT.
LOST SOME WEIGHT, THOUGH.
GRR!
GRR!
HE HASN'T CHANGED AT ALL!

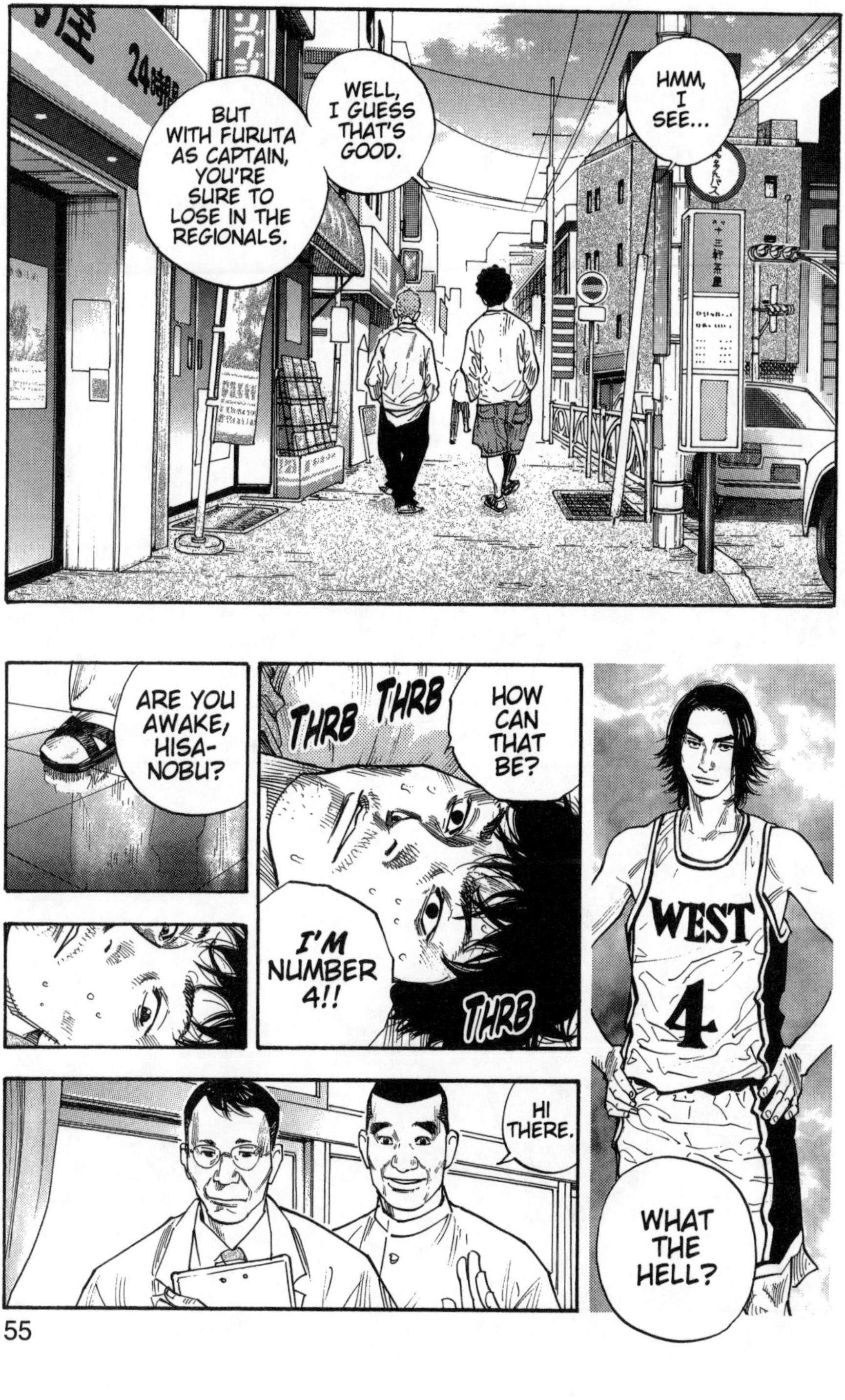
HMM, I SEE...
WELL, I GUESS THAT'S GOOD.
BUT WITH FURUTA AS CAPTAIN, YOU'RE SURE TO LOSE IN THE REGIONALS.
WEST
4
WHAT THE HELL?
HOW CAN THAT BE?
THRB THRB
I'M NUMBER 4!!
THRB
ARE YOU AWAKE, HISA-NOBU?
HI THERE.

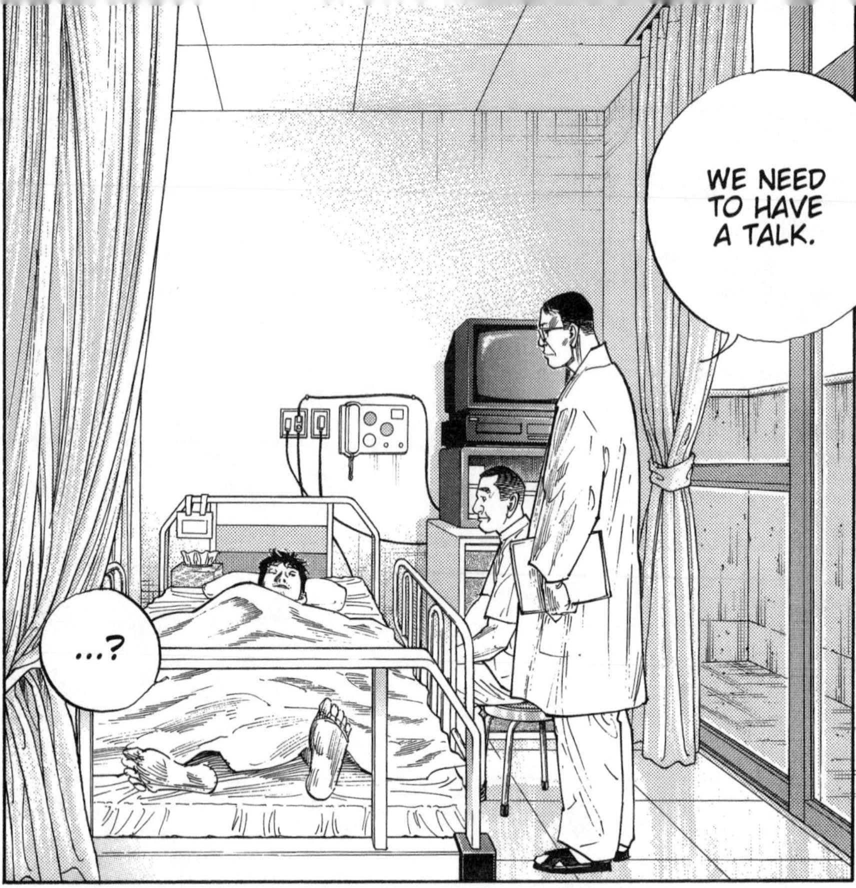
WE NEED TO HAVE A TALK.
...?
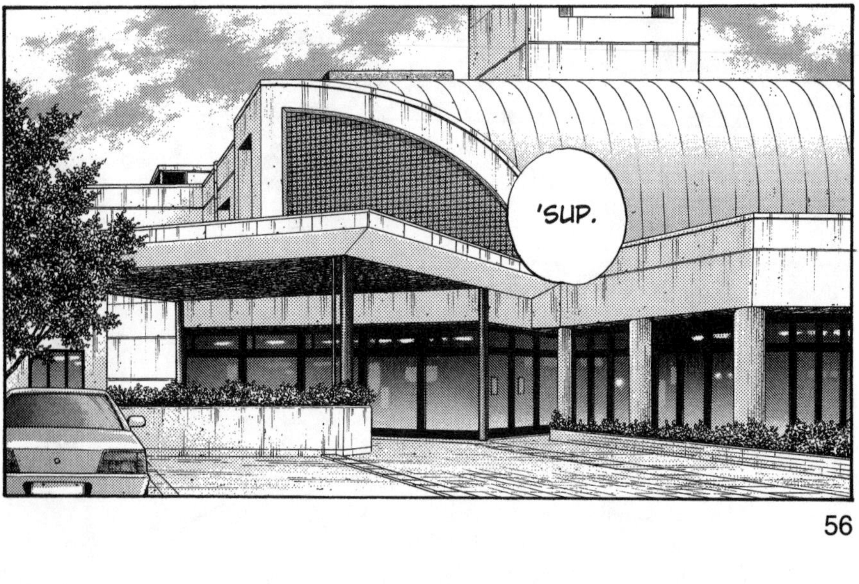
'SUP.

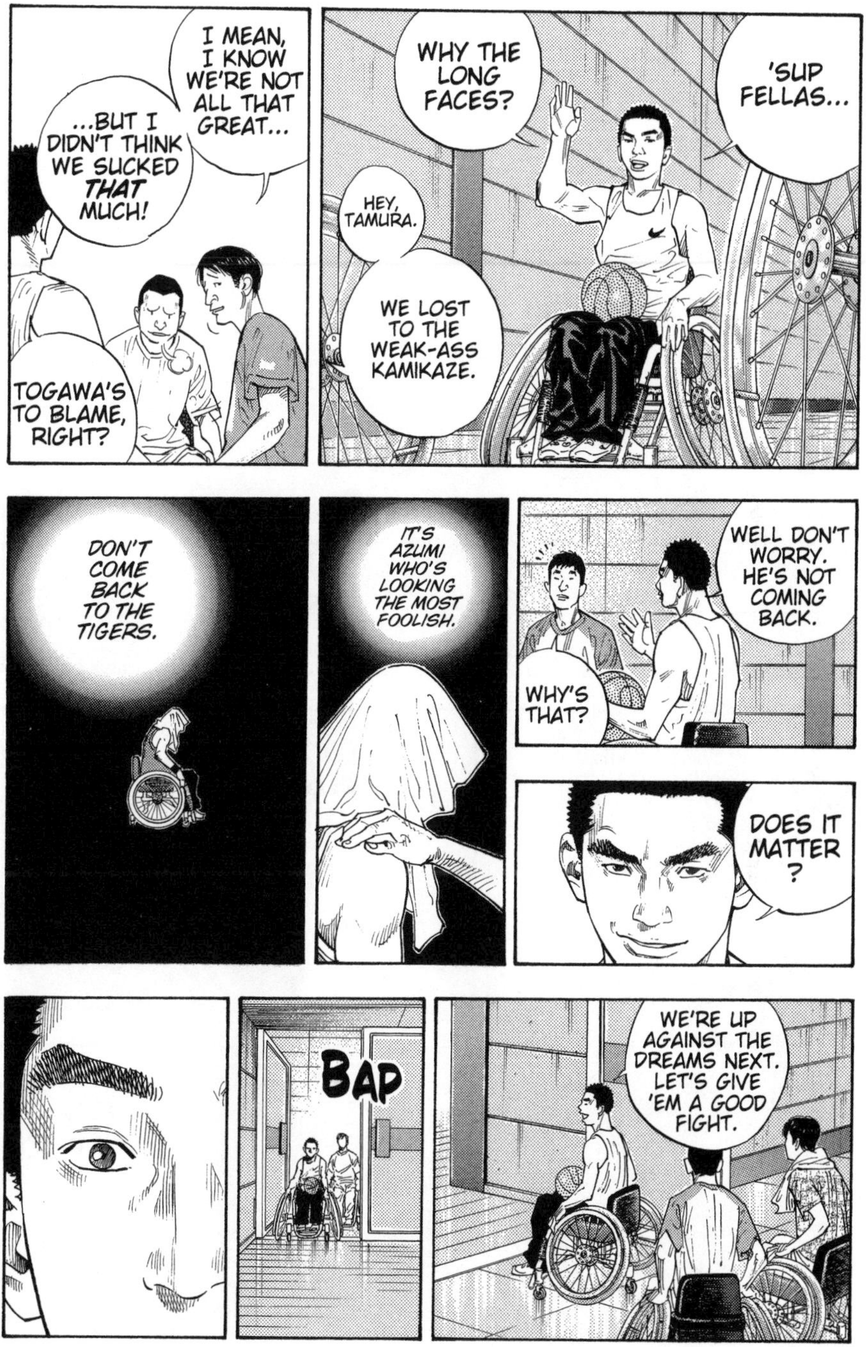
'SUP FELLAS...
WHY THE LONG FACES?
HEY, TAMURA.
WE LOST TO THE WEAK-ASS KAMIKAZE.
I MEAN, I KNOW WE'RE NOT ALL THAT GREAT...
...BUT I DIDN'T THINK WE SUCKED ***THAT*** MUCH!
TOGAWA'S TO BLAME, RIGHT?
WELL DON'T WORRY. HE'S NOT COMING BACK.
WHY'S THAT?
DOES IT MATTER?
IT'S AZUMI WHO'S LOOKING THE MOST FOOLISH.
DON'T COME BACK TO THE TIGERS.
WE'RE UP AGAINST THE DREAMS NEXT. LET'S GIVE 'EM A GOOD FIGHT.
BAP

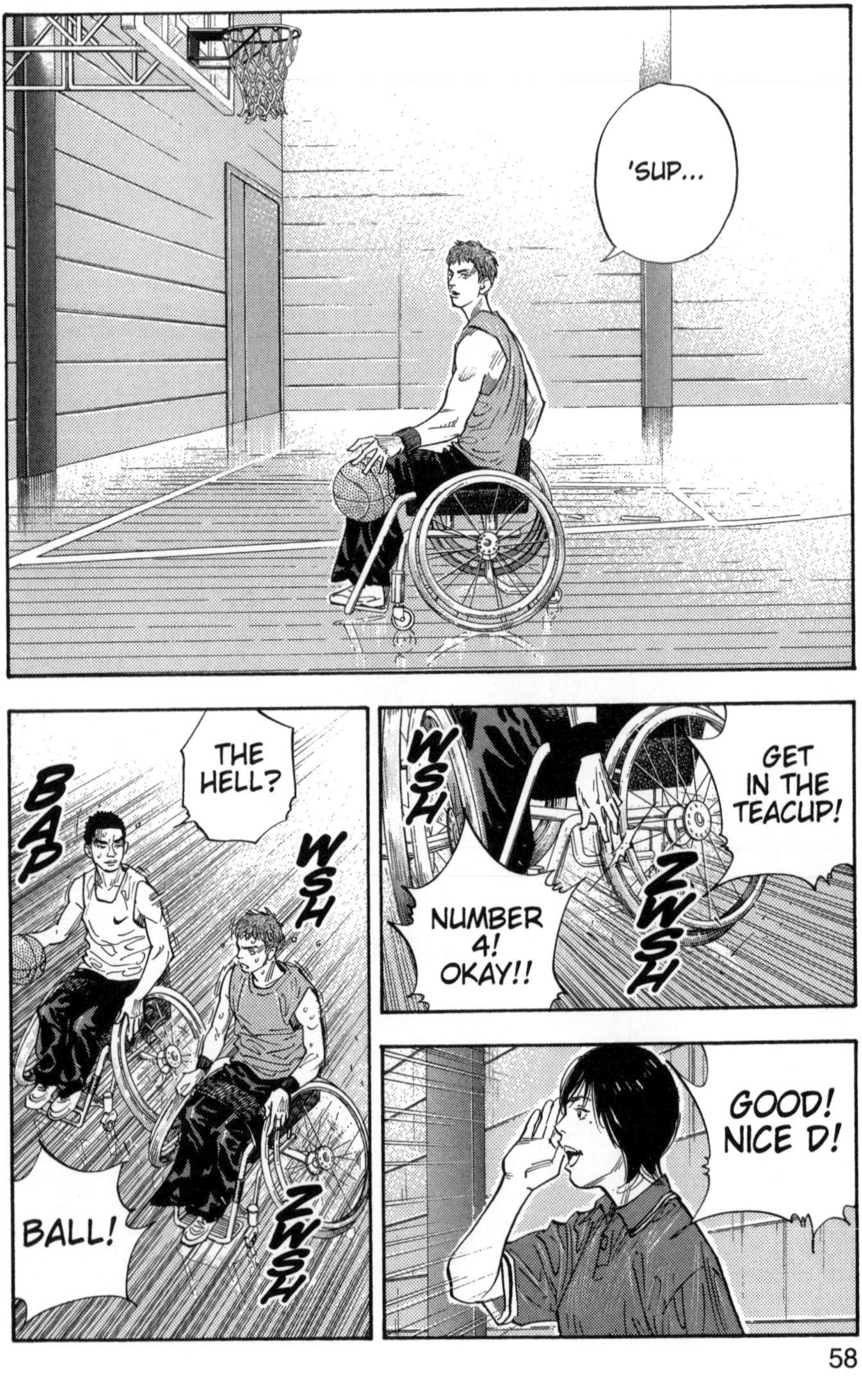
'SUP...
GET IN THE TEACUP!
ZWSH
NUMBER 4! OKAY!!
WSH
GOOD! NICE D!
THE HELL?
WSH
BAP
ZWSH
BALL!

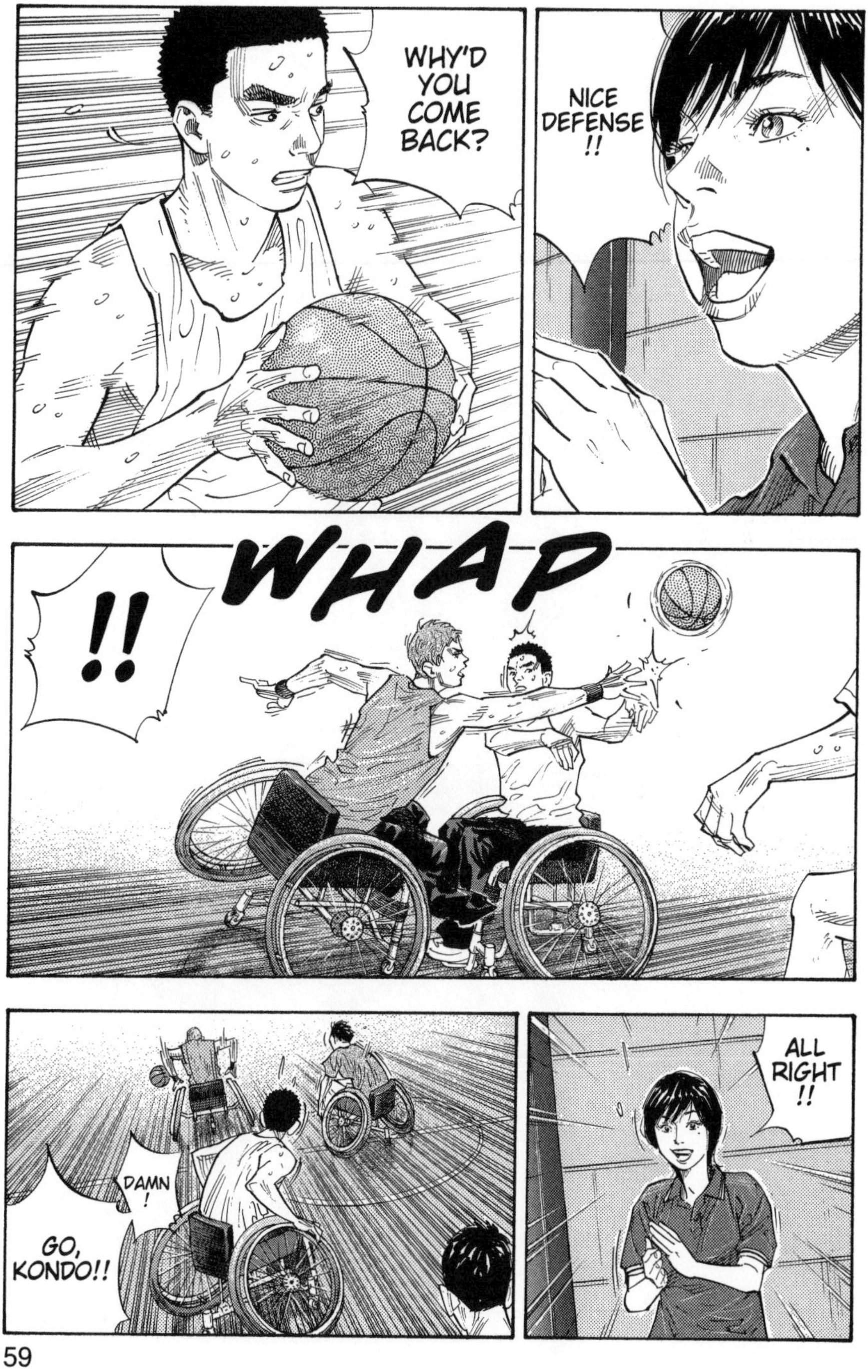
NICE DEFENSE !!
WHY'D YOU COME BACK?
WHAP
!!
ALL RIGHT !!
DAMN !
GO, KONDO!!

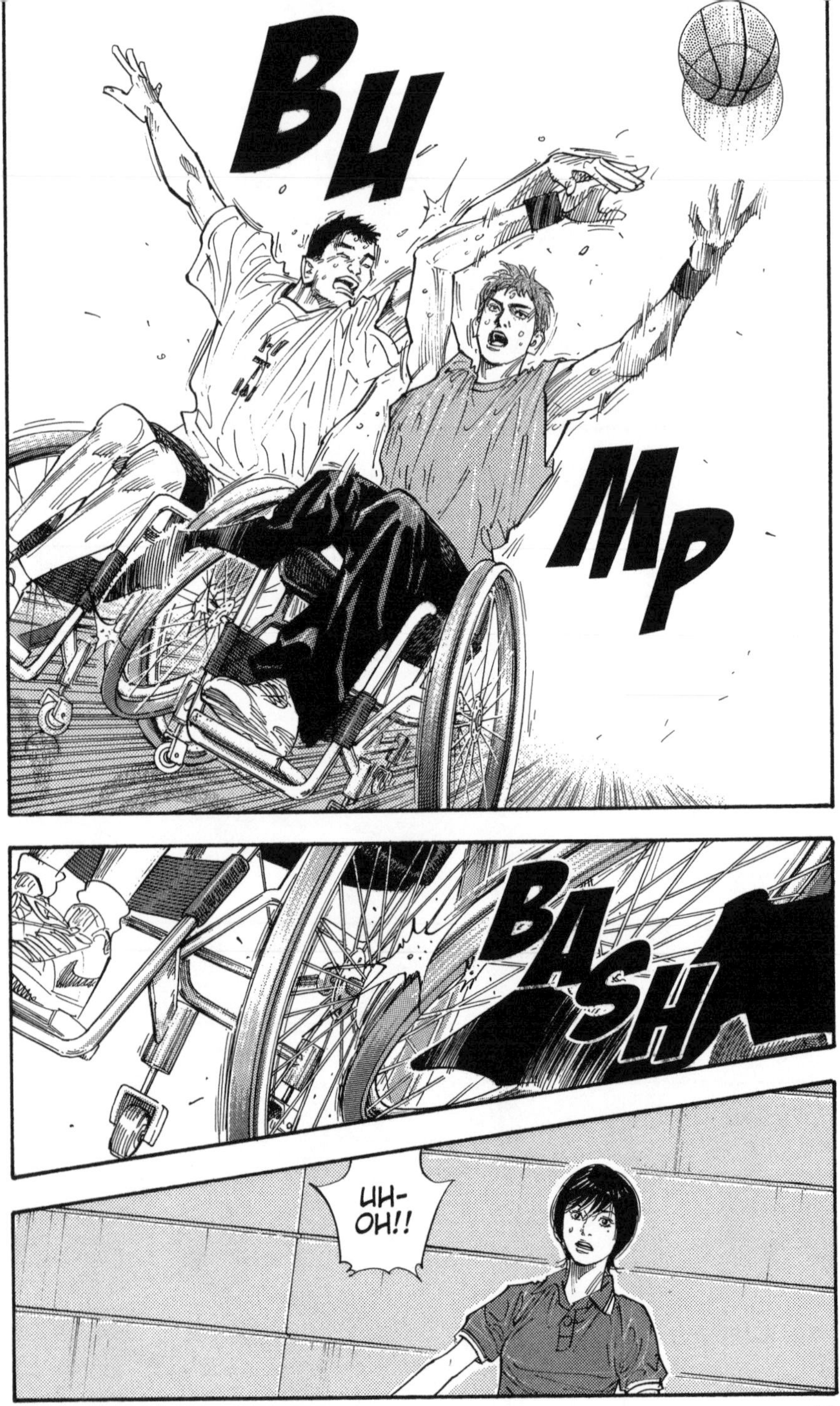
BU
MP
BASH
UH-OH!!

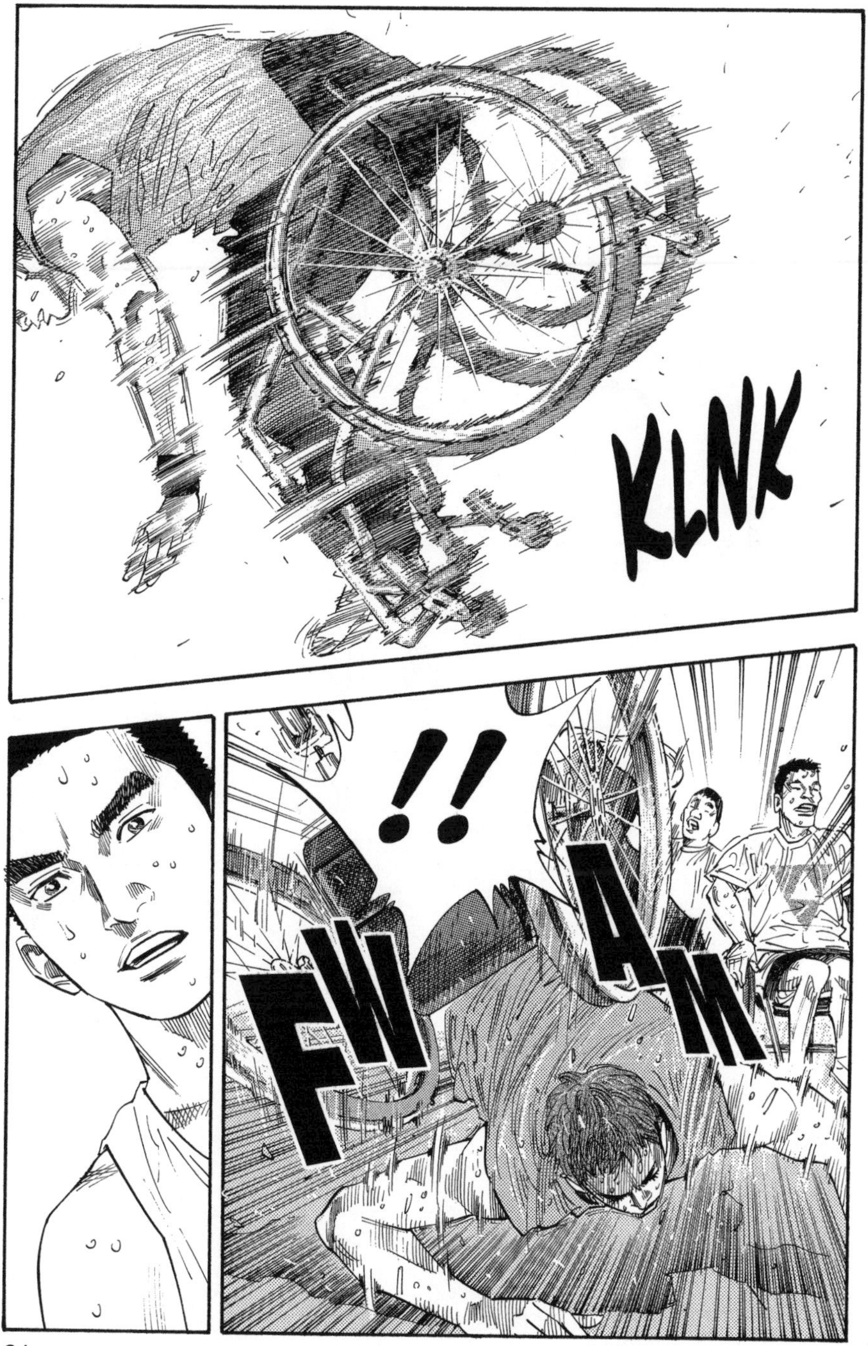
KLNK
!!
FWAM

NNGH
...

TUNK

KTAK

...UMPH!

WHOA!!

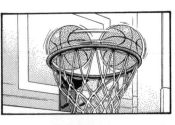

GO IN!

.....

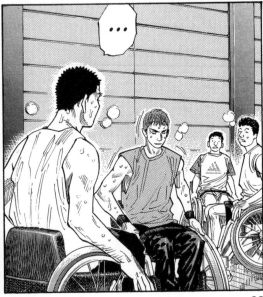

...

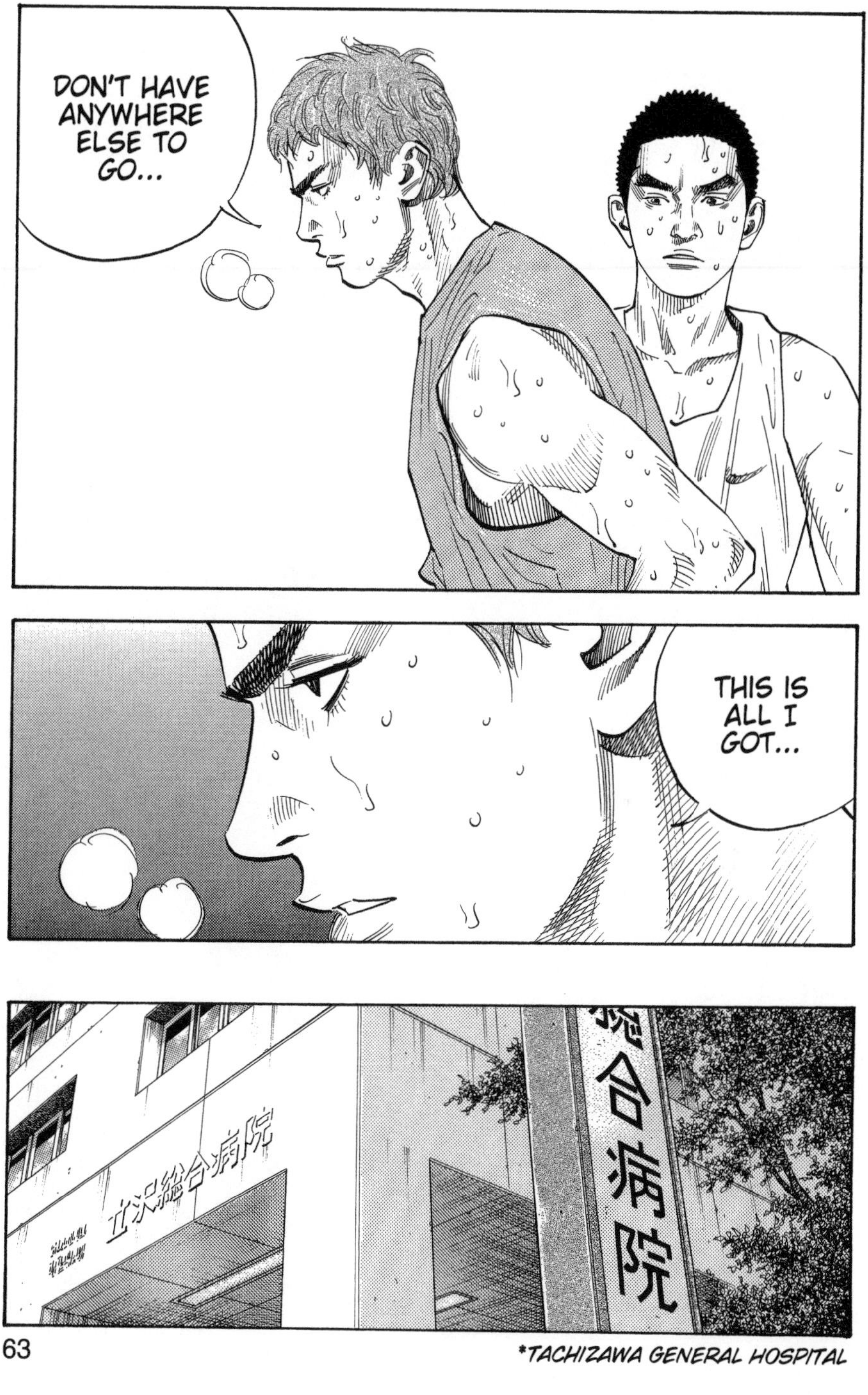
DON'T HAVE ANYWHERE ELSE TO GO...
THIS IS ALL I GOT...
立沢総合病院
総合病院

*TACHIZAWA GENERAL HOSPITAL

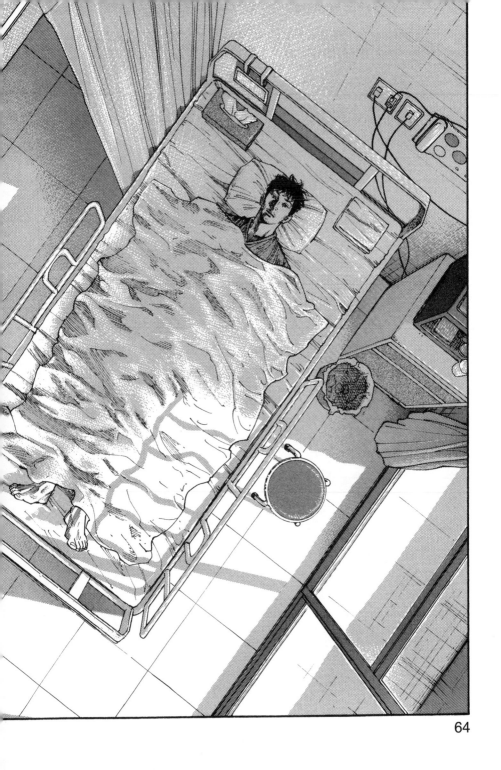

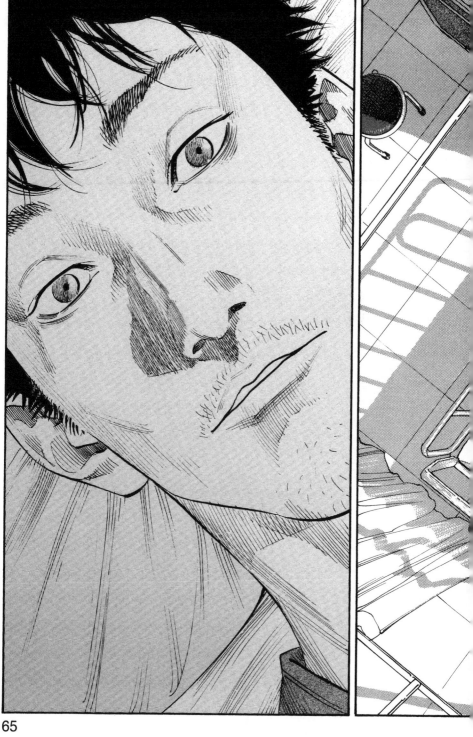

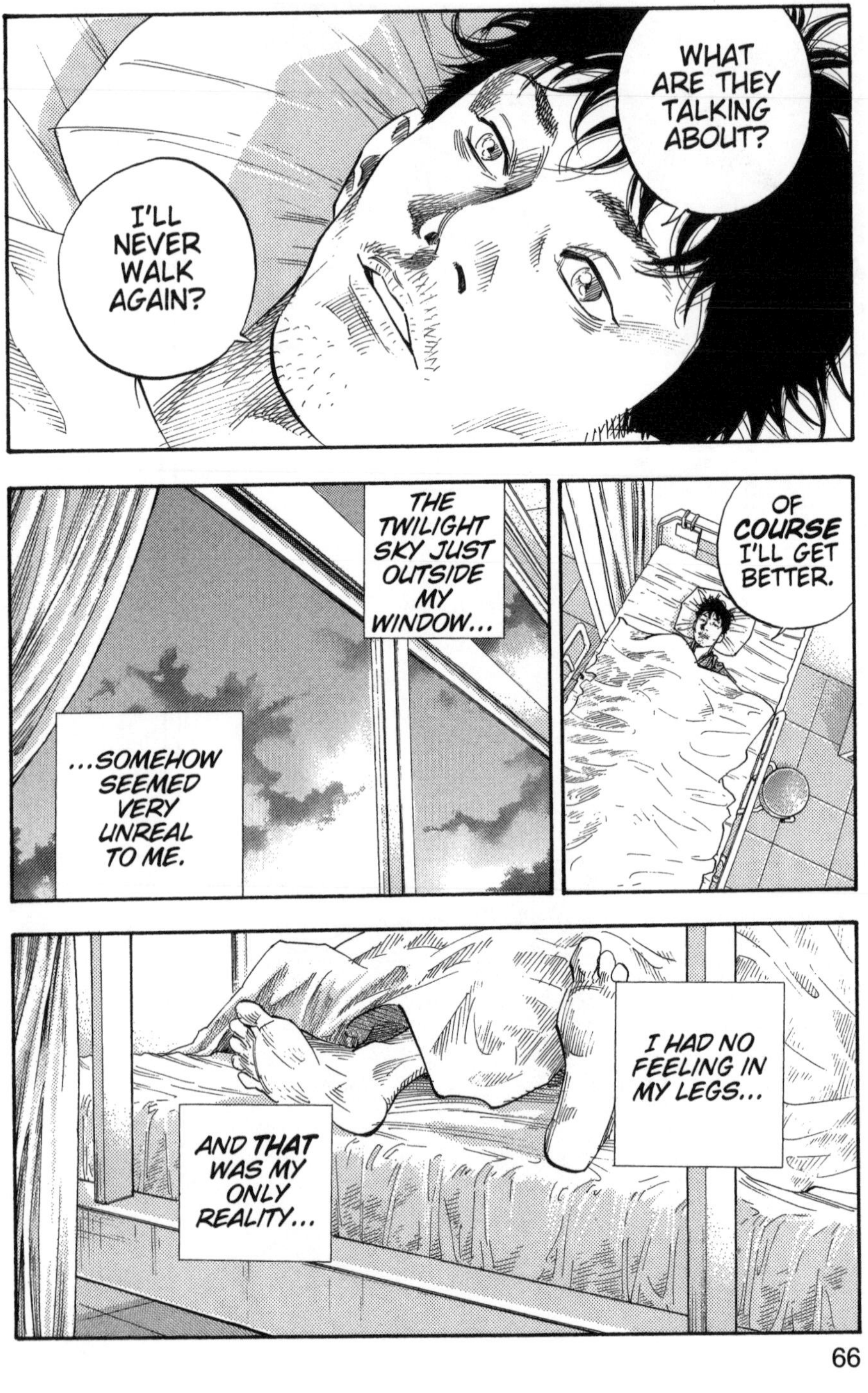
WHAT ARE THEY TALKING ABOUT?
I'LL NEVER WALK AGAIN?
OF COURSE I'LL GET BETTER.
THE TWILIGHT SKY JUST OUTSIDE MY WINDOW...
...SOMEHOW SEEMED VERY UNREAL TO ME.
I HAD NO FEELING IN MY LEGS...
AND THAT WAS MY ONLY REALITY...

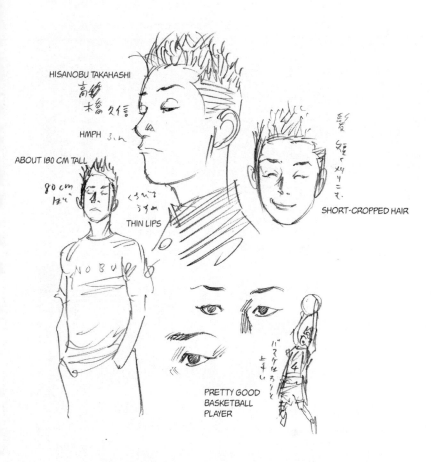

HISANOBU TAKAHASHI

高橋 久信

HMPH ふん

ABOUT 180 CM TALL

80cm ほど

THIN LIPS

くちびる うすめ

SHORT-CROPPED HAIR

髪 短く メリこむ

NOBU

PRETTY GOOD
BASKETBALL
PLAYER

バスケは わりと 上手い

REAL

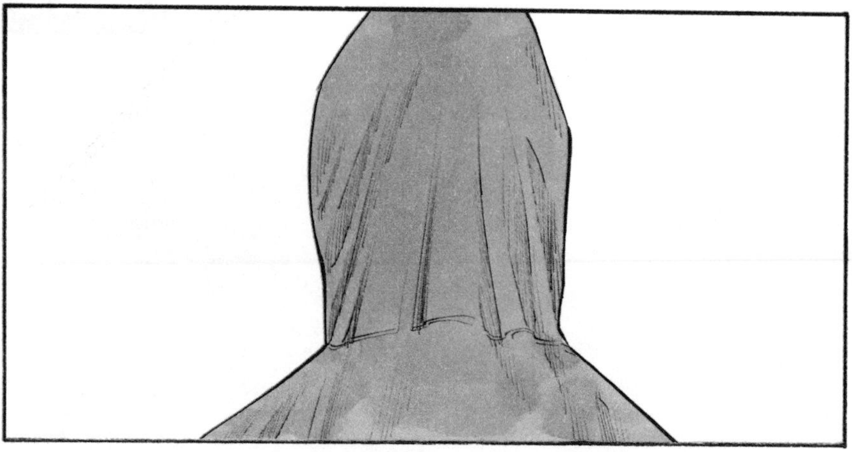

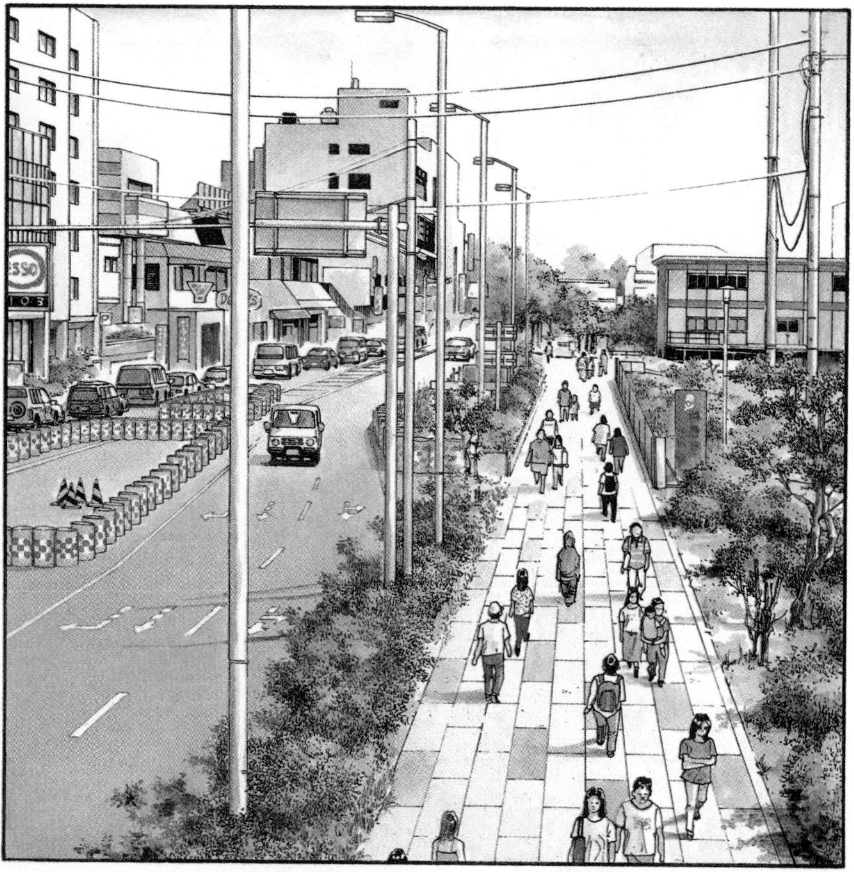
ESSO

9th

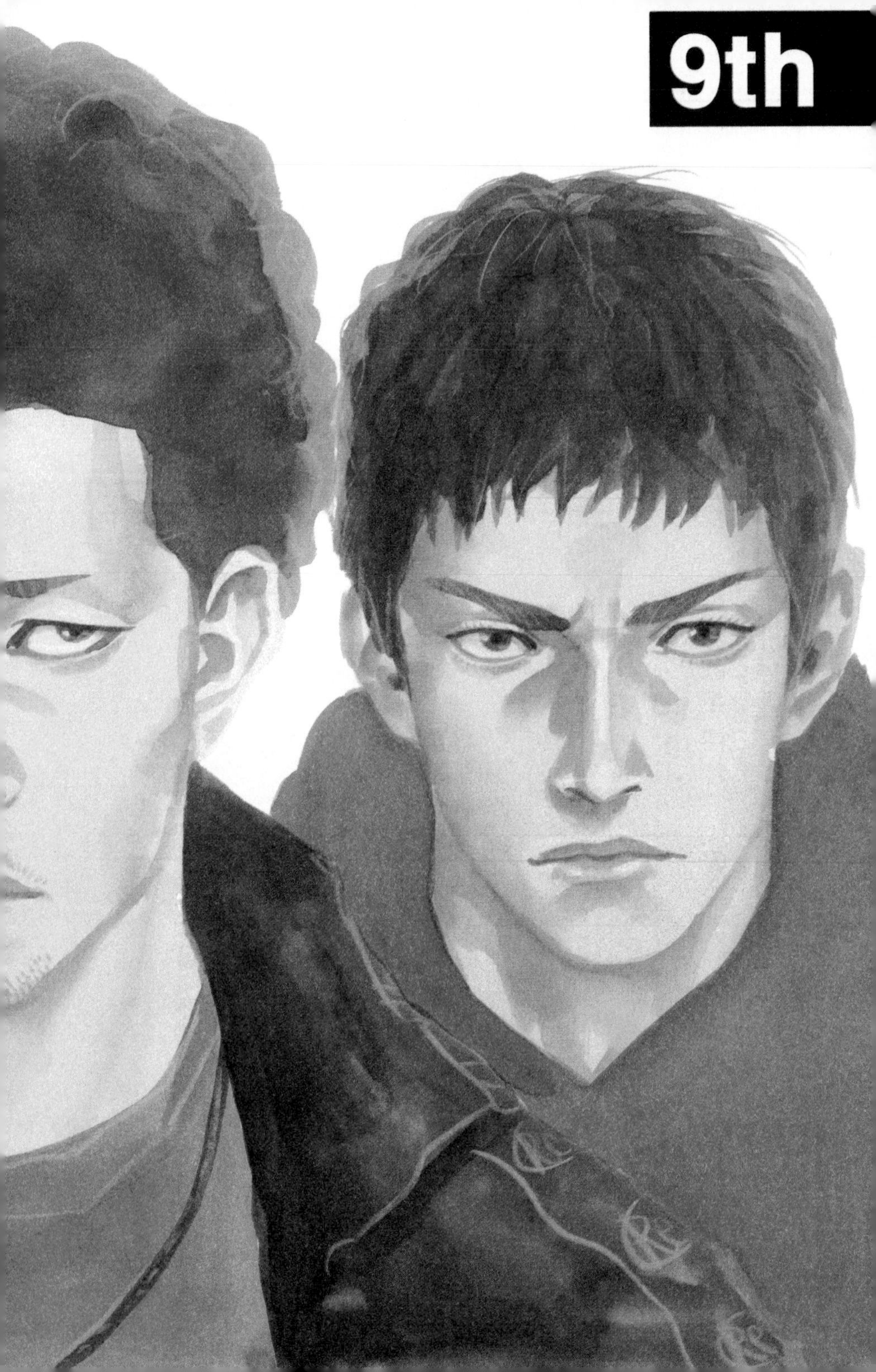

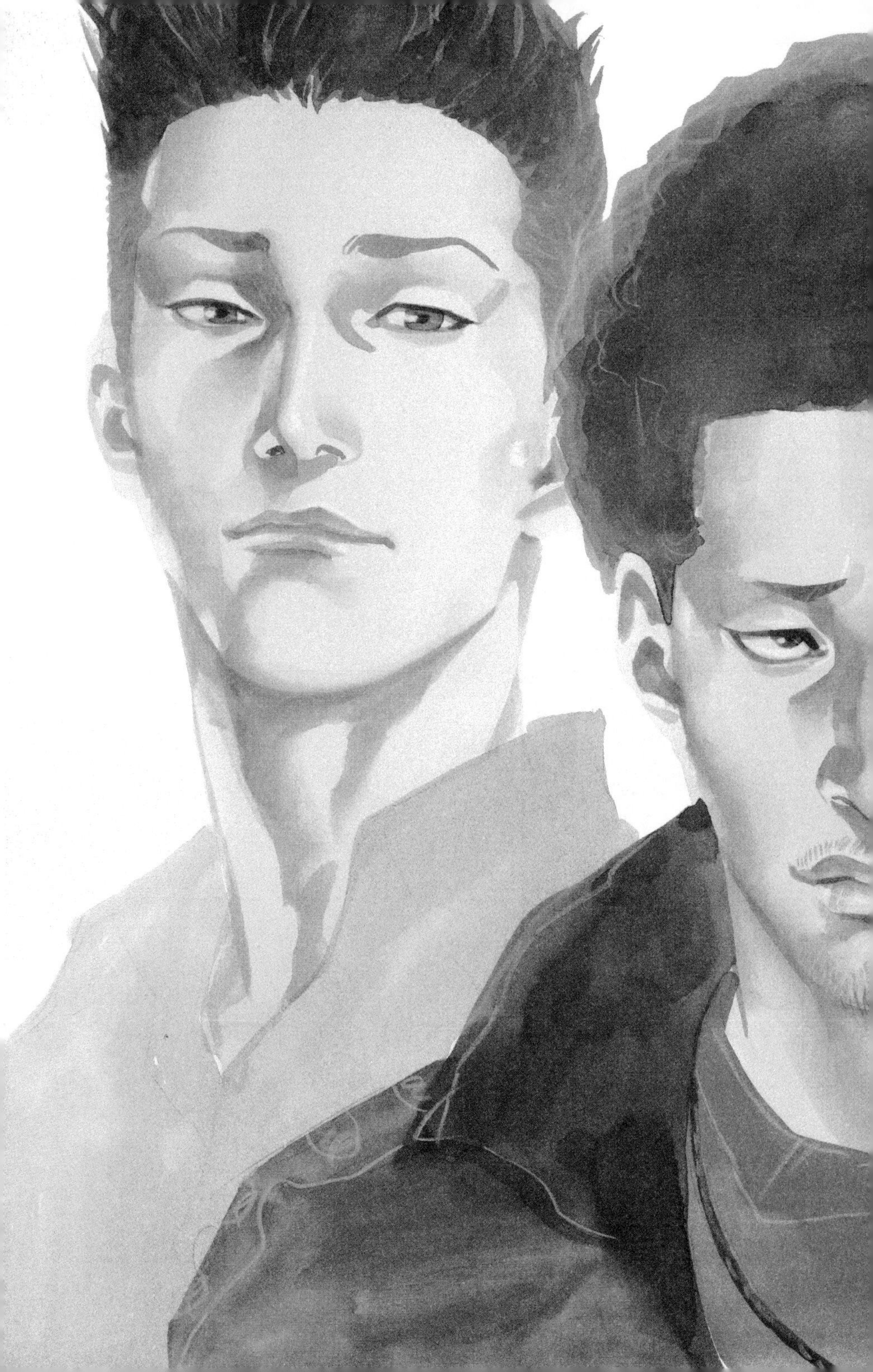

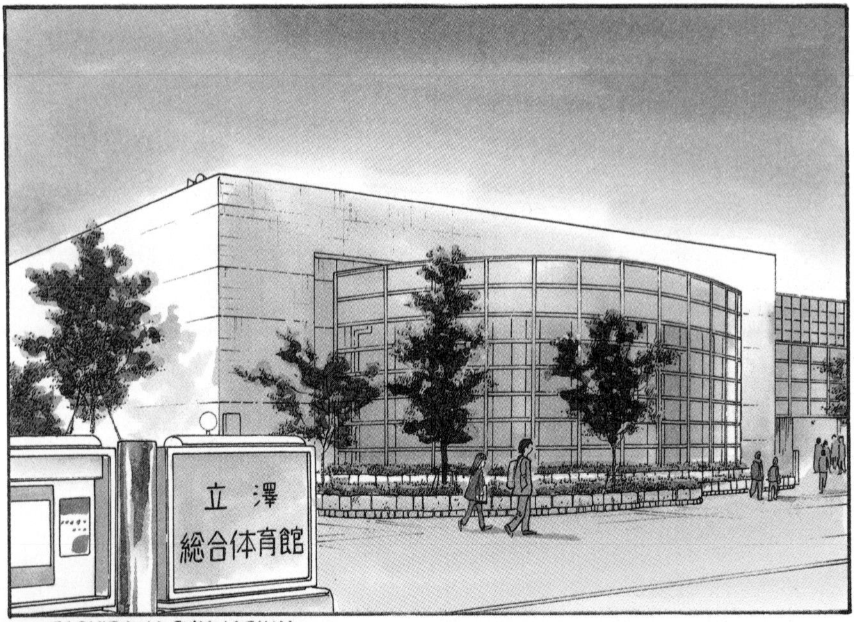
立澤
総合体育館

*TACHIZAWA GYMNASIUM

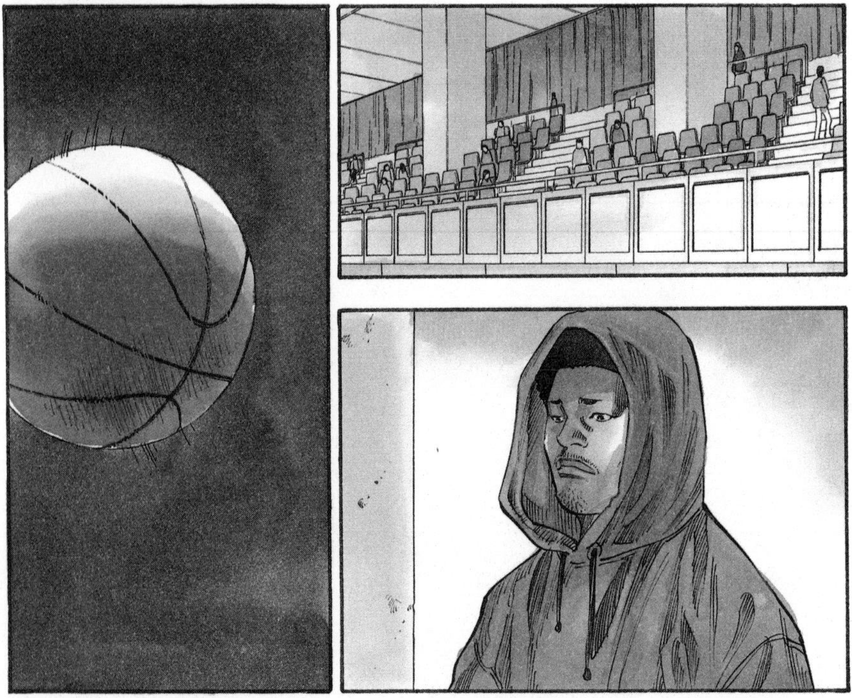

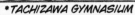

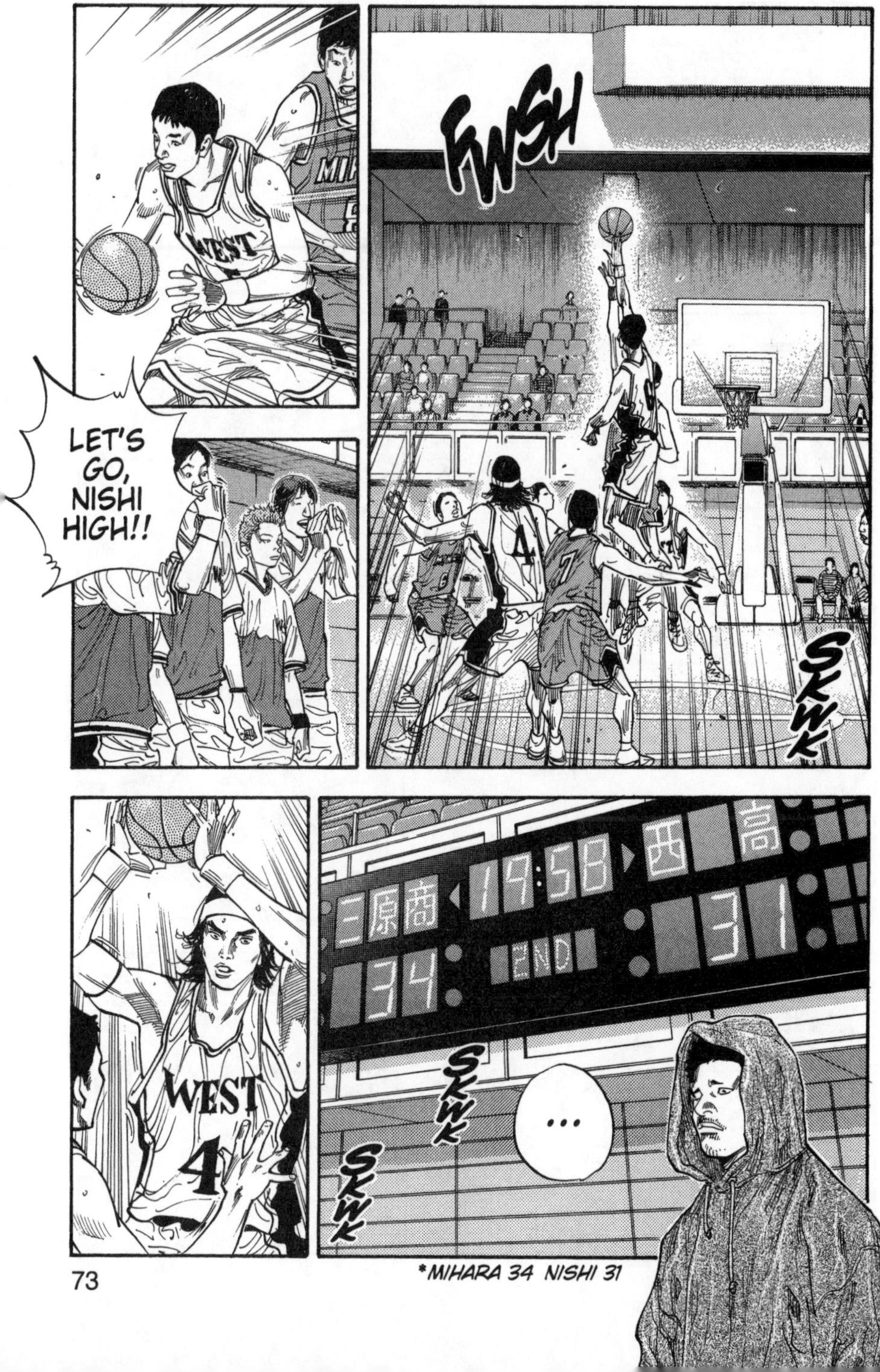
FWSH
SKWK
LET'S GO, NISHI HIGH!!
西高
14:58
三原商
31
2ND
34
SKWK
SKWK
...
*MIHARA 34 NISHI 31

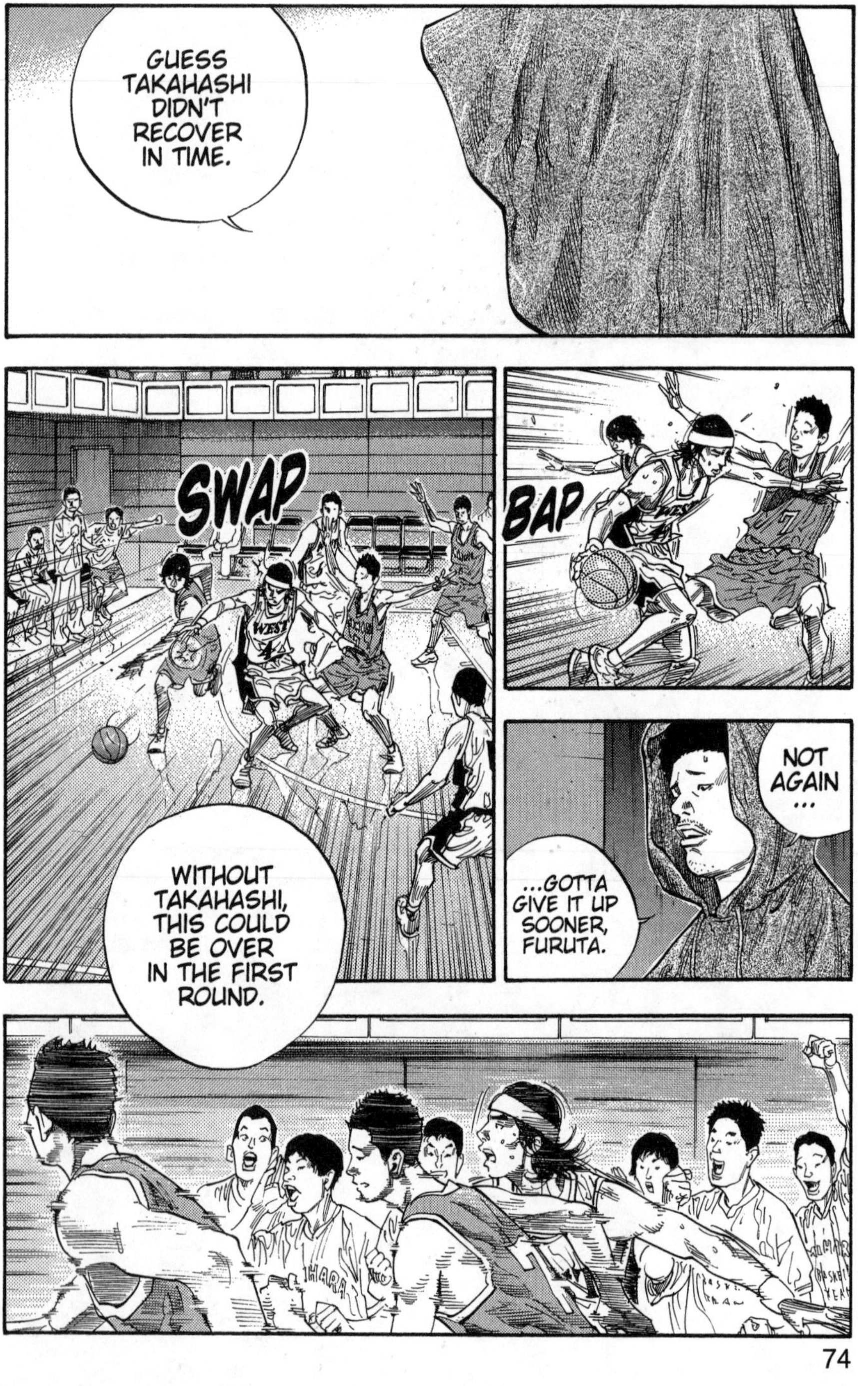
GUESS TAKAHASHI DIDN'T RECOVER IN TIME.
BAP
NOT AGAIN...
...GOTTA GIVE IT UP SOONER, FURUTA.
SWAP
WITHOUT TAKAHASHI, THIS COULD BE OVER IN THE FIRST ROUND.

AND THAT WOULD BE IT FOR THE THIRD-YEARS. NO MORE HIGH SCHOOL BALL.

...

HISANOBU, IT'S TIME WE GOT STARTED WITH YOUR PHYSICAL THERAPY.

AREN'T THEY...

*TACHIZAWA GENERAL HOSPITAL

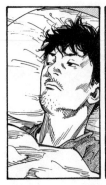

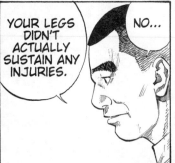

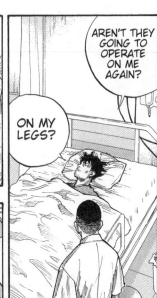

AREN'T THEY GOING TO OPERATE ON ME AGAIN?
ON MY LEGS?
NO...
YOUR LEGS DIDN'T ACTUALLY SUSTAIN ANY INJURIES.
...
IT TAKES TIME TO ACCEPT THE TRUTH.
THE TREATMENT PHASE IS OVER.
THE NEXT STEP IS TO WORK ON YOUR PHYSICAL REHABILITATION.

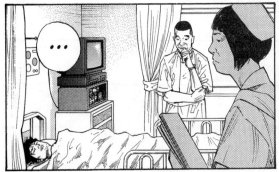

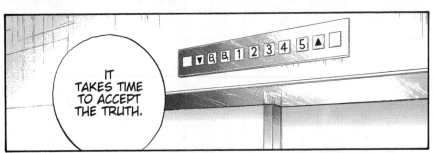

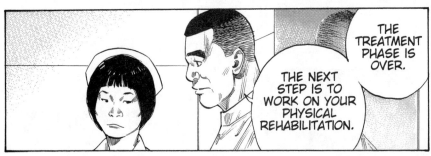

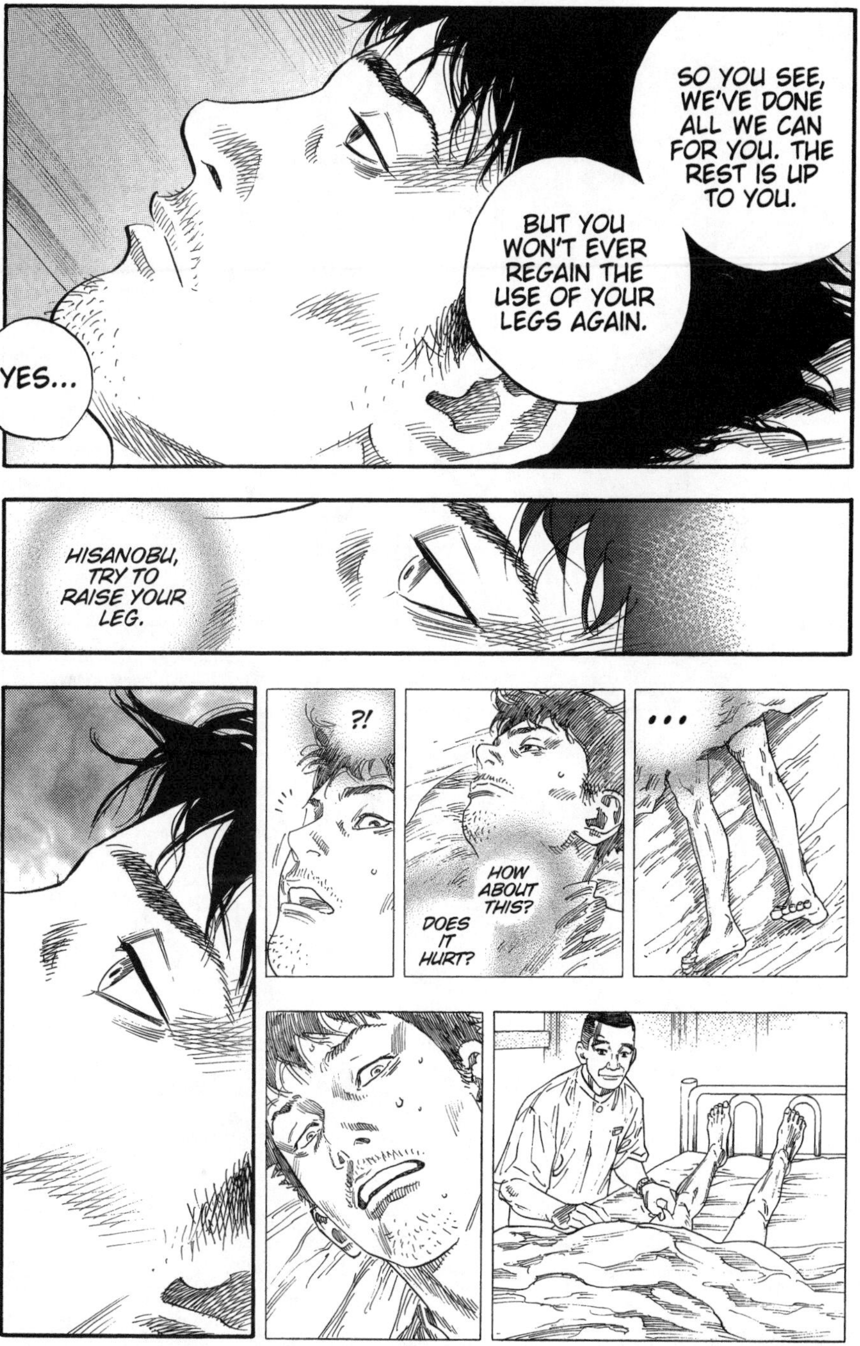
SO YOU SEE, WE'VE DONE ALL WE CAN FOR YOU. THE REST IS UP TO YOU.
BUT YOU WON'T EVER REGAIN THE USE OF YOUR LEGS AGAIN.
YES...
HISANOBU, TRY TO RAISE YOUR LEG.
...
HOW ABOUT THIS?
DOES IT HURT?
?!

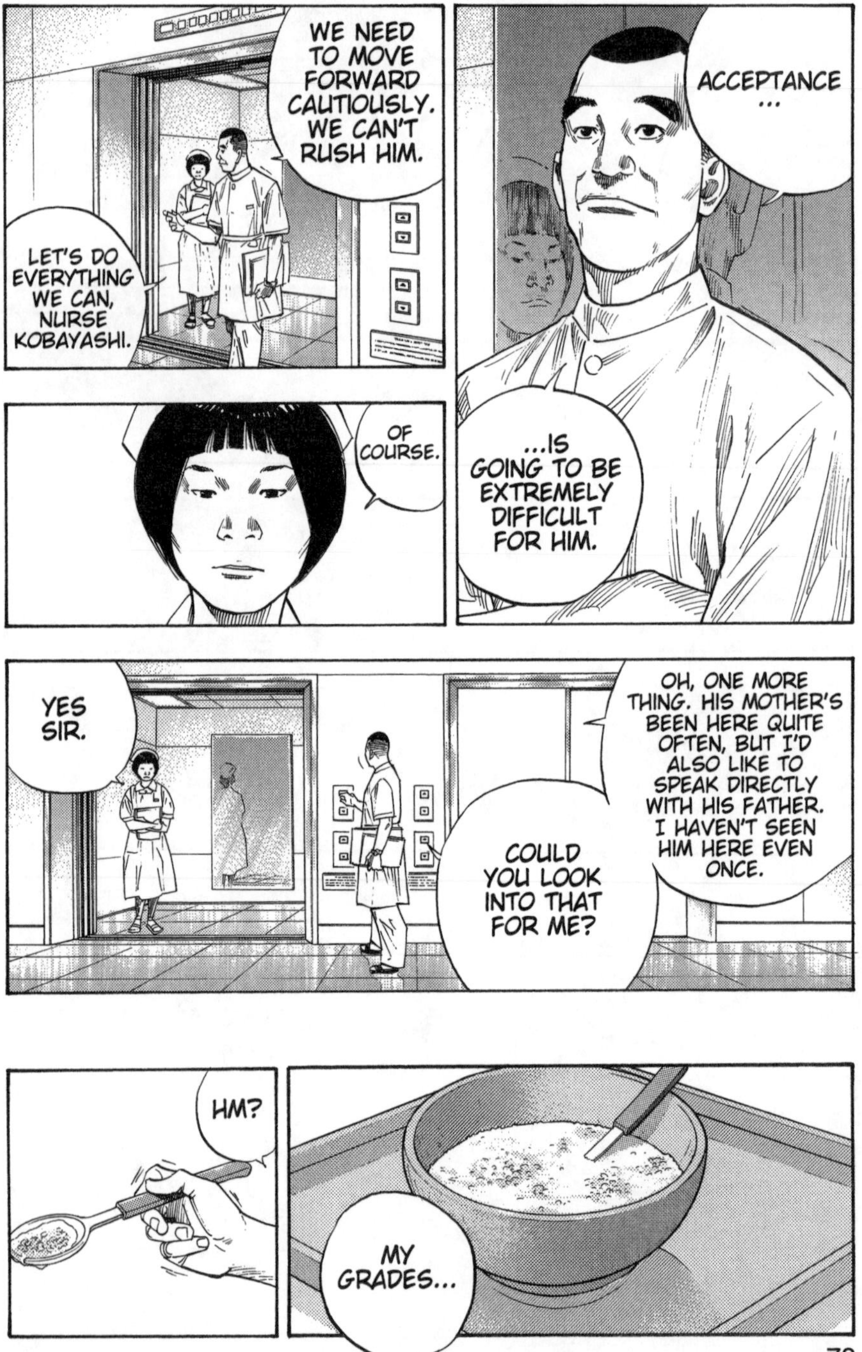
ACCEPTANCE...
...IS GOING TO BE EXTREMELY DIFFICULT FOR HIM.
WE NEED TO MOVE FORWARD CAUTIOUSLY. WE CAN'T RUSH HIM.
LET'S DO EVERYTHING WE CAN, NURSE KOBAYASHI.
OF COURSE.
OH, ONE MORE THING. HIS MOTHER'S BEEN HERE QUITE OFTEN, BUT I'D ALSO LIKE TO SPEAK DIRECTLY WITH HIS FATHER. I HAVEN'T SEEN HIM HERE EVEN ONCE.
COULD YOU LOOK INTO THAT FOR ME?
YES SIR.
MY GRADES...
HM?

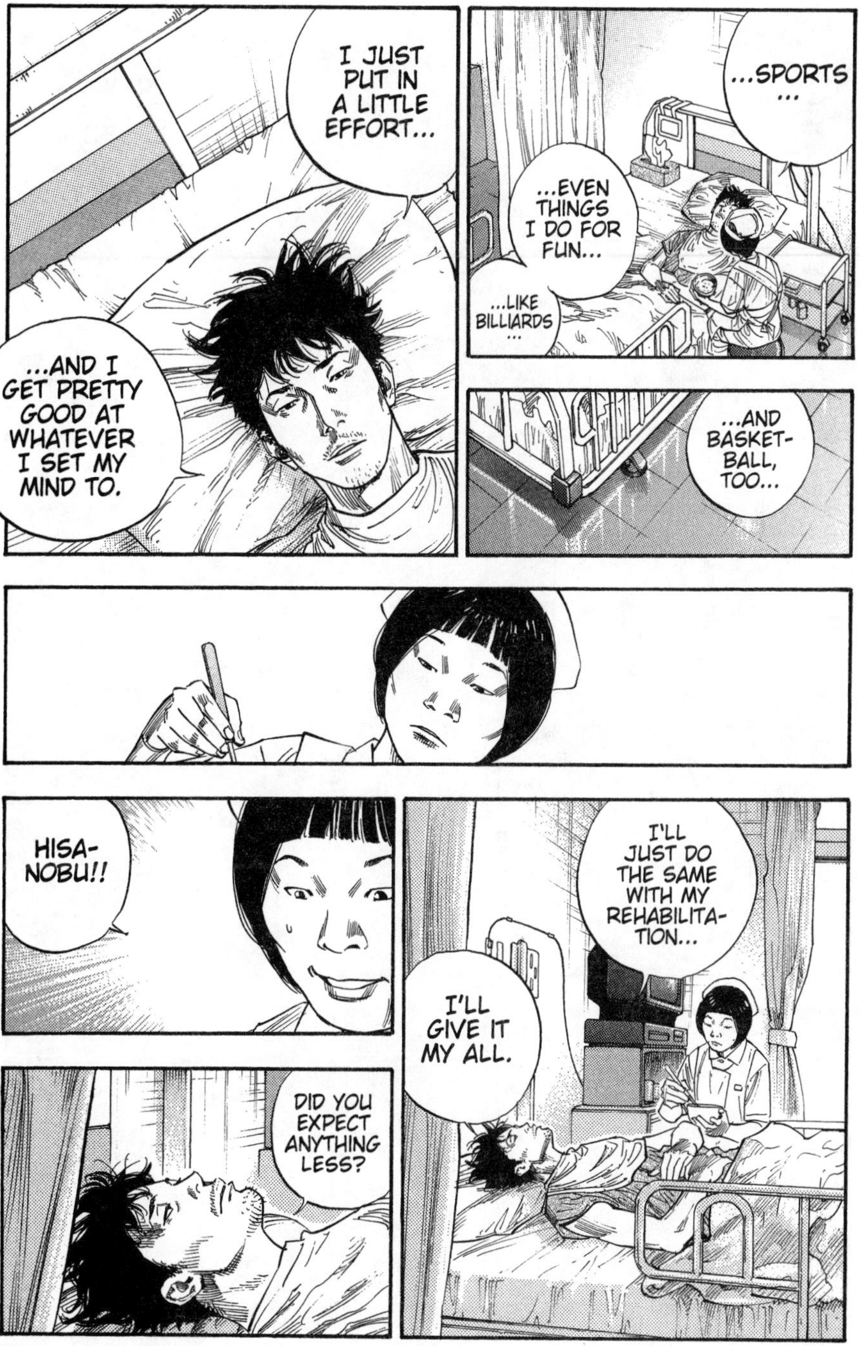
...SPORTS...
...EVEN THINGS I DO FOR FUN...
...LIKE BILLIARDS...
...AND BASKET-BALL, TOO...
I JUST PUT IN A LITTLE EFFORT...
...AND I GET PRETTY GOOD AT WHATEVER I SET MY MIND TO.
I'LL JUST DO THE SAME WITH MY REHABILITA-TION...
I'LL GIVE IT MY ALL.
HISA-NOBU!!
DID YOU EXPECT ANYTHING LESS?

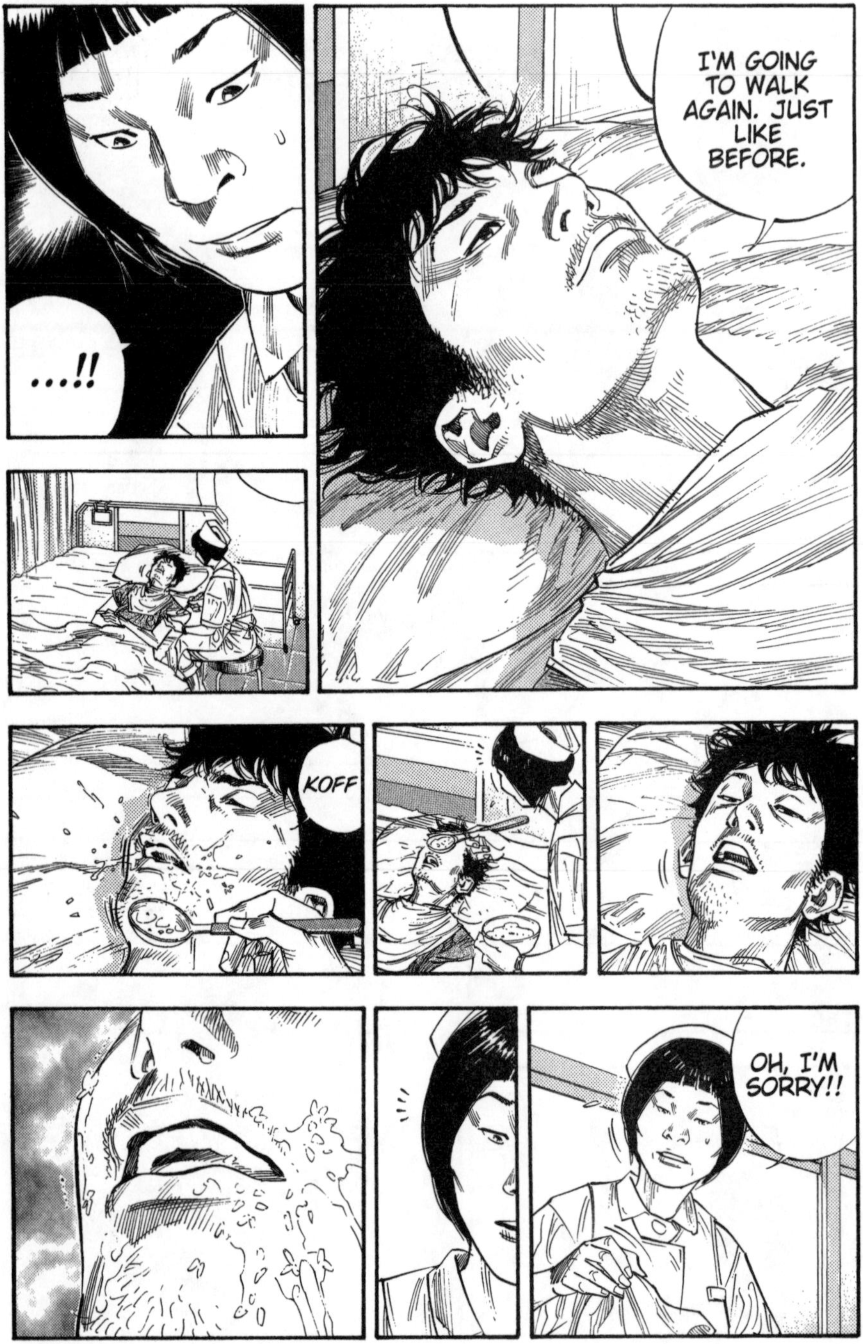
I'M GOING TO WALK AGAIN. JUST LIKE BEFORE.
...!!
KOFF
OH, I'M SORRY!!

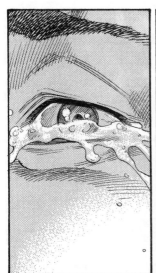

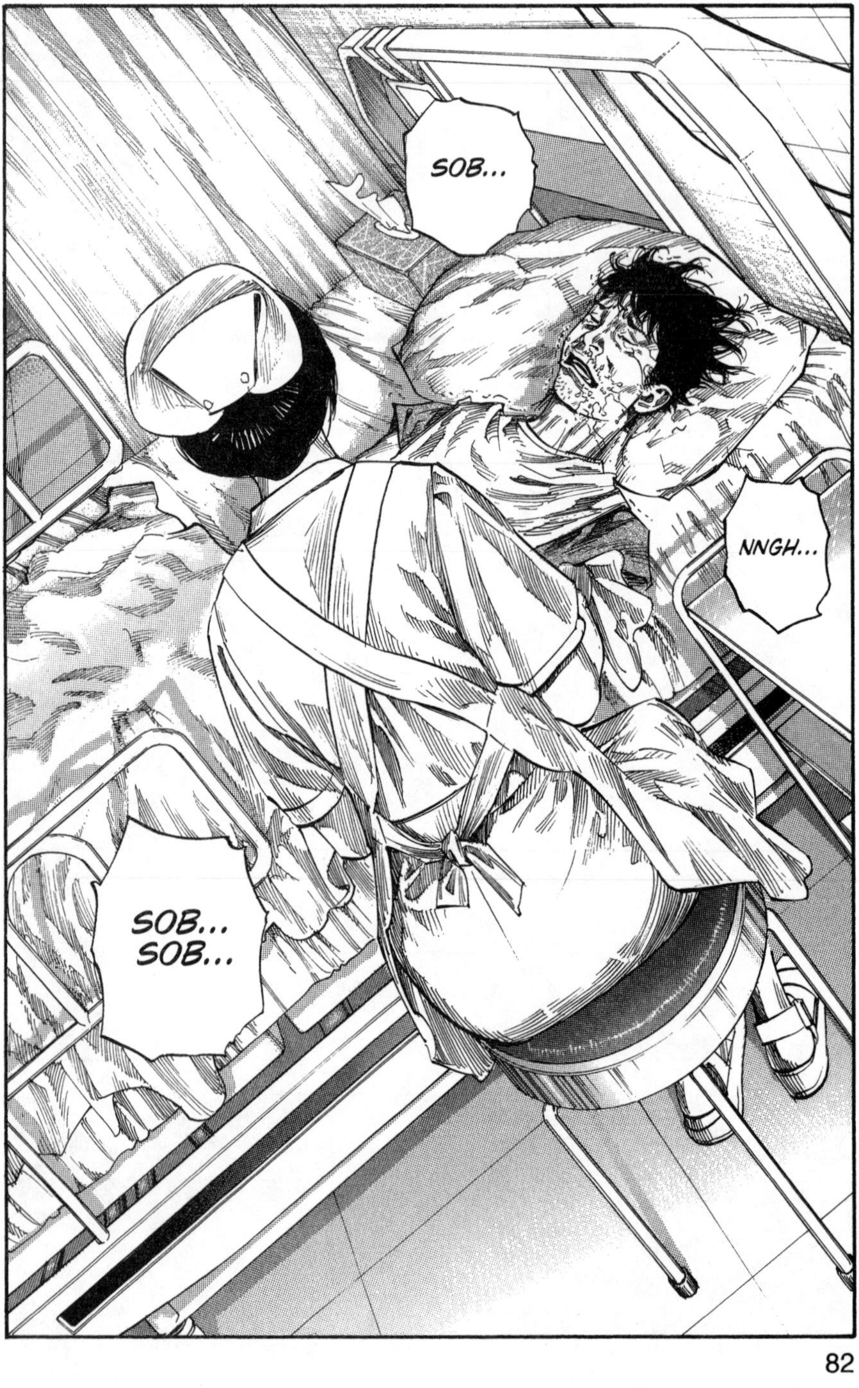
SOB...
NNGH...
SOB... SOB...

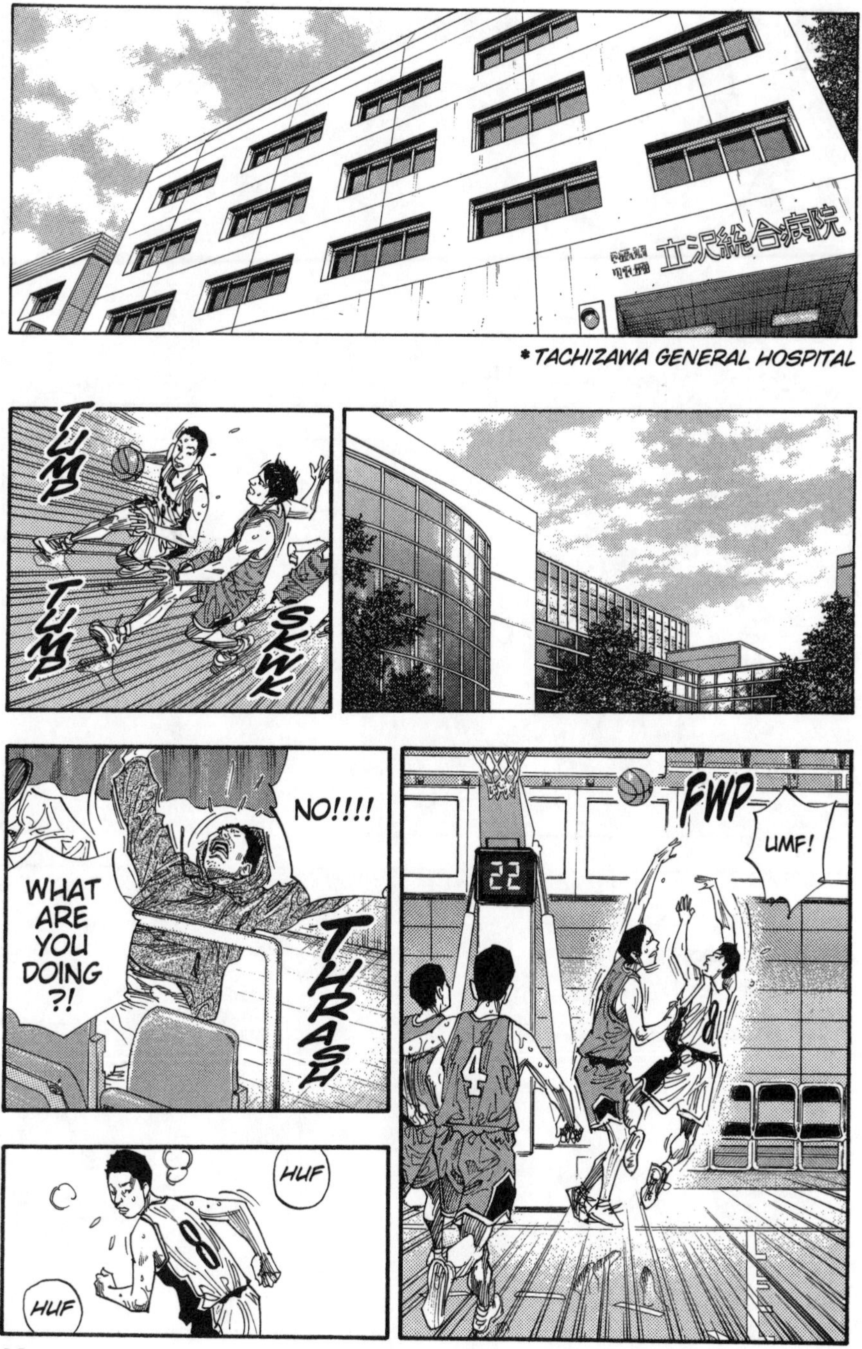
*TACHIZAWA GENERAL HOSPITAL
立沢総合病院
TUMP
TUMP
SKWK
FWP
UMF!
22
4
8
NO!!!!
WHAT ARE YOU DOING ?!
THRASH
HUF
HUF
8

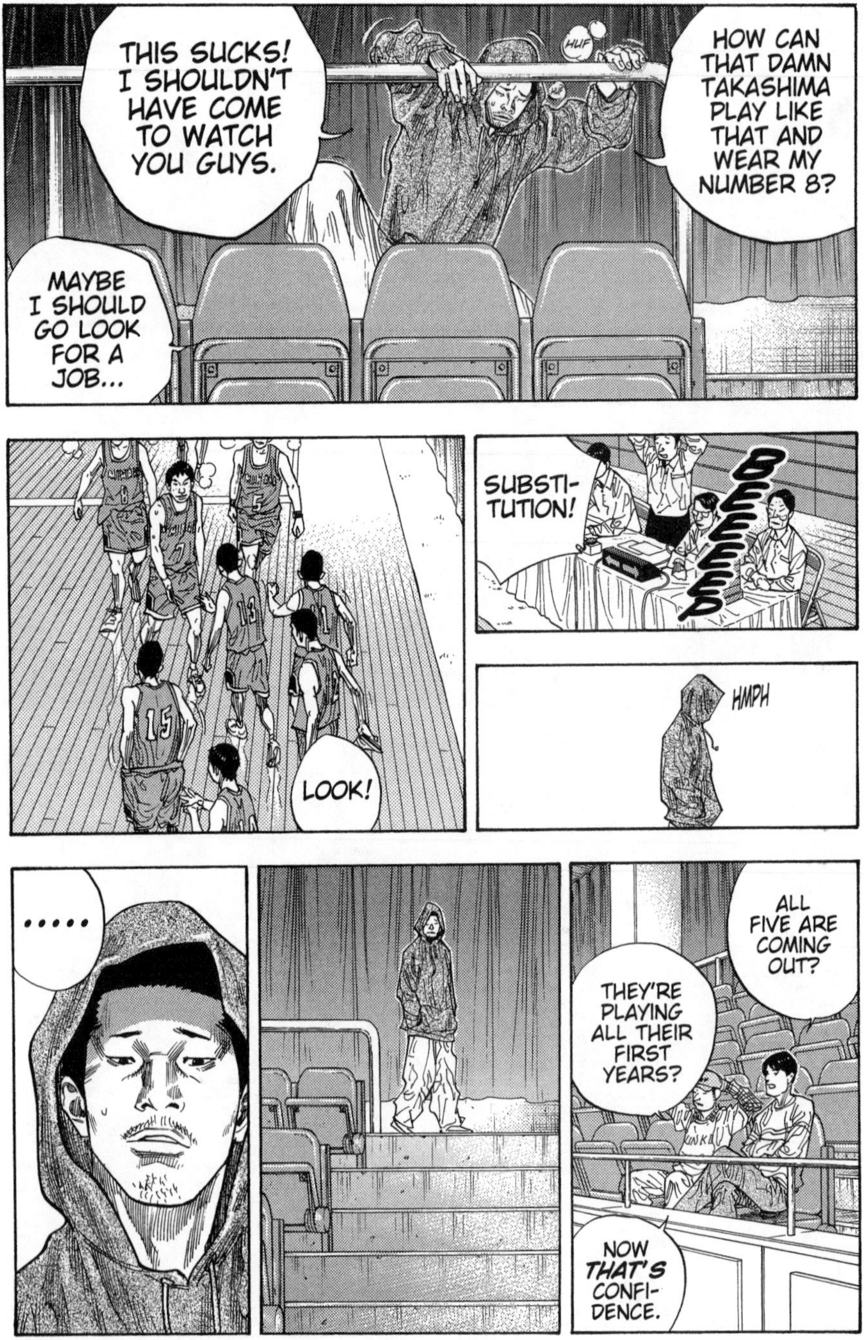
HOW CAN THAT DAMN TAKASHIMA PLAY LIKE THAT AND WEAR MY NUMBER 8?
HUF
THIS SUCKS! I SHOULDN'T HAVE COME TO WATCH YOU GUYS.
MAYBE I SHOULD GO LOOK FOR A JOB...
BEEEEEEP
SUBSTI-TUTION!
HMPH
LOOK!
ALL FIVE ARE COMING OUT?
THEY'RE PLAYING ALL THEIR FIRST YEARS?
NOW *THAT'S* CONFI-DENCE.
.....

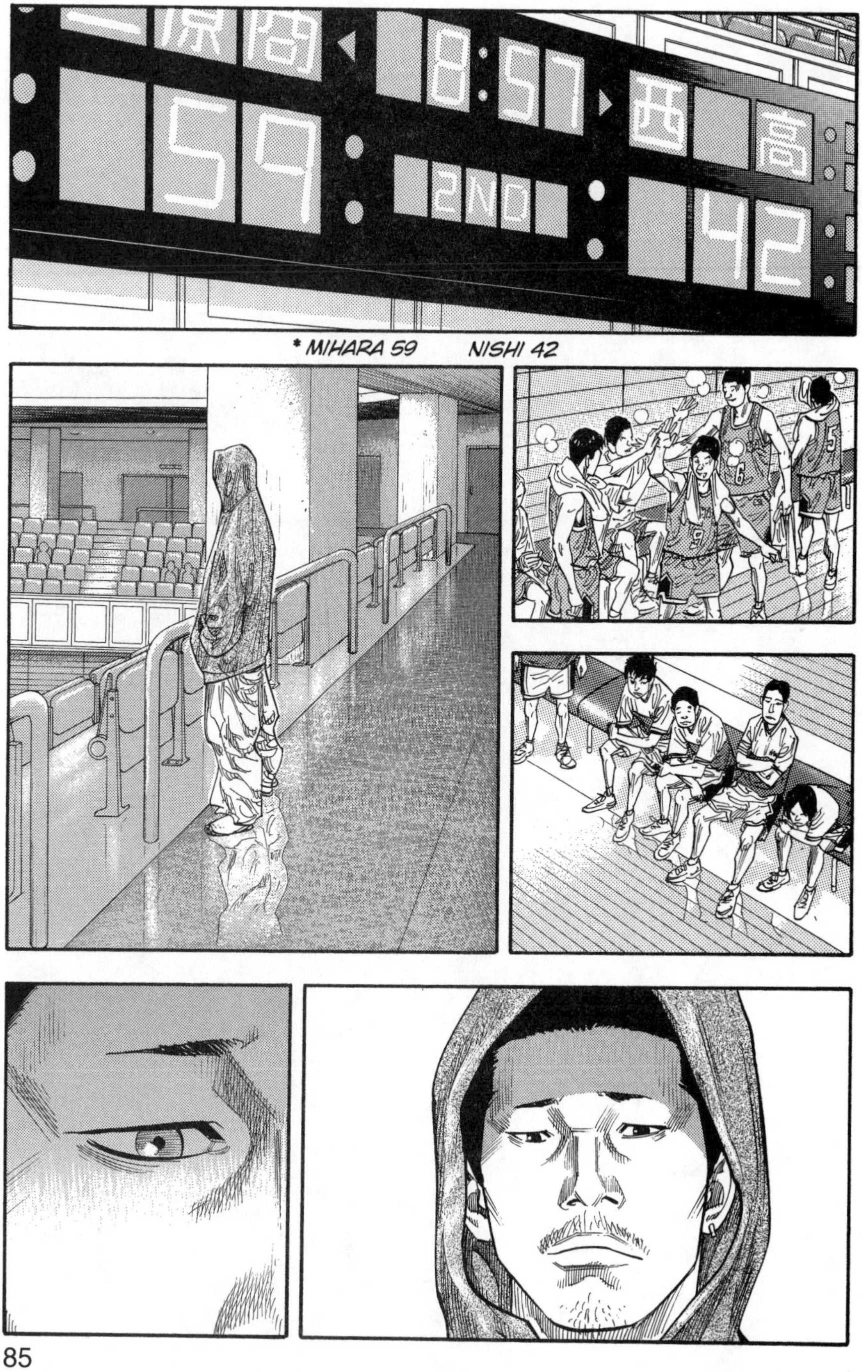
8:57
西 高
59
2ND
42

* MIHARA 59 NISHI 42

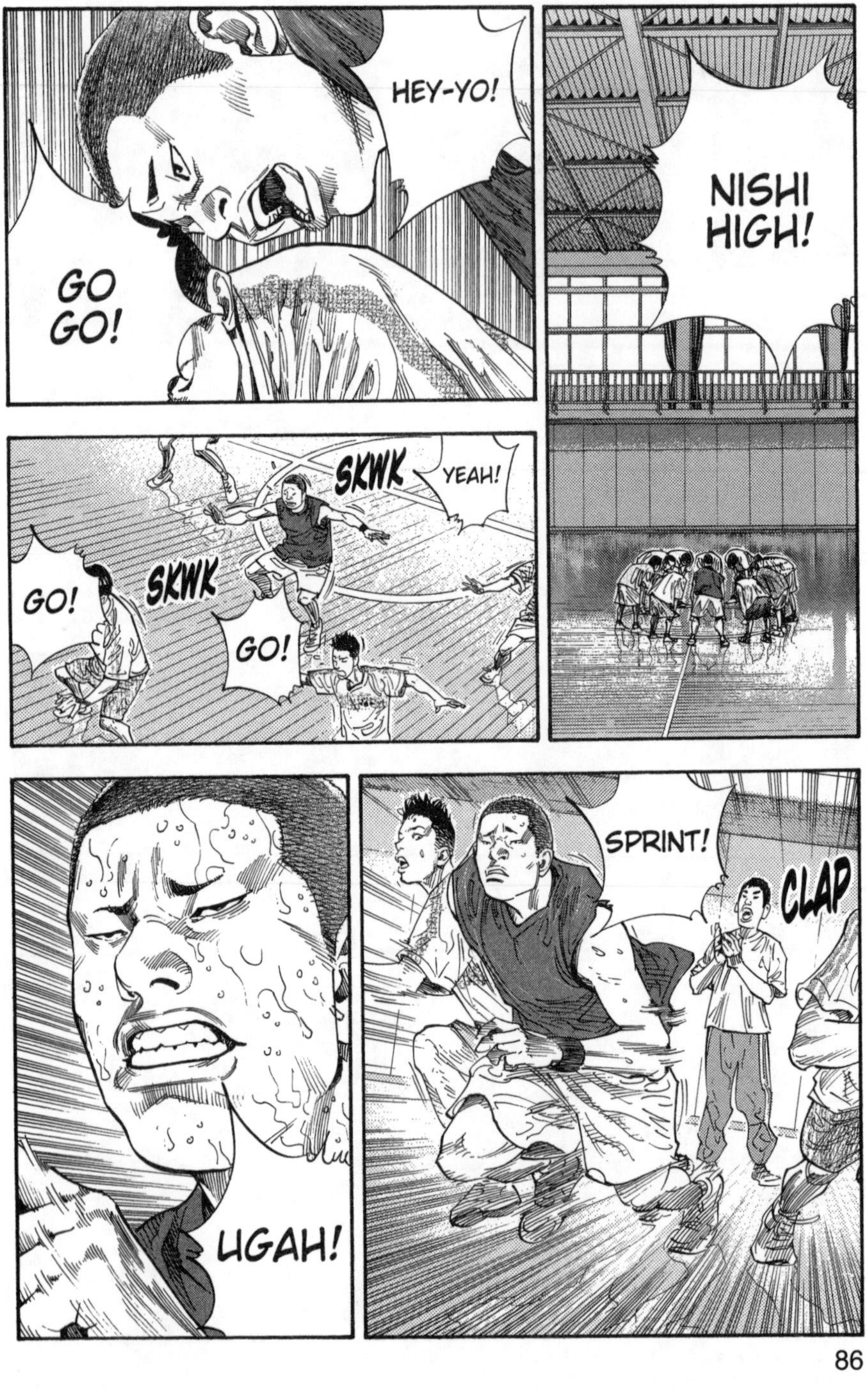
NISHI HIGH!
HEY-YO!
GO GO!
YEAH!
SKWK
SKWK
GO!
GO!
SPRINT!
CLAP
UGAH!

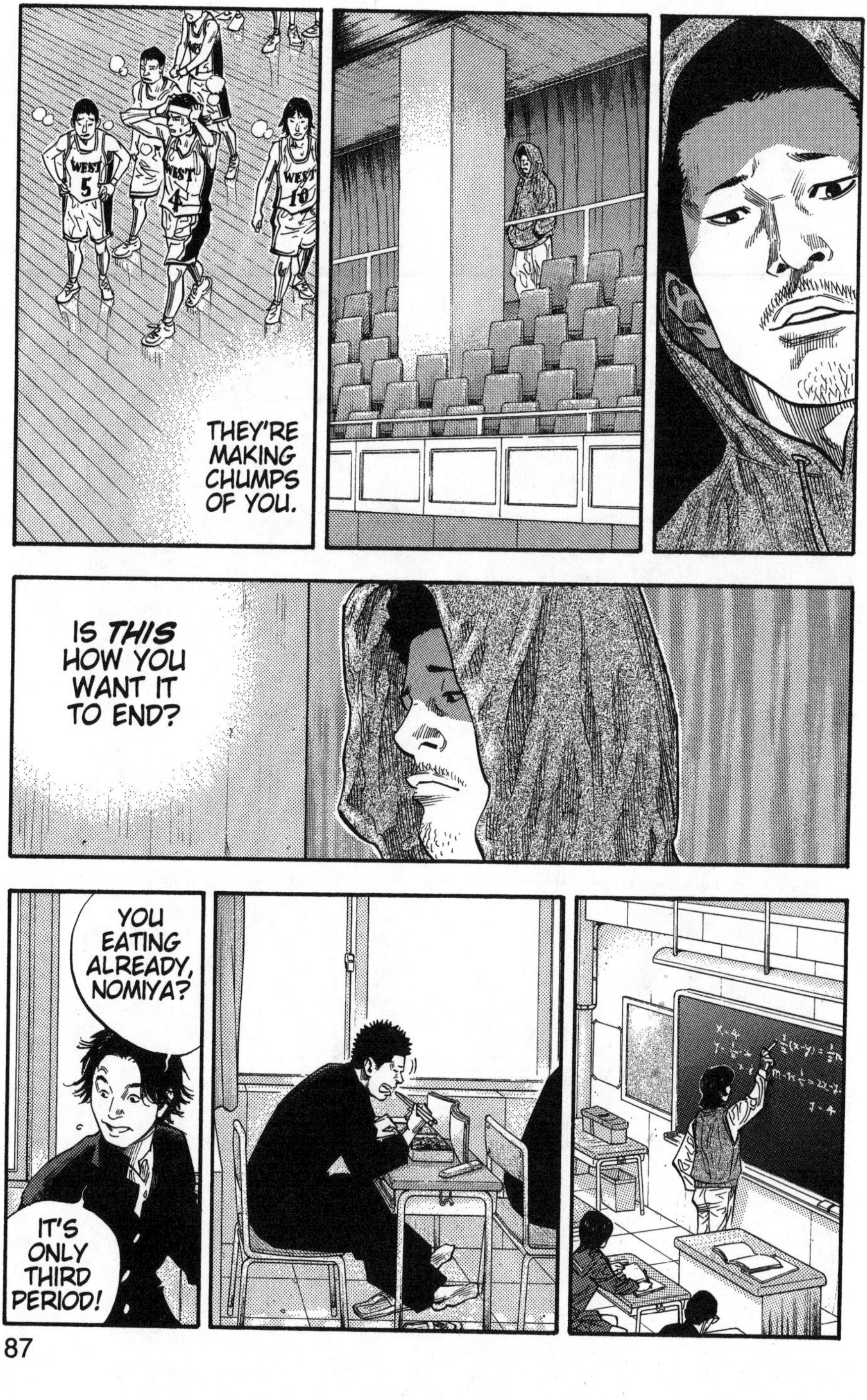
THEY'RE MAKING CHUMPS OF YOU.
IS *THIS* HOW YOU WANT IT TO END?
YOU EATING ALREADY, NOMIYA?
IT'S ONLY THIRD PERIOD!

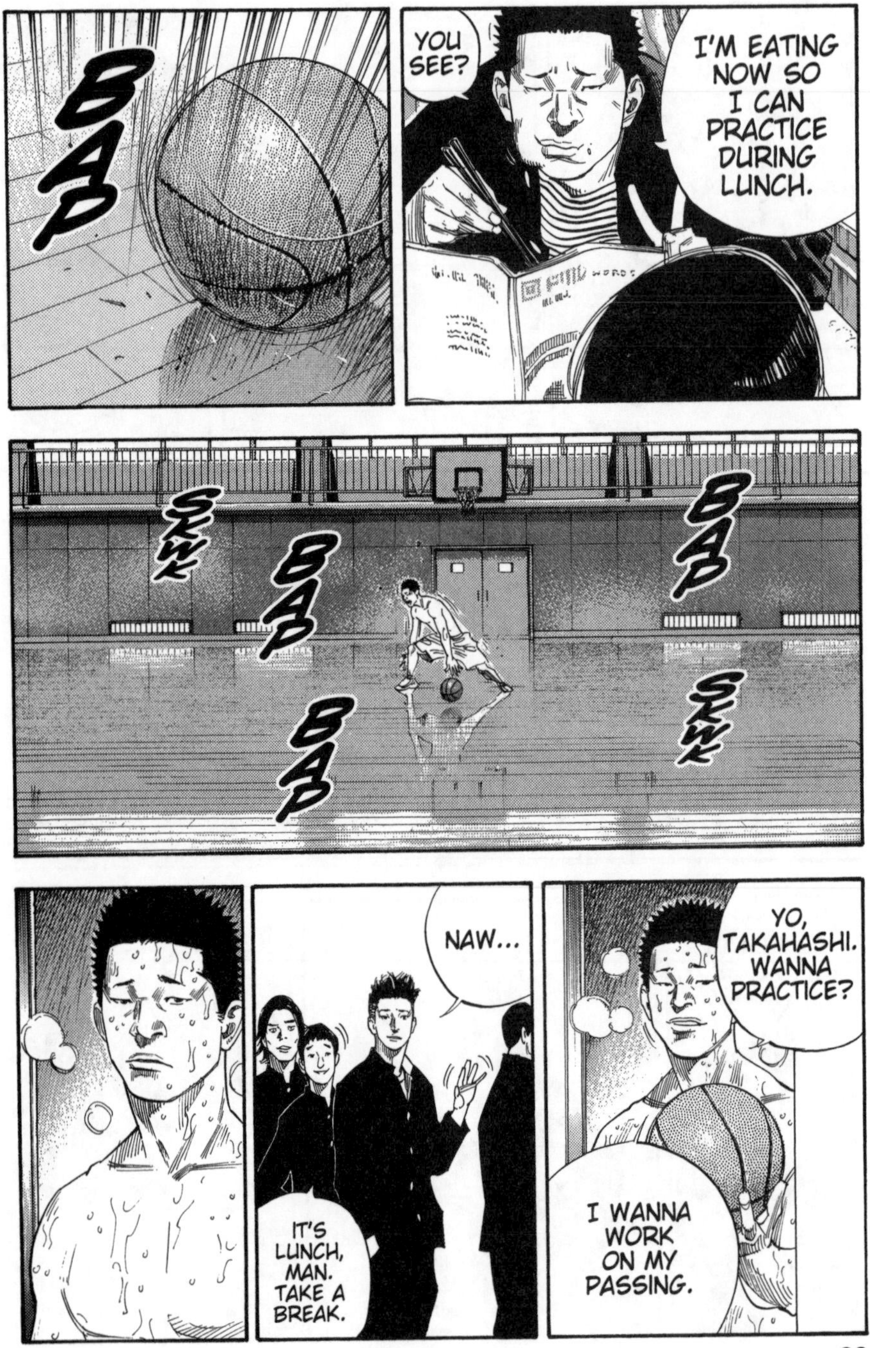
I'M EATING NOW SO I CAN PRACTICE DURING LUNCH.
YOU SEE?
BAP
BAP
SKWK
BAP
BAP
SKWK
YO, TAKAHASHI. WANNA PRACTICE?
I WANNA WORK ON MY PASSING.
NAW...
IT'S LUNCH, MAN. TAKE A BREAK.

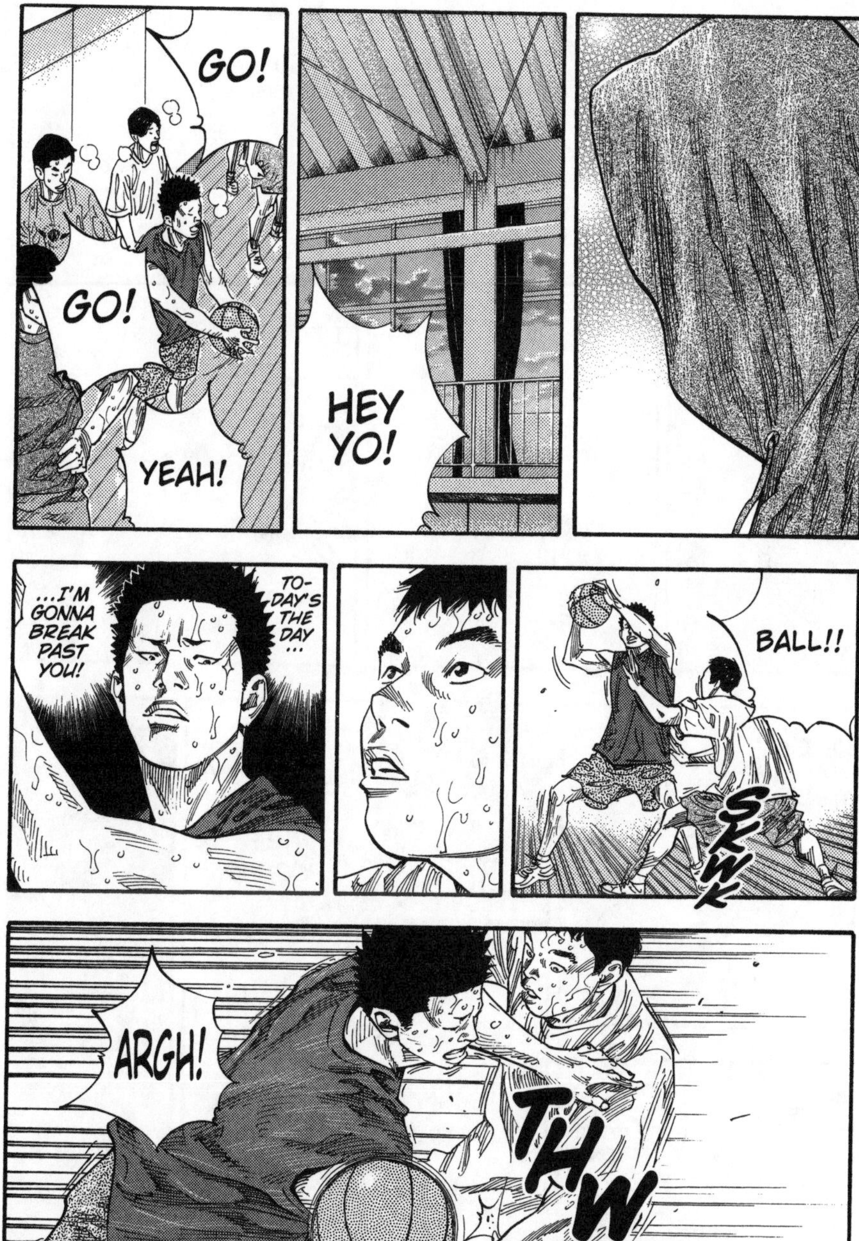
HEY YO!
GO!
GO!
YEAH!
BALL!!
SKWK
TO-DAY'S THE DAY...
...I'M GONNA BREAK PAST YOU!
ARGH!
THWP

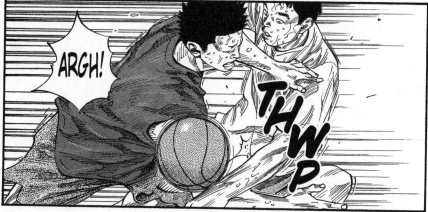

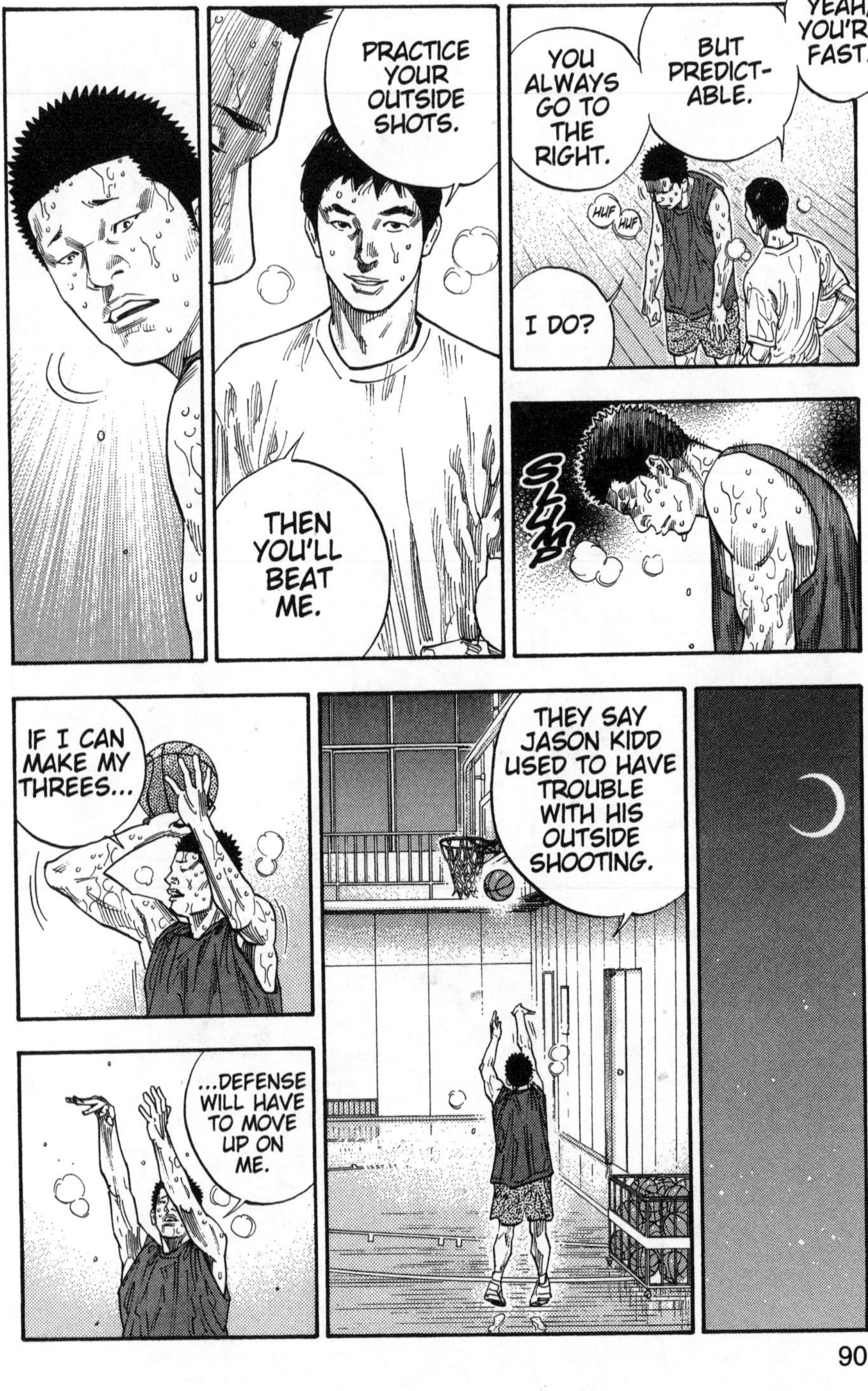
YEAH, YOU'RE FAST.
BUT PREDICT-ABLE.
YOU ALWAYS GO TO THE RIGHT.
HUF HUF
I DO?
SLUMP
PRACTICE YOUR OUTSIDE SHOTS.
THEN YOU'LL BEAT ME.
THEY SAY JASON KIDD USED TO HAVE TROUBLE WITH HIS OUTSIDE SHOOTING.
IF I CAN MAKE MY THREES...
...DEFENSE WILL HAVE TO MOVE UP ON ME.

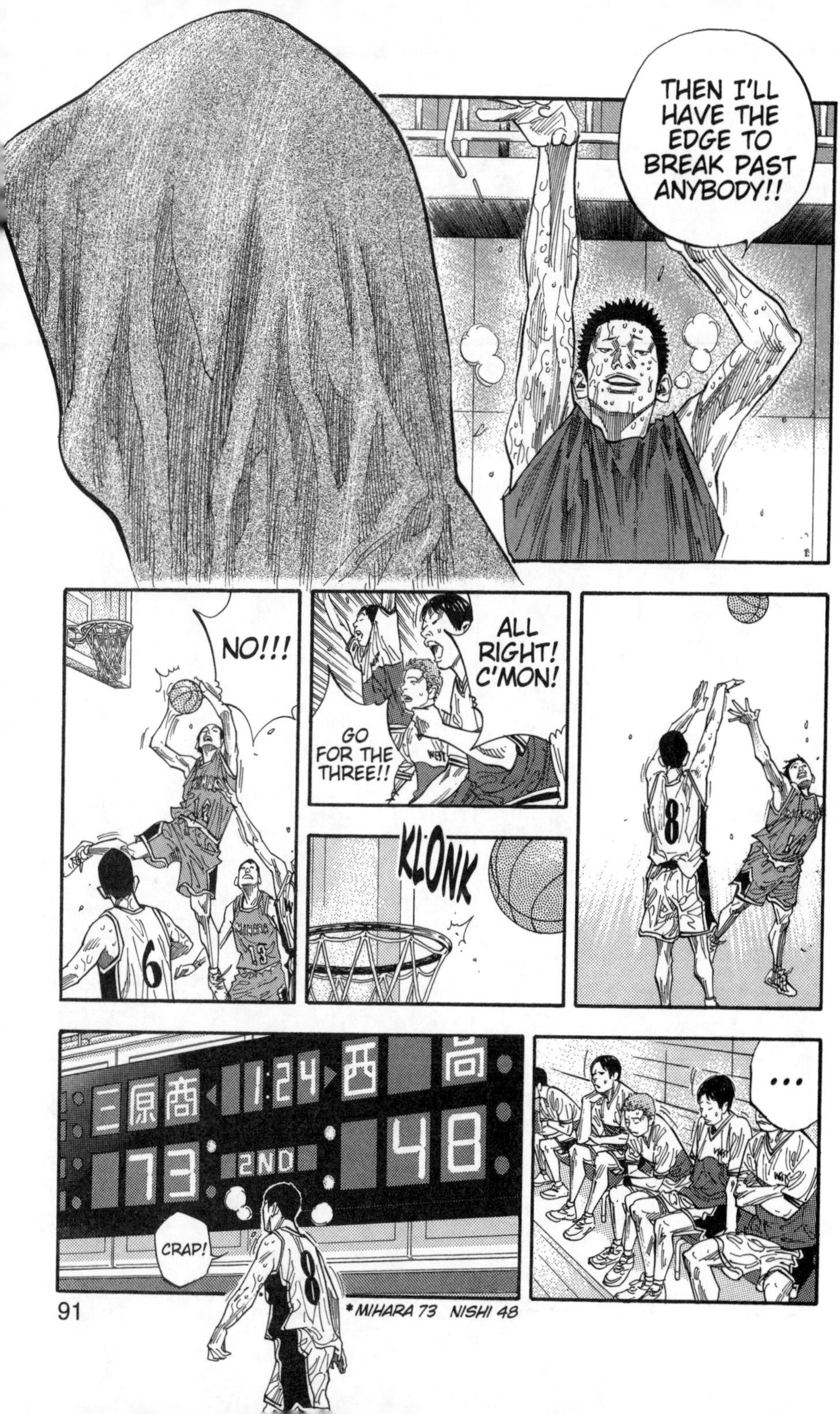
THEN I'LL HAVE THE EDGE TO BREAK PAST ANYBODY!!
ALL RIGHT! C'MON!
GO FOR THE THREE!!
KLONK
NO!!!
...
三原商
1:24
西
高
73
2ND
48
CRAP!
*MIHARA 73 NISHI 48

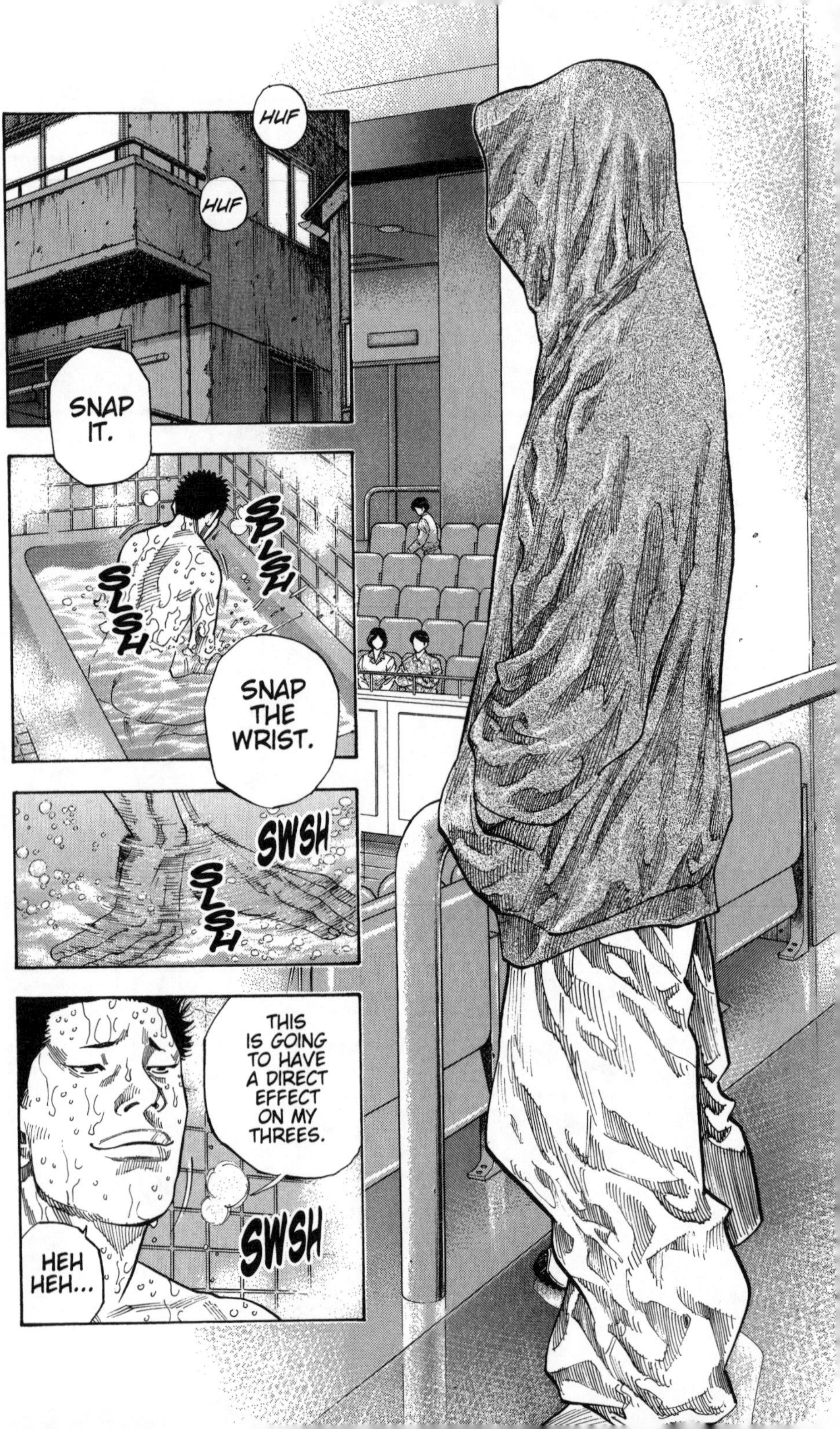
HUF
HUF
SNAP IT.
SPLSH
SLSH
SNAP THE WRIST.
SWSH
SLSH
THIS IS GOING TO HAVE A DIRECT EFFECT ON MY THREES.
SWSH
HEH HEH...

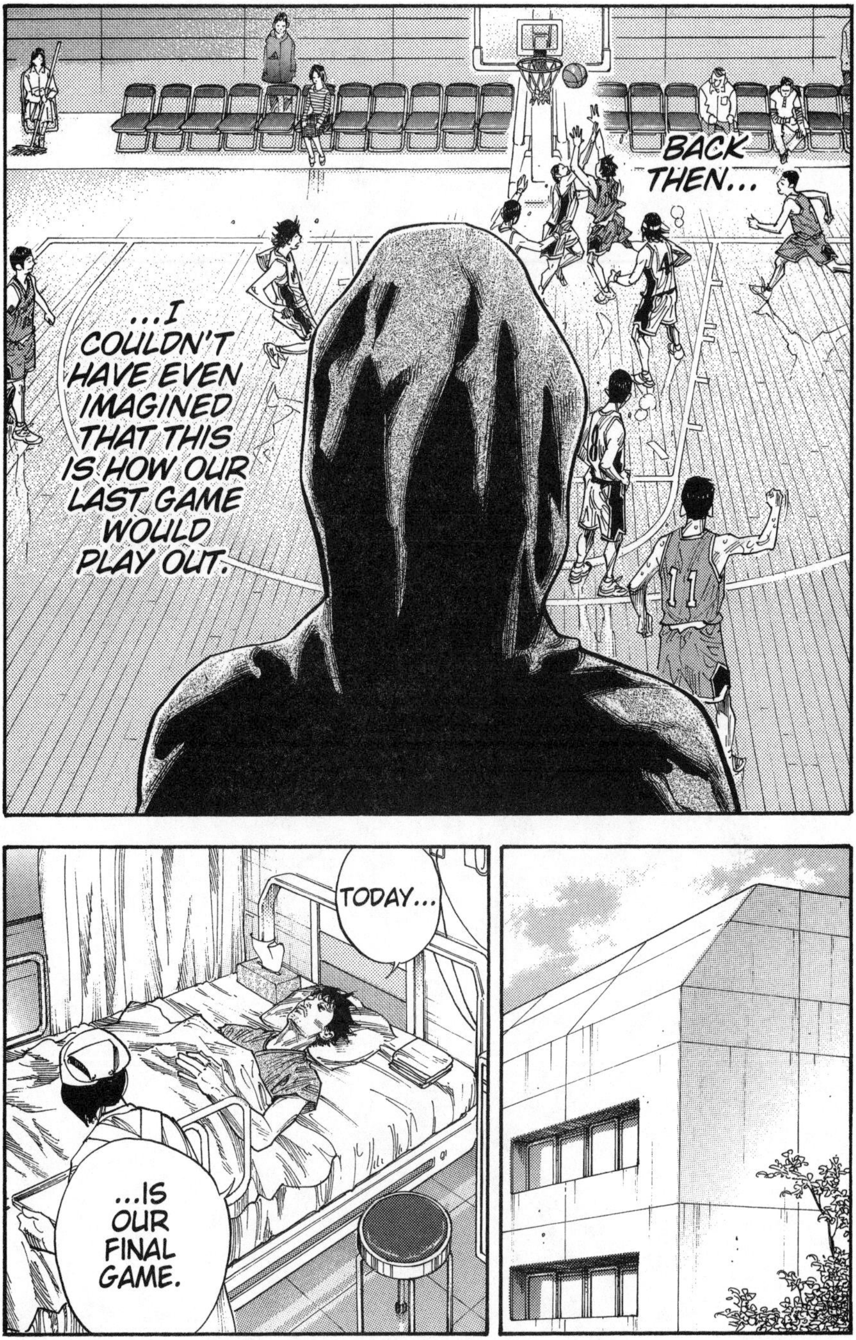
BACK THEN...
...I COULDN'T HAVE EVEN IMAGINED THAT THIS IS HOW OUR LAST GAME WOULD PLAY OUT.
TODAY...
...IS OUR FINAL GAME.

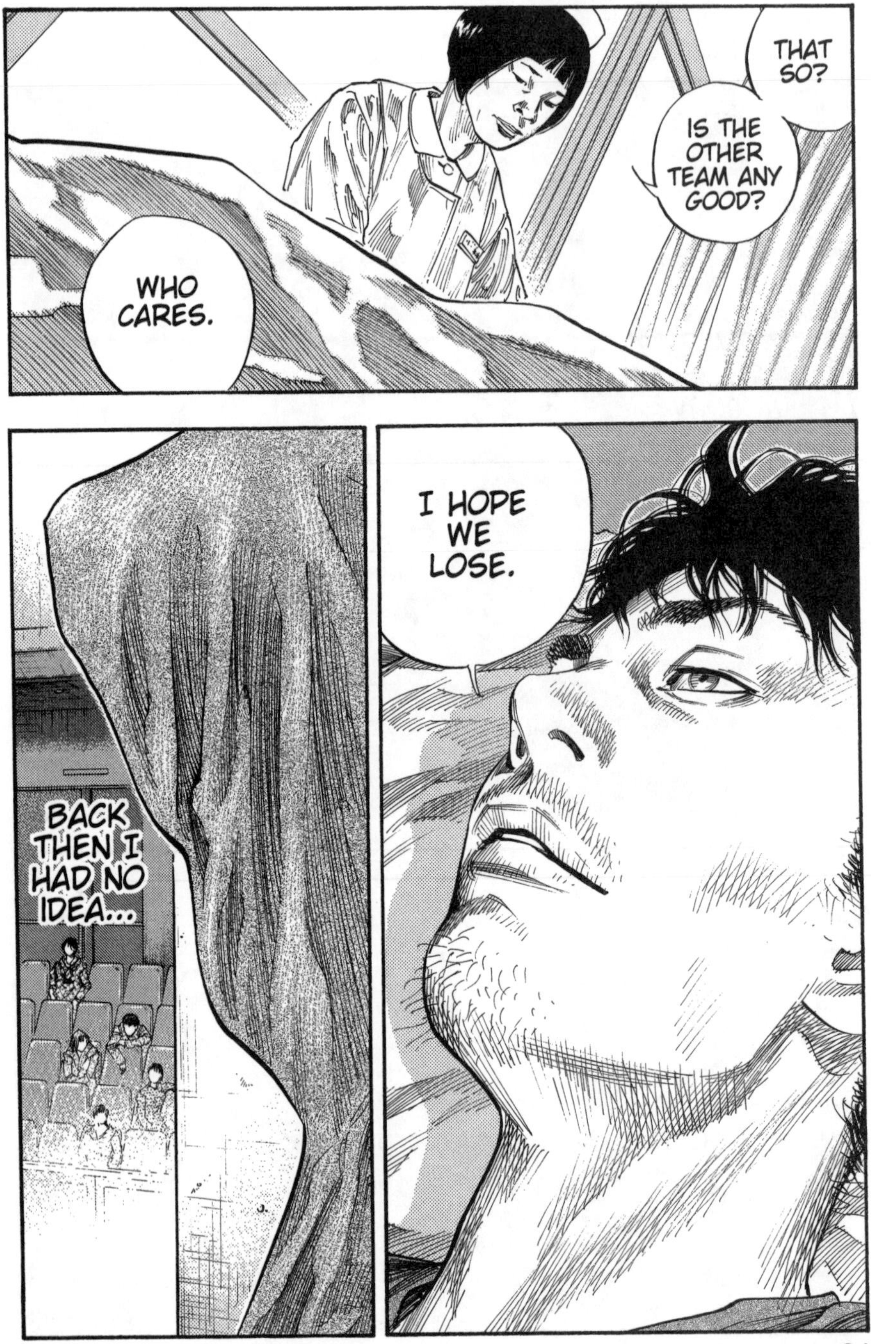
THAT SO?
IS THE OTHER TEAM ANY GOOD?
WHO CARES.
I HOPE WE LOSE.
BACK THEN I HAD NO IDEA...

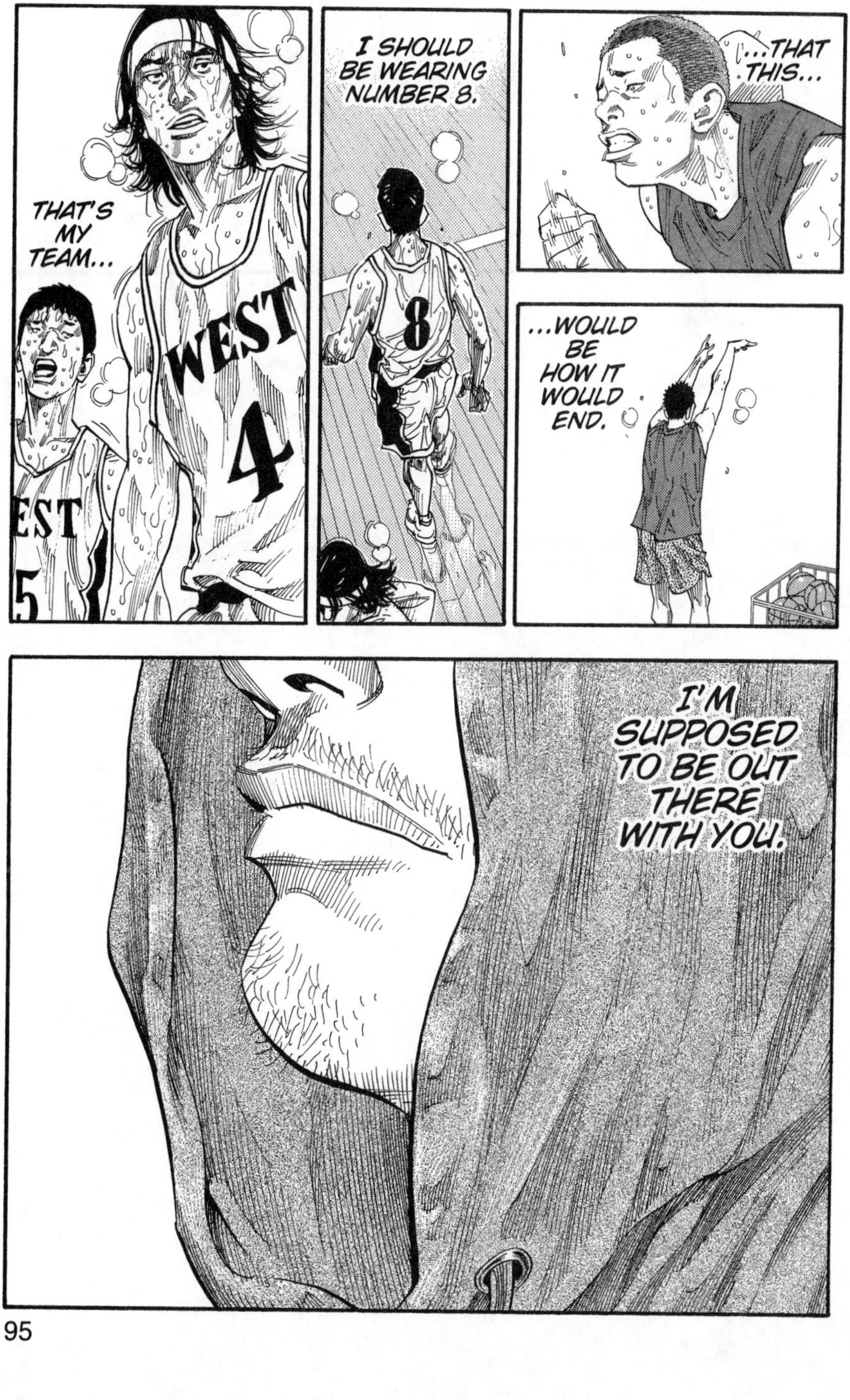
...THAT THIS...
...WOULD BE HOW IT WOULD END.
I SHOULD BE WEARING NUMBER 8.
THAT'S MY TEAM...
I'M SUPPOSED TO BE OUT THERE WITH YOU.

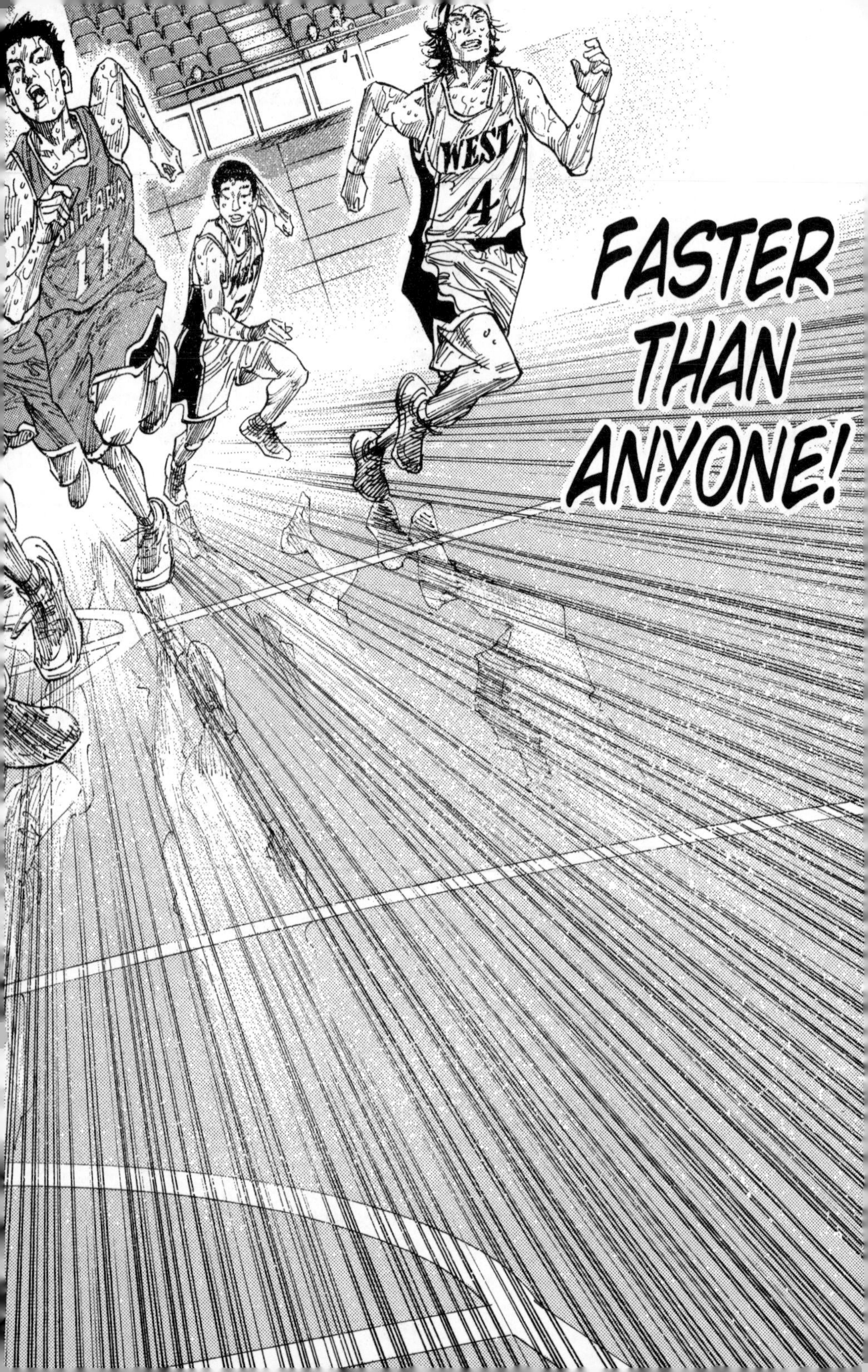
FASTER THAN ANYONE!

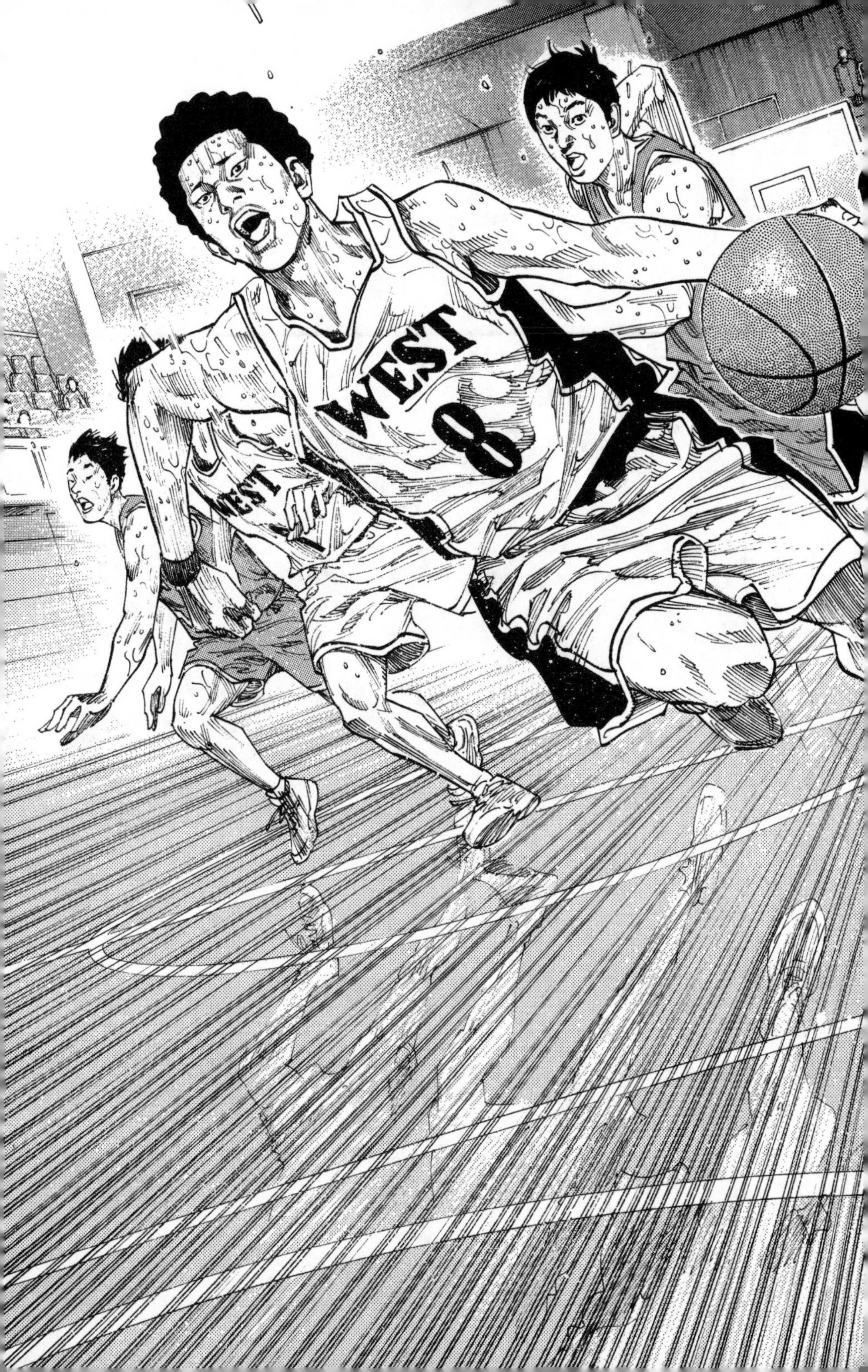
WEST
8
WEST

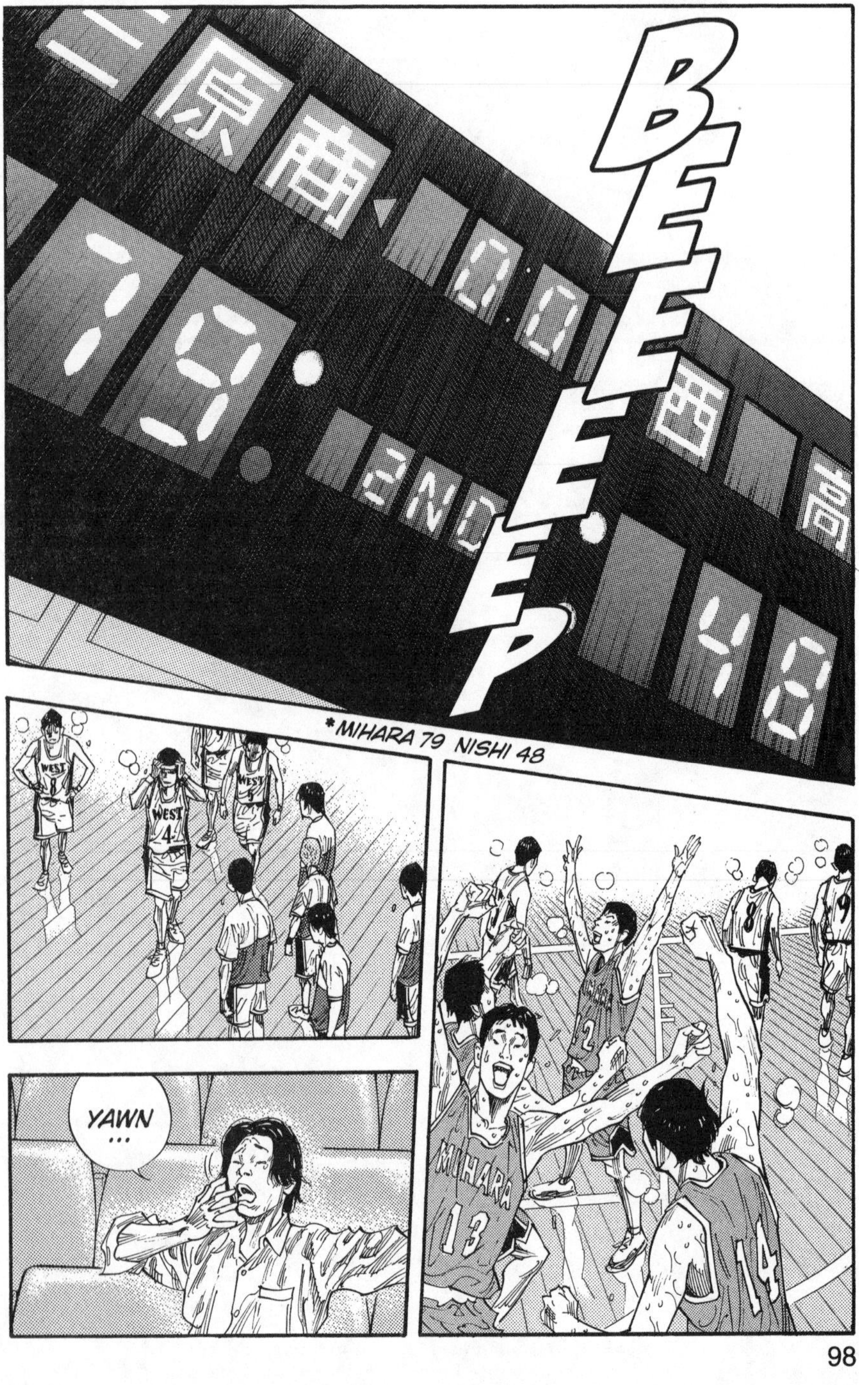
BEEEEEEP
*MIHARA 79 NISHI 48
YAWN ...

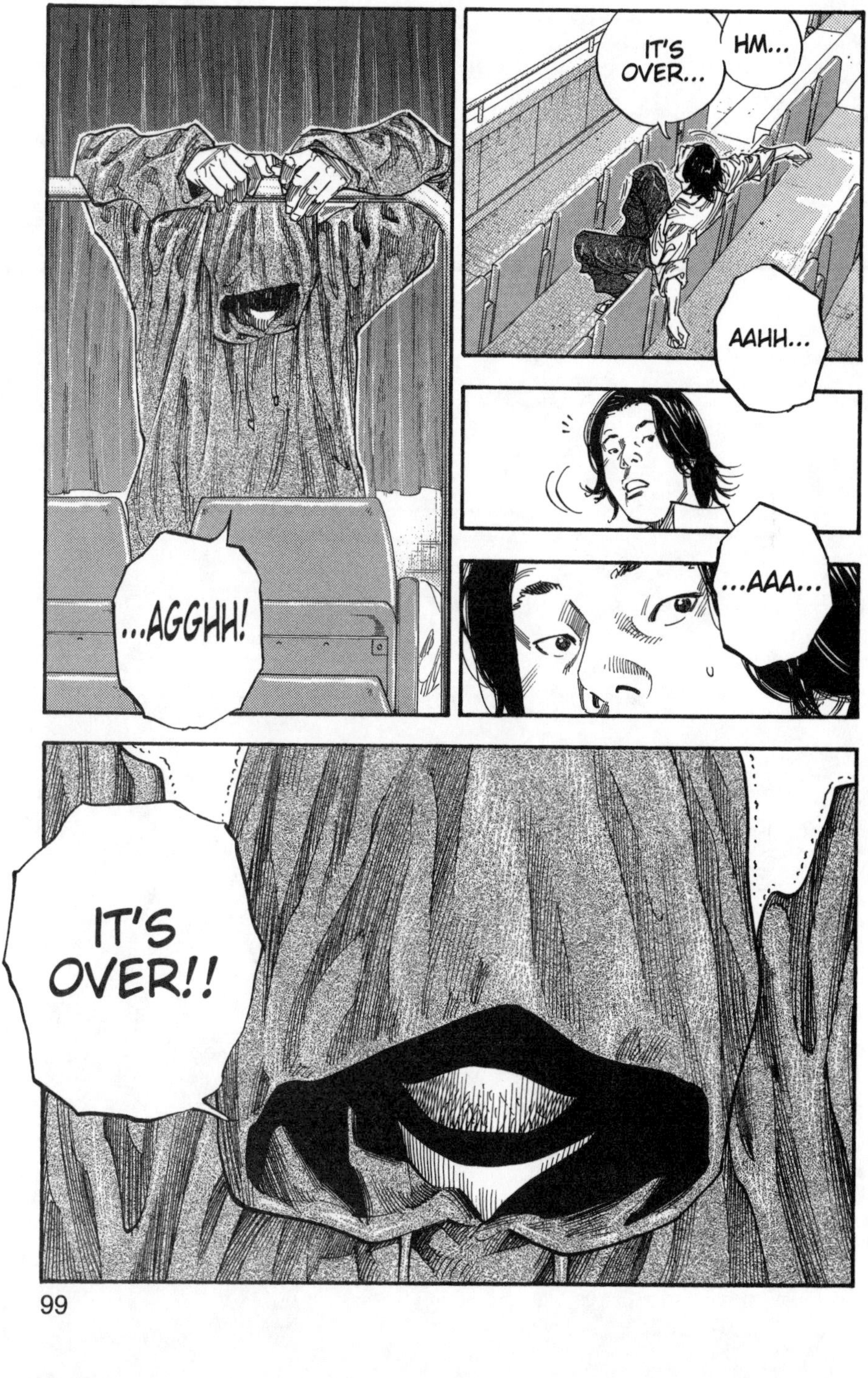

HM...
IT'S OVER...
AAHH...
...AAA...
...AGGHH!
IT'S OVER!!

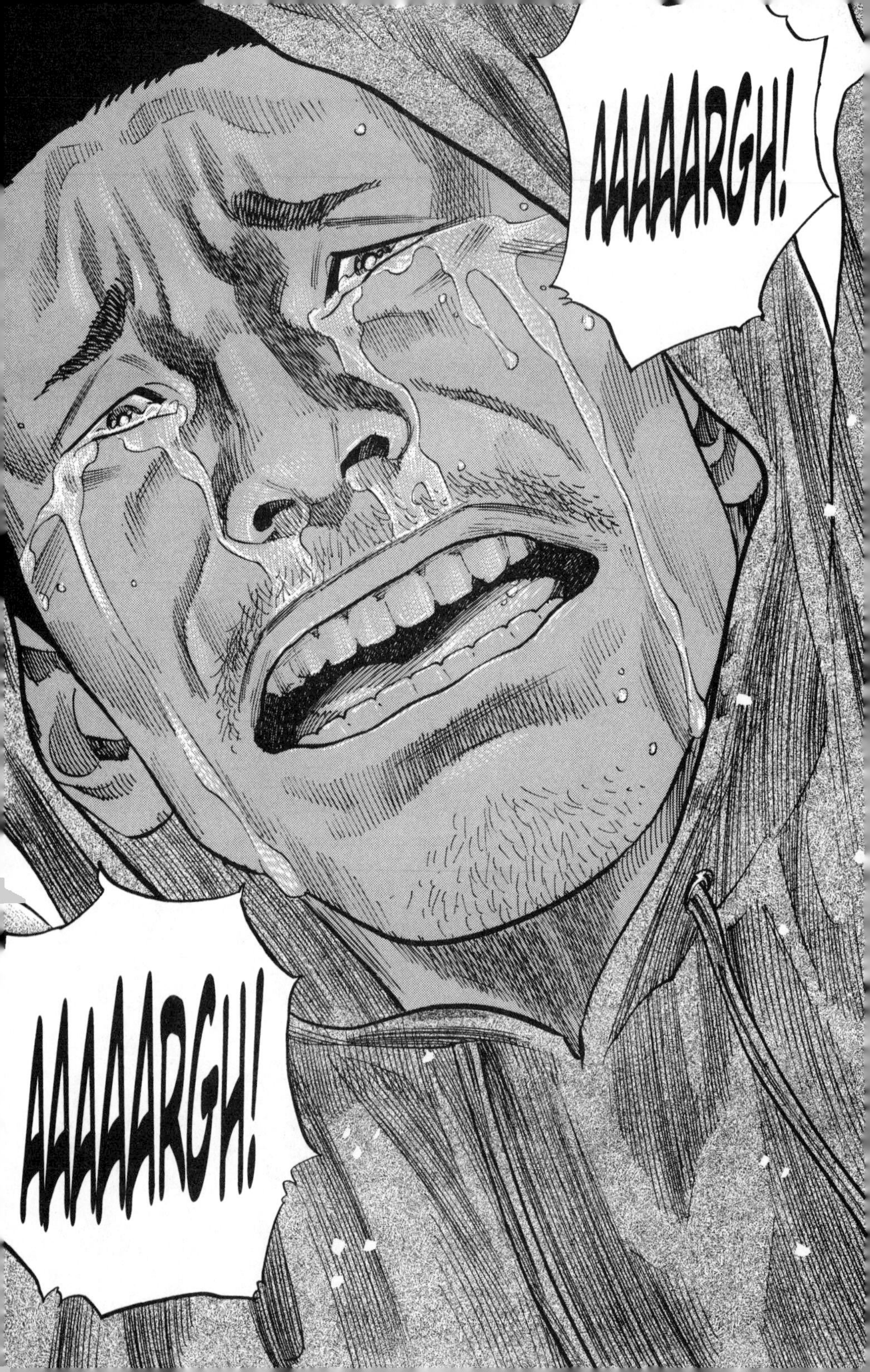
AAAAARGH!
AAAAARGH!

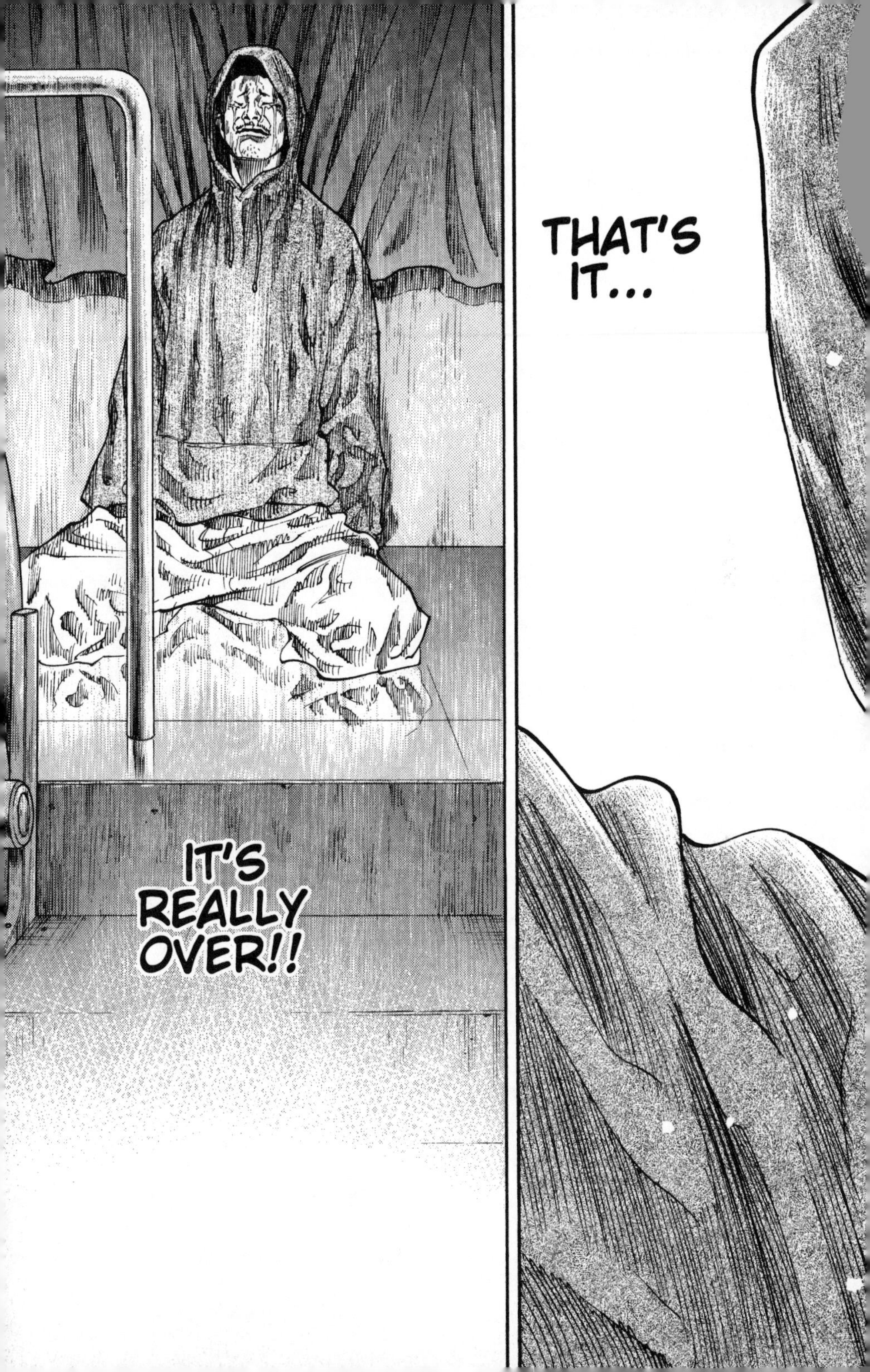
THAT'S IT...
IT'S REALLY OVER!!

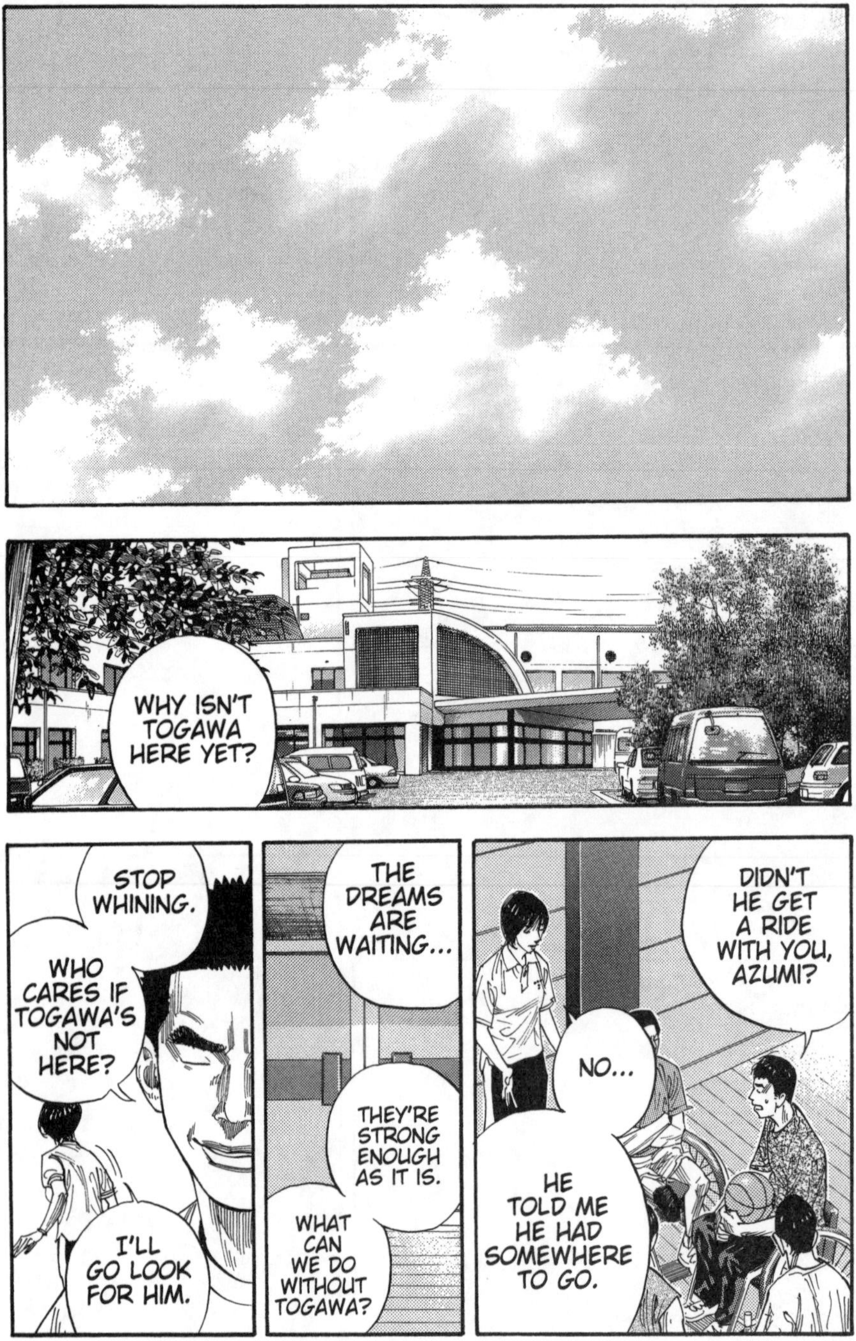
WHY ISN'T TOGAWA HERE YET?
DIDN'T HE GET A RIDE WITH YOU, AZUMI?
NO...
HE TOLD ME HE HAD SOMEWHERE TO GO.
THE DREAMS ARE WAITING...
THEY'RE STRONG ENOUGH AS IT IS.
WHAT CAN WE DO WITHOUT TOGAWA?
STOP WHINING.
WHO CARES IF TOGAWA'S NOT HERE?
I'LL GO LOOK FOR HIM.

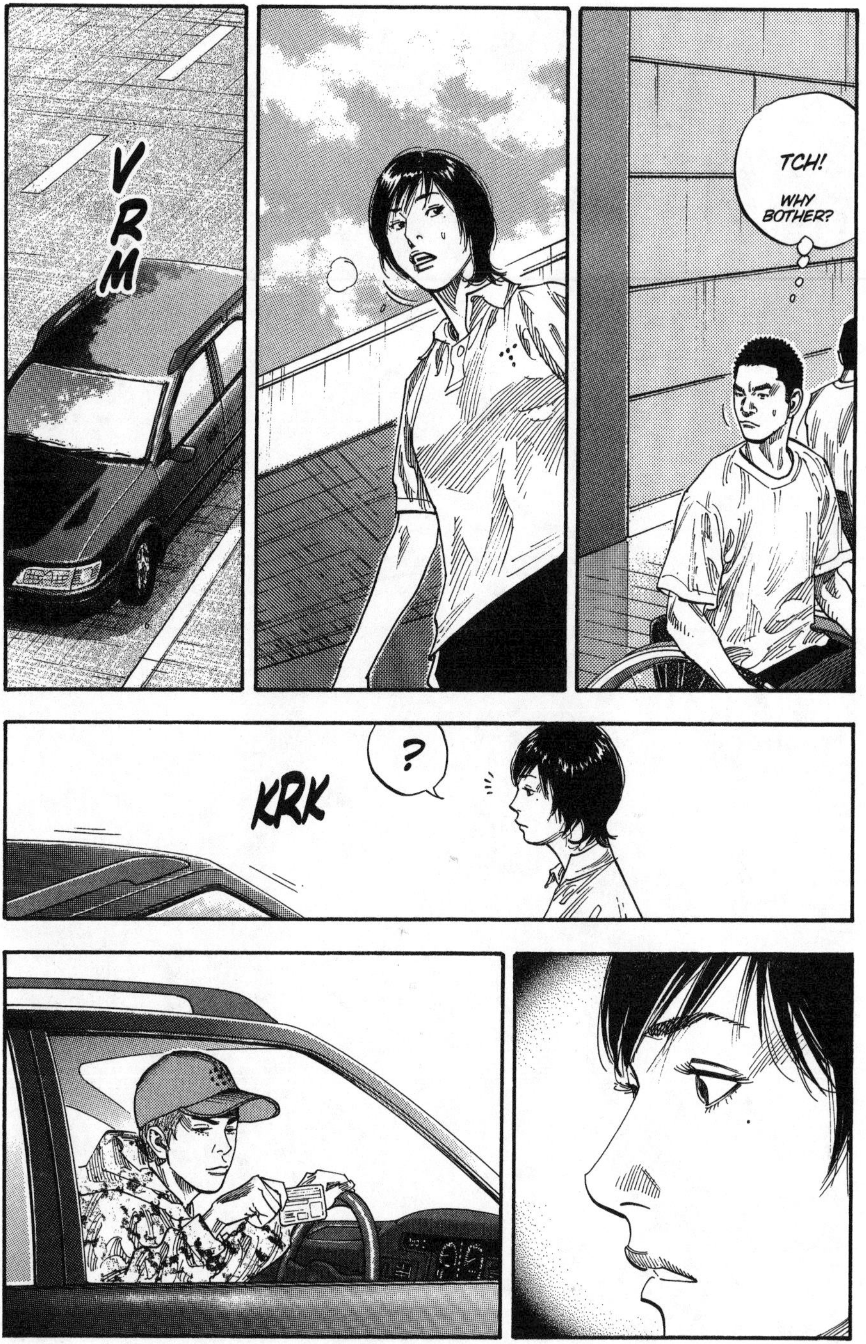
TCH!
WHY BOTHER?
VRM
?
KRK

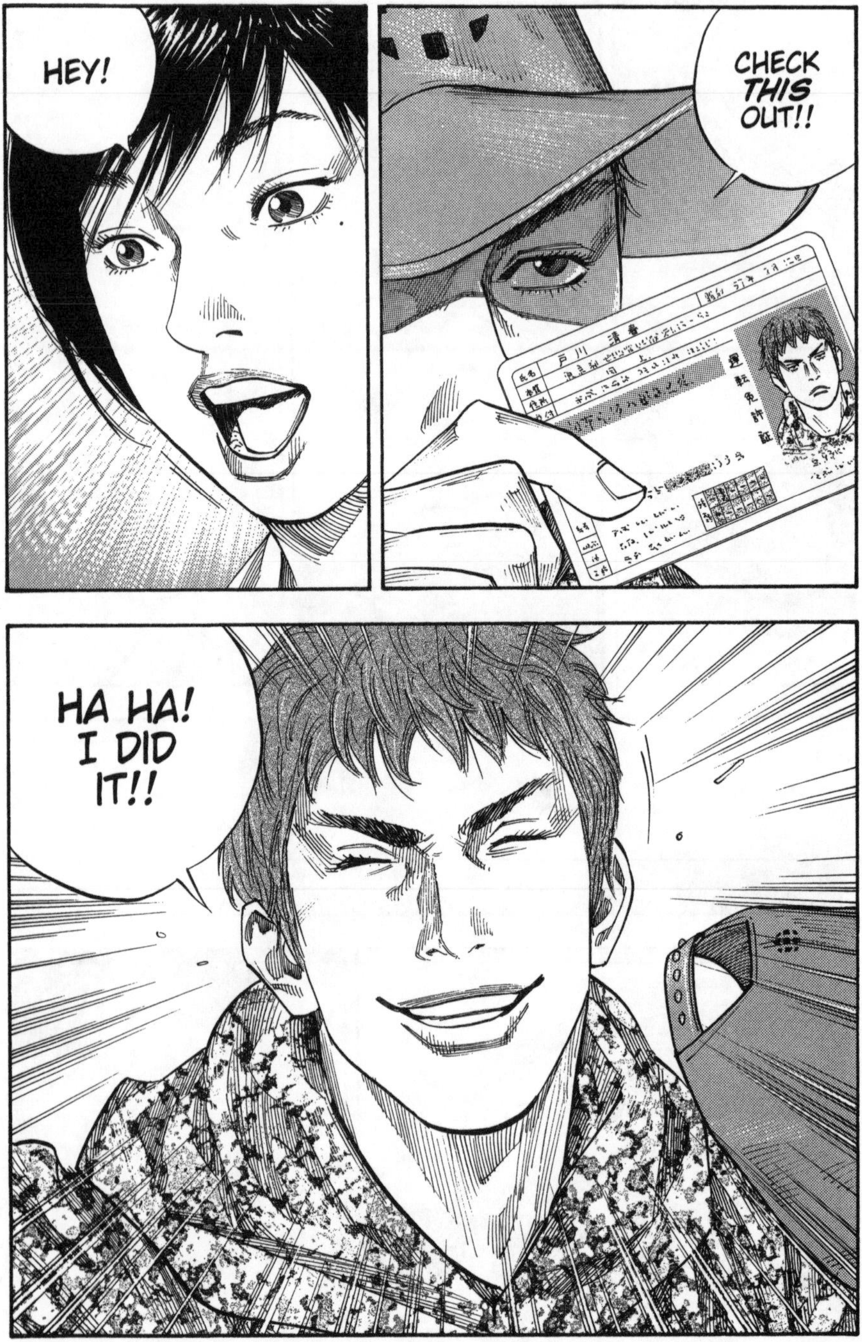
CHECK THIS OUT!!
HEY!
HA HA! I DID IT!!

REAL

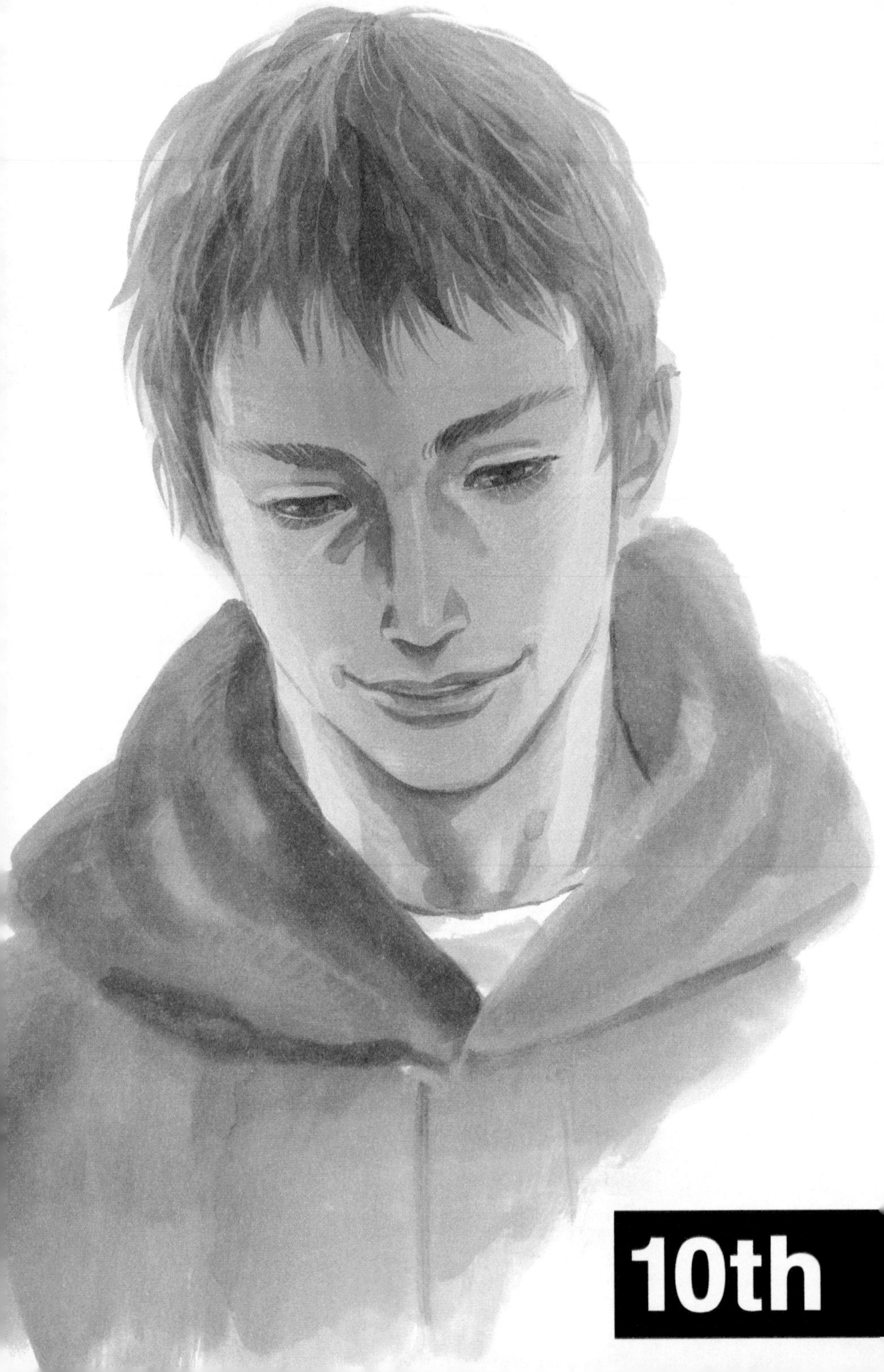

10th

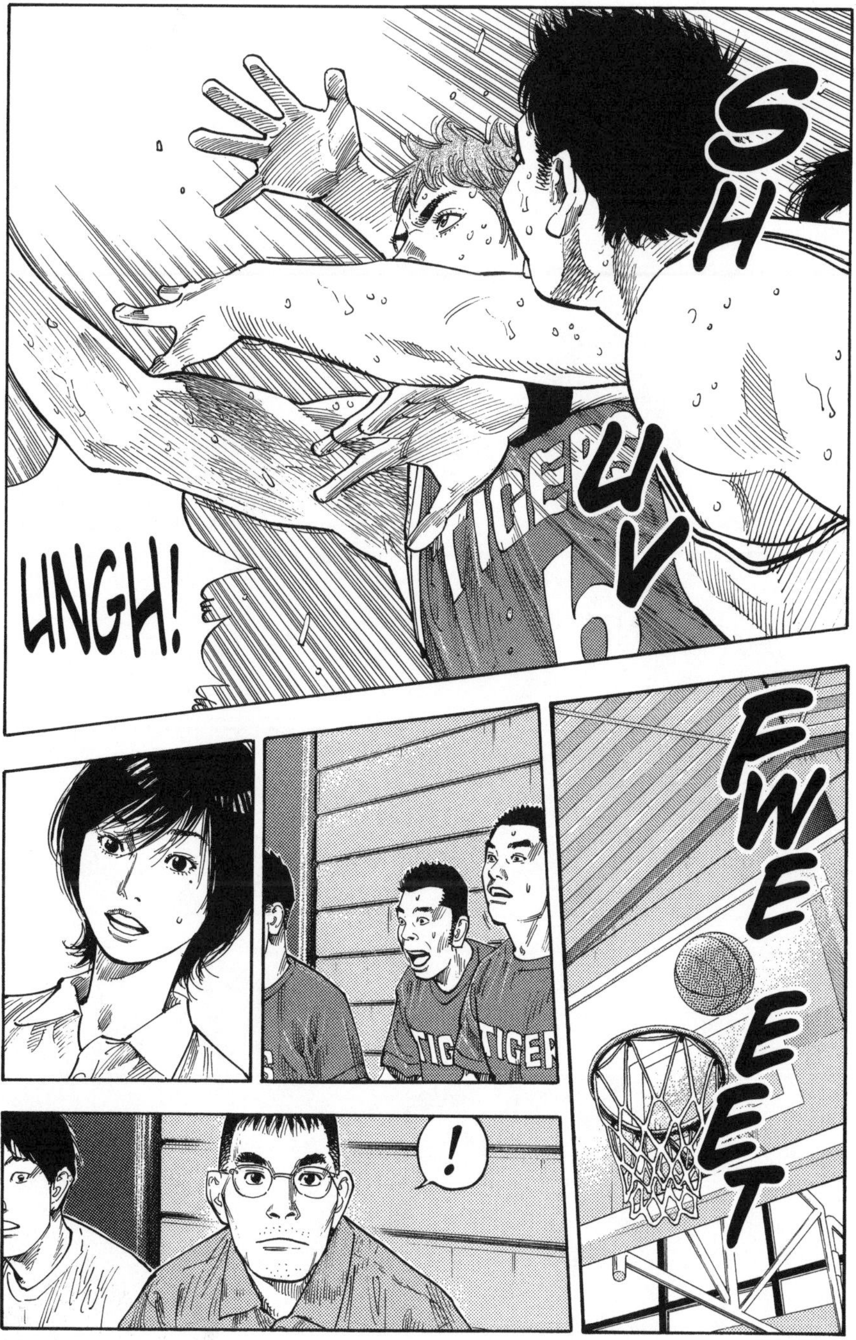
SHUVV
UNGH!
FWEEEET
!

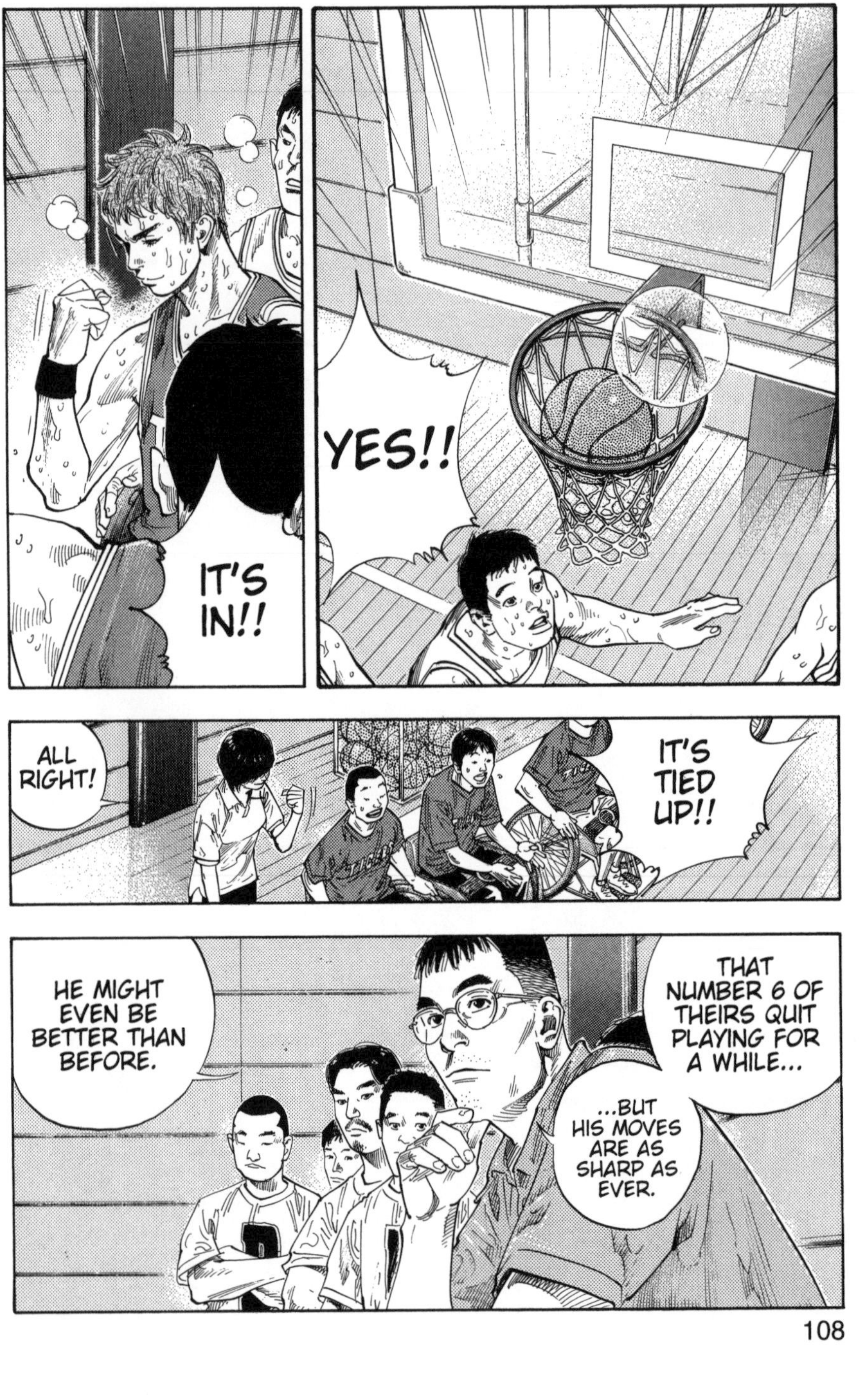
YES!!
IT'S IN!!
IT'S TIED UP!!
ALL RIGHT!
THAT NUMBER 6 OF THEIRS QUIT PLAYING FOR A WHILE...
...BUT HIS MOVES ARE AS SHARP AS EVER.
HE MIGHT EVEN BE BETTER THAN BEFORE.

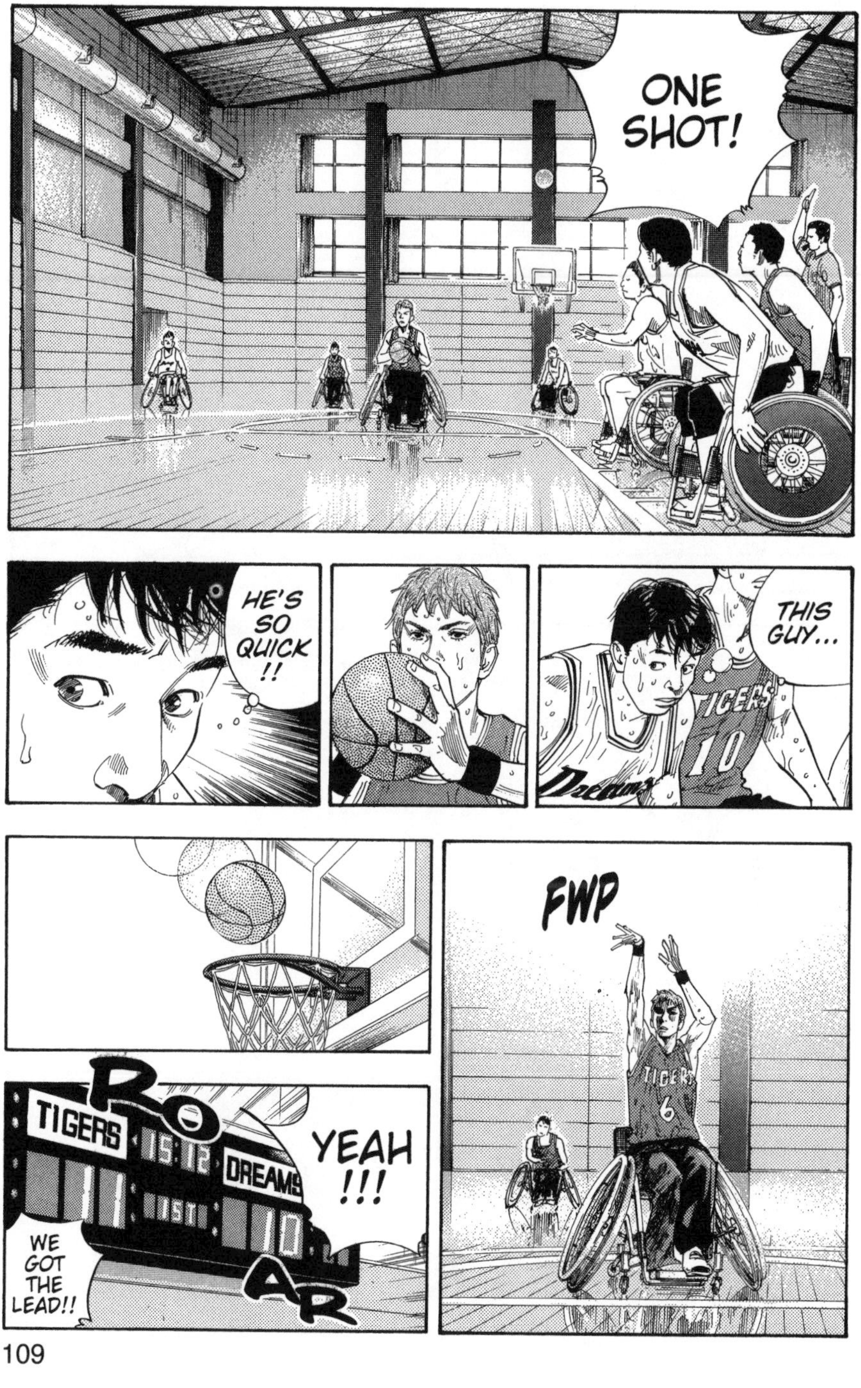
ONE SHOT!
THIS GUY...
TIGERS 10
HE'S SO QUICK !!
FWP
TIGERS 6
TIGERS 15:12 DREAMS
11 1ST 10
ROAR
YEAH !!!
WE GOT THE LEAD!!

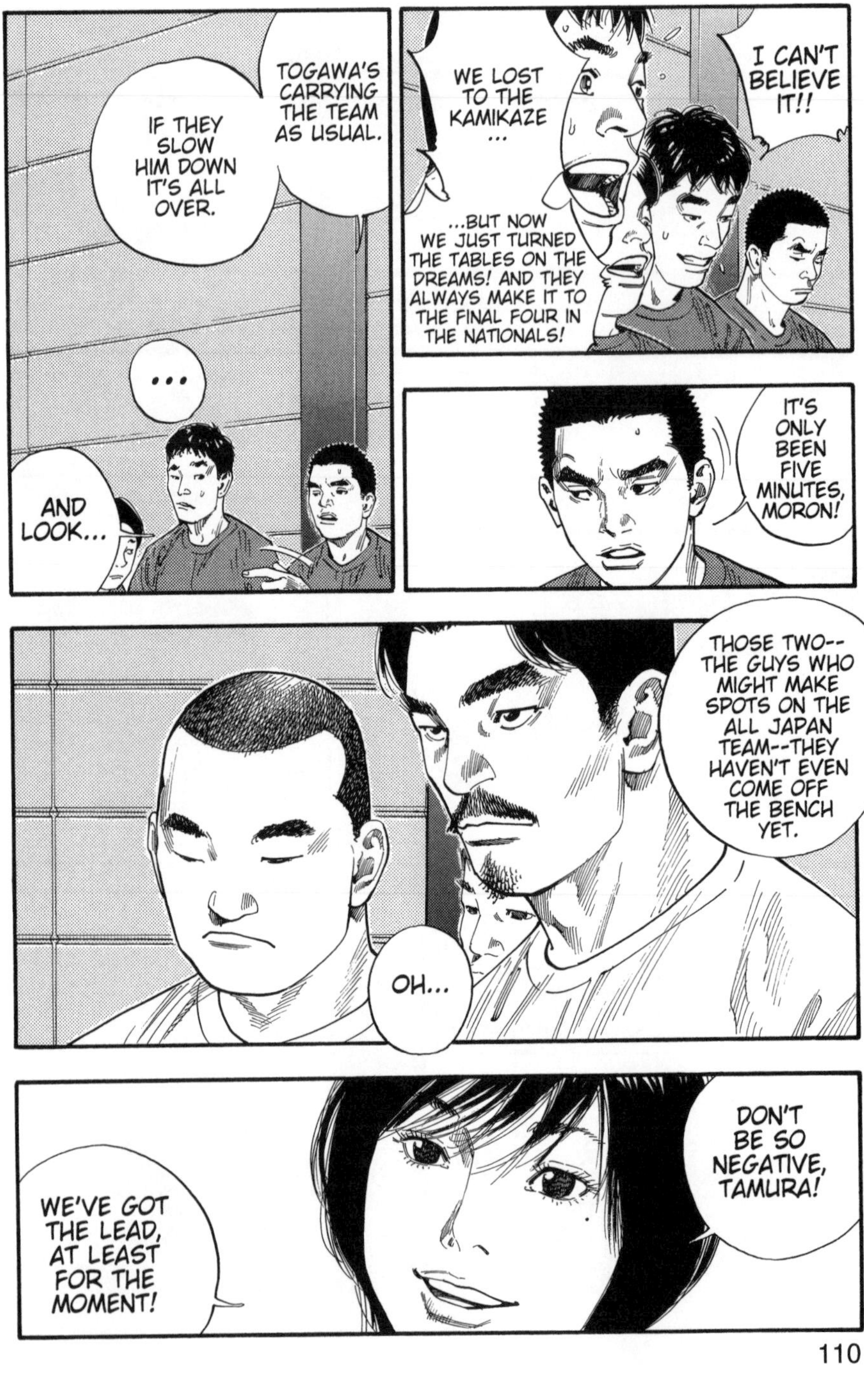
I CAN'T BELIEVE IT!!
WE LOST TO THE KAMIKAZE ...
...BUT NOW WE JUST TURNED THE TABLES ON THE DREAMS! AND THEY ALWAYS MAKE IT TO THE FINAL FOUR IN THE NATIONALS!
IT'S ONLY BEEN FIVE MINUTES, MORON!
TOGAWA'S CARRYING THE TEAM AS USUAL.
IF THEY SLOW HIM DOWN IT'S ALL OVER.
...
AND LOOK...
THOSE TWO--THE GUYS WHO MIGHT MAKE SPOTS ON THE ALL JAPAN TEAM--THEY HAVEN'T EVEN COME OFF THE BENCH YET.
OH...
DON'T BE SO NEGATIVE, TAMURA!
WE'VE GOT THE LEAD, AT LEAST FOR THE MOMENT!

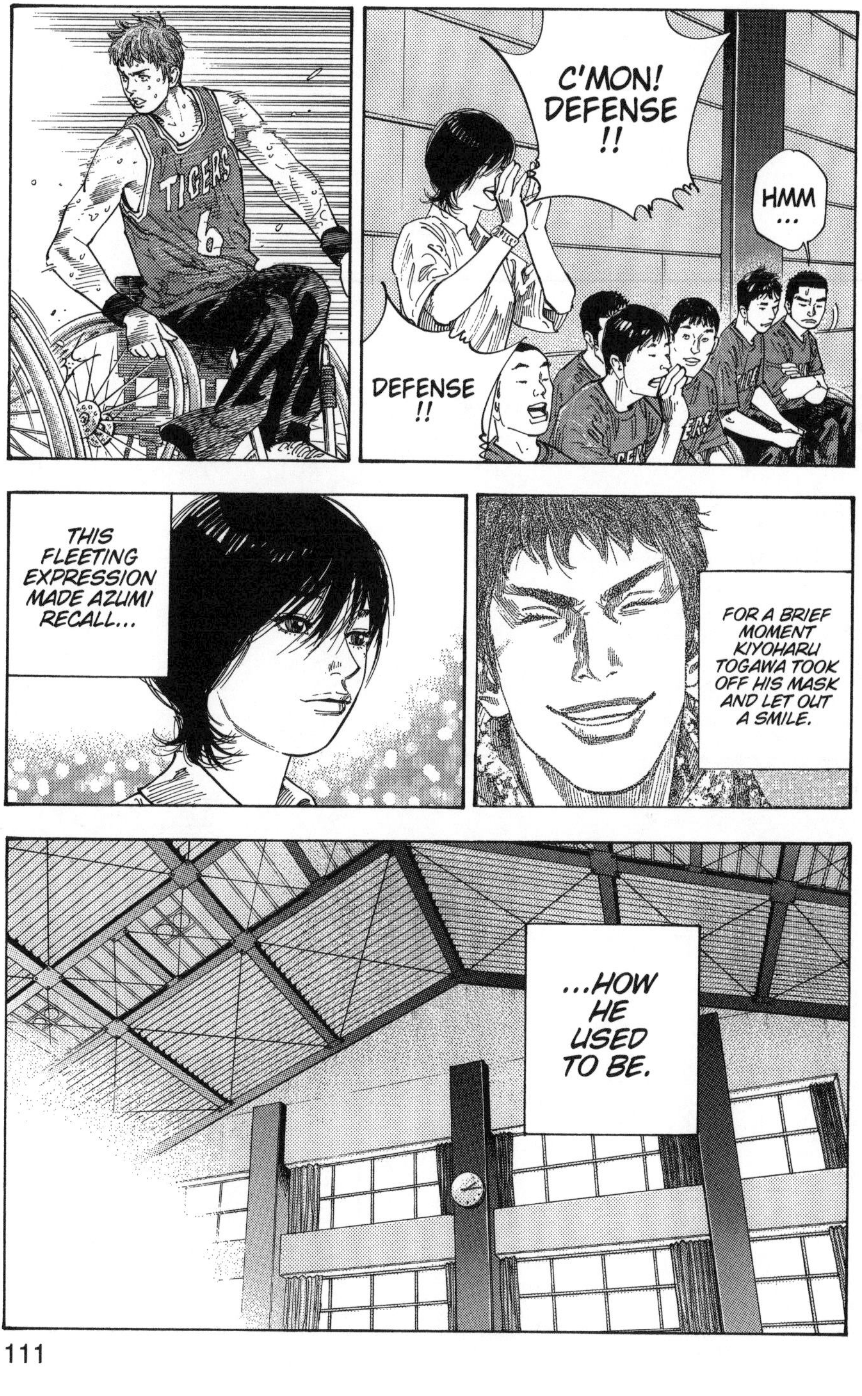
C'MON! DEFENSE !!
HMM ...
DEFENSE !!
FOR A BRIEF MOMENT KIYOHARU TOGAWA TOOK OFF HIS MASK AND LET OUT A SMILE.
THIS FLEETING EXPRESSION MADE AZUMI RECALL...
...HOW HE USED TO BE.

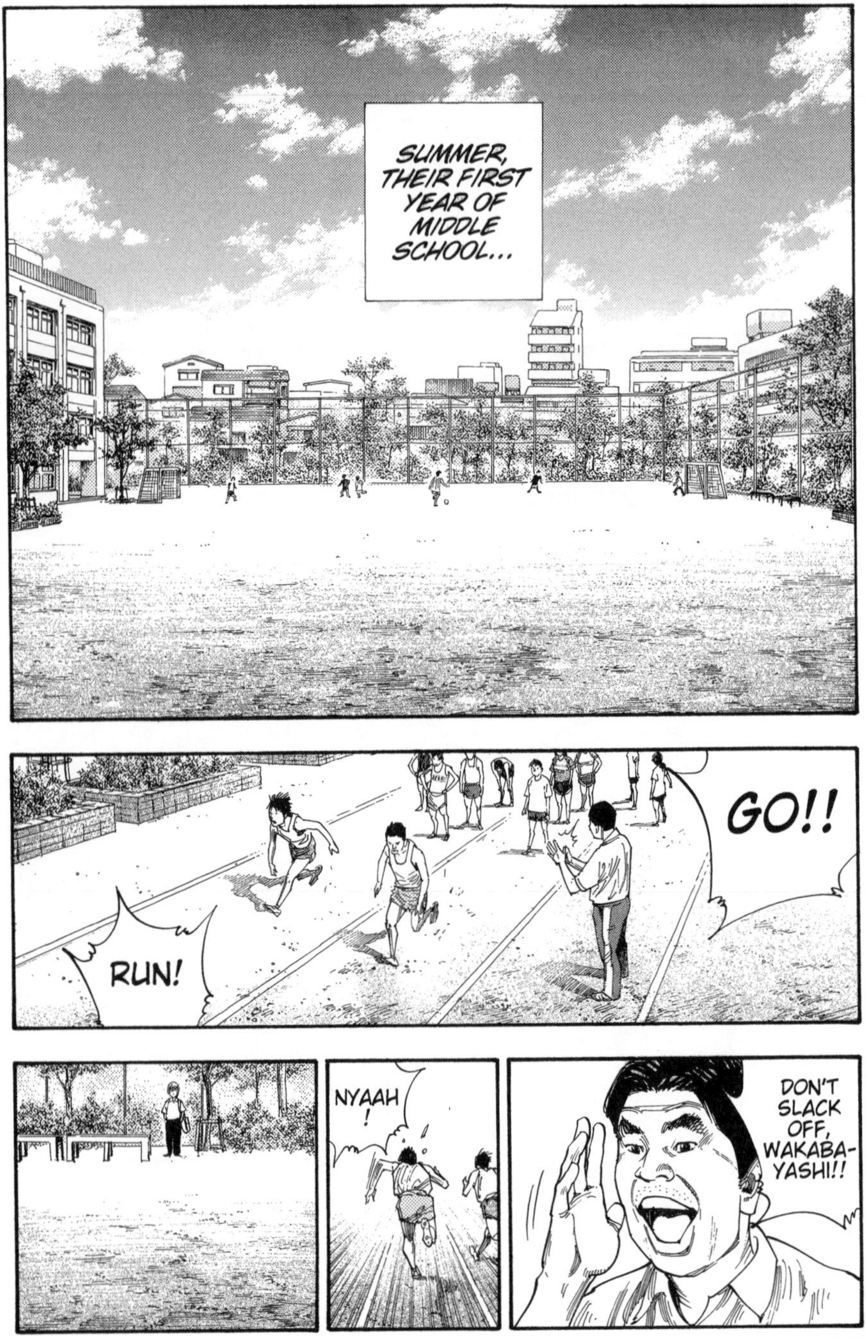
SUMMER, THEIR FIRST YEAR OF MIDDLE SCHOOL...
GO!!
RUN!
DON'T SLACK OFF, WAKABA-YASHI!!
NYAAH!

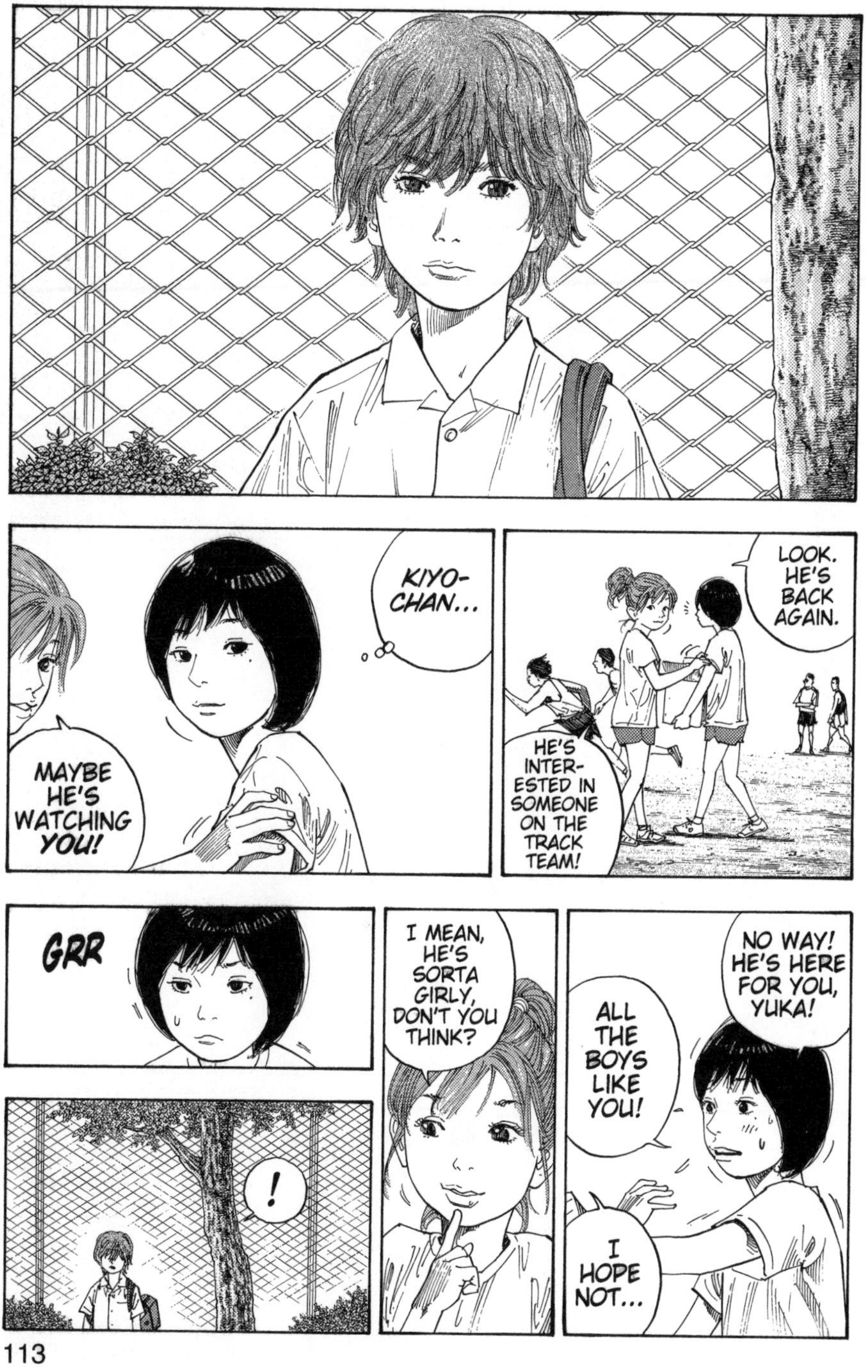
LOOK. HE'S BACK AGAIN.
HE'S INTERESTED IN SOMEONE ON THE TRACK TEAM!
KIYO-CHAN...
MAYBE HE'S WATCHING YOU!
NO WAY! HE'S HERE FOR YOU, YUKA!
ALL THE BOYS LIKE YOU!
I HOPE NOT...
I MEAN, HE'S SORTA GIRLY, DON'T YOU THINK?
GRR
!

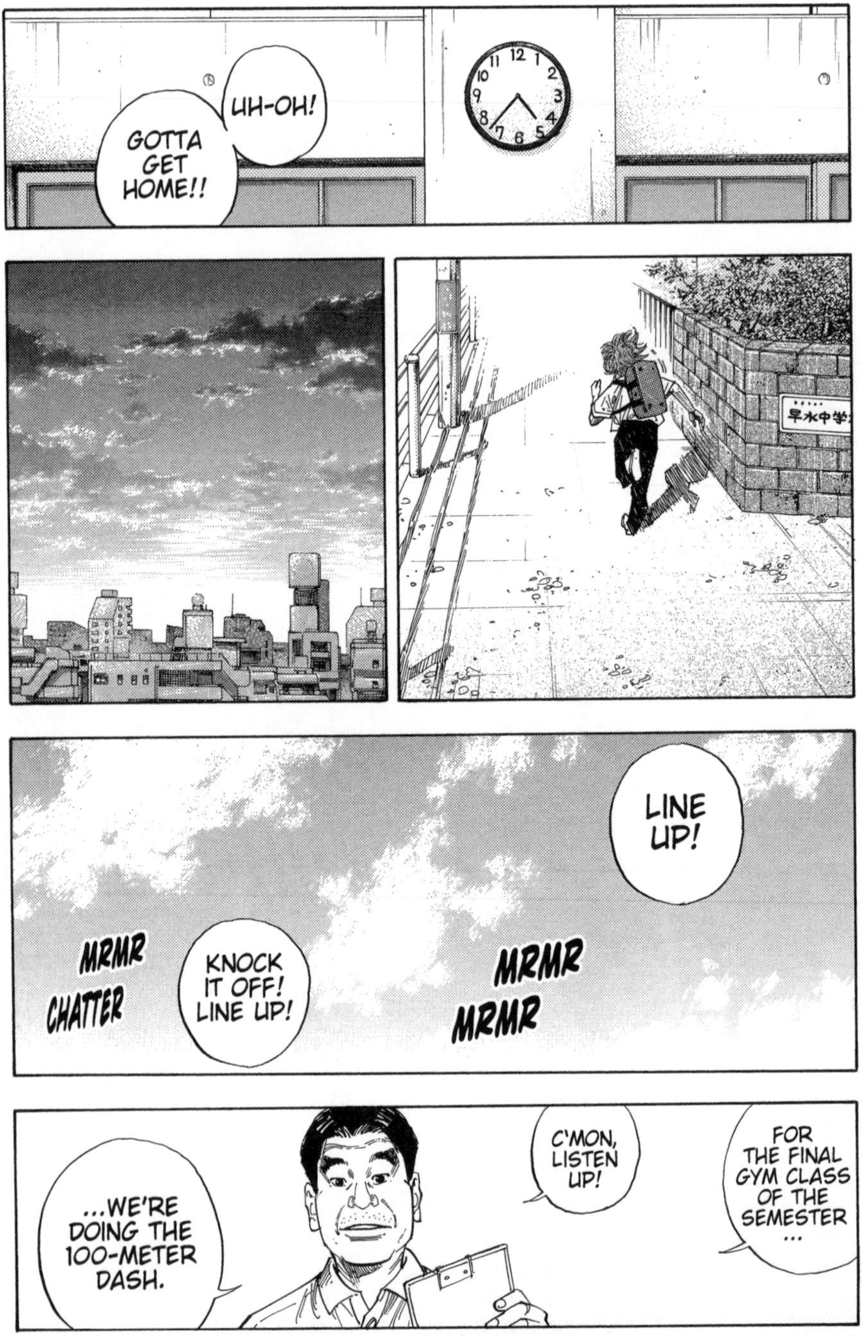
UH-OH!
GOTTA GET HOME!!
早水中学
LINE UP!
MRMR
KNOCK IT OFF! LINE UP!
MRMR
MRMR
CHATTER
FOR THE FINAL GYM CLASS OF THE SEMESTER...
C'MON, LISTEN UP!
...WE'RE DOING THE 100-METER DASH.

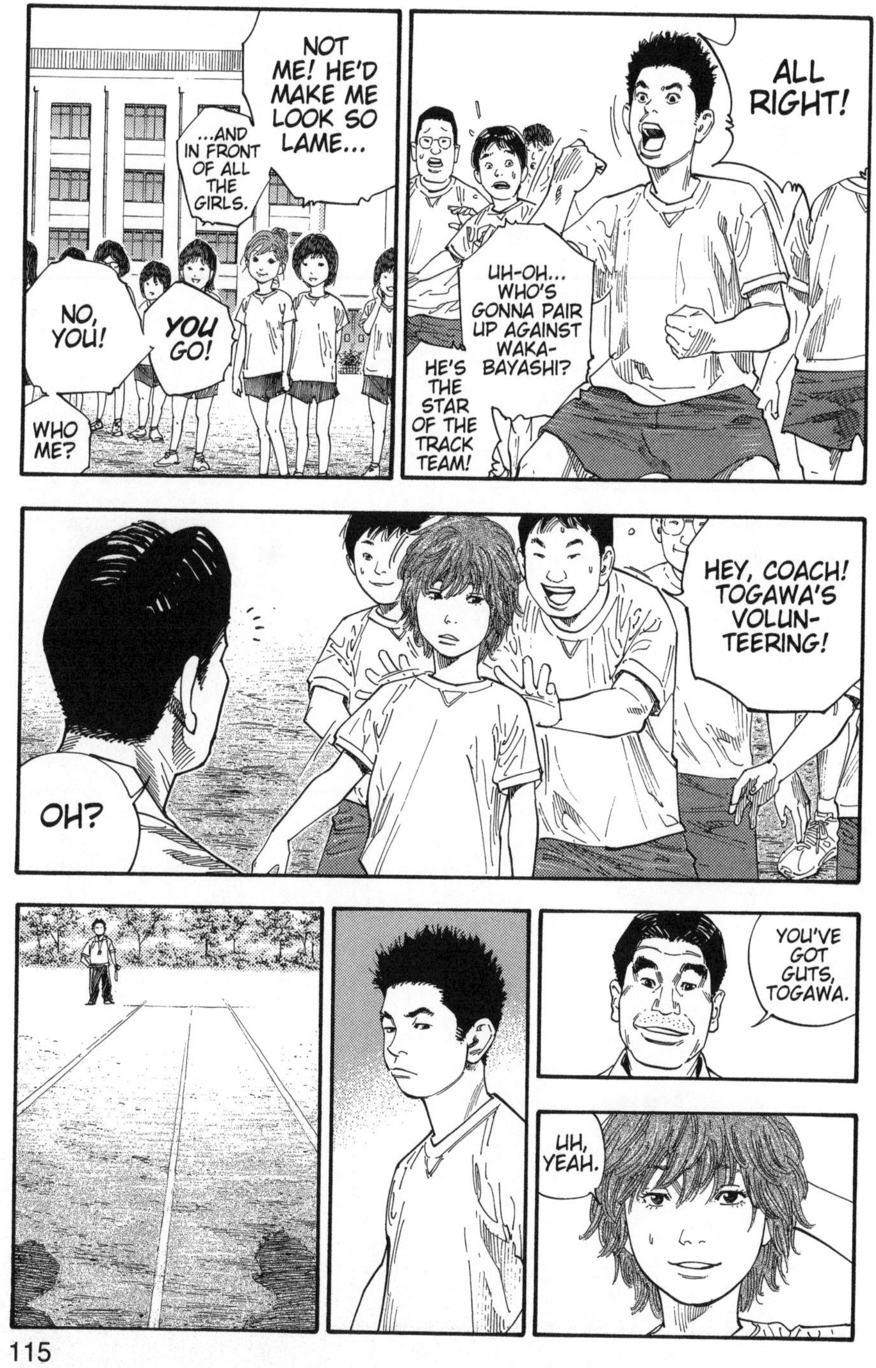
ALL RIGHT!
UH-OH... WHO'S GONNA PAIR UP AGAINST WAKA-BAYASHI?
HE'S THE STAR OF THE TRACK TEAM!
NOT ME! HE'D MAKE ME LOOK SO LAME...
...AND IN FRONT OF ALL THE GIRLS.
YOU GO!
NO, YOU!
WHO ME?
HEY, COACH! TOGAWA'S VOLUN-TEERING!
OH?
YOU'VE GOT GUTS, TOGAWA.
UH, YEAH.

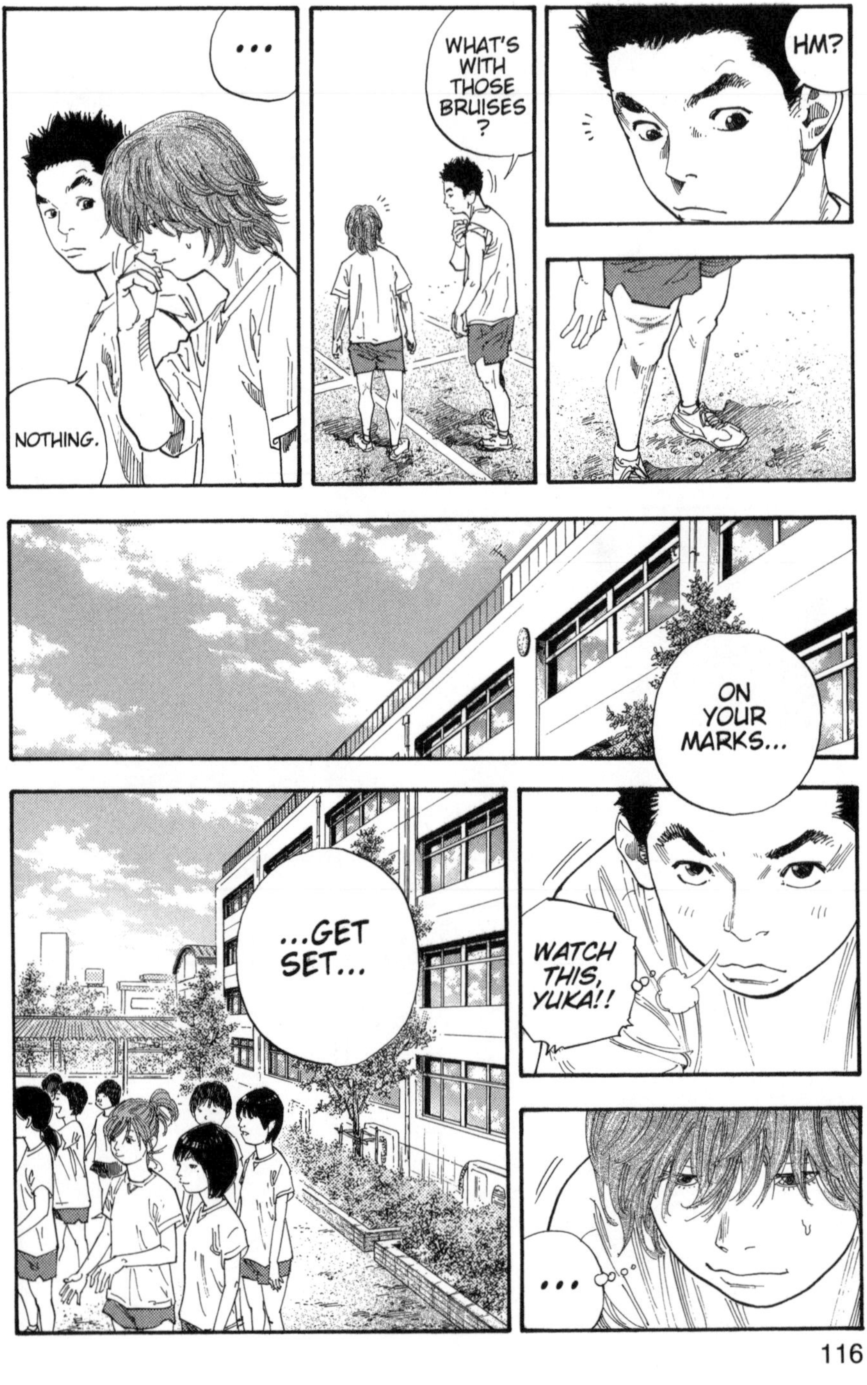
HM?
WHAT'S WITH THOSE BRUISES?
...
NOTHING.
ON YOUR MARKS...
WATCH THIS, YUKA!!
...
...GET SET...

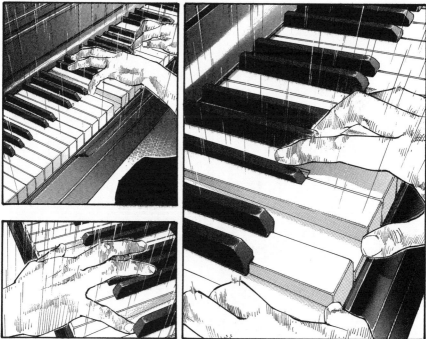

117

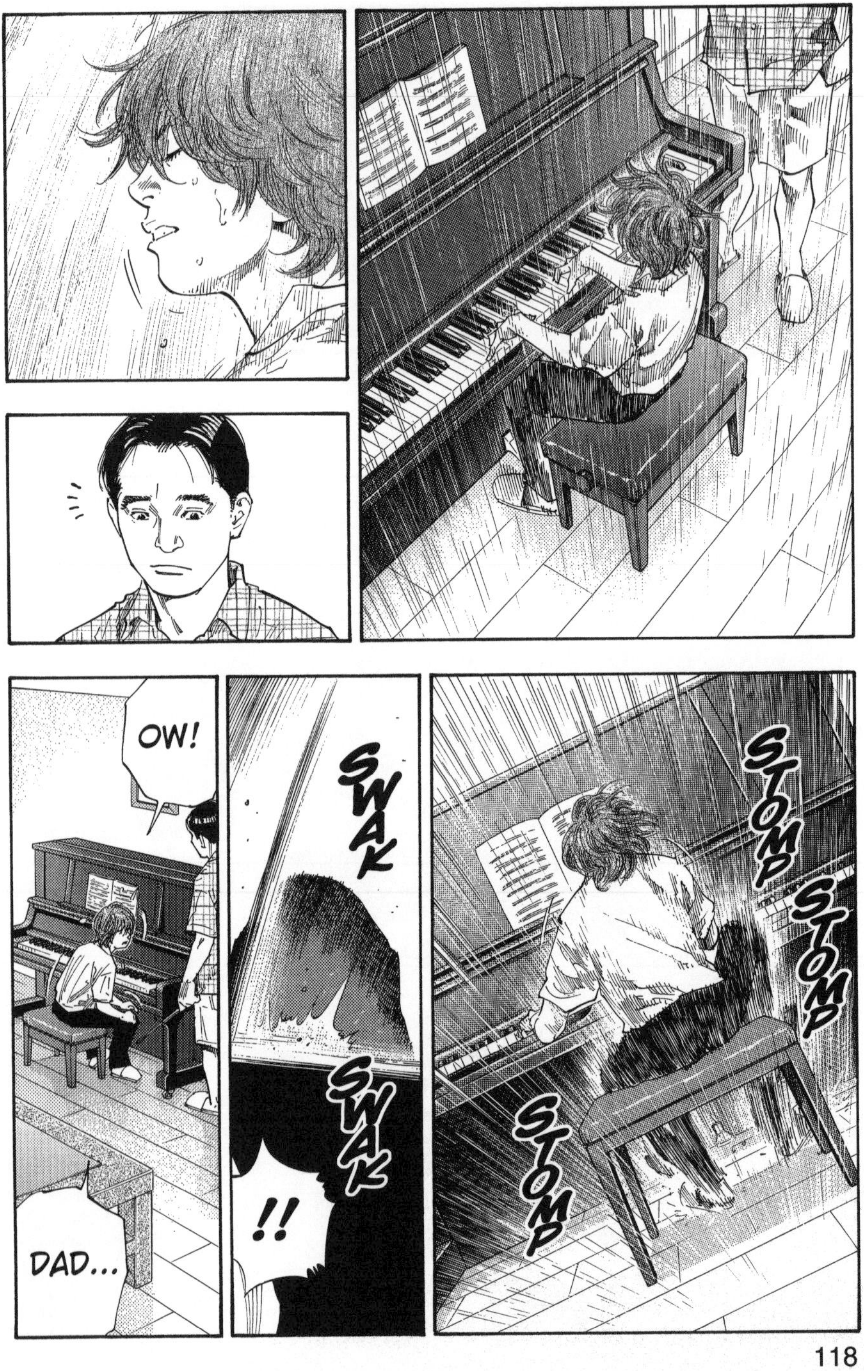
STOMP
STOMP
STOMP
SWAK
SWAK
!!
OW!
DAD...

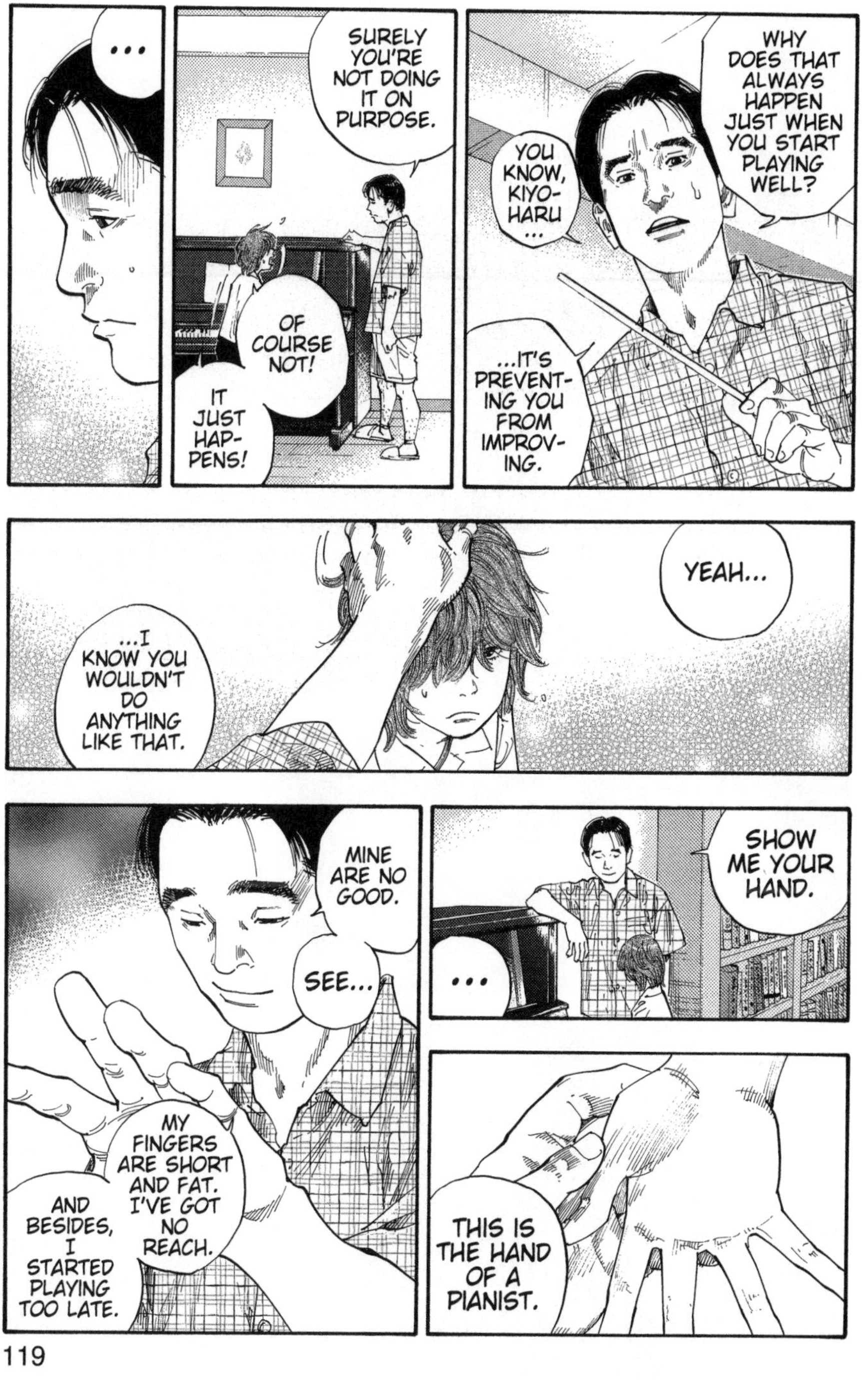
WHY DOES THAT ALWAYS HAPPEN JUST WHEN YOU START PLAYING WELL?
YOU KNOW, KIYO-HARU...
...IT'S PREVENT-ING YOU FROM IMPROV-ING.
SURELY YOU'RE NOT DOING IT ON PURPOSE.
OF COURSE NOT!
IT JUST HAP-PENS!
...
YEAH...
...I KNOW YOU WOULDN'T DO ANYTHING LIKE THAT.
SHOW ME YOUR HAND.
...
THIS IS THE HAND OF A PIANIST.
MINE ARE NO GOOD.
SEE...
MY FINGERS ARE SHORT AND FAT. I'VE GOT NO REACH.
AND BESIDES, I STARTED PLAYING TOO LATE.

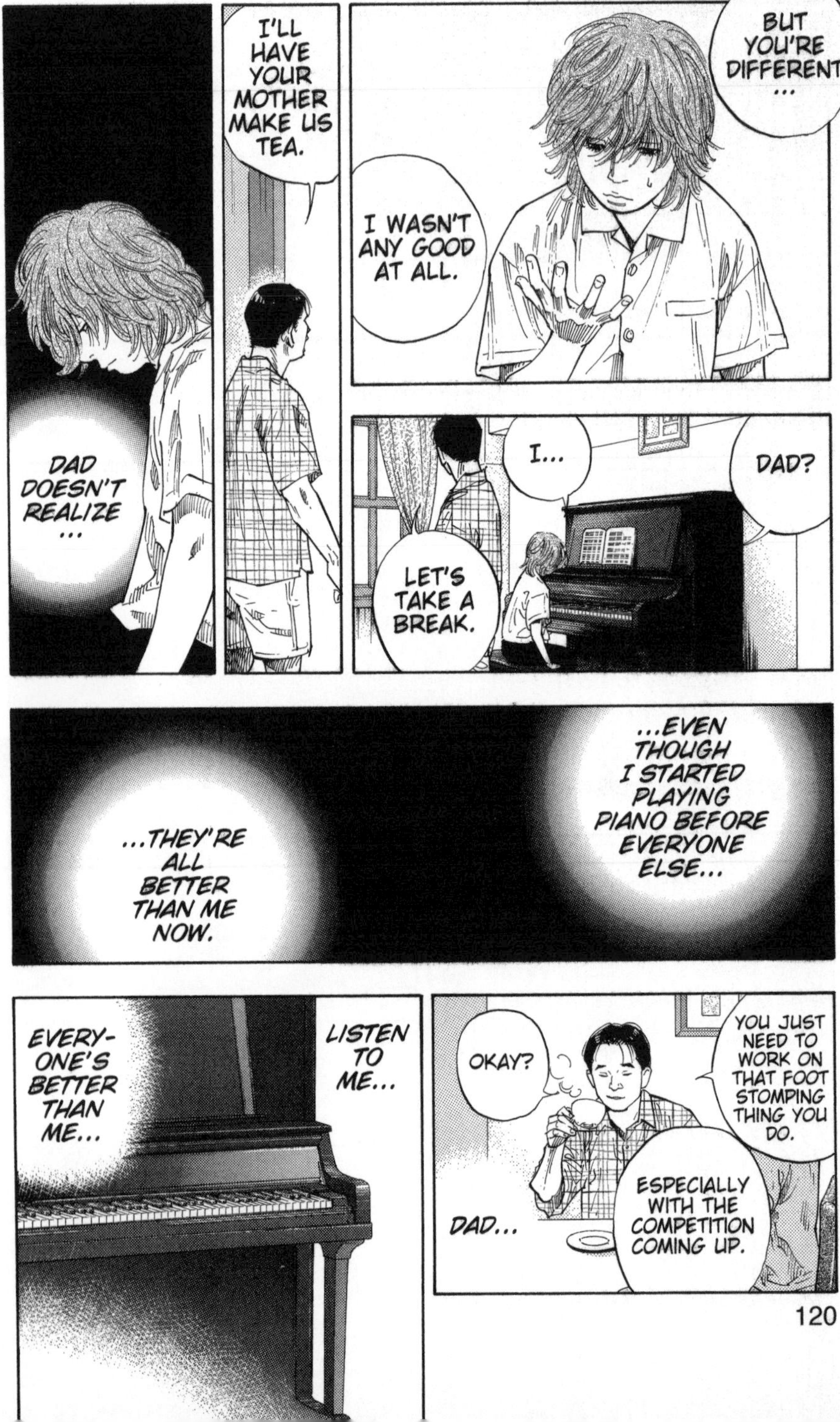
BUT YOU'RE DIFFERENT...
I WASN'T ANY GOOD AT ALL.
DAD?
I...
LET'S TAKE A BREAK.
I'LL HAVE YOUR MOTHER MAKE US TEA.
DAD DOESN'T REALIZE...
...EVEN THOUGH I STARTED PLAYING PIANO BEFORE EVERYONE ELSE...
...THEY'RE ALL BETTER THAN ME NOW.
YOU JUST NEED TO WORK ON THAT FOOT STOMPING THING YOU DO.
OKAY?
ESPECIALLY WITH THE COMPETITION COMING UP.
DAD...
LISTEN TO ME...
EVERY-ONE'S BETTER THAN ME...

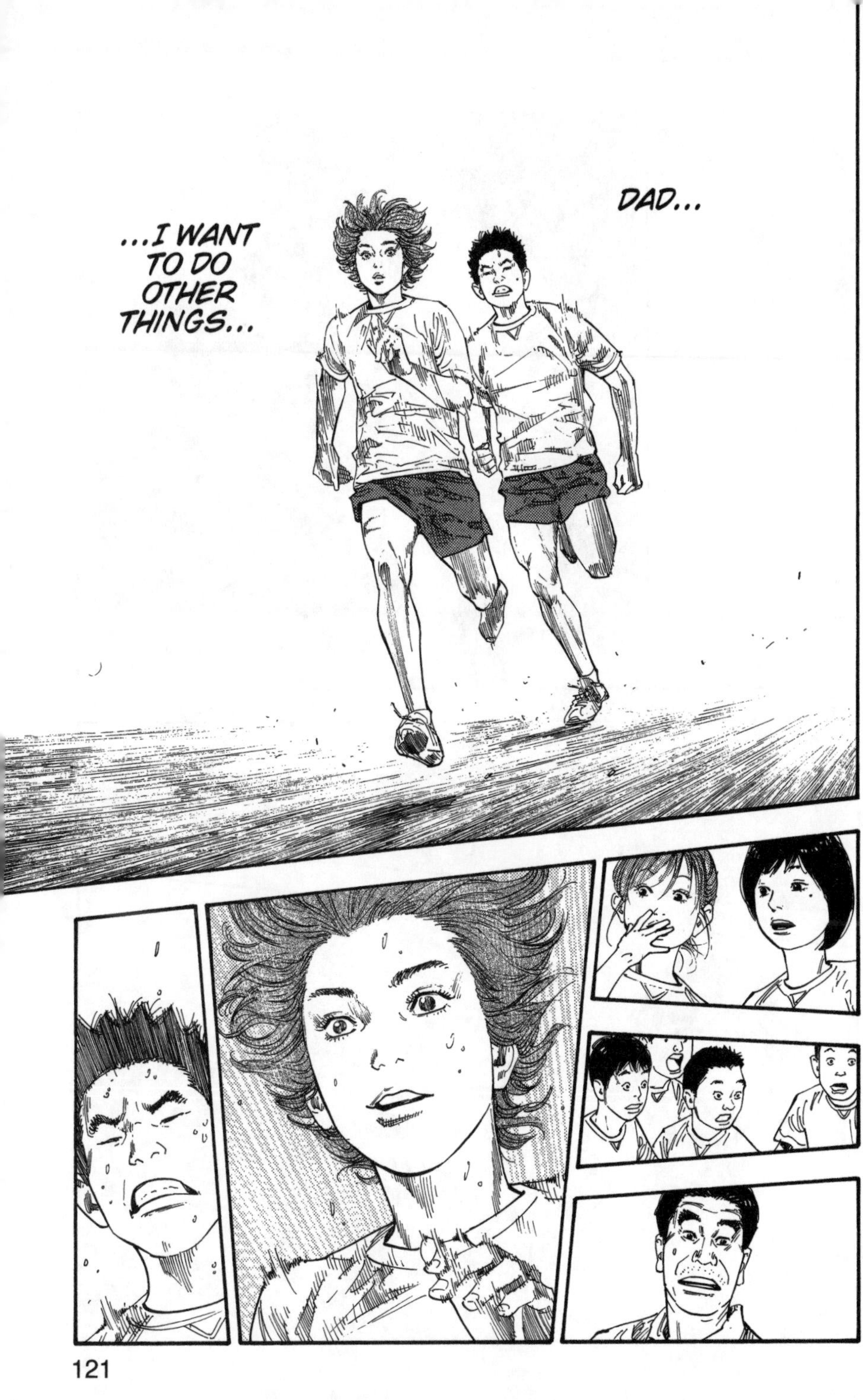
DAD...
...I WANT TO DO OTHER THINGS...

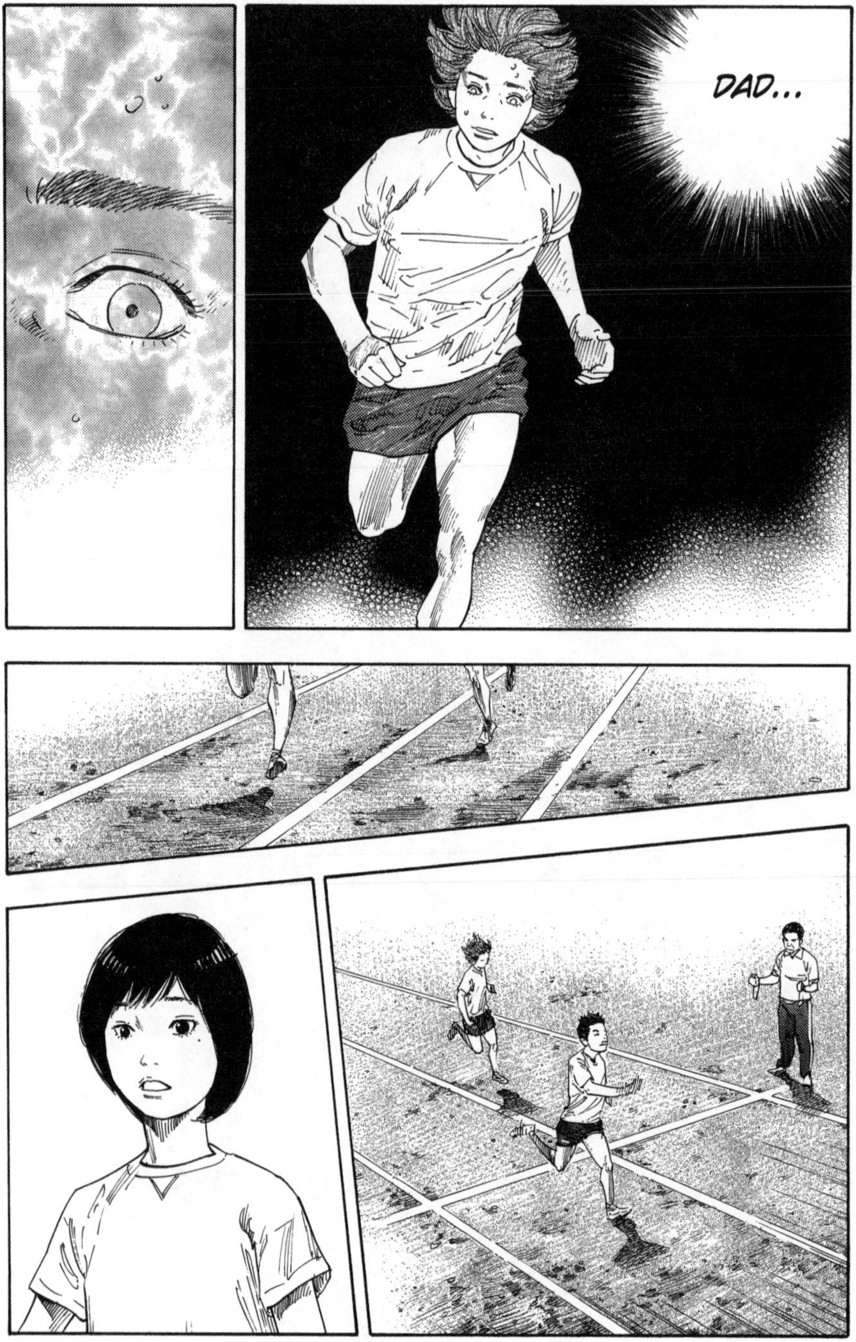
DAD...

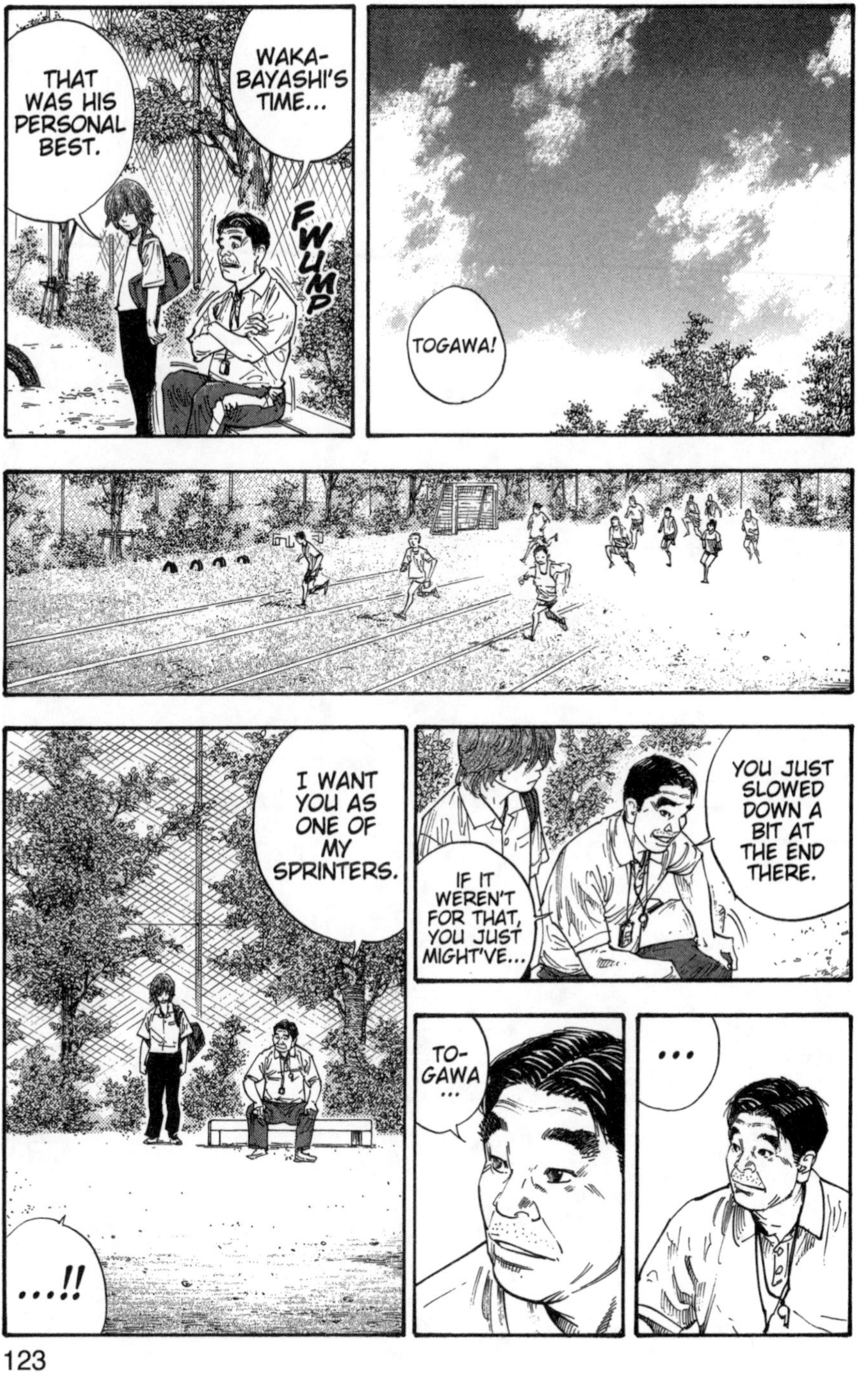
TOGAWA!
WAKA-BAYASHI'S TIME...
FWUMP
THAT WAS HIS PERSONAL BEST.
YOU JUST SLOWED DOWN A BIT AT THE END THERE.
IF IT WEREN'T FOR THAT, YOU JUST MIGHT'VE...
...
TO-GAWA...
I WANT YOU AS ONE OF MY SPRINTERS.
...!!

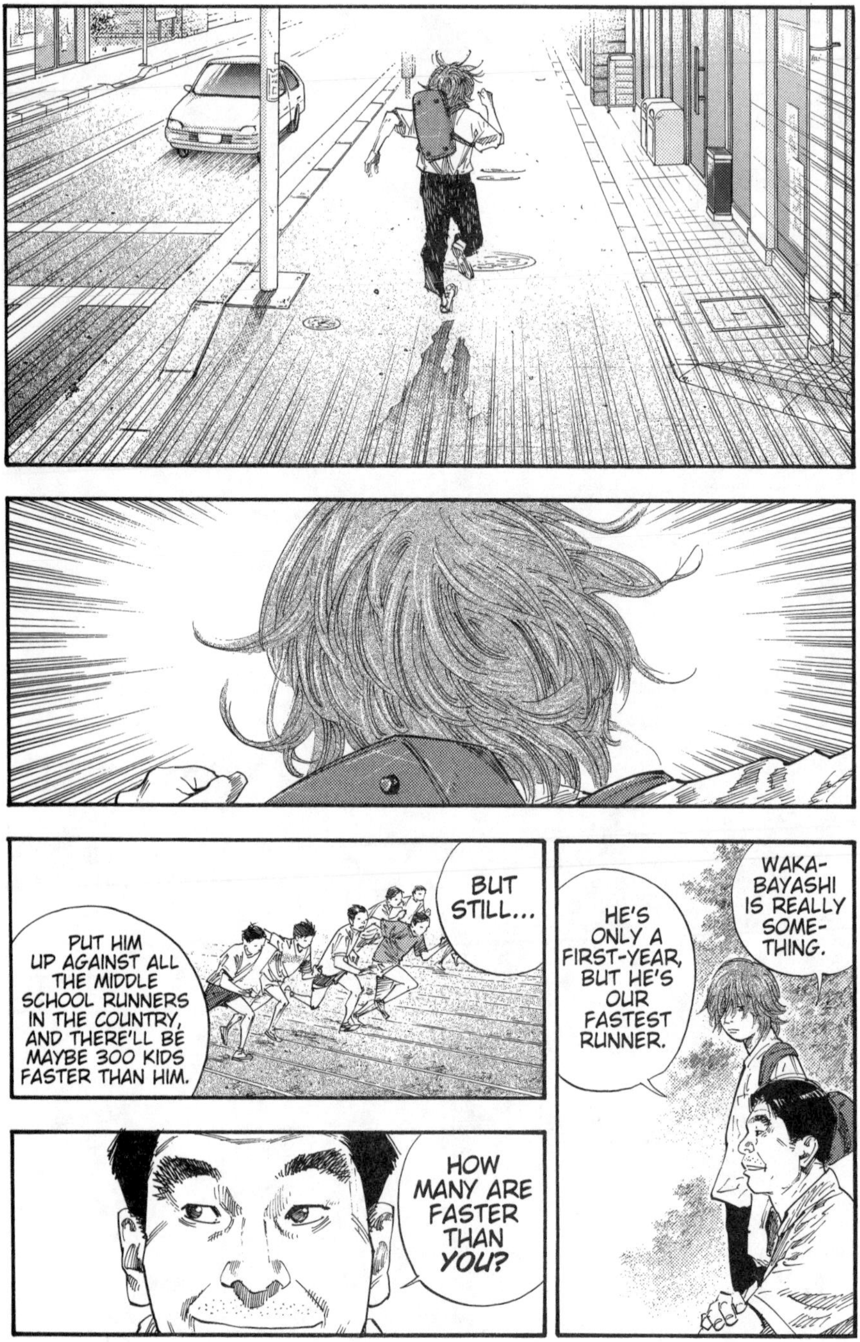
WAKA-BAYASHI IS REALLY SOME-THING.
HE'S ONLY A FIRST-YEAR, BUT HE'S OUR FASTEST RUNNER.
BUT STILL...
PUT HIM UP AGAINST ALL THE MIDDLE SCHOOL RUNNERS IN THE COUNTRY, AND THERE'LL BE MAYBE 300 KIDS FASTER THAN HIM.
HOW MANY ARE FASTER THAN *YOU?*

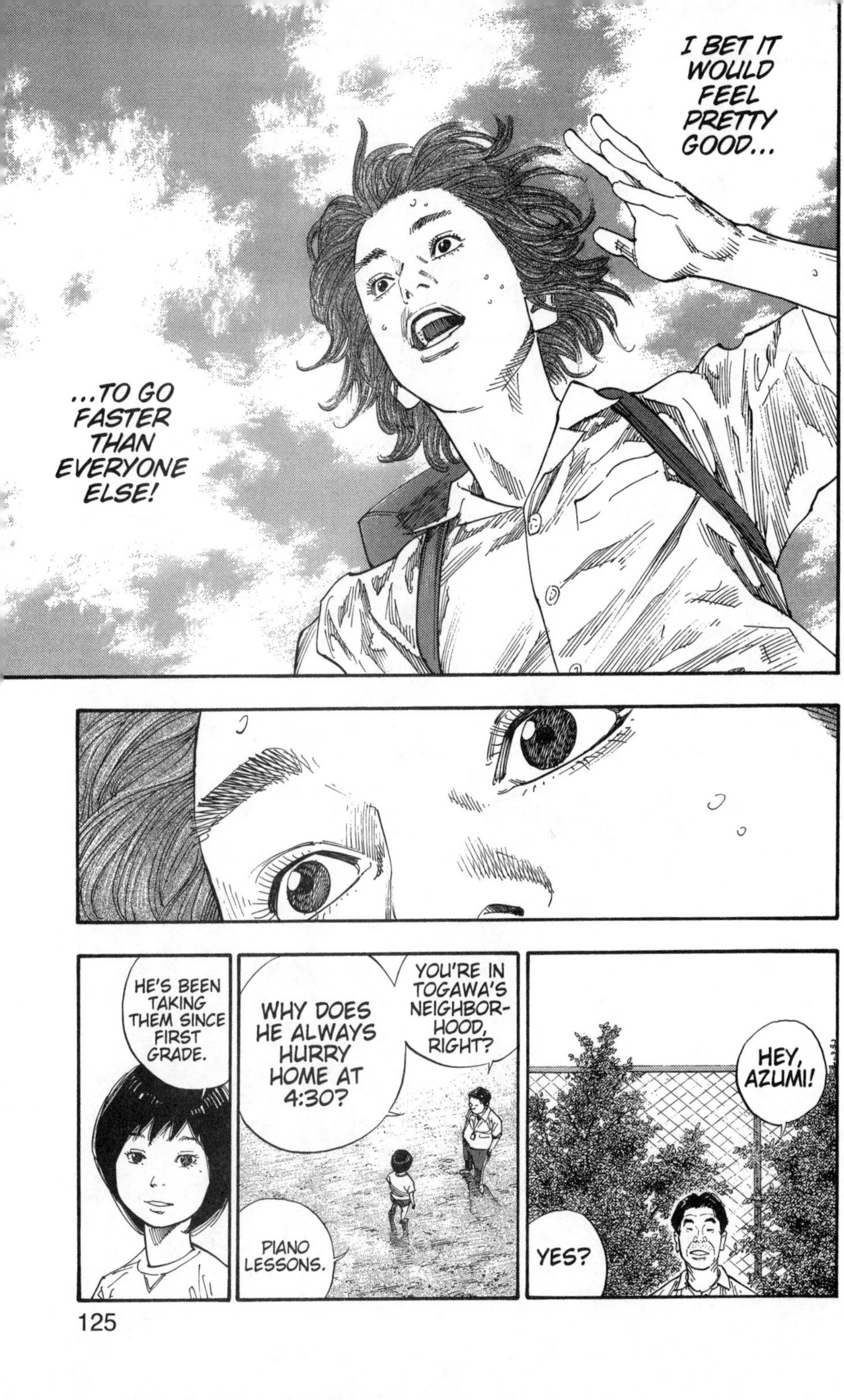
I BET IT WOULD FEEL PRETTY GOOD...
...TO GO FASTER THAN EVERYONE ELSE!
HEY, AZUMI!
YES?
YOU'RE IN TOGAWA'S NEIGHBOR-HOOD, RIGHT?
WHY DOES HE ALWAYS HURRY HOME AT 4:30?
PIANO LESSONS.
HE'S BEEN TAKING THEM SINCE FIRST GRADE.

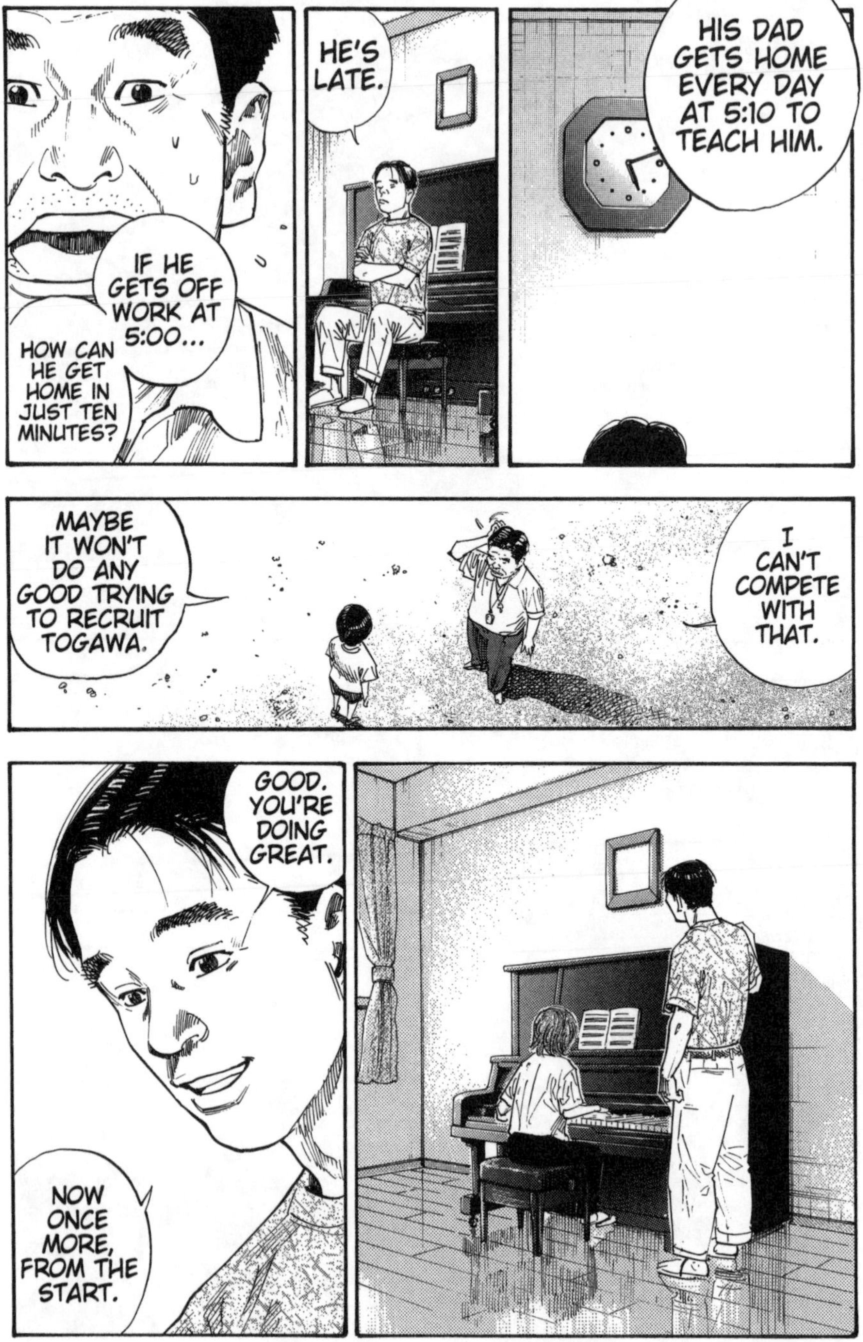
HIS DAD GETS HOME EVERY DAY AT 5:10 TO TEACH HIM.
HE'S LATE.
IF HE GETS OFF WORK AT 5:00...
HOW CAN HE GET HOME IN JUST TEN MINUTES?
I CAN'T COMPETE WITH THAT.
MAYBE IT WON'T DO ANY GOOD TRYING TO RECRUIT TOGAWA.
GOOD. YOU'RE DOING GREAT.
NOW ONCE MORE, FROM THE START.

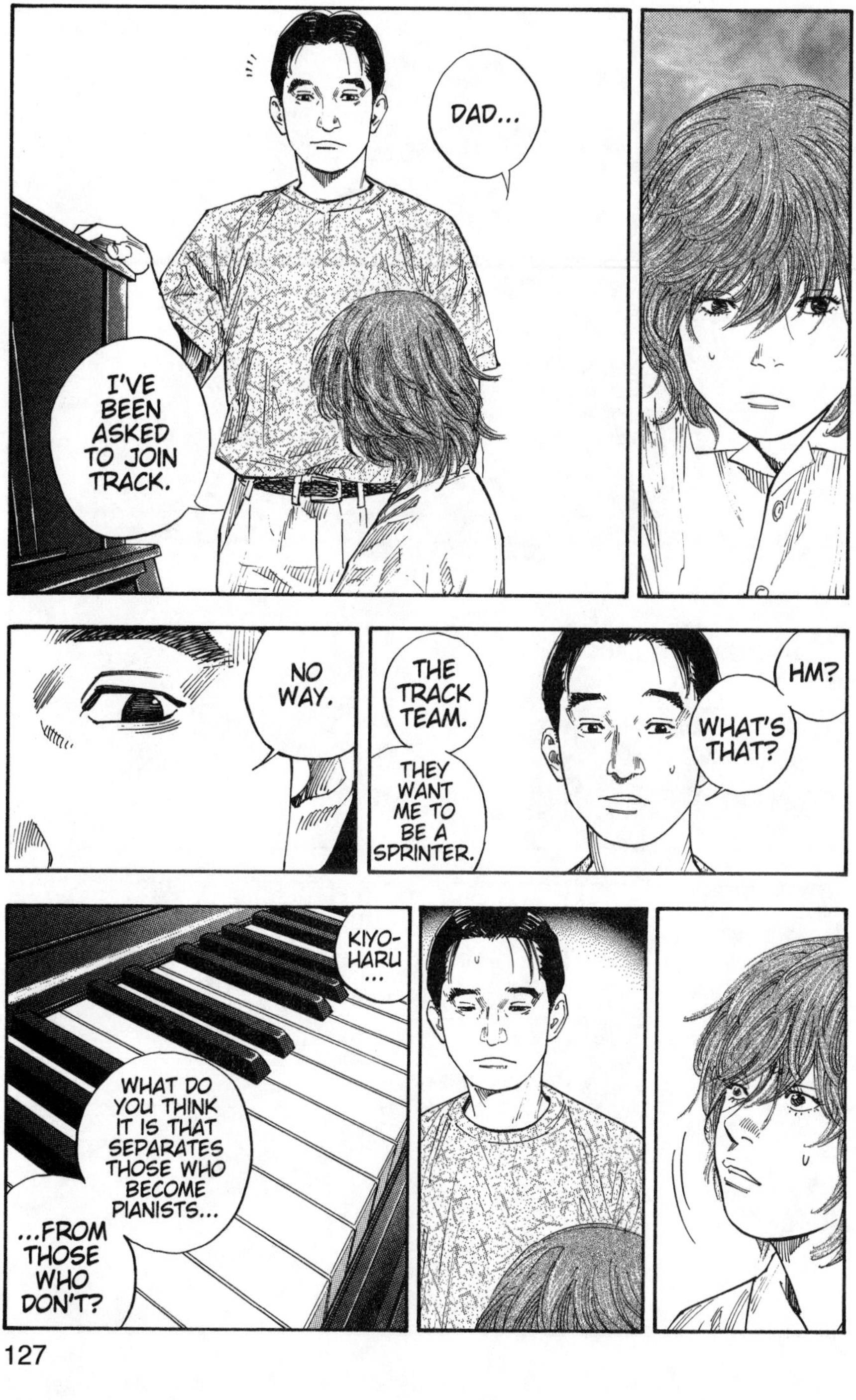
DAD...
I'VE BEEN ASKED TO JOIN TRACK.
HM?
WHAT'S THAT?
THE TRACK TEAM.
THEY WANT ME TO BE A SPRINTER.
NO WAY.
KIYO-HARU...
WHAT DO YOU THINK IT IS THAT SEPARATES THOSE WHO BECOME PIANISTS...
...FROM THOSE WHO DON'T?

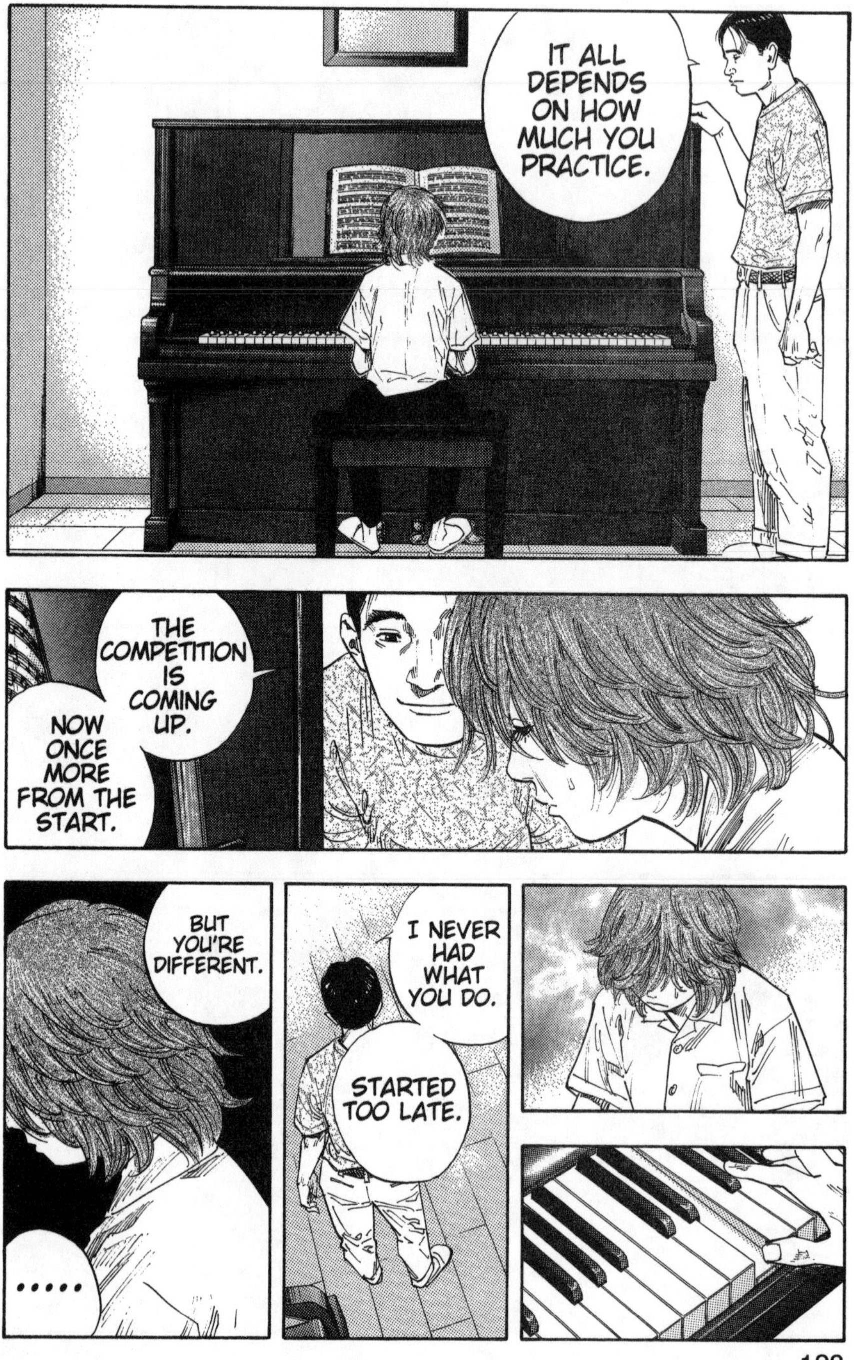
IT ALL DEPENDS ON HOW MUCH YOU PRACTICE.
THE COMPETITION IS COMING UP.
NOW ONCE MORE FROM THE START.
I NEVER HAD WHAT YOU DO.
STARTED TOO LATE.
BUT YOU'RE DIFFERENT.
.....

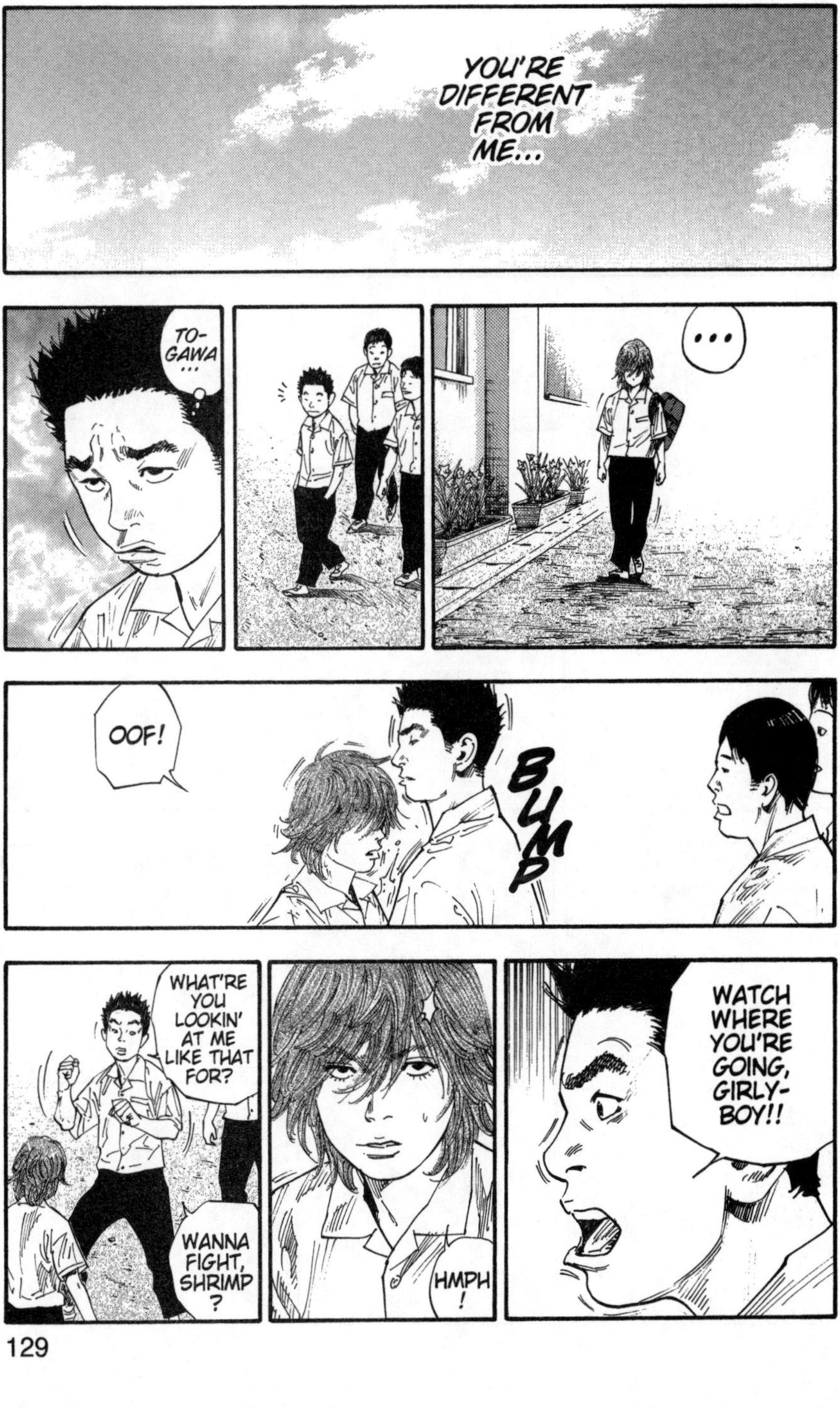
YOU'RE DIFFERENT FROM ME...
...
TO-GAWA...
BUMP
OOF!
WATCH WHERE YOU'RE GOING, GIRLY-BOY!!
HMPH!
WHAT'RE YOU LOOKIN' AT ME LIKE THAT FOR?
WANNA FIGHT, SHRIMP?

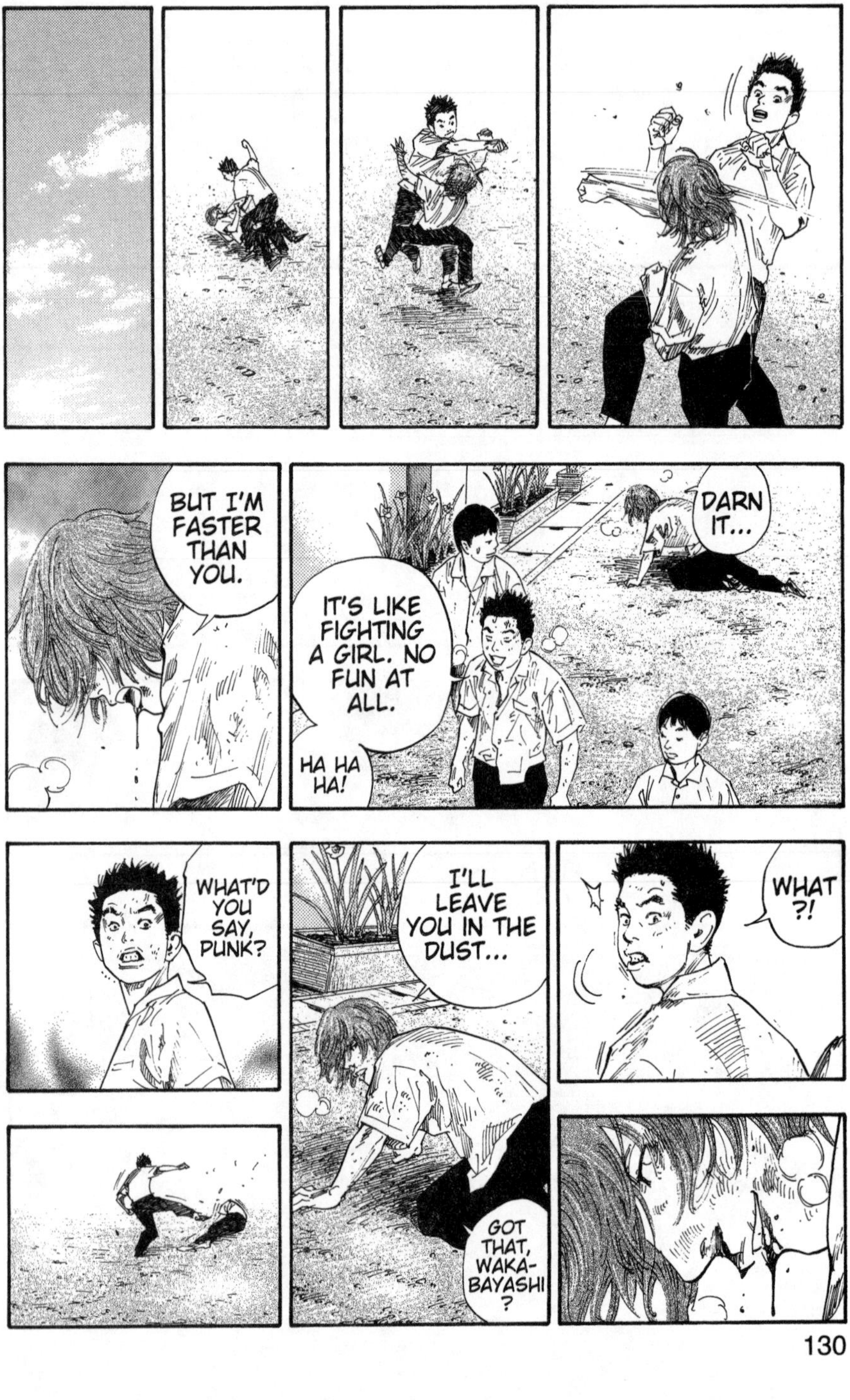
DARN IT...
IT'S LIKE FIGHTING A GIRL. NO FUN AT ALL.
HA HA HA!
BUT I'M FASTER THAN YOU.
WHAT?!
I'LL LEAVE YOU IN THE DUST...
GOT THAT, WAKA-BAYASHI?
WHAT'D YOU SAY, PUNK?

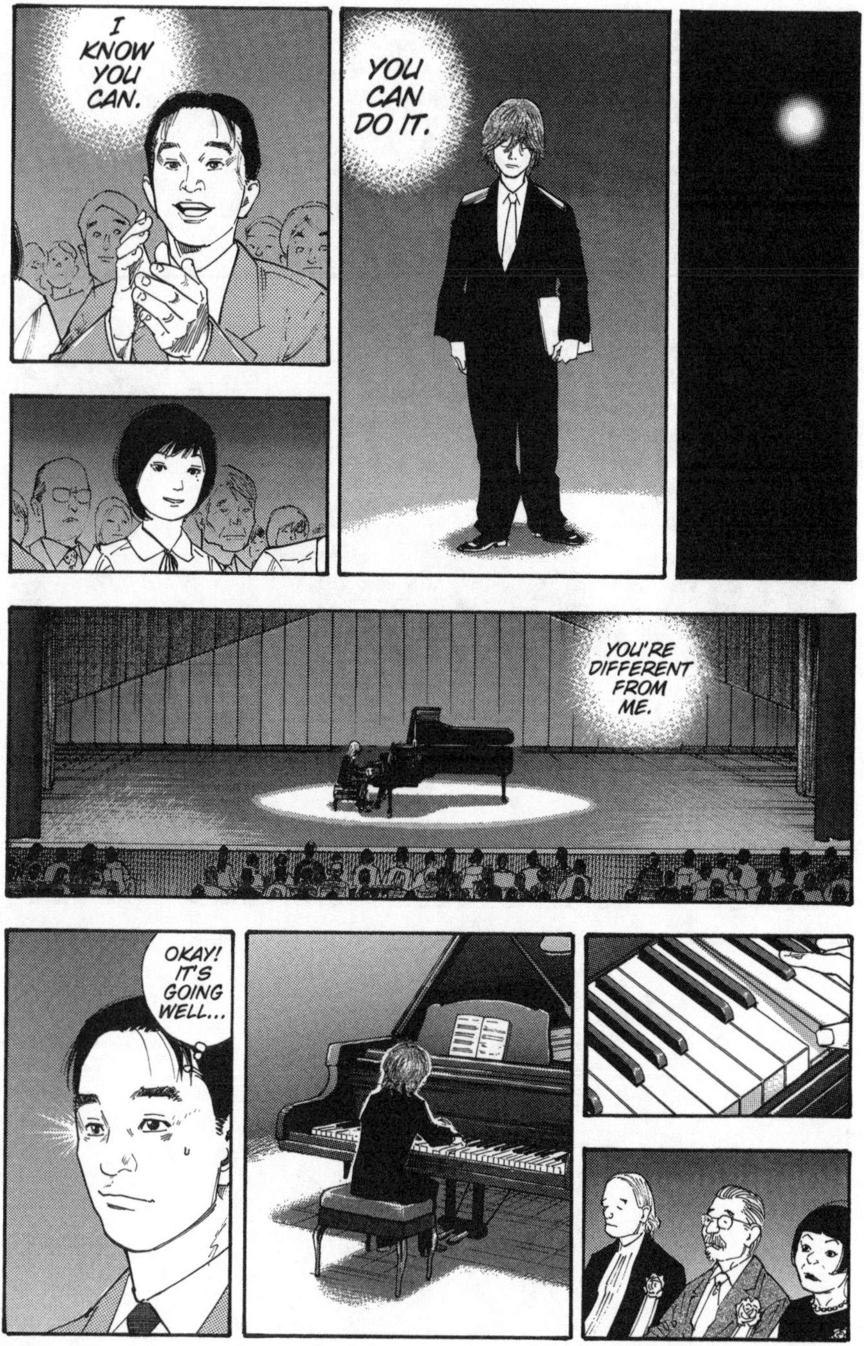
YOU CAN DO IT.
I KNOW YOU CAN.
YOU'RE DIFFERENT FROM ME.
OKAY! IT'S GOING WELL...

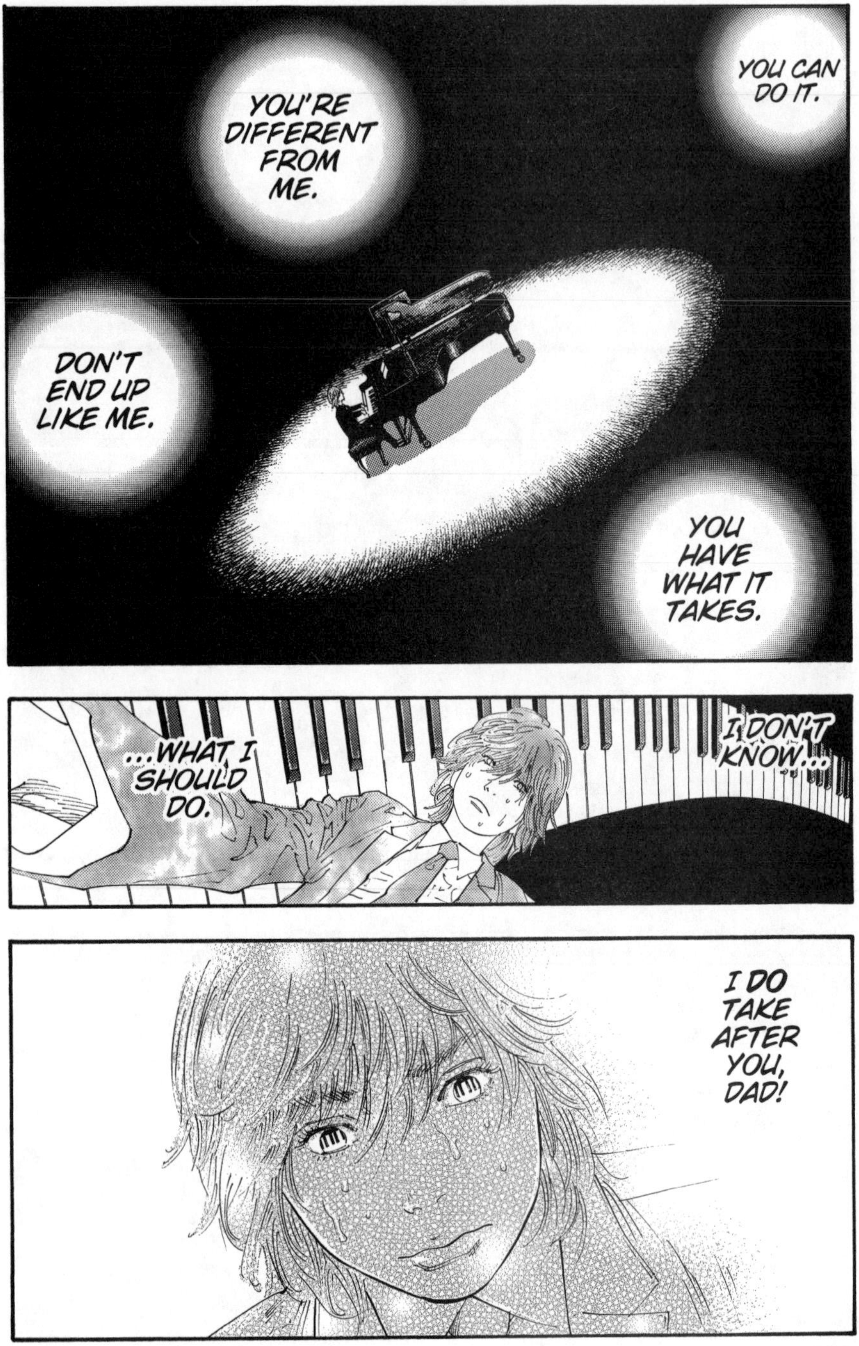
YOU CAN DO IT.
YOU'RE DIFFERENT FROM ME.
YOU HAVE WHAT IT TAKES.
DON'T END UP LIKE ME.
I DON'T KNOW...
...WHAT I SHOULD DO.
I DO TAKE AFTER YOU, DAD!

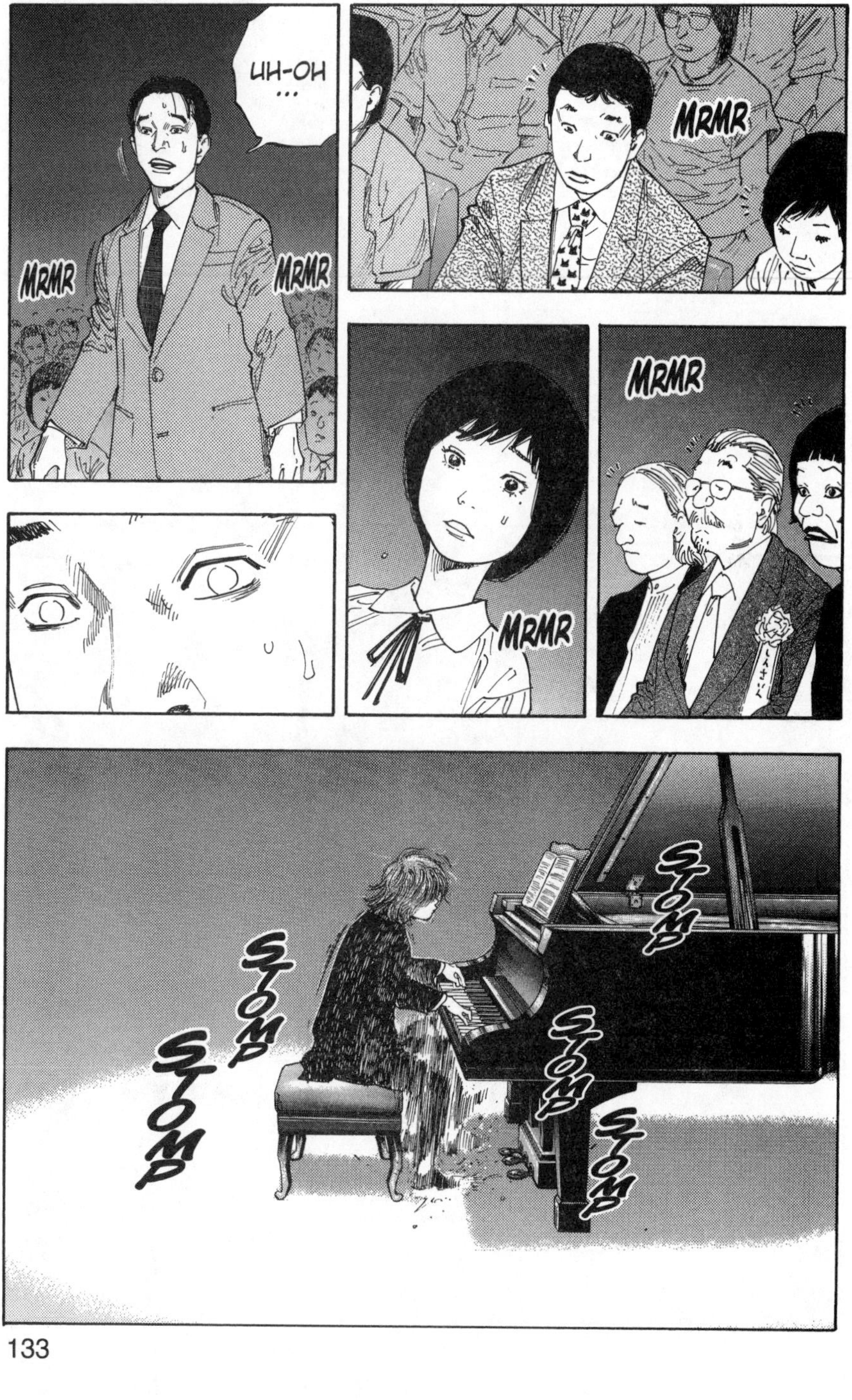
MRMR
MRMR
MRMR
UH-OH ...
MRMR
MRMR
STOMP
STOMP
STOMP
STOMP
STOMP

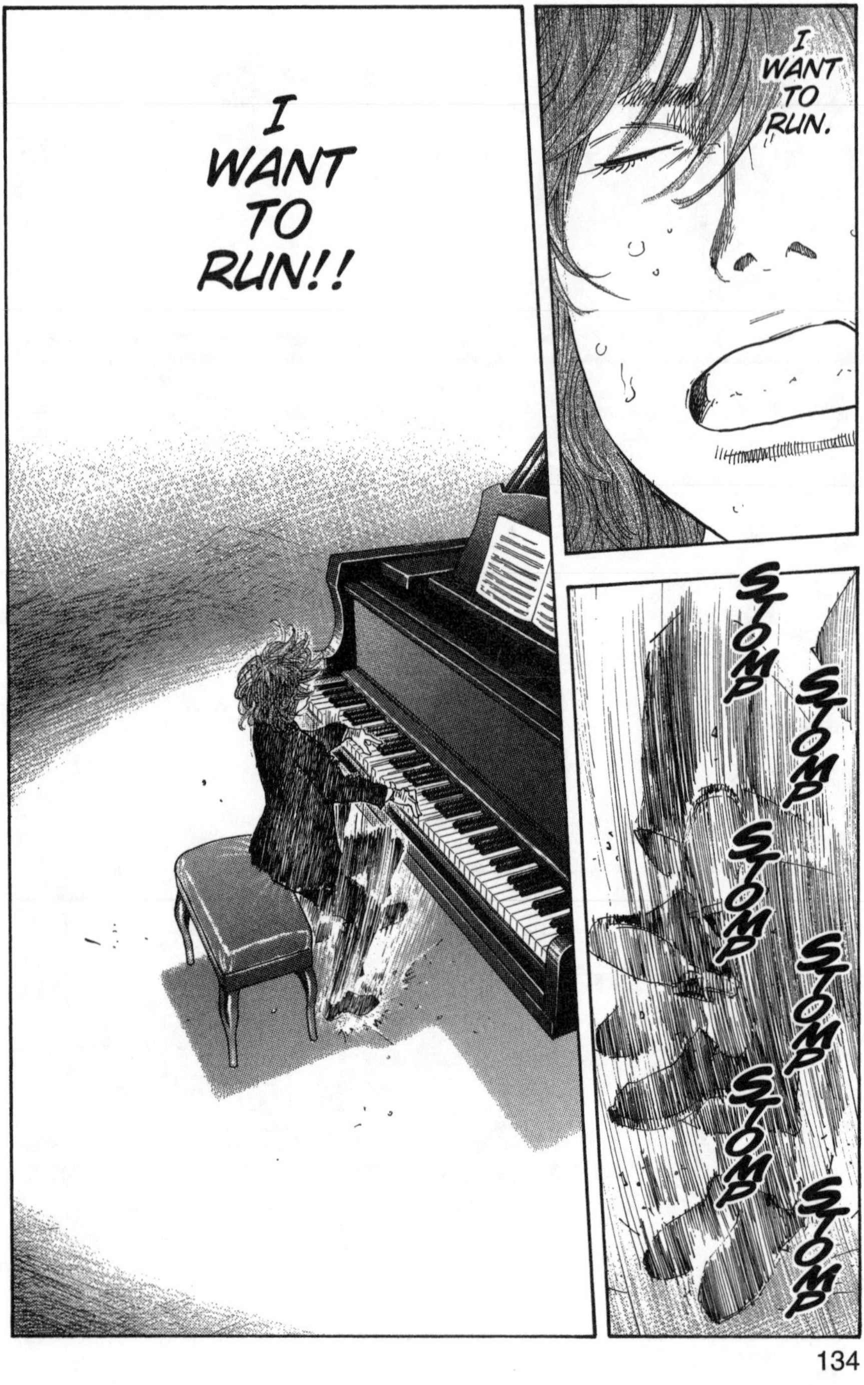
I WANT TO RUN.
STOMP STOMP STOMP STOMP STOMP STOMP STOMP
I WANT TO RUN!!

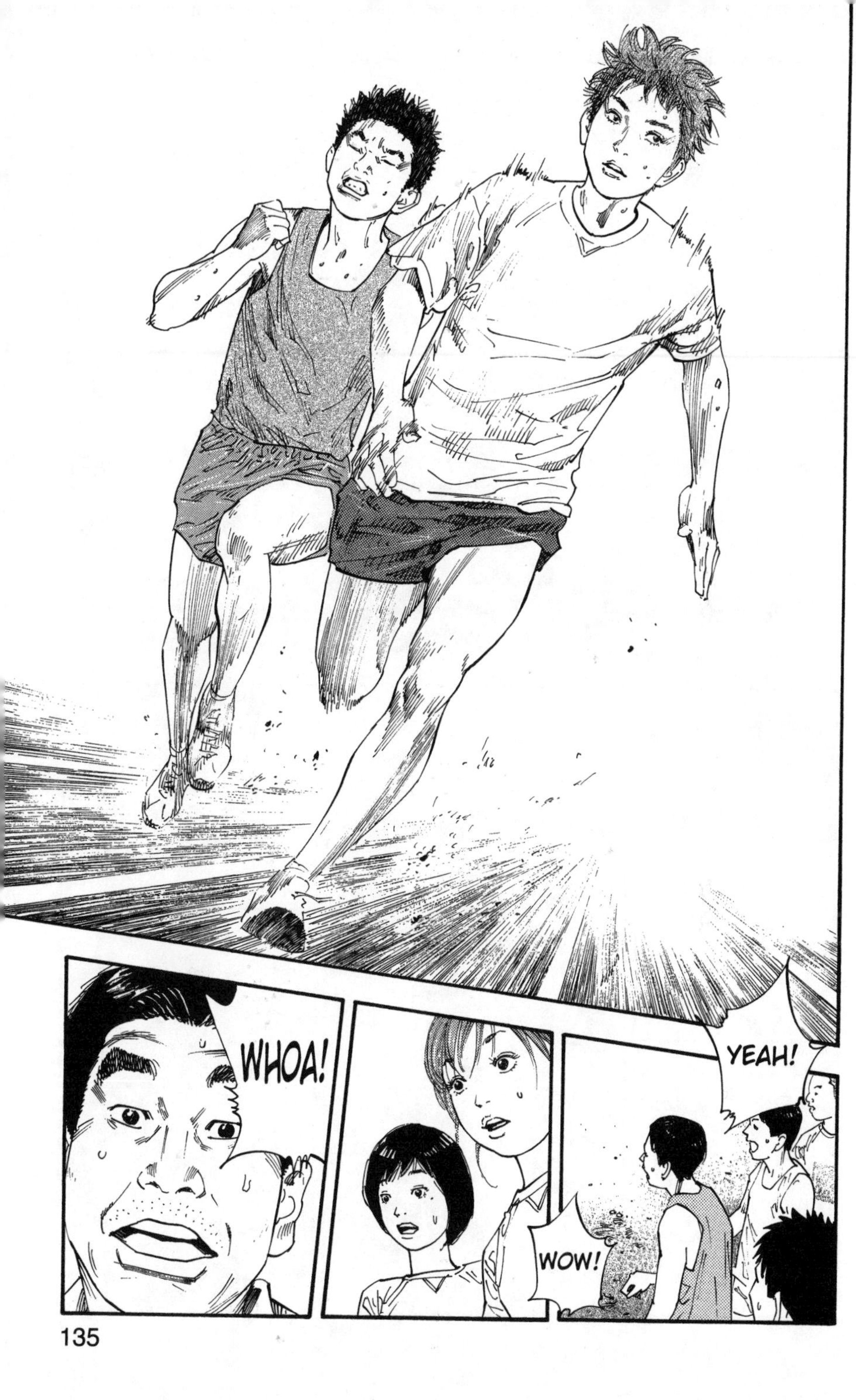
YEAH!
WOW!
WHOA!

WOW!!!
WHAT'S HIS TIME?!
...
HUF
HUF
...
HUF
HUF
HUF
HUF
COACH?
HUF
HOW MANY GUYS ARE AHEAD OF ME NOW?
HUF
IN ALL OF JAPAN...
...I'D SAY ABOUT 50!!
HUF
HUF

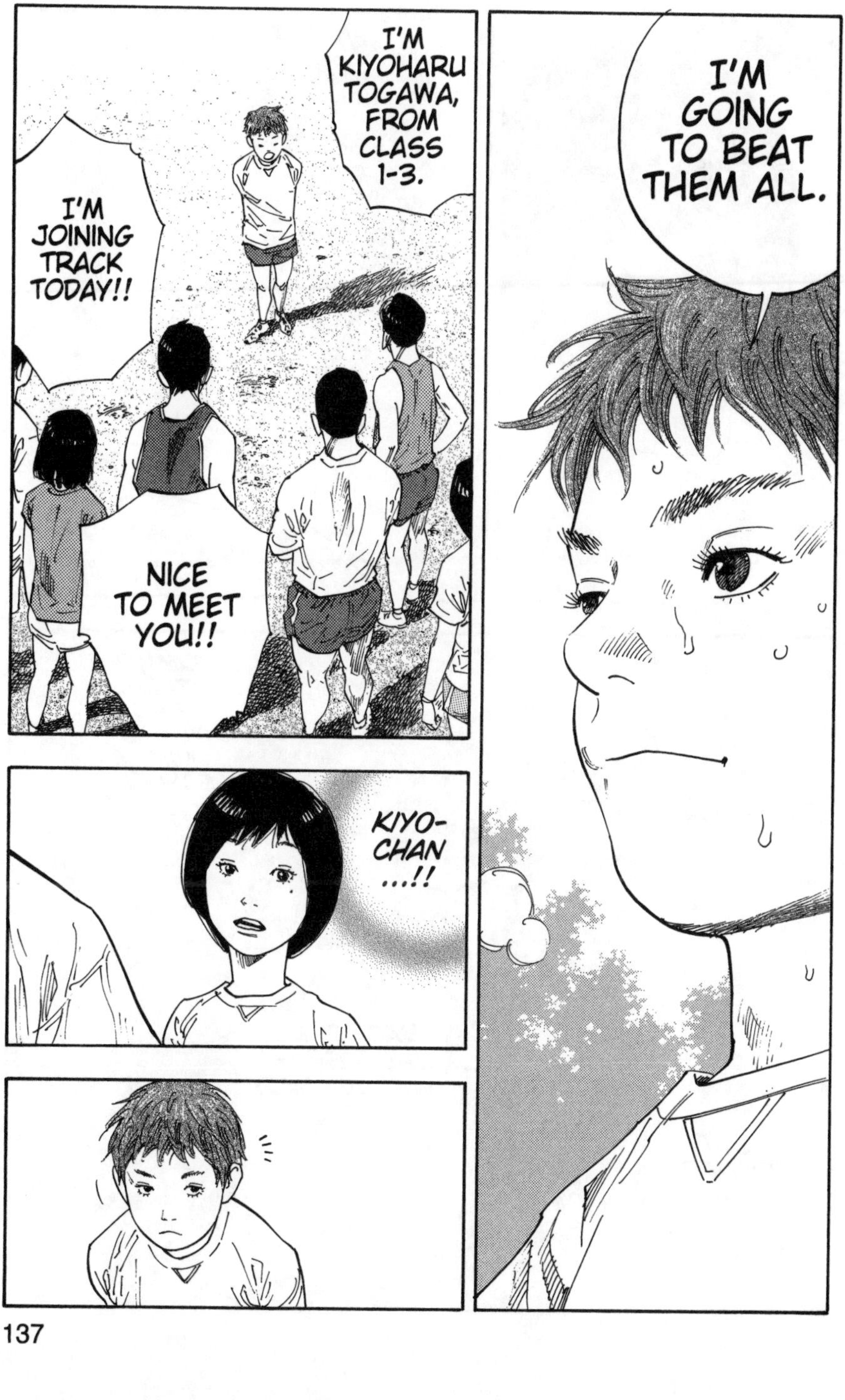
I'M GOING TO BEAT THEM ALL.
I'M KIYOHARU TOGAWA, FROM CLASS 1-3.
I'M JOINING TRACK TODAY!!
NICE TO MEET YOU!!
KIYO-CHAN ...!!

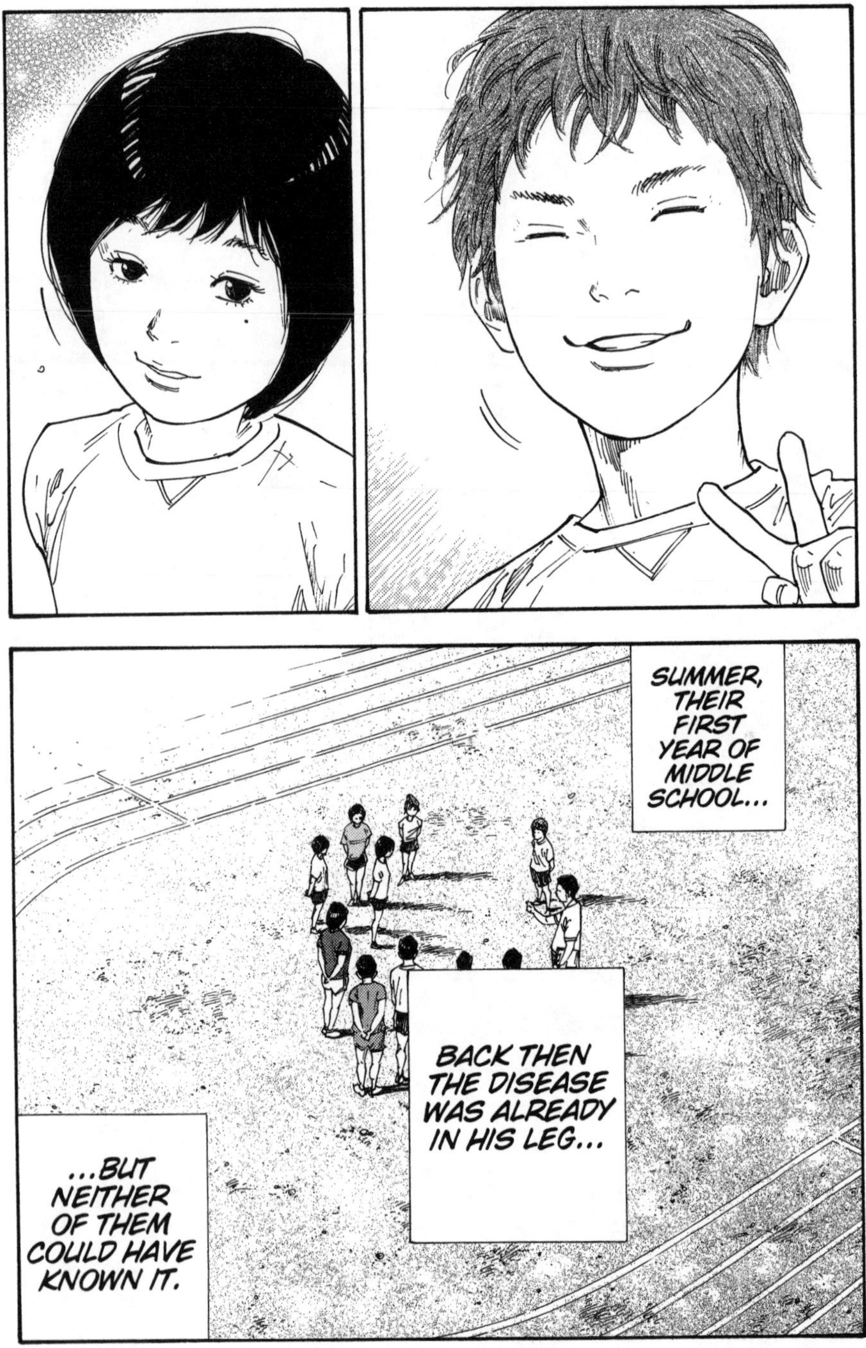
SUMMER, THEIR FIRST YEAR OF MIDDLE SCHOOL...
BACK THEN THE DISEASE WAS ALREADY IN HIS LEG...
...BUT NEITHER OF THEM COULD HAVE KNOWN IT.

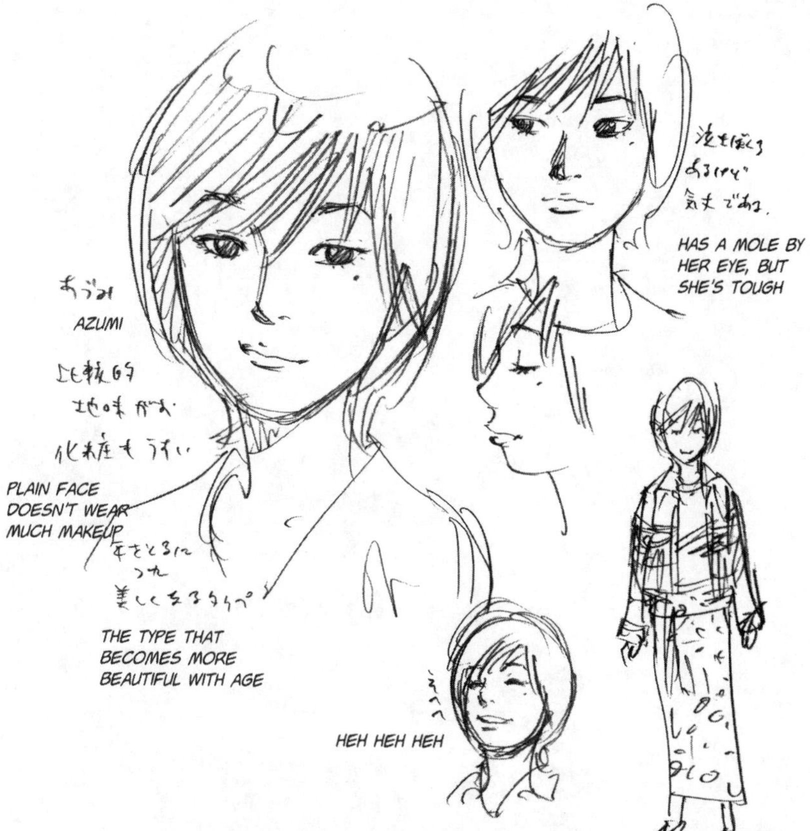
泣きぼくろあるけど気丈である。
HAS A MOLE BY HER EYE, BUT SHE'S TOUGH
あづみ
AZUMI
比較的地味がお
化粧もうすい
PLAIN FACE
DOESN'T WEAR MUCH MAKEUP
年をとるにつれ美しくなるタイプ
THE TYPE THAT BECOMES MORE BEAUTIFUL WITH AGE
えへへ
HEH HEH HEH

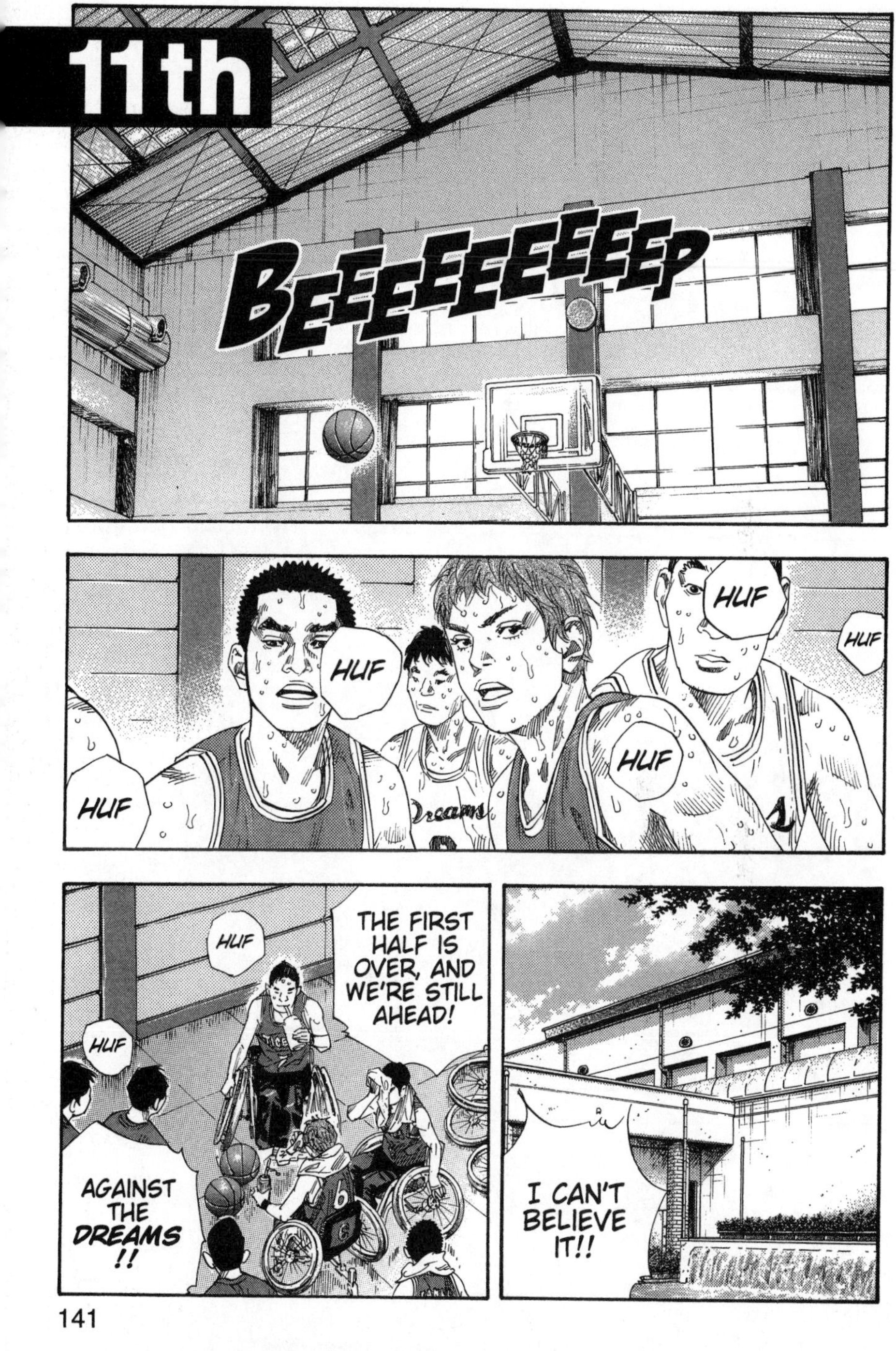
11th
BEEEEEEEEEP
HUF
HUF
HUF
HUF
HUF
I CAN'T BELIEVE IT!!
THE FIRST HALF IS OVER, AND WE'RE STILL AHEAD!
HUF
HUF
AGAINST THE DREAMS!!

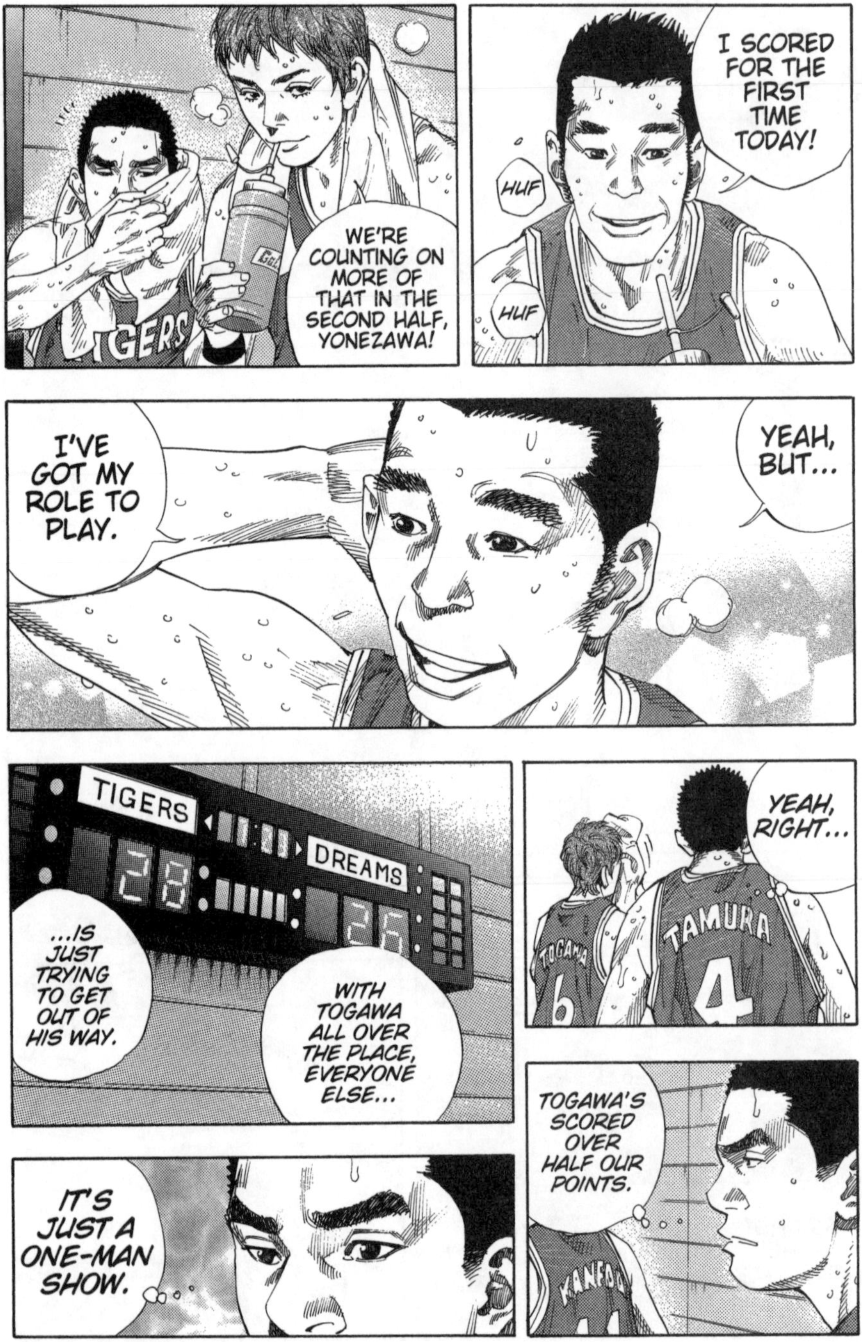
I SCORED FOR THE FIRST TIME TODAY!
HUF
HUF
WE'RE COUNTING ON MORE OF THAT IN THE SECOND HALF, YONEZAWA!
TIGERS
YEAH, BUT...
I'VE GOT MY ROLE TO PLAY.
YEAH, RIGHT...
TAMURA
4
TOGAWA
6
TIGERS
DREAMS
28
26
WITH TOGAWA ALL OVER THE PLACE, EVERYONE ELSE...
...IS JUST TRYING TO GET OUT OF HIS WAY.
TOGAWA'S SCORED OVER HALF OUR POINTS.
IT'S JUST A ONE-MAN SHOW.

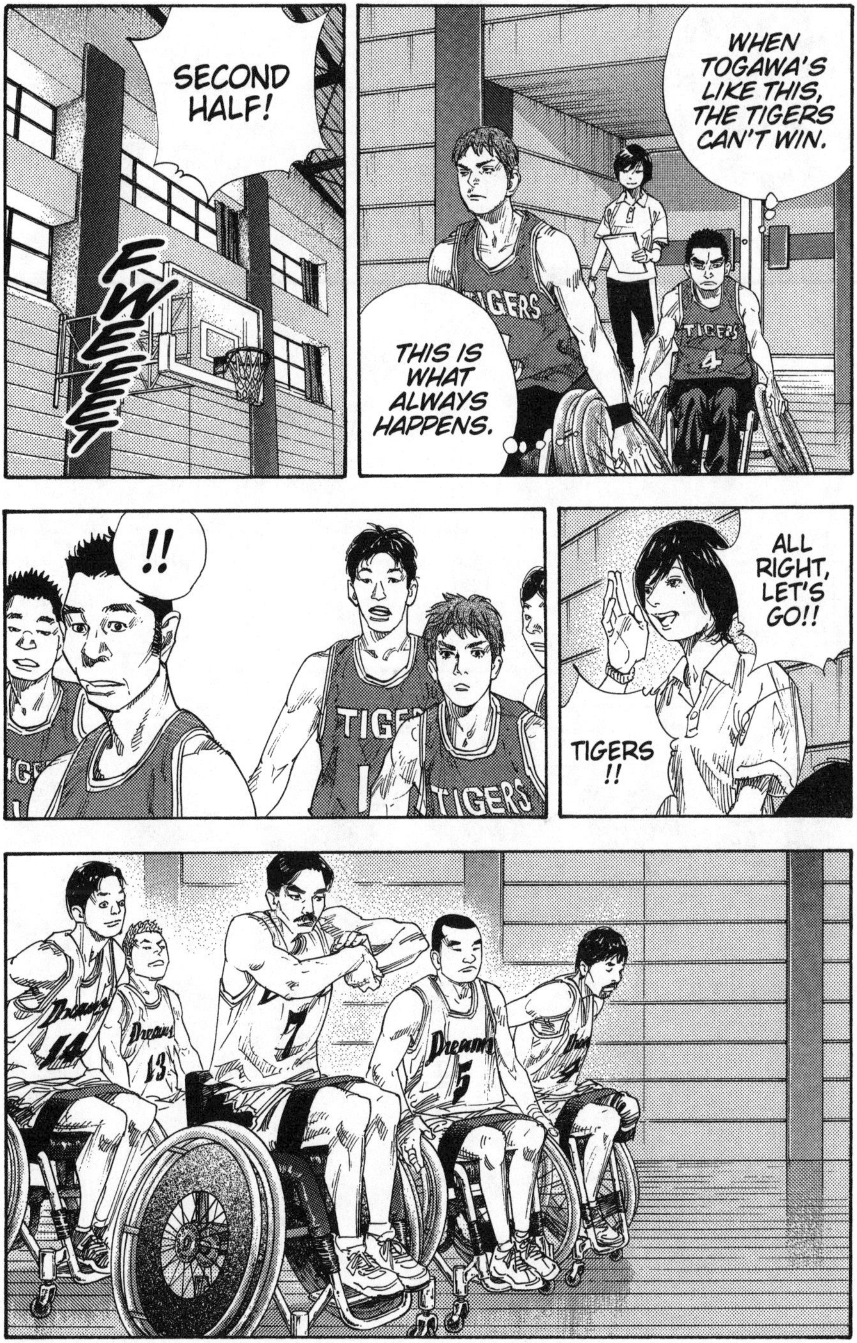
WHEN TOGAWA'S LIKE THIS, THE TIGERS CAN'T WIN.
THIS IS WHAT ALWAYS HAPPENS.
SECOND HALF!
FWEEEET
ALL RIGHT, LET'S GO!!
TIGERS!!
!!

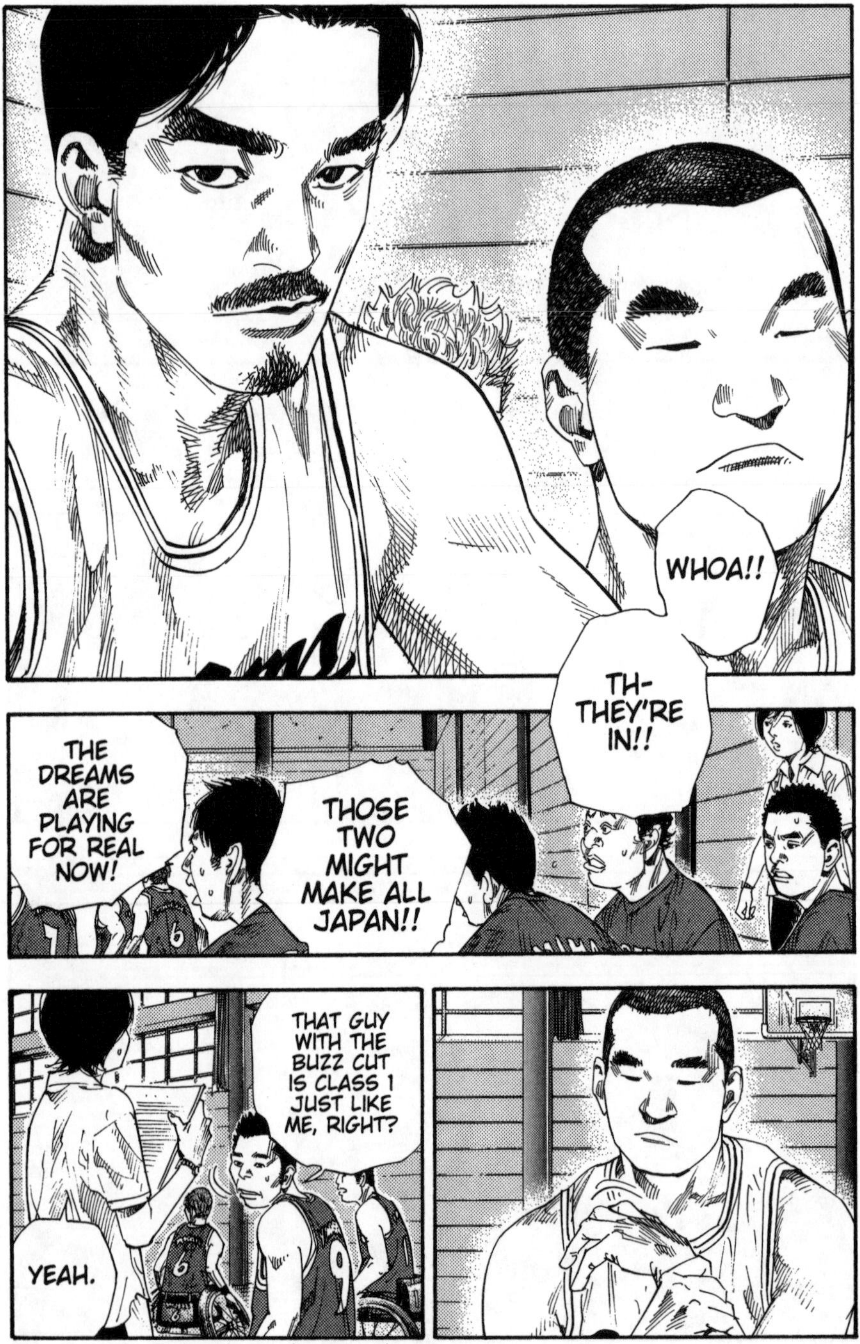
WHOA!!
TH-THEY'RE IN!!
THOSE TWO MIGHT MAKE ALL JAPAN!!
THE DREAMS ARE PLAYING FOR REAL NOW!
THAT GUY WITH THE BUZZ CUT IS CLASS 1 JUST LIKE ME, RIGHT?
YEAH.

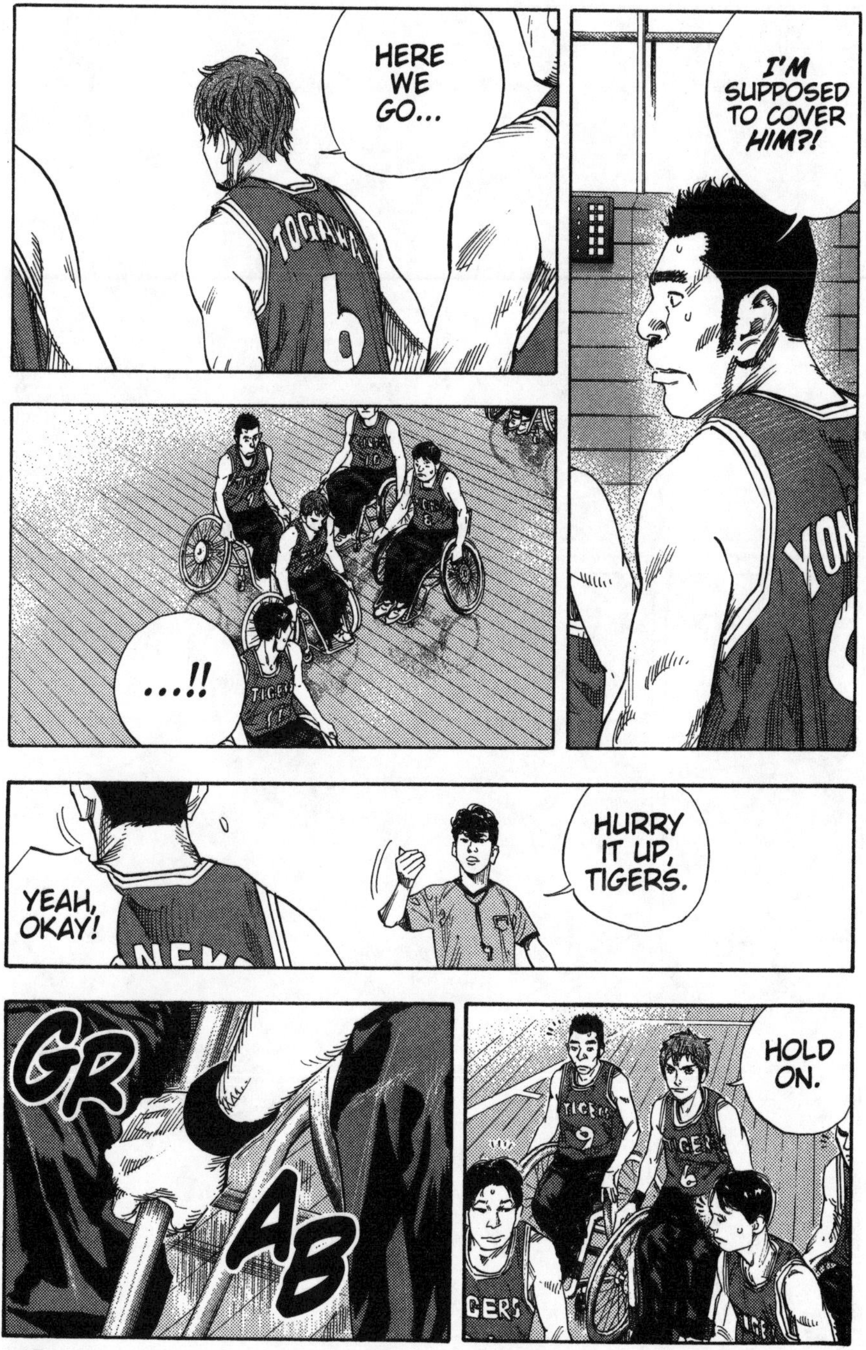
I'M SUPPOSED TO COVER HIM?!
HERE WE GO...
...!!
HURRY IT UP, TIGERS.
YEAH, OKAY!
HOLD ON.
GR
AB

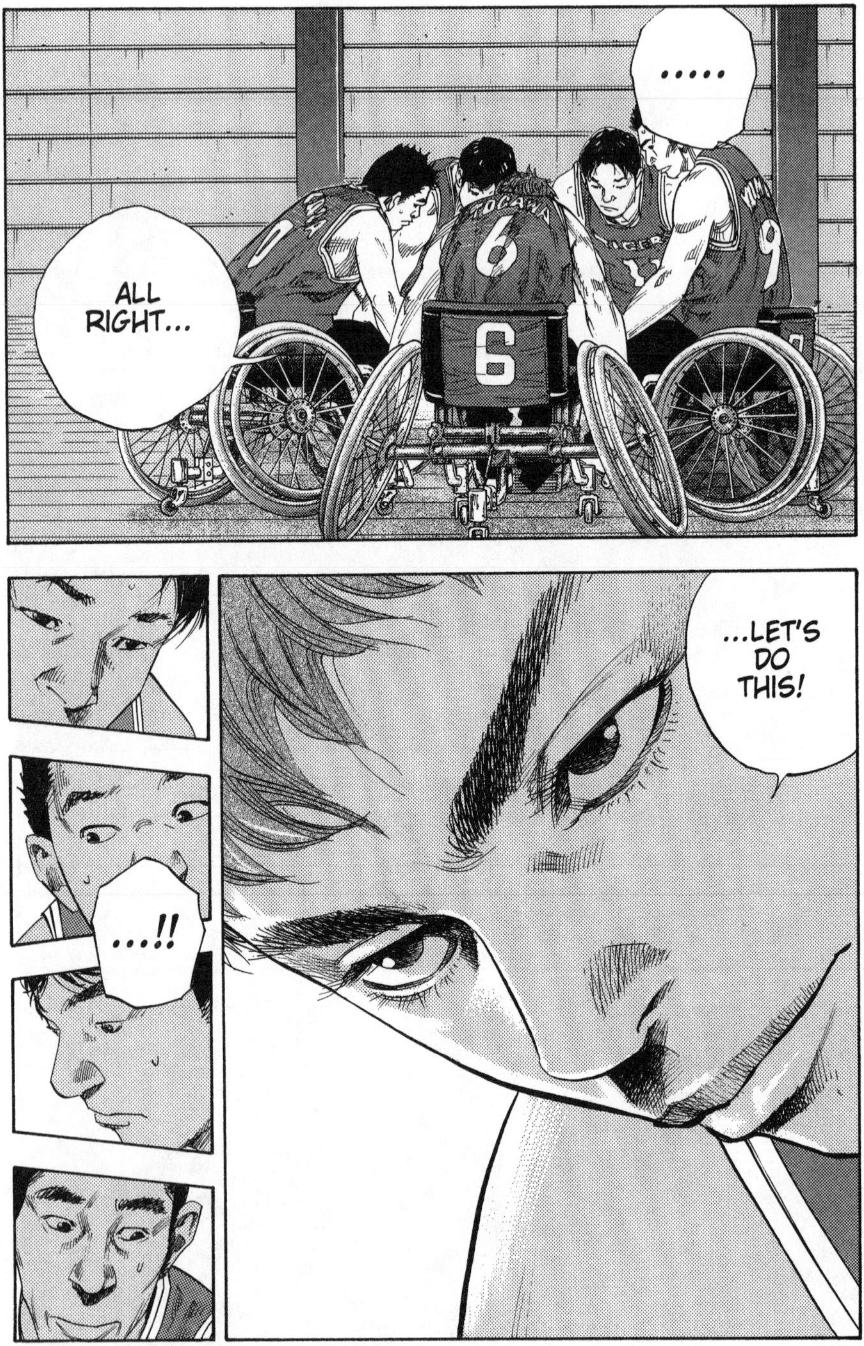
.....
ALL RIGHT...
...LET'S DO THIS!
...!!

THE TIGERS AREN'T USUALLY MUCH OF A TEAM.
WHEELCHAIR BASKETBALL IS A ROUGH AND DEMANDING SPORT.
BUT ON THIS DAY THEY WERE FULL OF FIGHTING SPIRIT.
GET A MOVE ON, TIGERS!!
I WANT TO WIN.

WE'RE GONNA WIN.

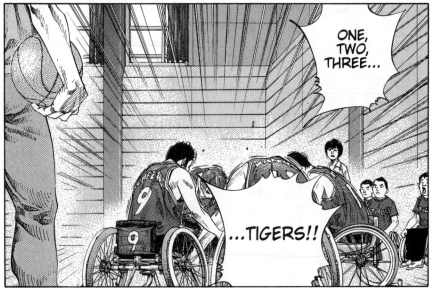

ONE, TWO, THREE...

...TIGERS!!

...!!

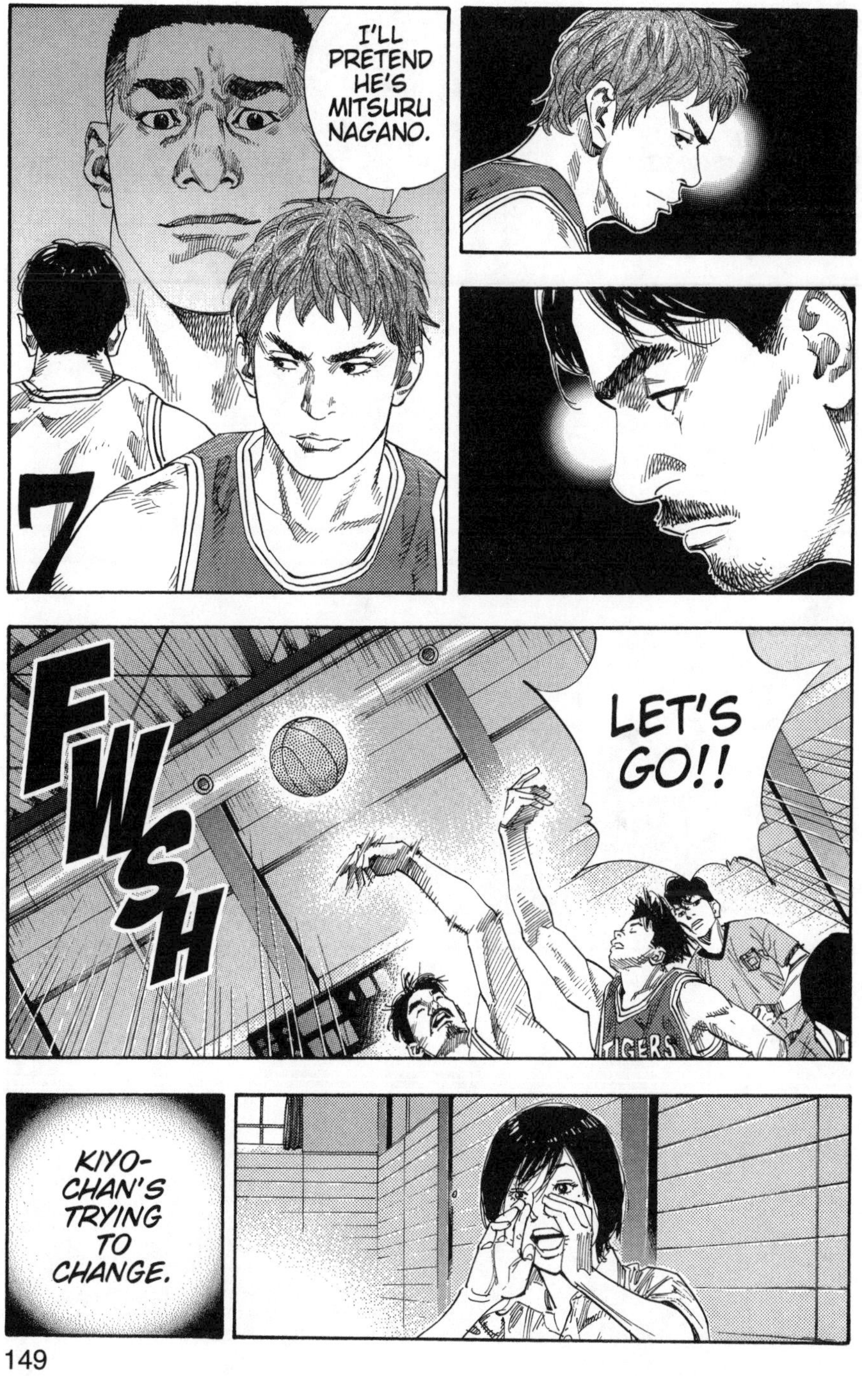
I'LL PRETEND HE'S MITSURU NAGANO.
LET'S GO!!
FWSH
KIYO-CHAN'S TRYING TO CHANGE.

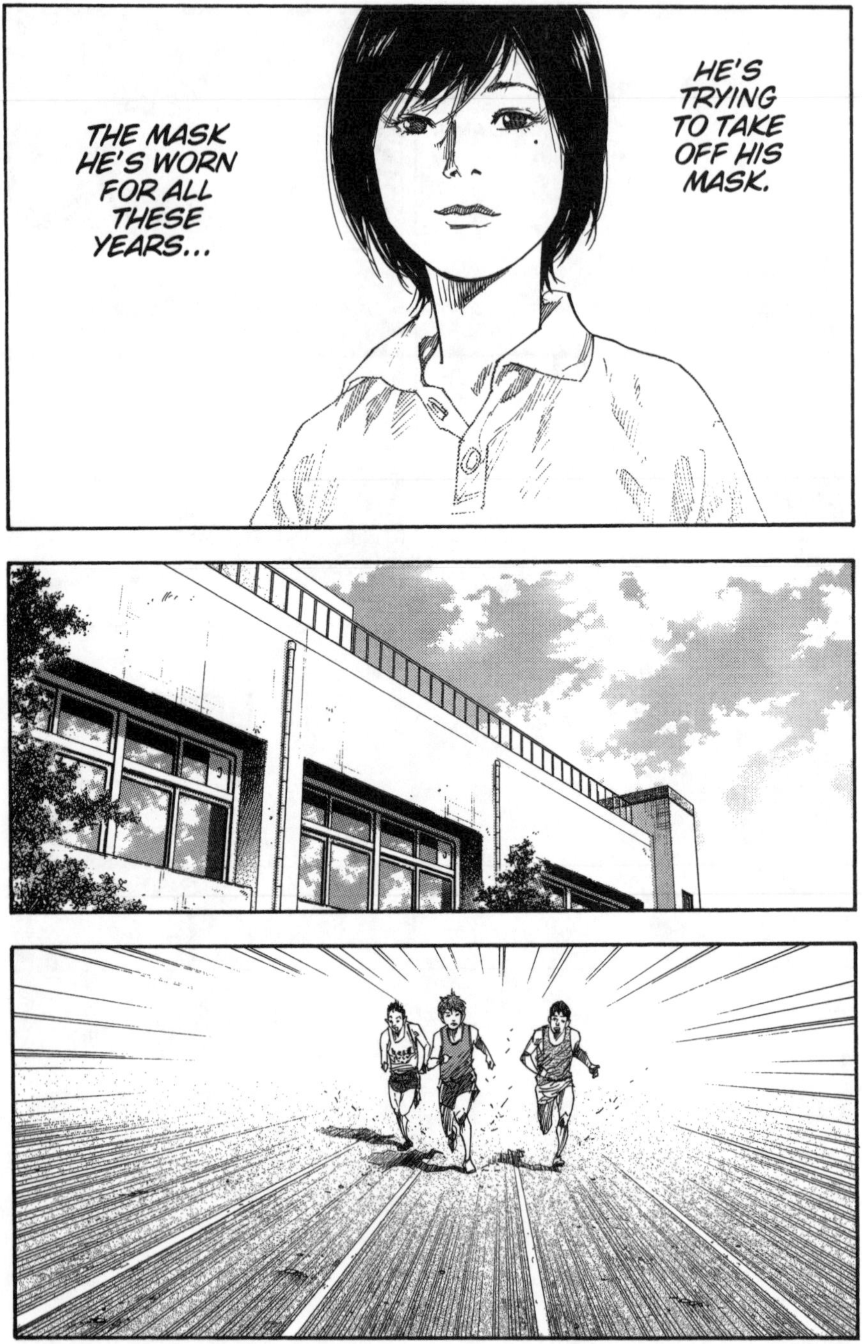
HE'S TRYING TO TAKE OFF HIS MASK.
THE MASK HE'S WORN FOR ALL THESE YEARS...

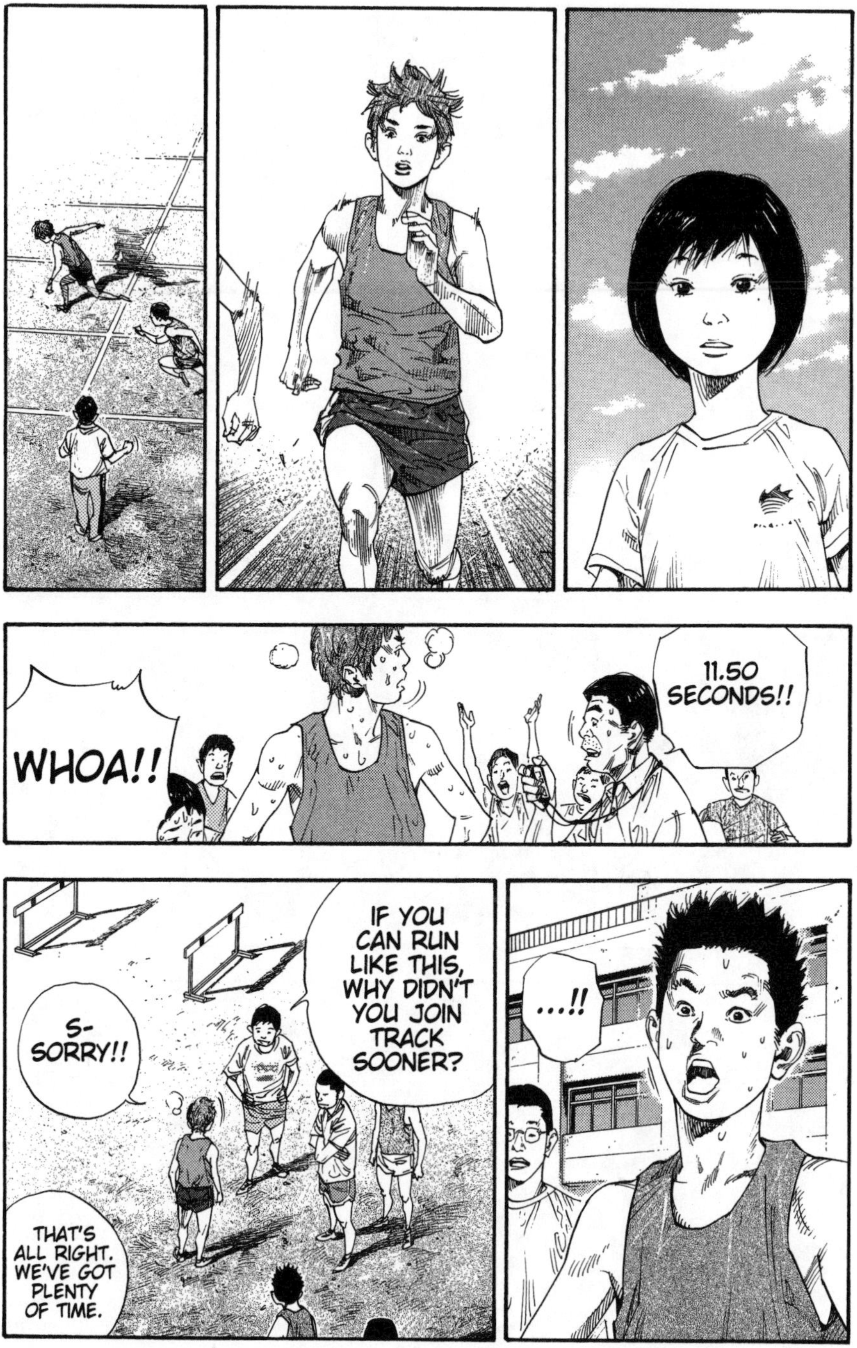
11.50 SECONDS!!
WHOA!!
...!!
IF YOU CAN RUN LIKE THIS, WHY DIDN'T YOU JOIN TRACK SOONER?
S-SORRY!!
THAT'S ALL RIGHT. WE'VE GOT PLENTY OF TIME.

I THINK HE LOOKS CUTE WITH HIS HAIR CUT LIKE THAT.

HUH?

YUKA...

KIYO-HARU!

DEPENDING ON HOW HARD YOU PRACTICE, YOU MIGHT EVEN MAKE IT TO NATIONALS, TOGAWA.

TH-THANKS...

I'LL DO...MY BEST...

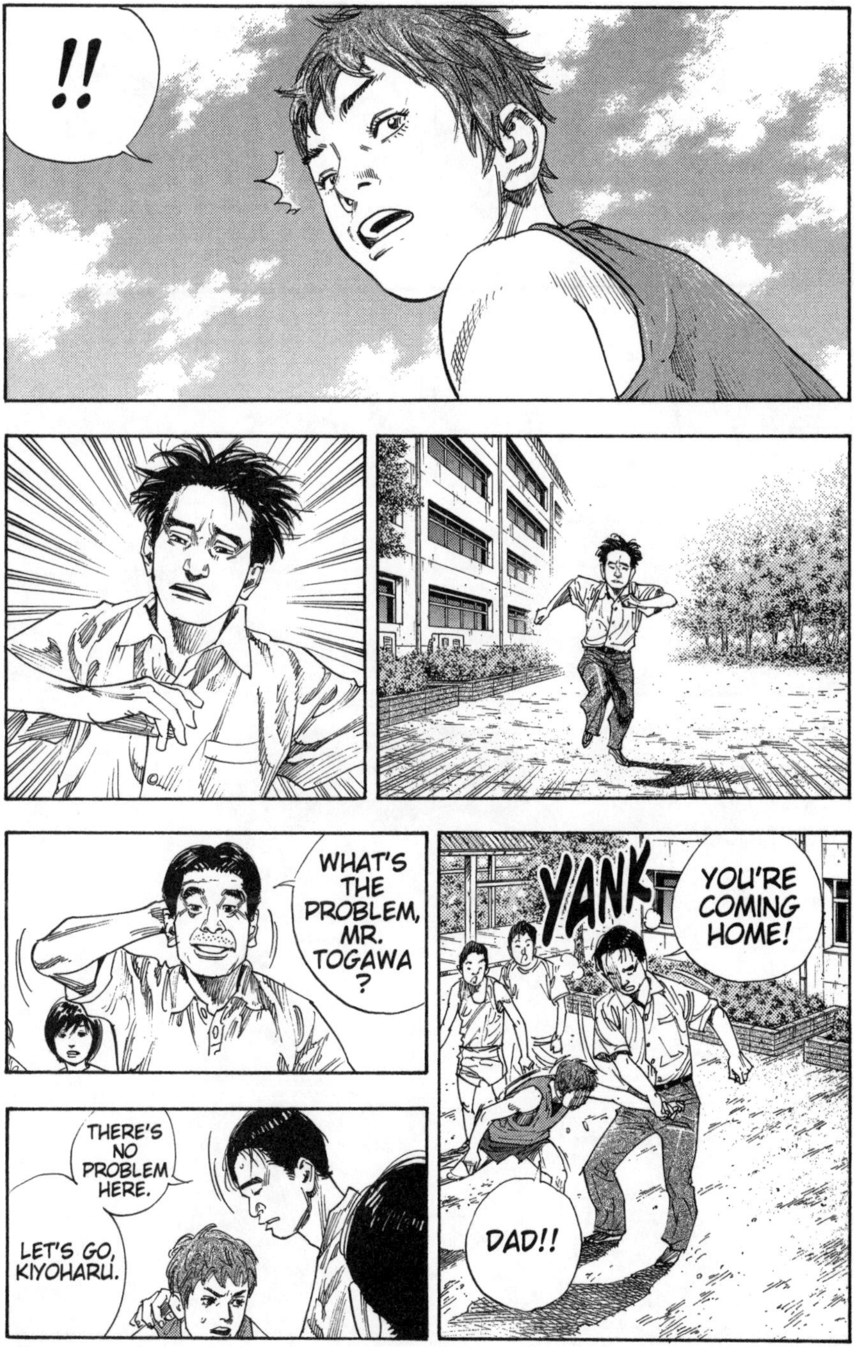
!!
YANK
YOU'RE COMING HOME!
DAD!!
WHAT'S THE PROBLEM, MR. TOGAWA?
THERE'S NO PROBLEM HERE.
LET'S GO, KIYOHARU.

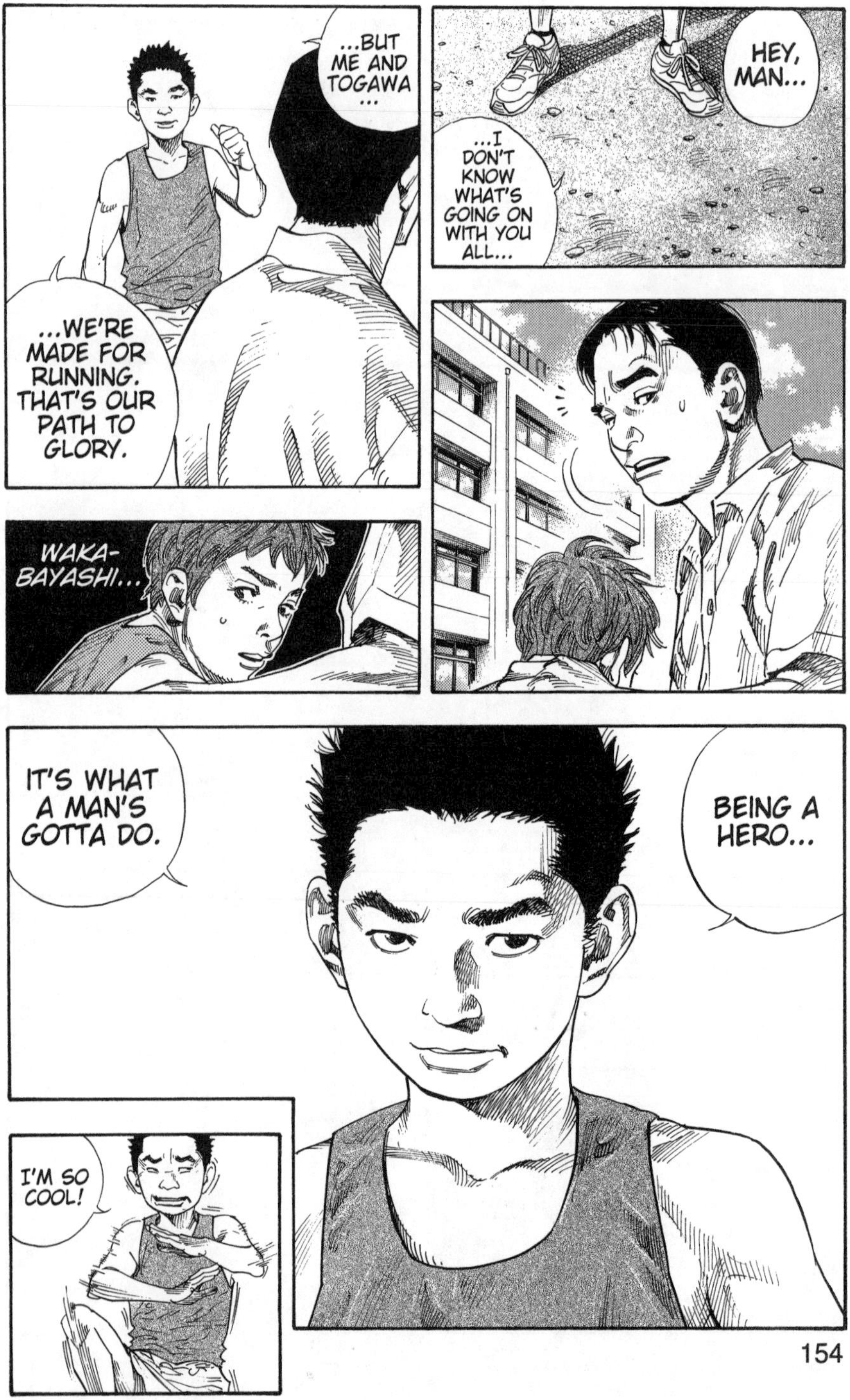
HEY, MAN...
...I DON'T KNOW WHAT'S GOING ON WITH YOU ALL...
...BUT ME AND TOGAWA...
...WE'RE MADE FOR RUNNING. THAT'S OUR PATH TO GLORY.
WAKA-BAYASHI...
BEING A HERO...
IT'S WHAT A MAN'S GOTTA DO.
I'M SO COOL!

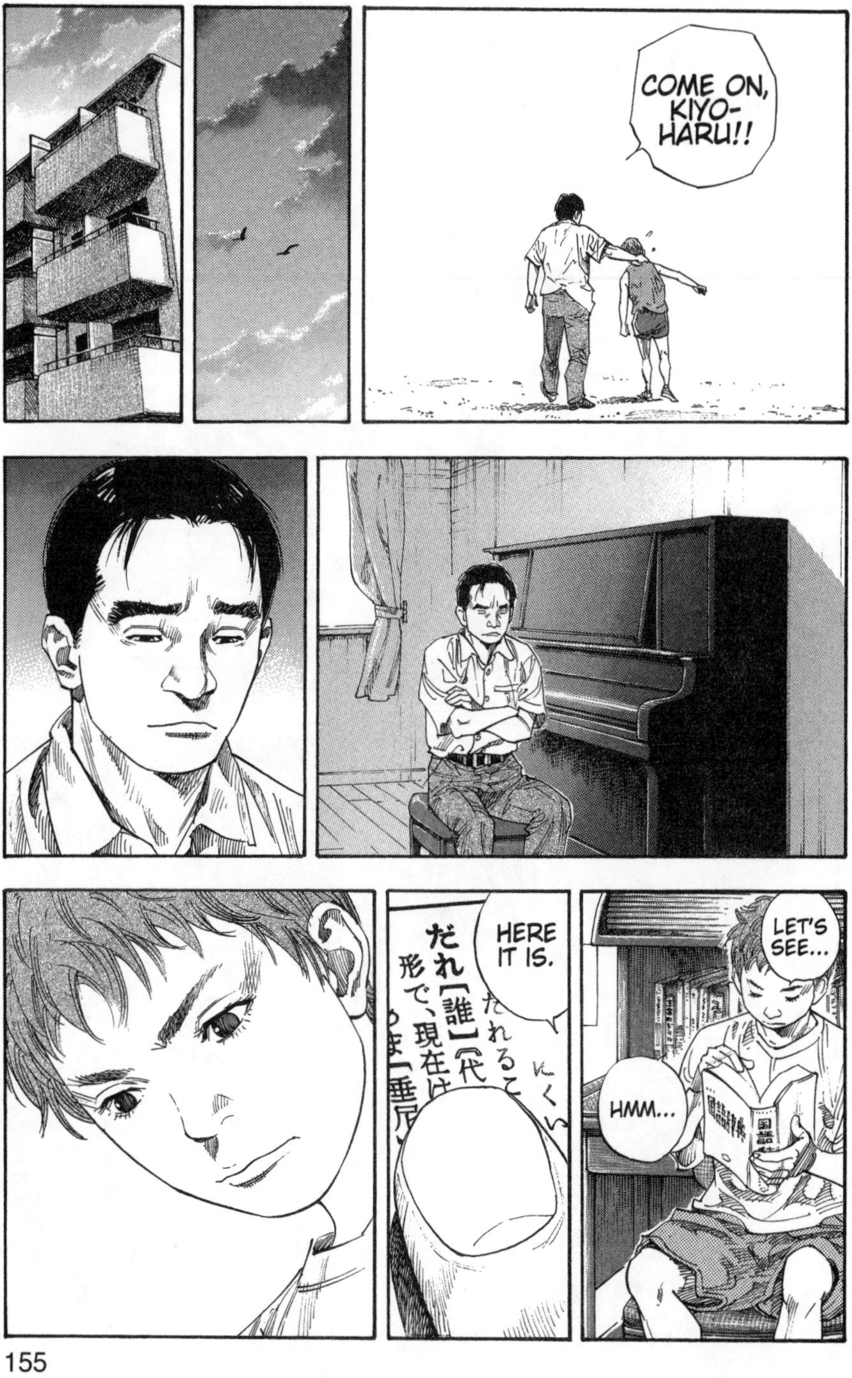
COME ON, KIYO-HARU!!
LET'S SEE...
HMM...
国語辞典
HERE IT IS.
だれ【誰】〔代
形で、現在は

SWP

．．．．．

I'LL HAVE
YOUR MOM
MAKE US
SOME
TEA.

PLINK

．．．．．

156

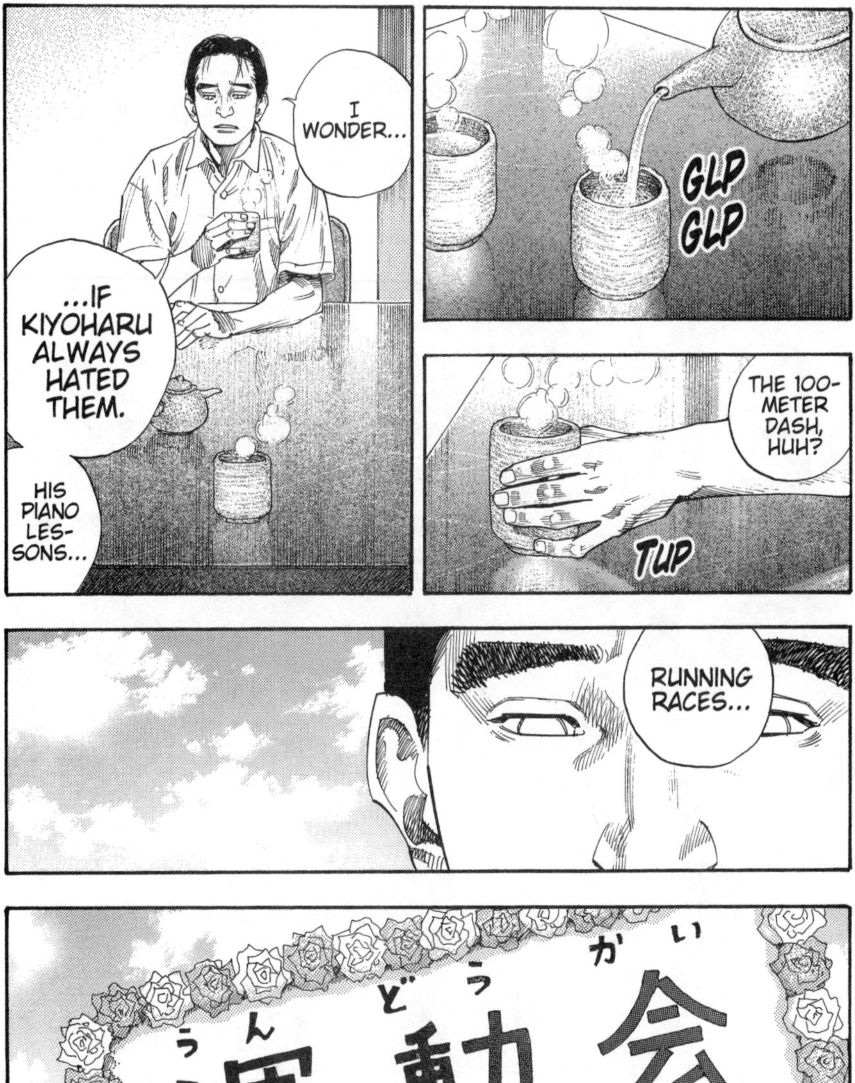
GLP
GLP
THE 100-METER DASH, HUH?
TUP
I WONDER...
...IF KIYOHARU ALWAYS HATED THEM.
HIS PIANO LESSONS...
RUNNING RACES...
うんどうかい
*SPORTS FESTIVAL
WOULD KIYOHARU TOGAWA'S FATHER...
...PLEASE COME TO THE TENT AREA...
藤子小学
YOUR RELAY IS ABOUT TO BEGIN.

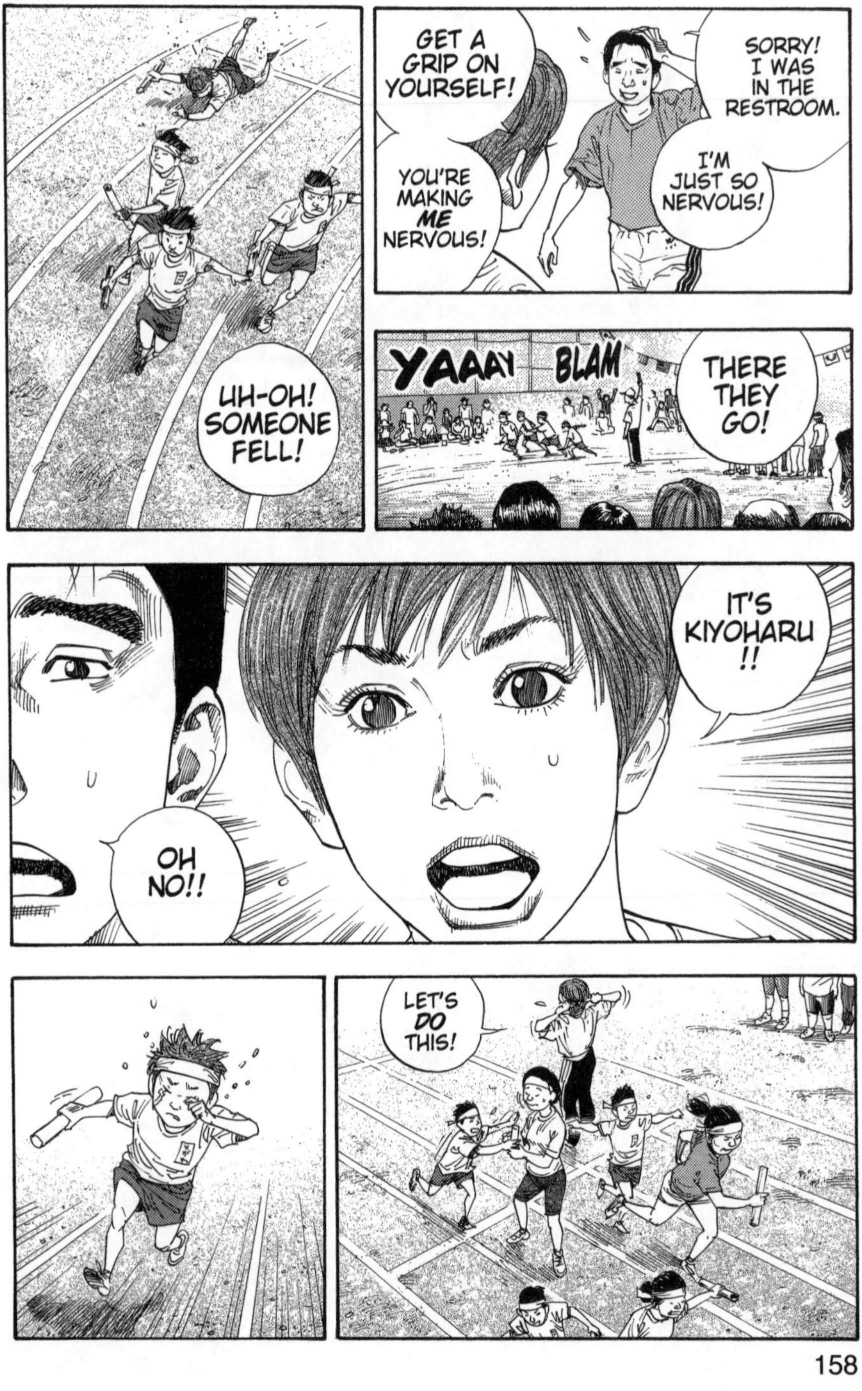
SORRY! I WAS IN THE RESTROOM.
I'M JUST SO NERVOUS!
GET A GRIP ON YOURSELF!
YOU'RE MAKING *ME* NERVOUS!
THERE THEY GO!
BLAM
YAAAY
UH-OH! SOMEONE FELL!
IT'S KIYOHARU!!
OH NO!!
LET'S *DO* THIS!

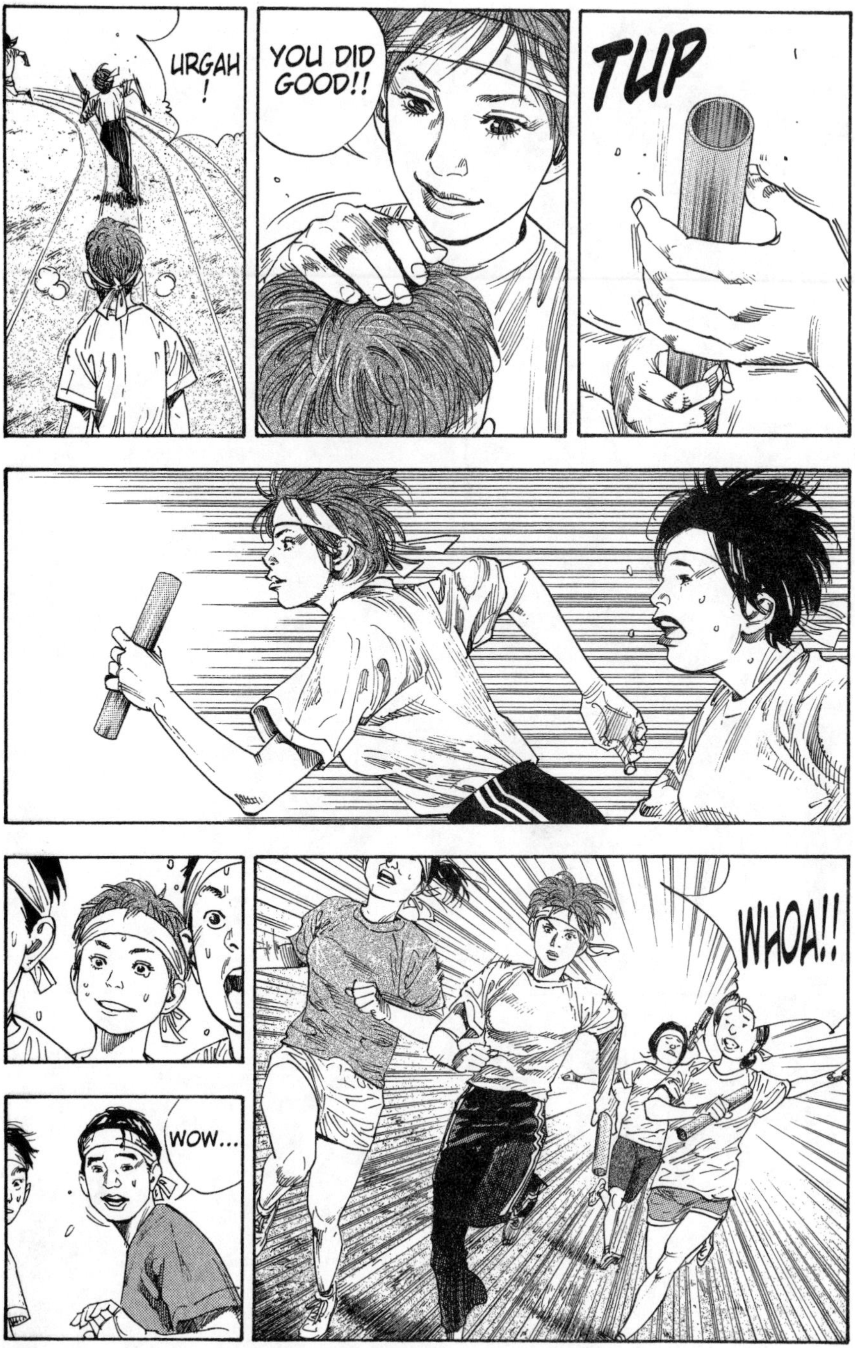
TUP
YOU DID GOOD!!
URGAH!
WHOA!!
WOW...

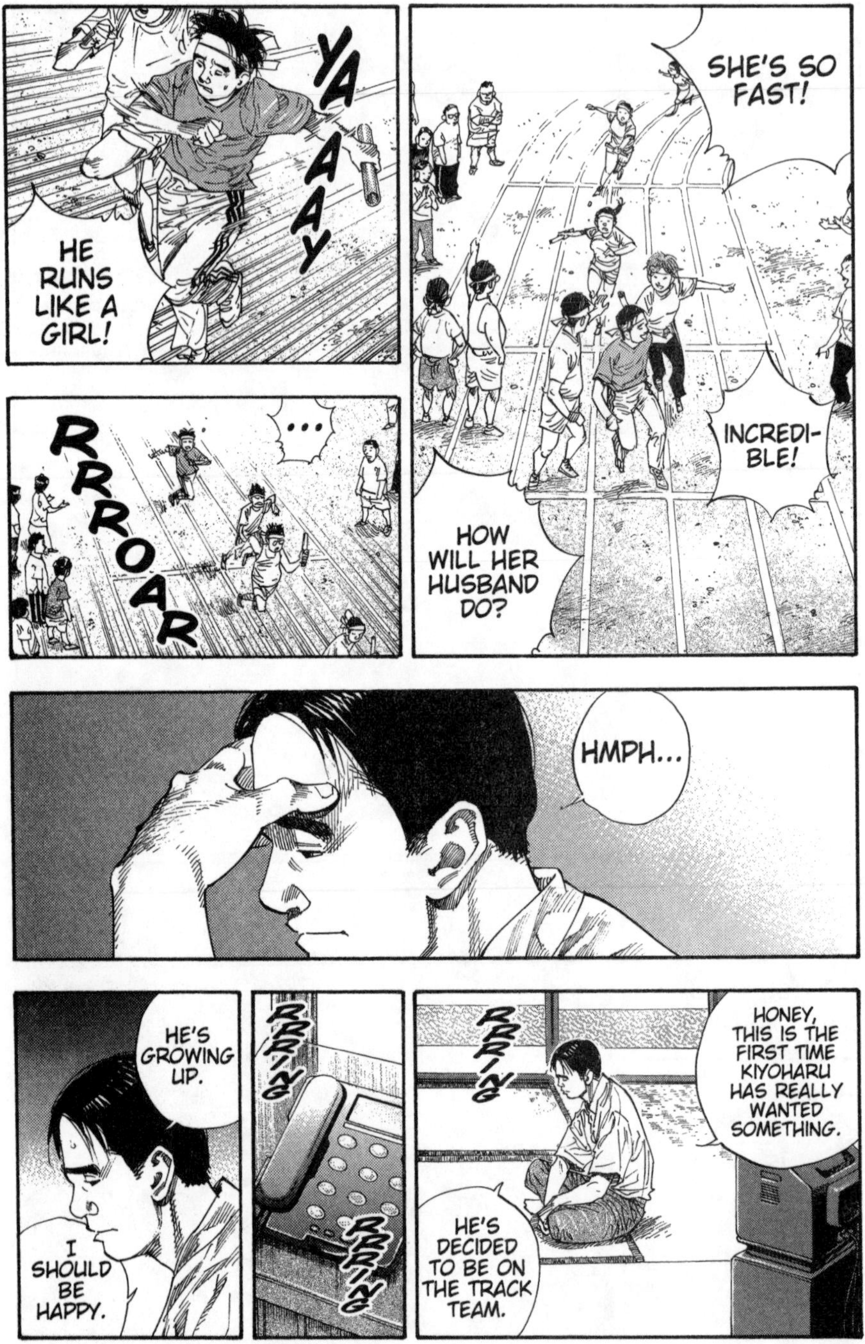
SHE'S SO FAST!
INCREDI-BLE!
HOW WILL HER HUSBAND DO?
YAAAAY
HE RUNS LIKE A GIRL!
...
RRRROAR
HMPH...
RRRING
HONEY, THIS IS THE FIRST TIME KIYOHARU HAS REALLY WANTED SOMETHING.
HE'S DECIDED TO BE ON THE TRACK TEAM.
RRRING
RRRING
HE'S GROWING UP.
I SHOULD BE HAPPY.

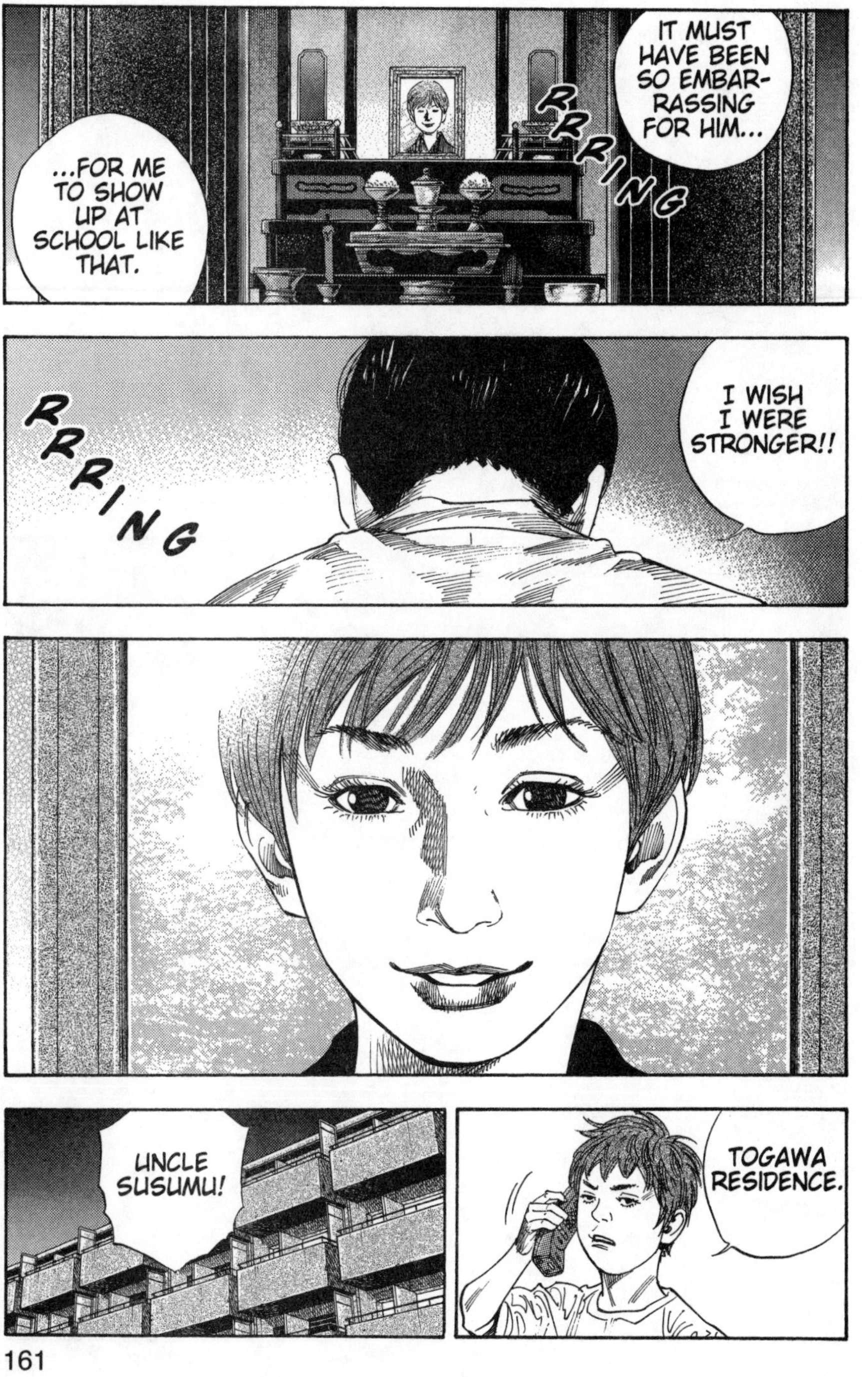
IT MUST HAVE BEEN SO EMBARRASSING FOR HIM...
RRRING
...FOR ME TO SHOW UP AT SCHOOL LIKE THAT.
I WISH I WERE STRONGER!!
RRRING
TOGAWA RESIDENCE.
UNCLE SUSUMU!

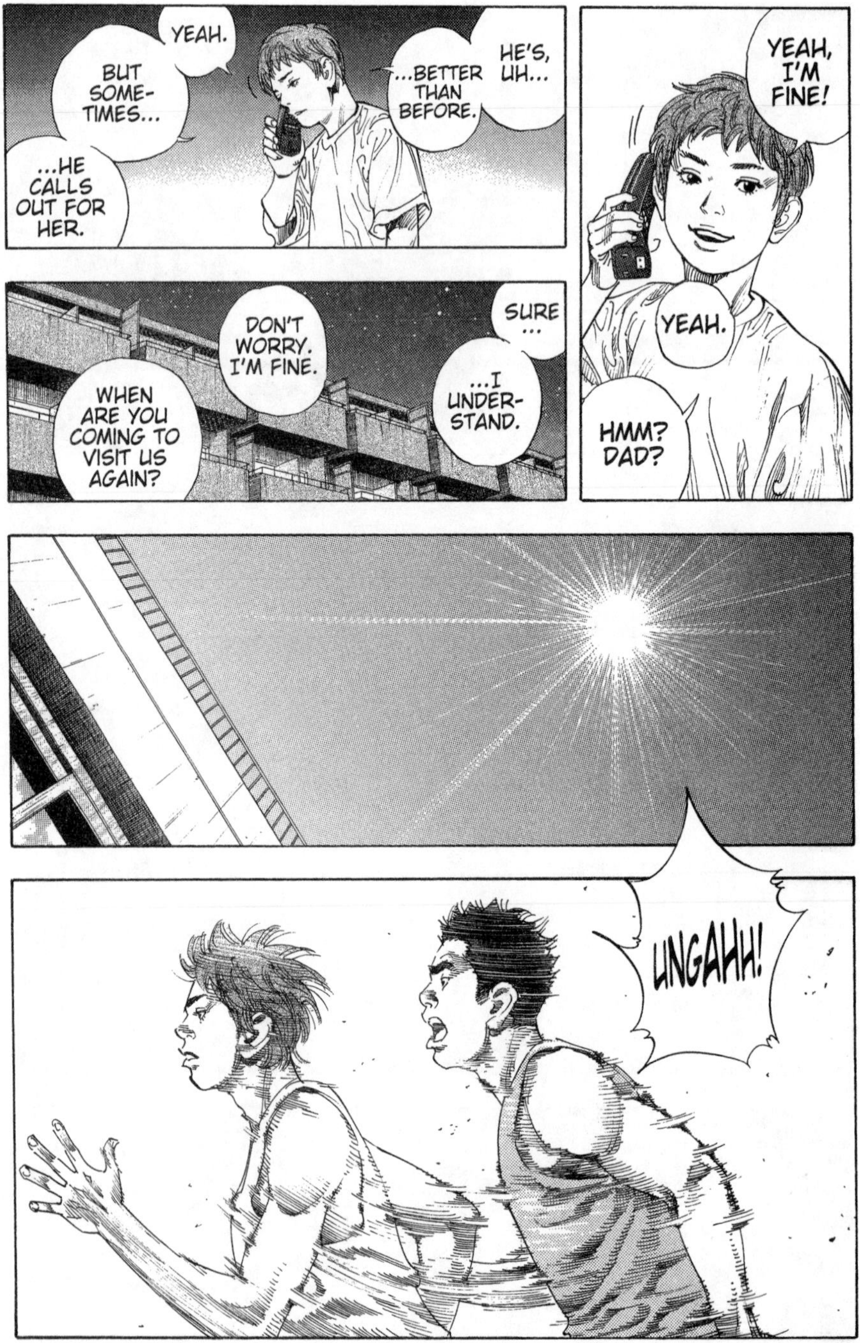
YEAH, I'M FINE!
YEAH.
HMM? DAD?
HE'S, UH...
...BETTER THAN BEFORE.
YEAH.
BUT SOMETIMES...
...HE CALLS OUT FOR HER.
SURE...
...I UNDERSTAND.
DON'T WORRY. I'M FINE.
WHEN ARE YOU COMING TO VISIT US AGAIN?
UNGAHH!

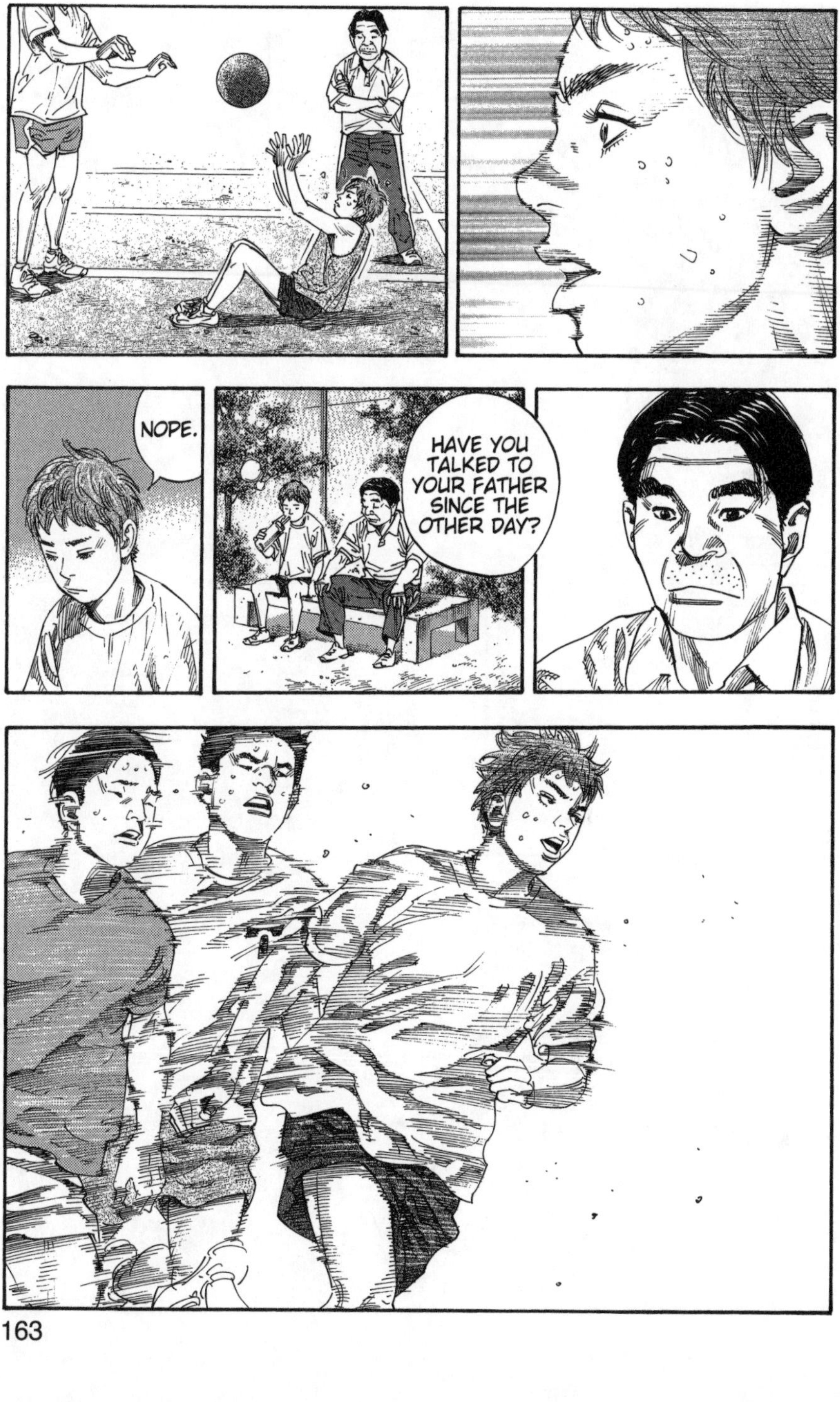
HAVE YOU TALKED TO YOUR FATHER SINCE THE OTHER DAY?
NOPE.

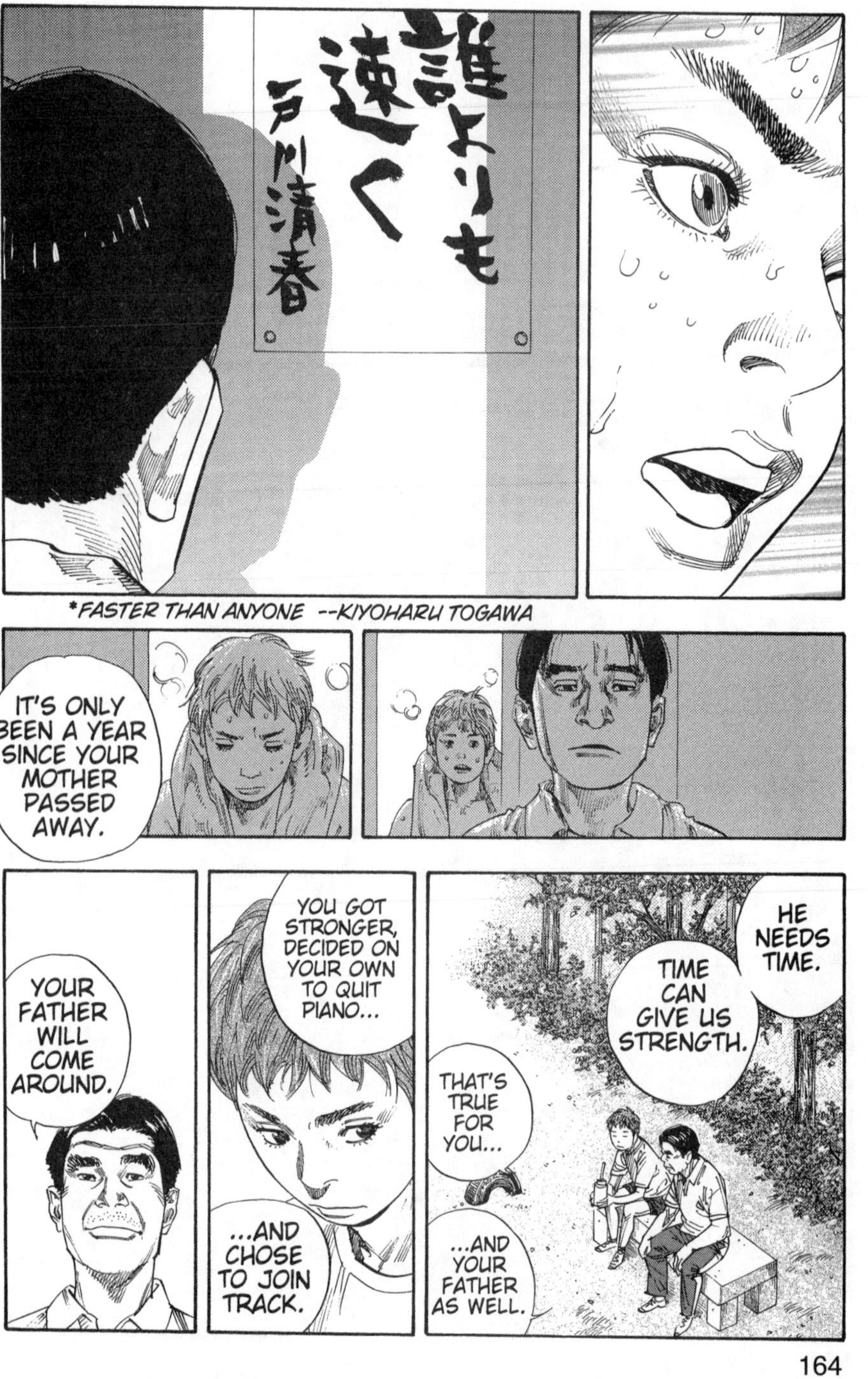
誰よりも速く
戸川清春
*FASTER THAN ANYONE --KIYOHARU TOGAWA
IT'S ONLY BEEN A YEAR SINCE YOUR MOTHER PASSED AWAY.
HE NEEDS TIME.
TIME CAN GIVE US STRENGTH.
THAT'S TRUE FOR YOU...
...AND YOUR FATHER AS WELL.
YOU GOT STRONGER, DECIDED ON YOUR OWN TO QUIT PIANO...
...AND CHOSE TO JOIN TRACK.
YOUR FATHER WILL COME AROUND.

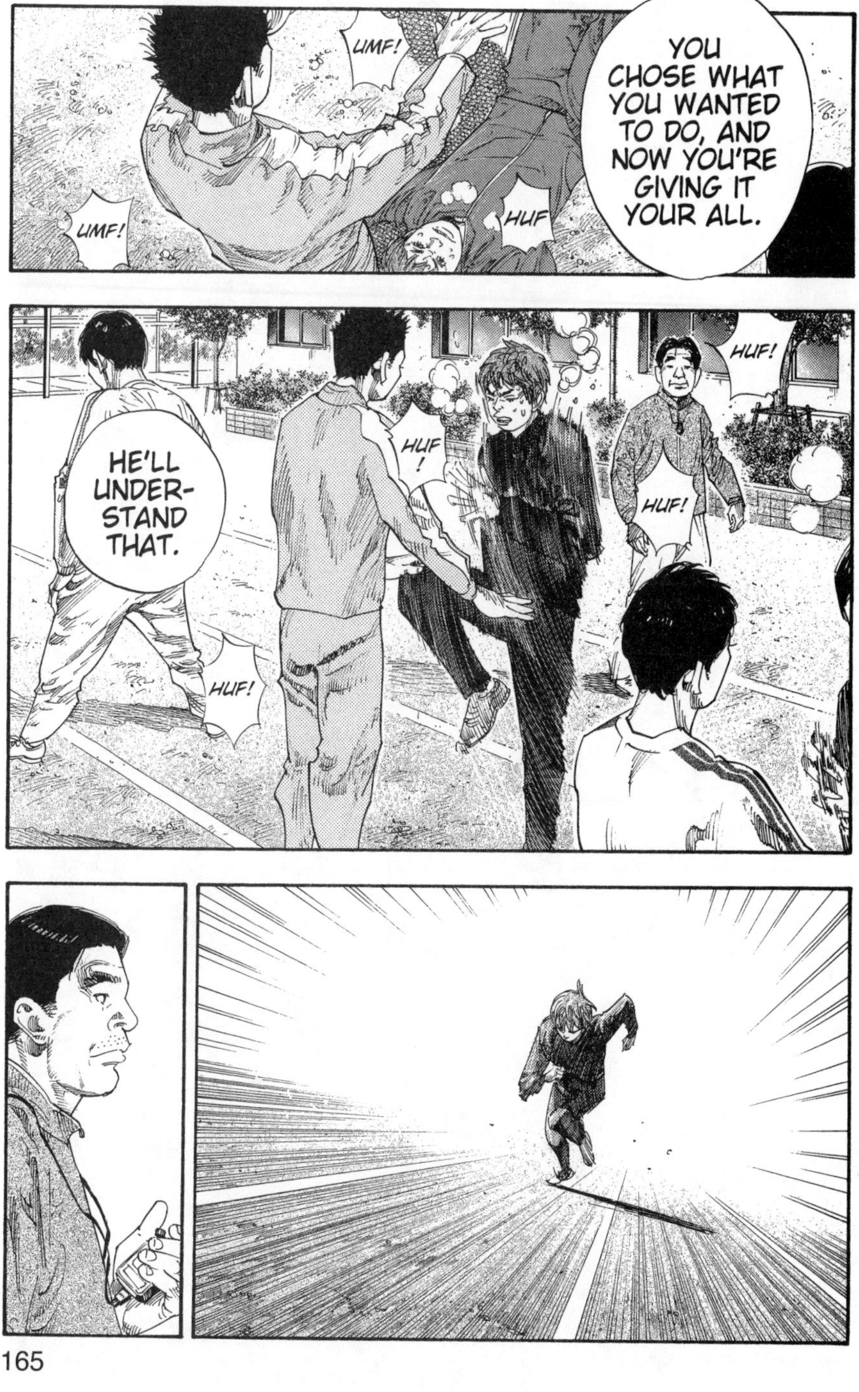
YOU CHOSE WHAT YOU WANTED TO DO, AND NOW YOU'RE GIVING IT YOUR ALL.
UMF!
HUF
UMF!
HUF!
HUF!
HUF !
HE'LL UNDER-STAND THAT.
HUF!

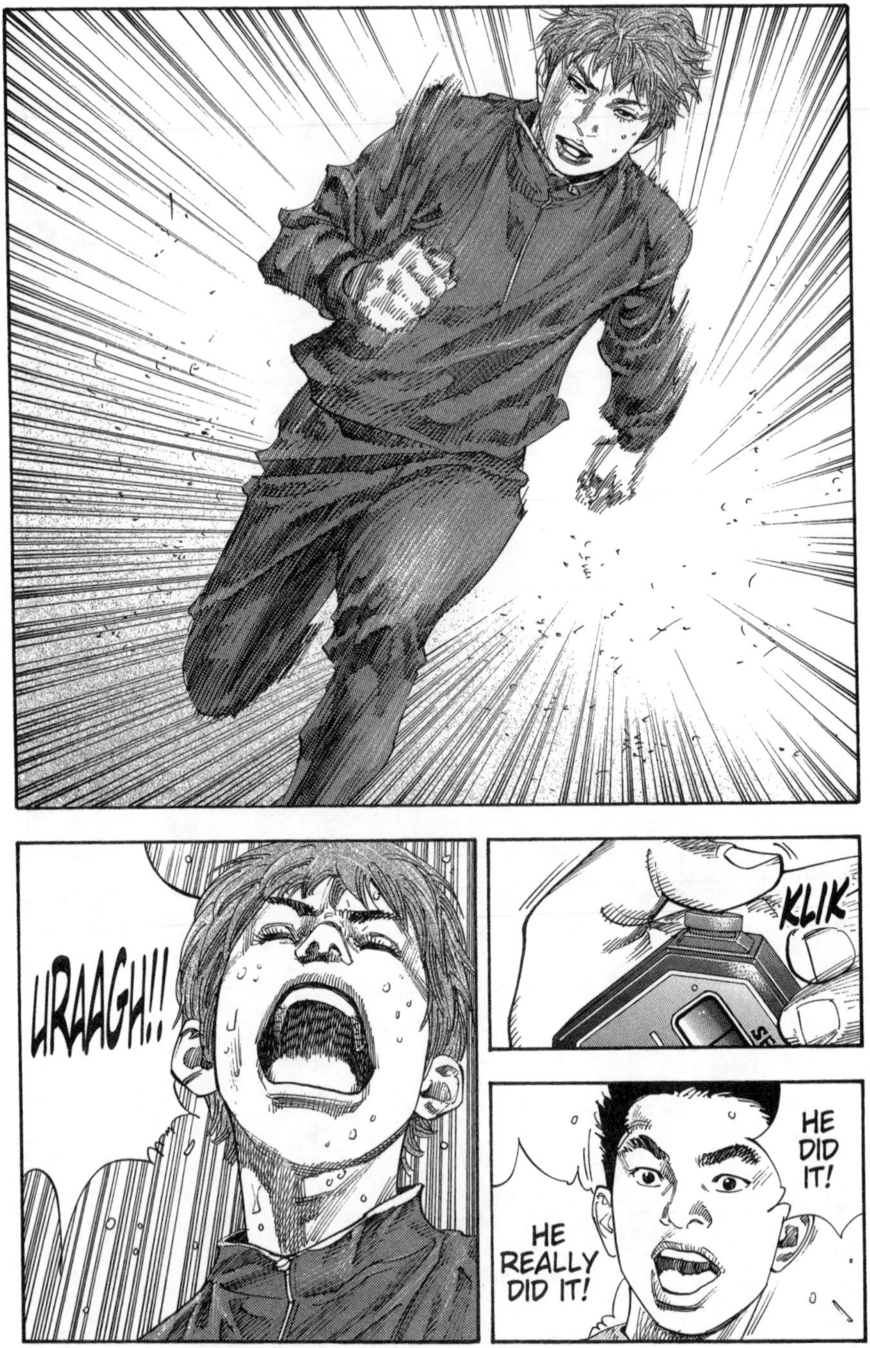
KLIK
HE DID IT!
HE REALLY DID IT!
URAAGH!!

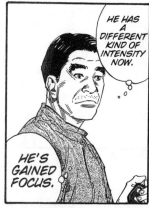

HUF
HUF
HUF
HUF
HE HAS A DIFFERENT KIND OF INTENSITY NOW.
HE'S GAINED FOCUS.
A KID LIKE THIS ONLY COMES AROUND ONCE EVERY FEW YEARS.
11.48
SKRCH
KIYOHARU, WHAT'S GOING ON WITH YOUR LEG?
SORE MUSCLES.
MAYBE I'VE BEEN TRAINING TOO HARD.

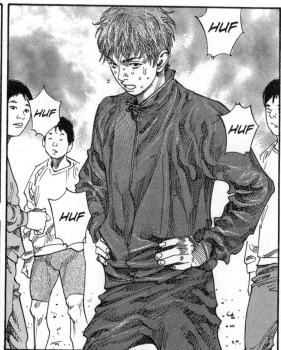

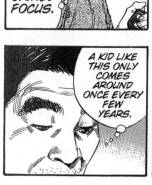

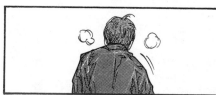

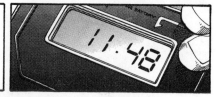

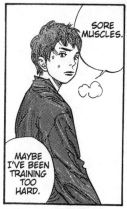

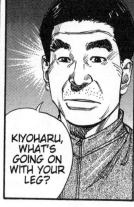

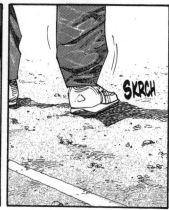

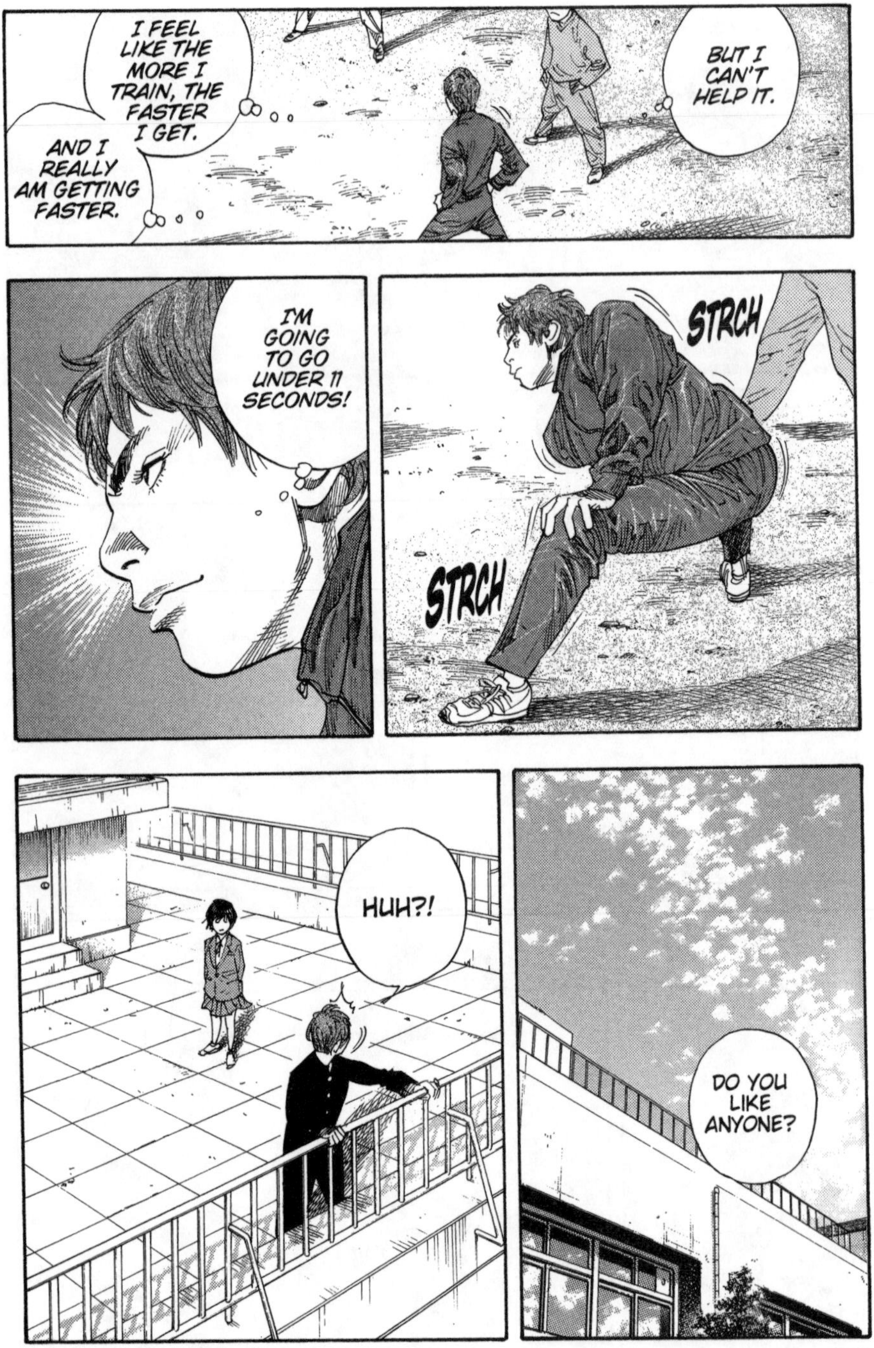
BUT I CAN'T HELP IT.
I FEEL LIKE THE MORE I TRAIN, THE FASTER I GET.
AND I REALLY AM GETTING FASTER.
STRCH
STRCH
I'M GOING TO GO UNDER 11 SECONDS!
DO YOU LIKE ANYONE?
HUH?!

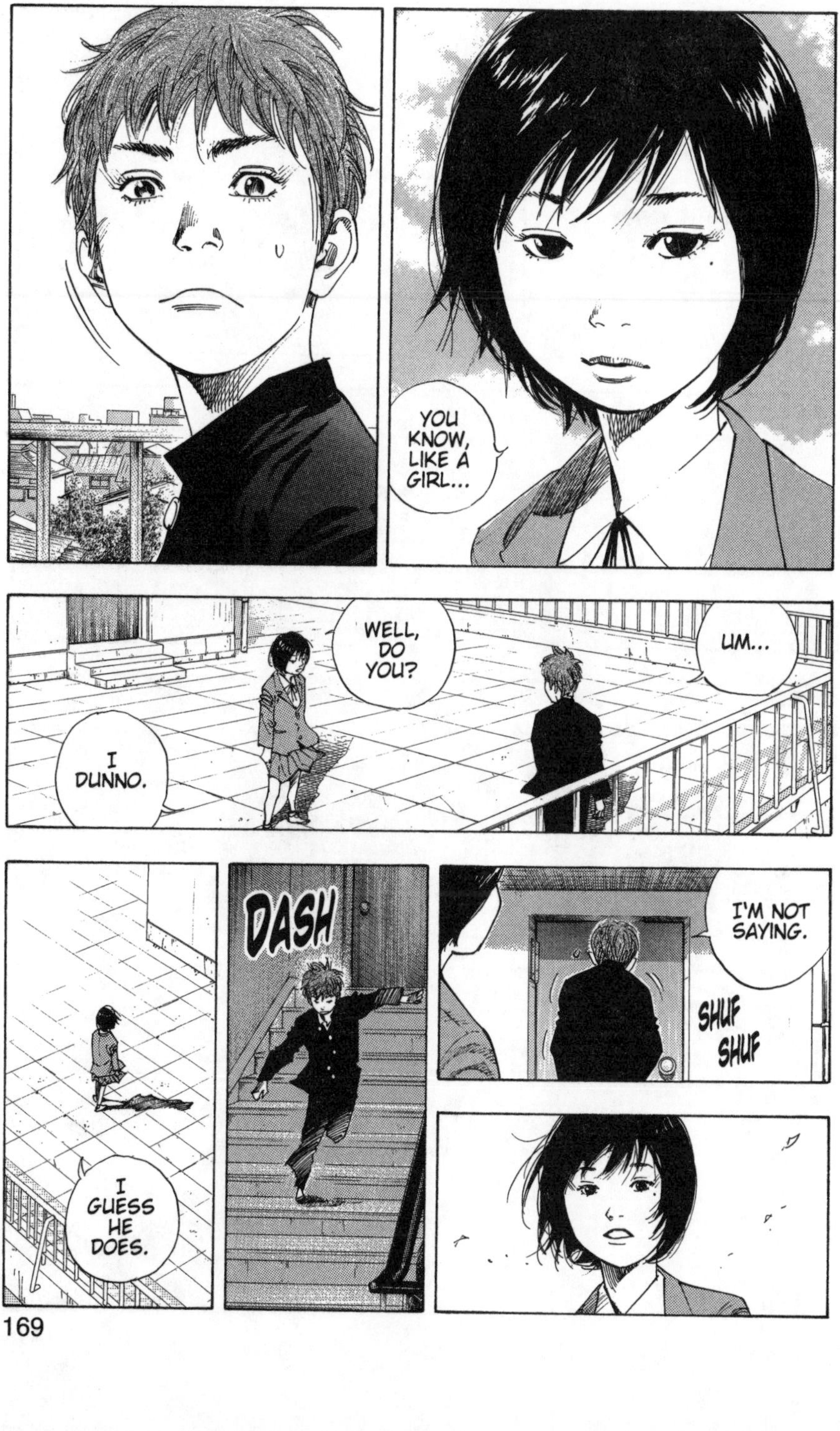
YOU KNOW, LIKE A GIRL...
UM...
WELL, DO YOU?
I DUNNO.
I'M NOT SAYING.
SHUF SHUF
DASH
I GUESS HE DOES.

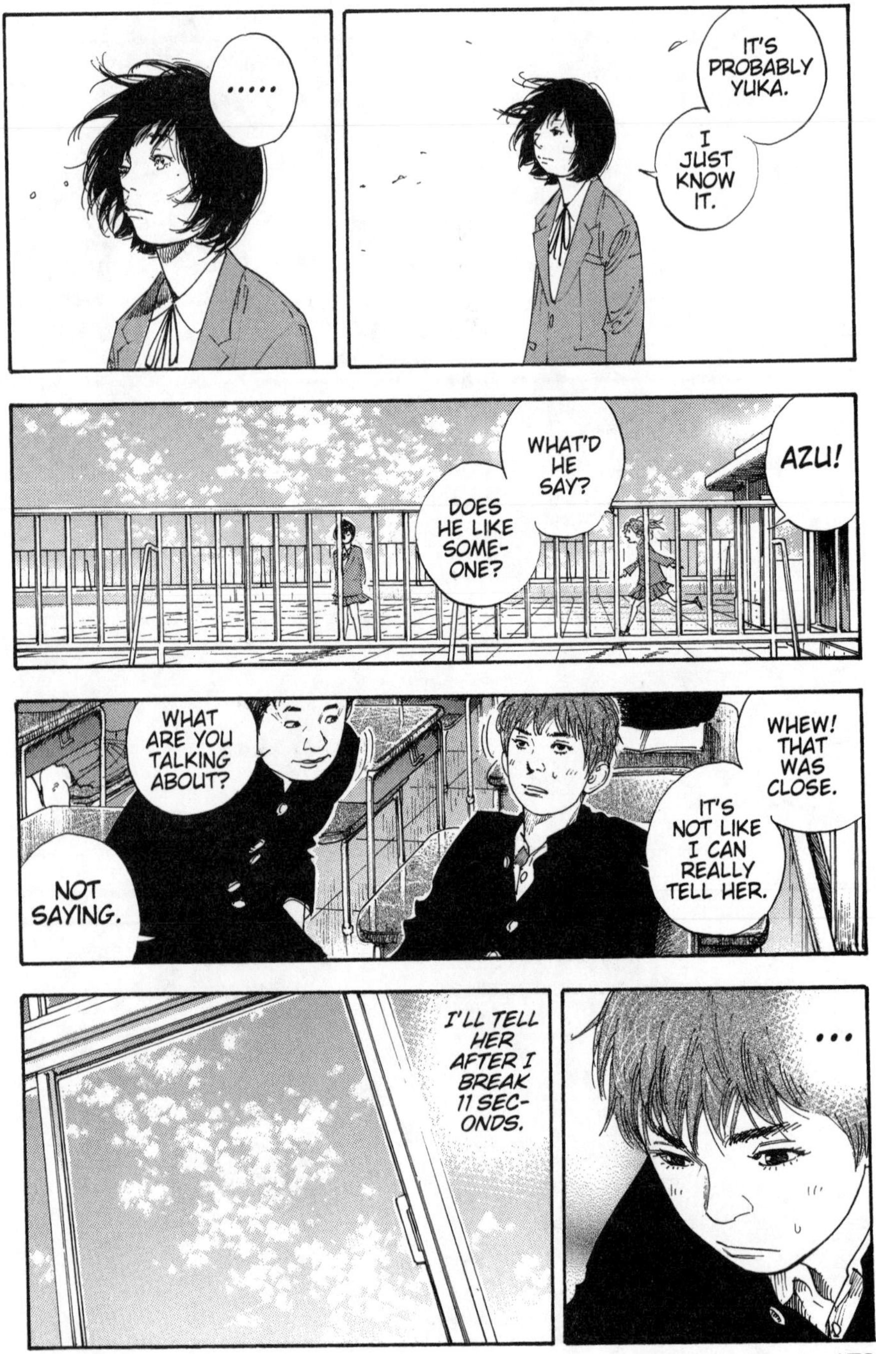
IT'S PROBABLY YUKA.
I JUST KNOW IT.
......
AZU!
WHAT'D HE SAY?
DOES HE LIKE SOMEONE?
WHEW! THAT WAS CLOSE.
IT'S NOT LIKE I CAN REALLY TELL HER.
WHAT ARE YOU TALKING ABOUT?
NOT SAYING.
...
I'LL TELL HER AFTER I BREAK 11 SECONDS.

AFTER
I BREAK
11 SECONDS
...

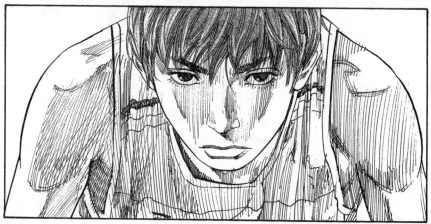

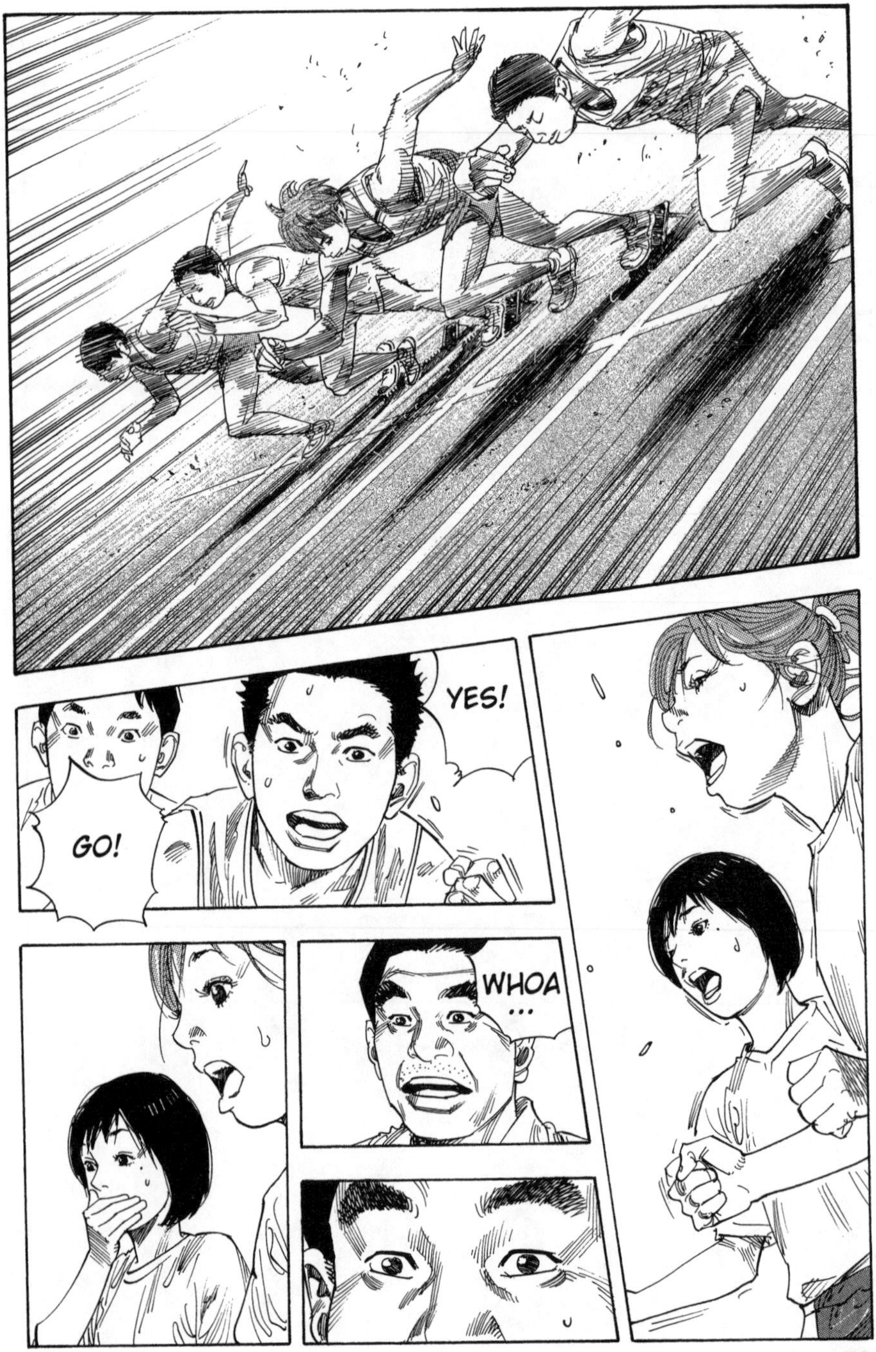
YES!
GO!
WHOA ...

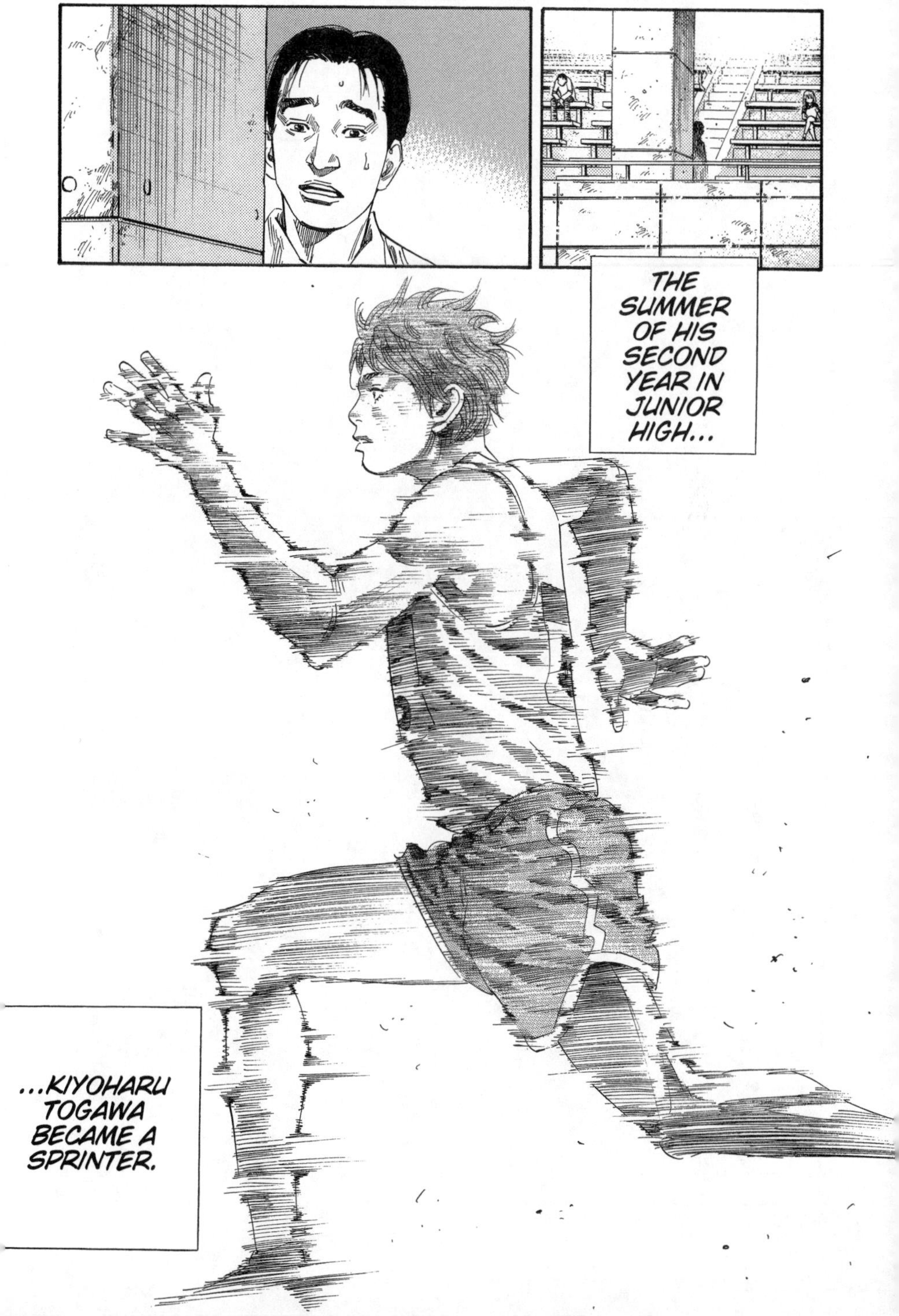
THE SUMMER OF HIS SECOND YEAR IN JUNIOR HIGH...
...KIYOHARU TOGAWA BECAME A SPRINTER.

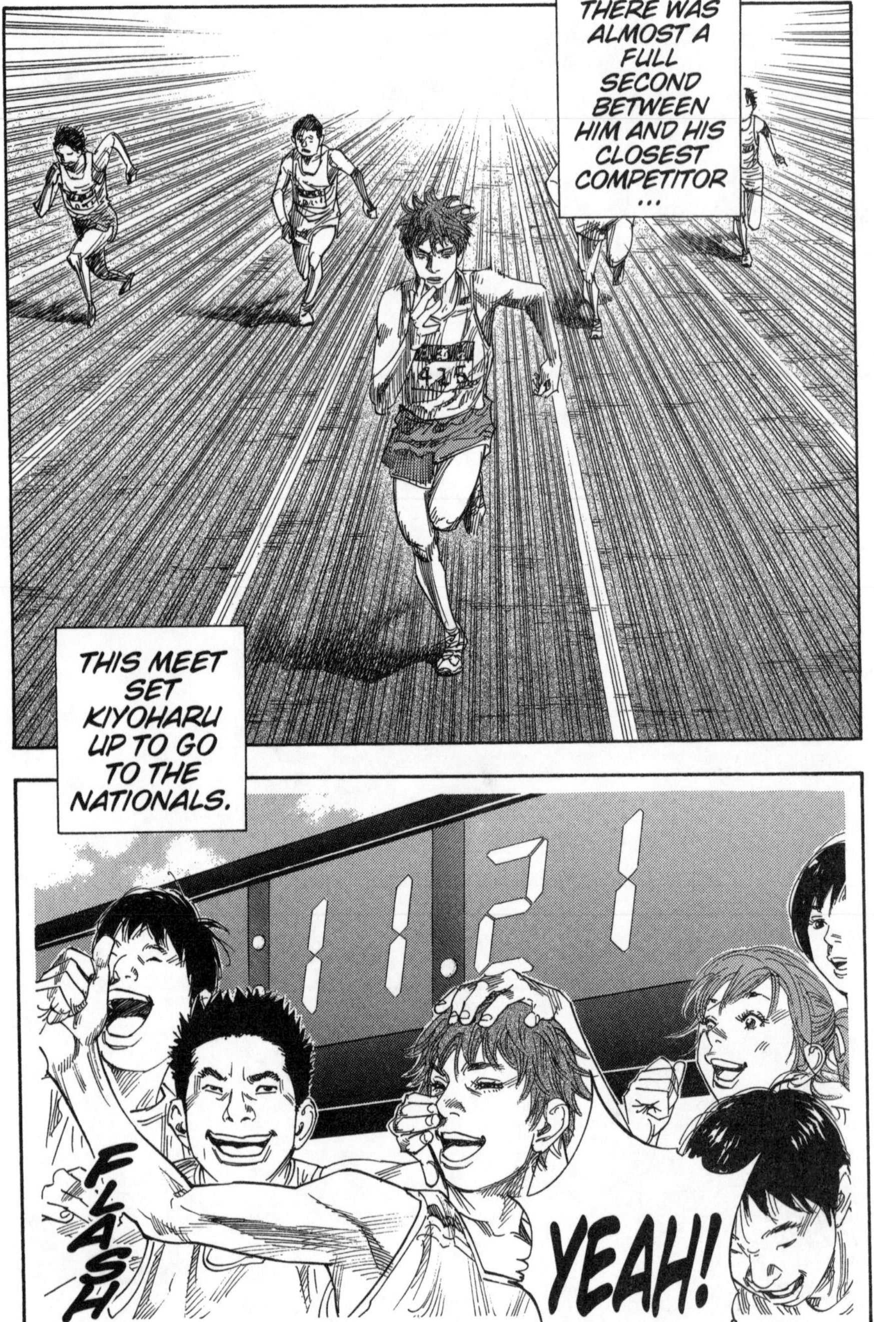
THERE WAS ALMOST A FULL SECOND BETWEEN HIM AND HIS CLOSEST COMPETITOR ...
THIS MEET SET KIYOHARU UP TO GO TO THE NATIONALS.
YEAH!
FLASH

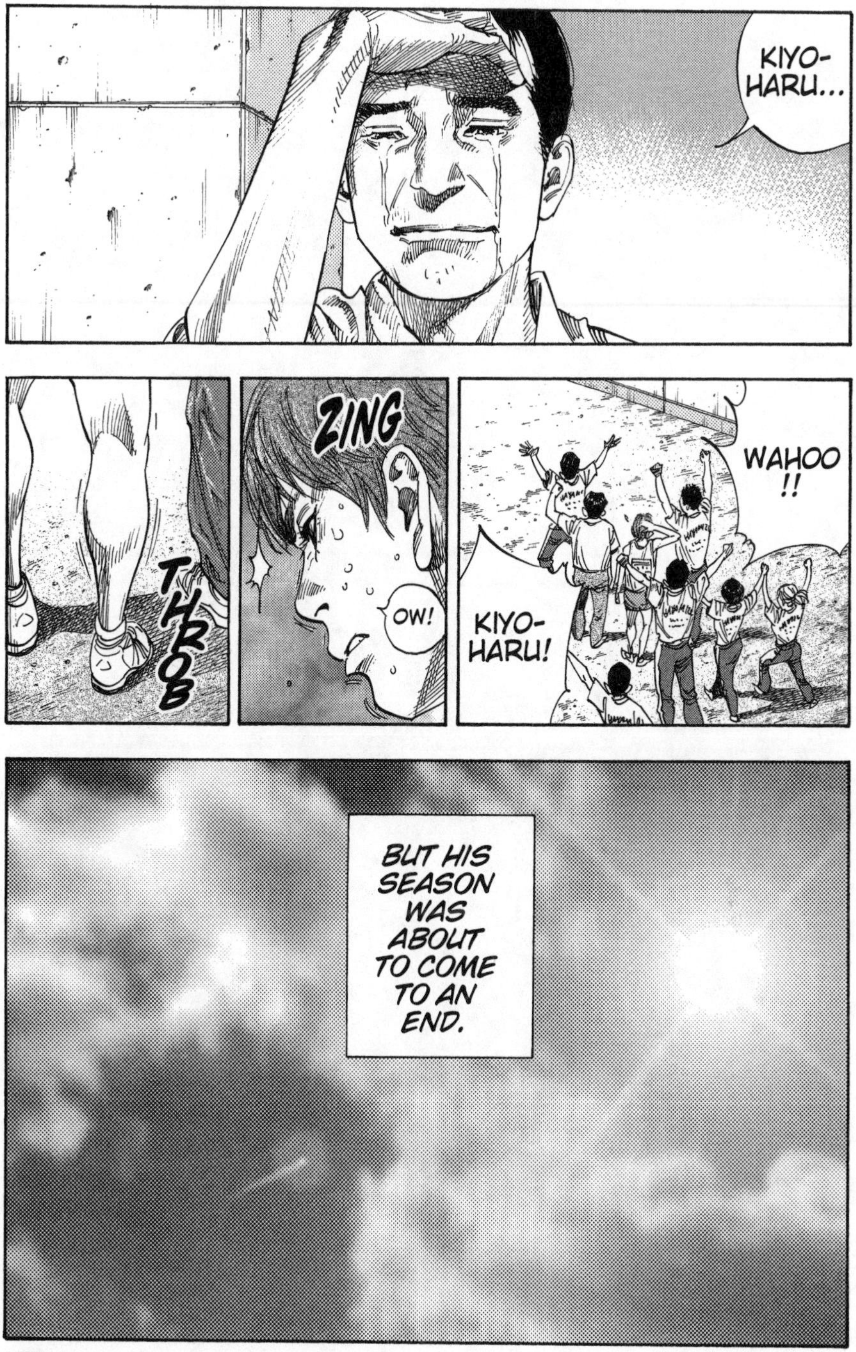
KIYO-HARU...
WAHOO!!
KIYO-HARU!
ZING
OW!
THROB
BUT HIS SEASON WAS ABOUT TO COME TO AN END.

12th

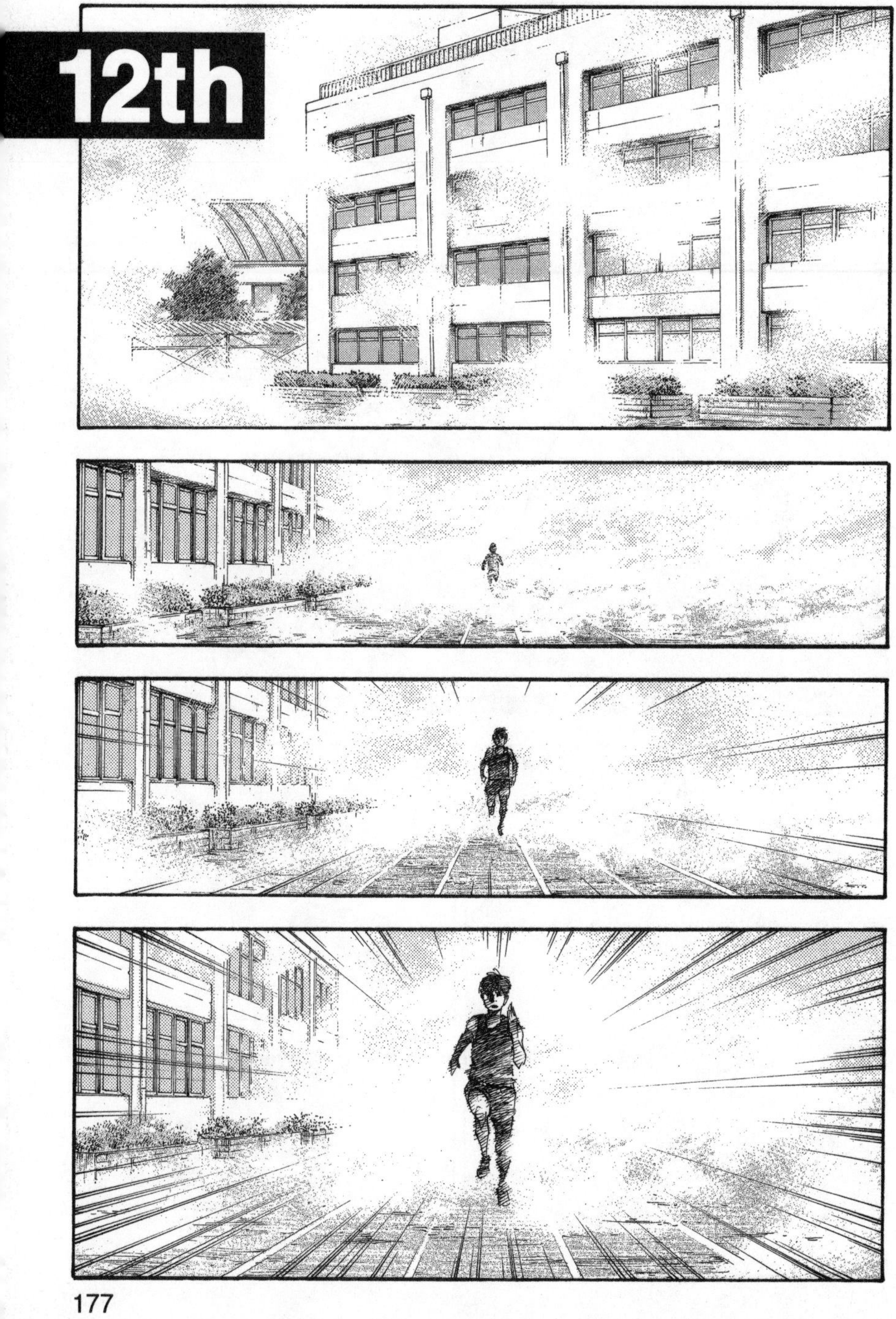

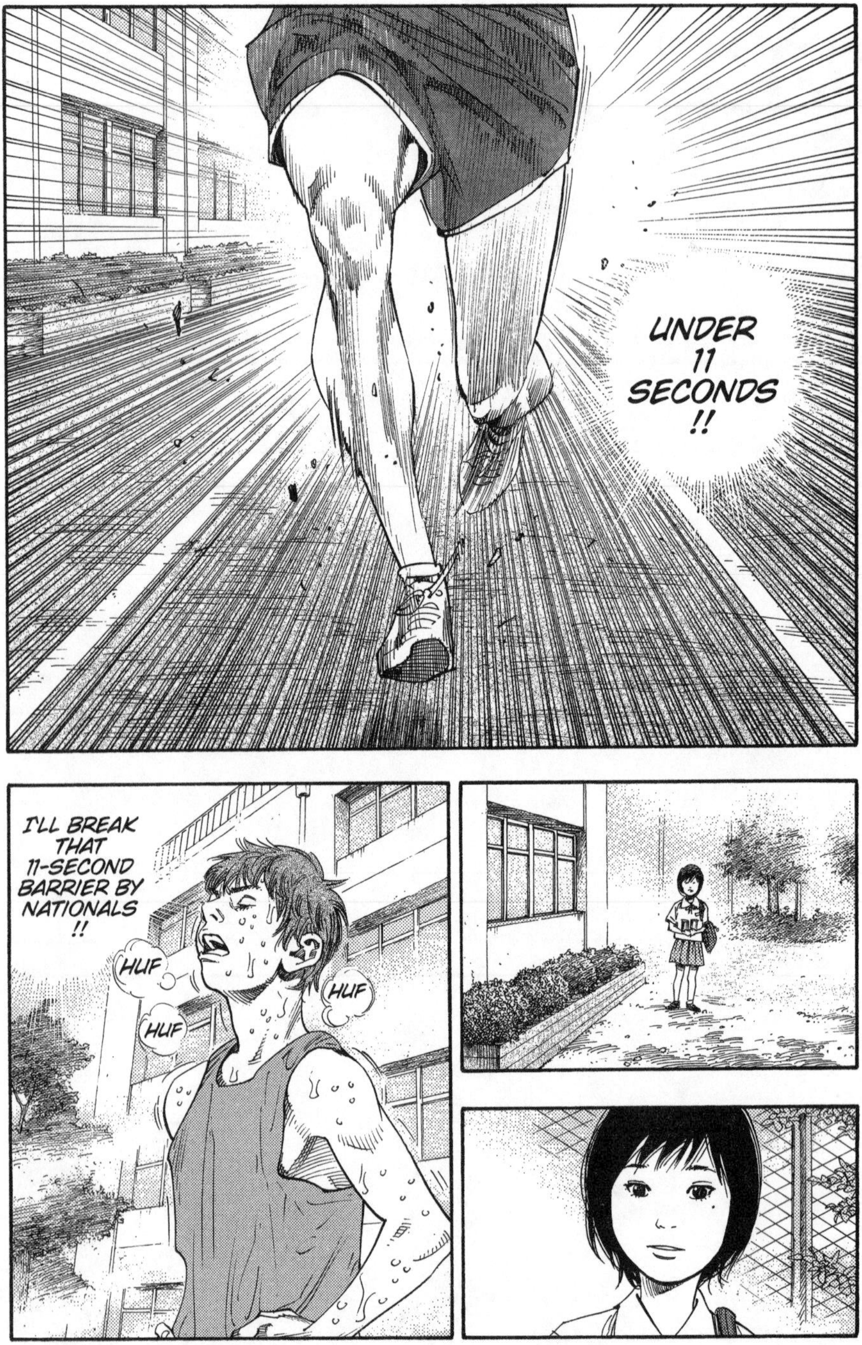
UNDER 11 SECONDS !!
I'LL BREAK THAT 11-SECOND BARRIER BY NATIONALS !!
HUF
HUF
HUF

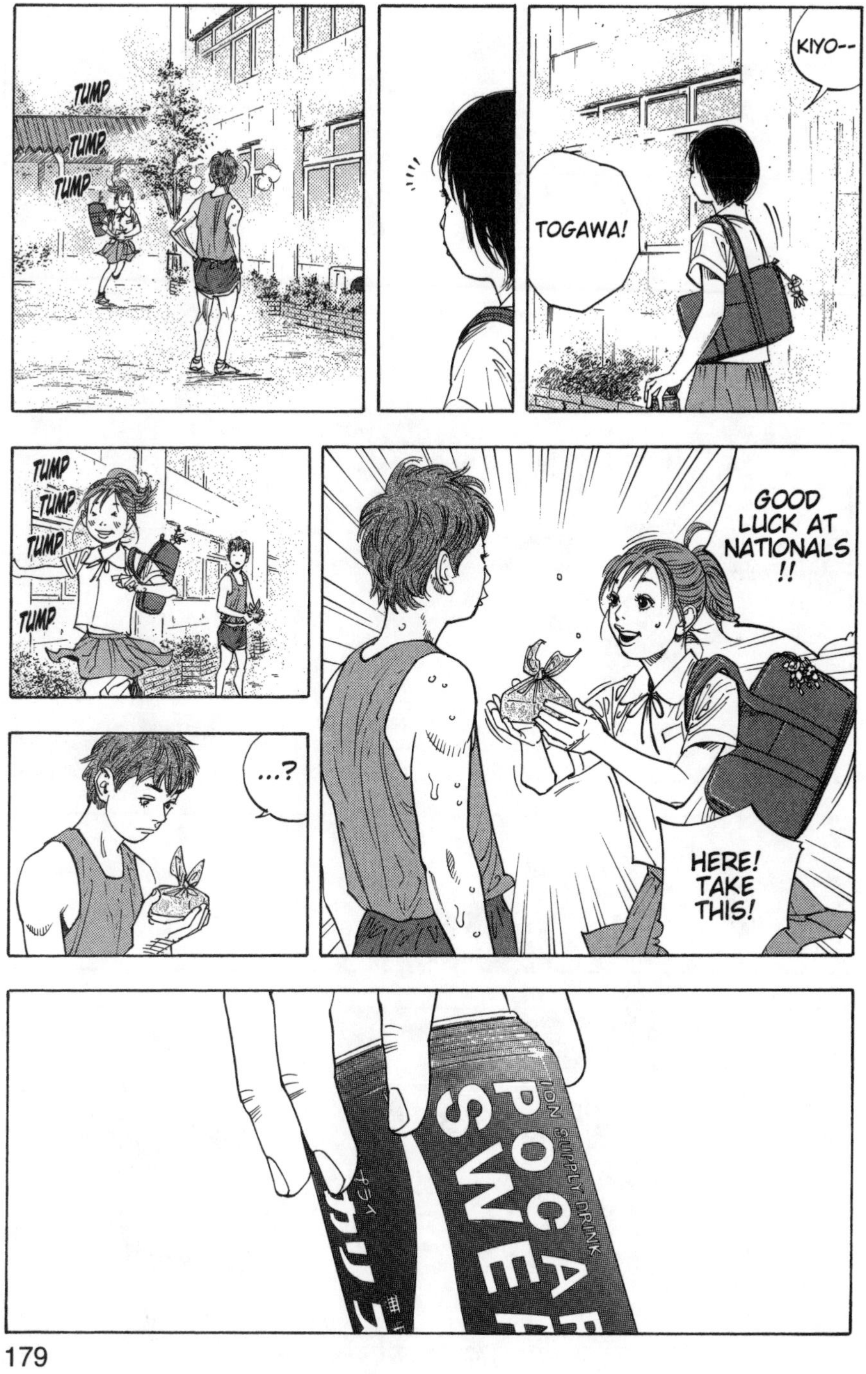
KIYO--
TOGAWA!
TUMP
TUMP
TUMP
GOOD LUCK AT NATIONALS !!
HERE! TAKE THIS!
TUMP
TUMP
TUMP
TUMP
...?
ION SUPPLY DRINK
POCA
SWE

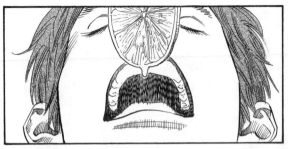

MNCH
MNCH

THAT'S
SOUR!

BUT
IT'S
GOOD!

歓 迎
平成○年度
全国中学校選抜大会

*NATIONAL MIDDLE SCHOOL ATHLETICS INVITATIONAL

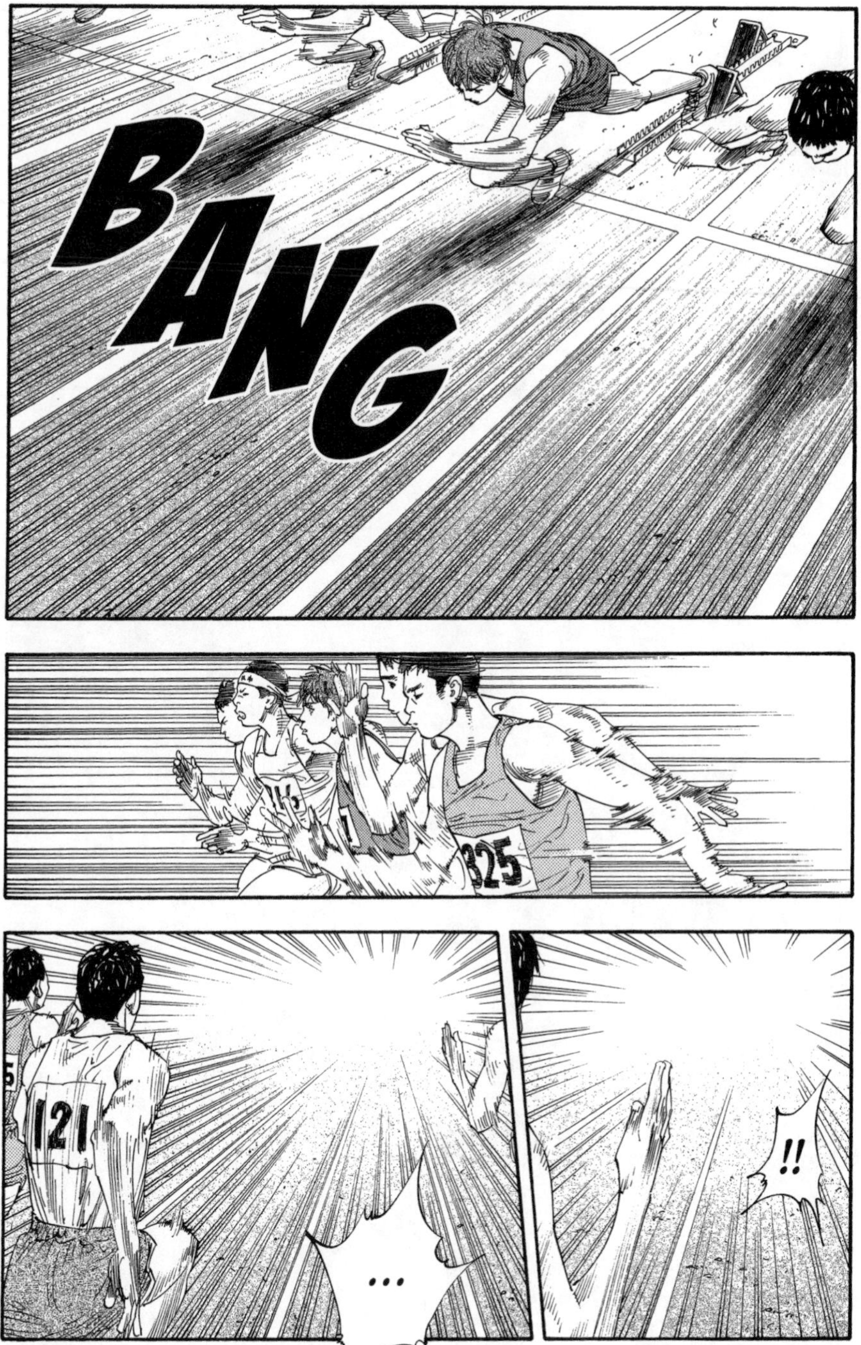
BANG
325
121
!!
...

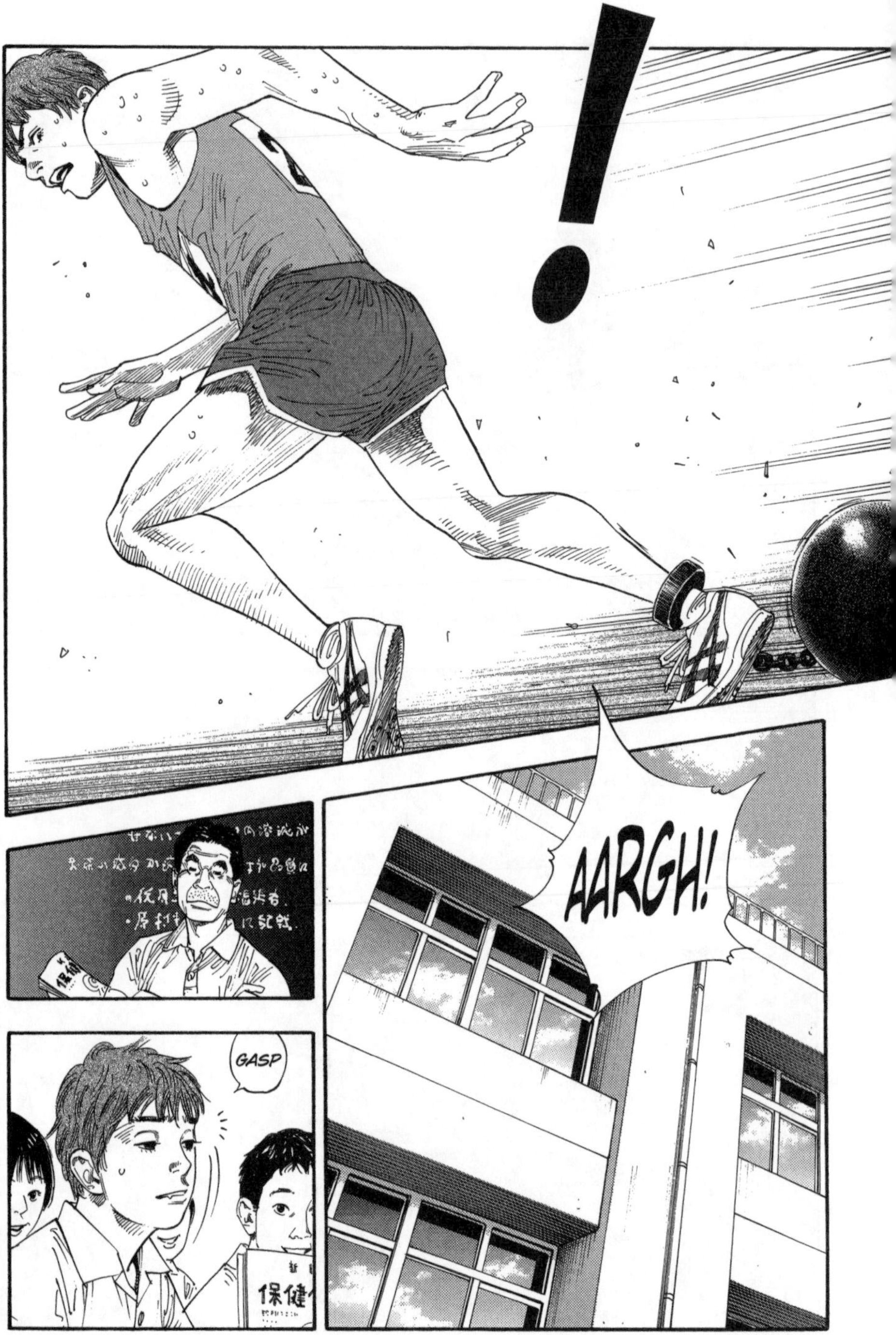
!
AARGH!
GASP

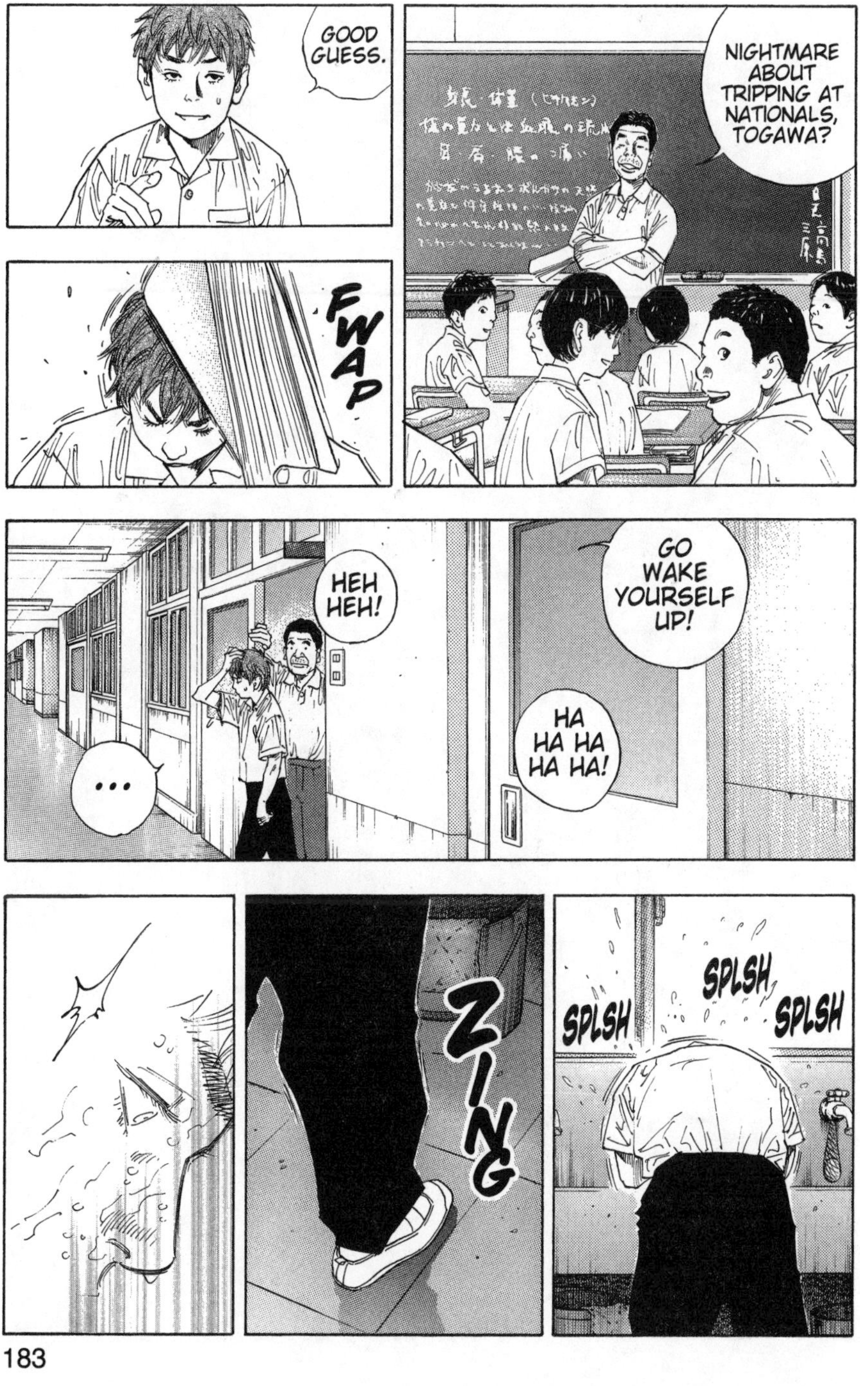

NIGHTMARE ABOUT TRIPPING AT NATIONALS, TOGAWA?
GOOD GUESS.
FWAP
GO WAKE YOURSELF UP!
HA HA HA HA HA!
HEH HEH!
...
SPLSH
SPLSH
SPLSH
ZING

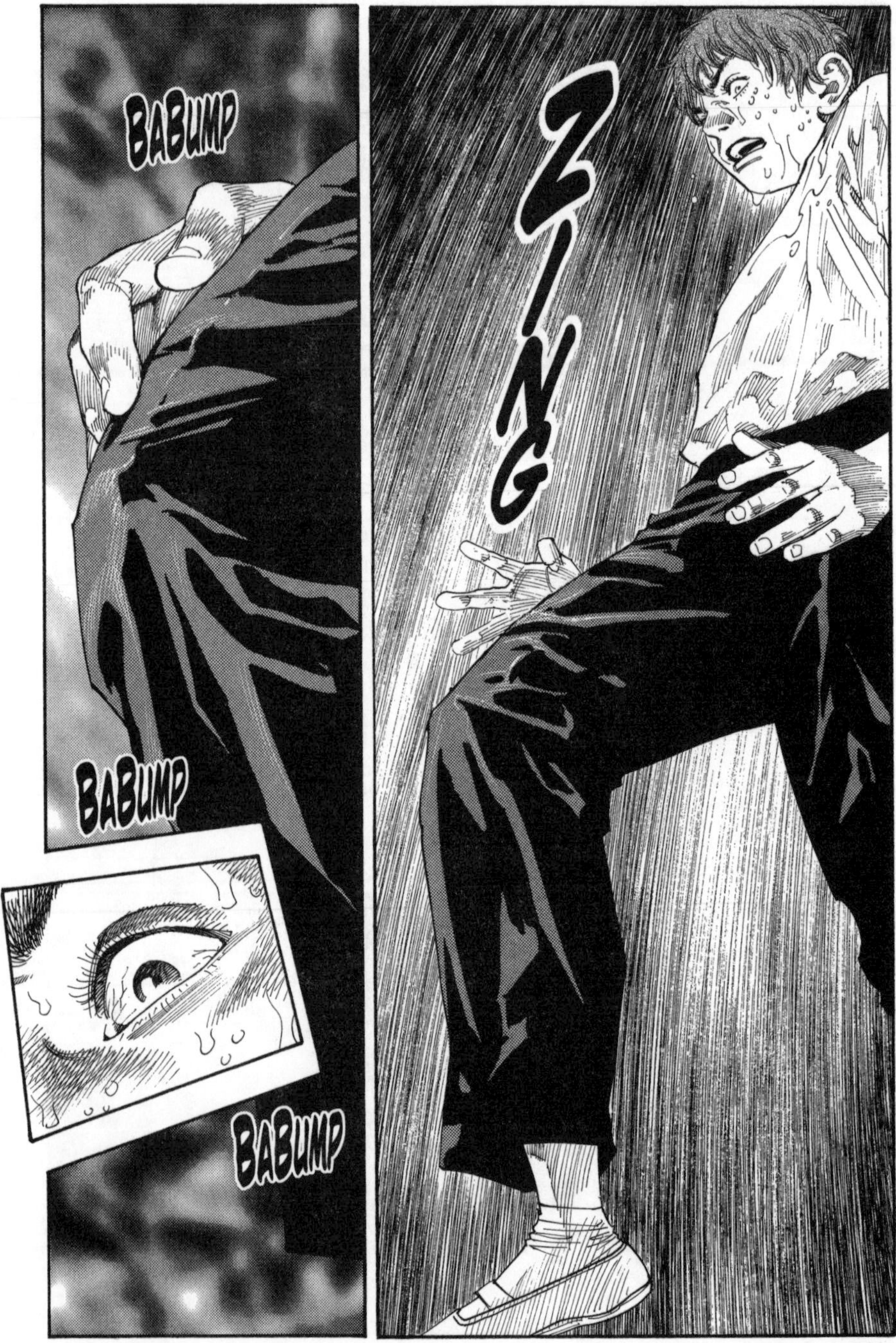
ZING
BABUMP
BABUMP
BABUMP

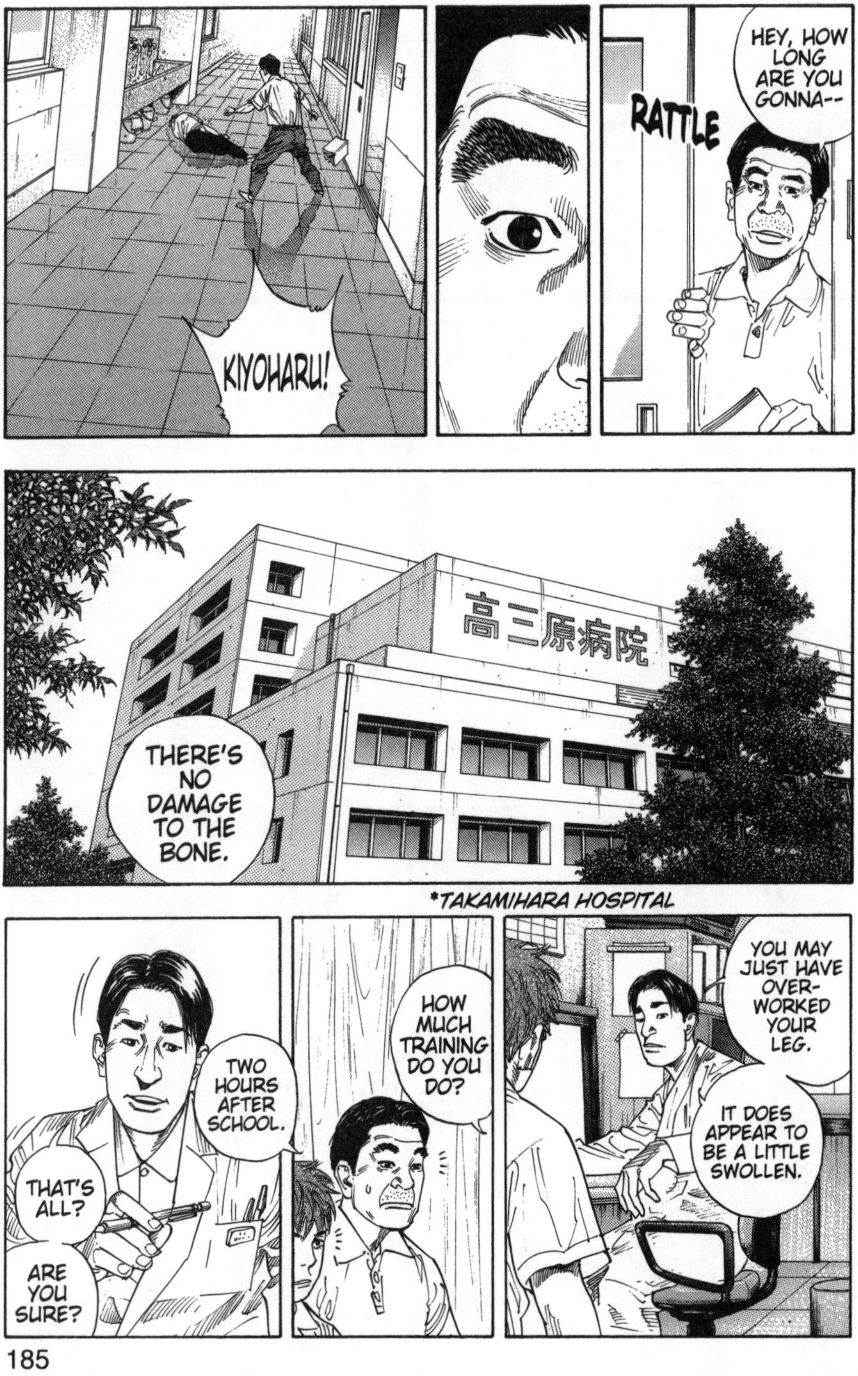
HEY, HOW LONG ARE YOU GONNA--
RATTLE
KIYOHARU!
高三原病院
THERE'S NO DAMAGE TO THE BONE.
*TAKAMIHARA HOSPITAL
YOU MAY JUST HAVE OVER-WORKED YOUR LEG.
IT DOES APPEAR TO BE A LITTLE SWOLLEN.
HOW MUCH TRAINING DO YOU DO?
TWO HOURS AFTER SCHOOL.
THAT'S ALL?
ARE YOU SURE?

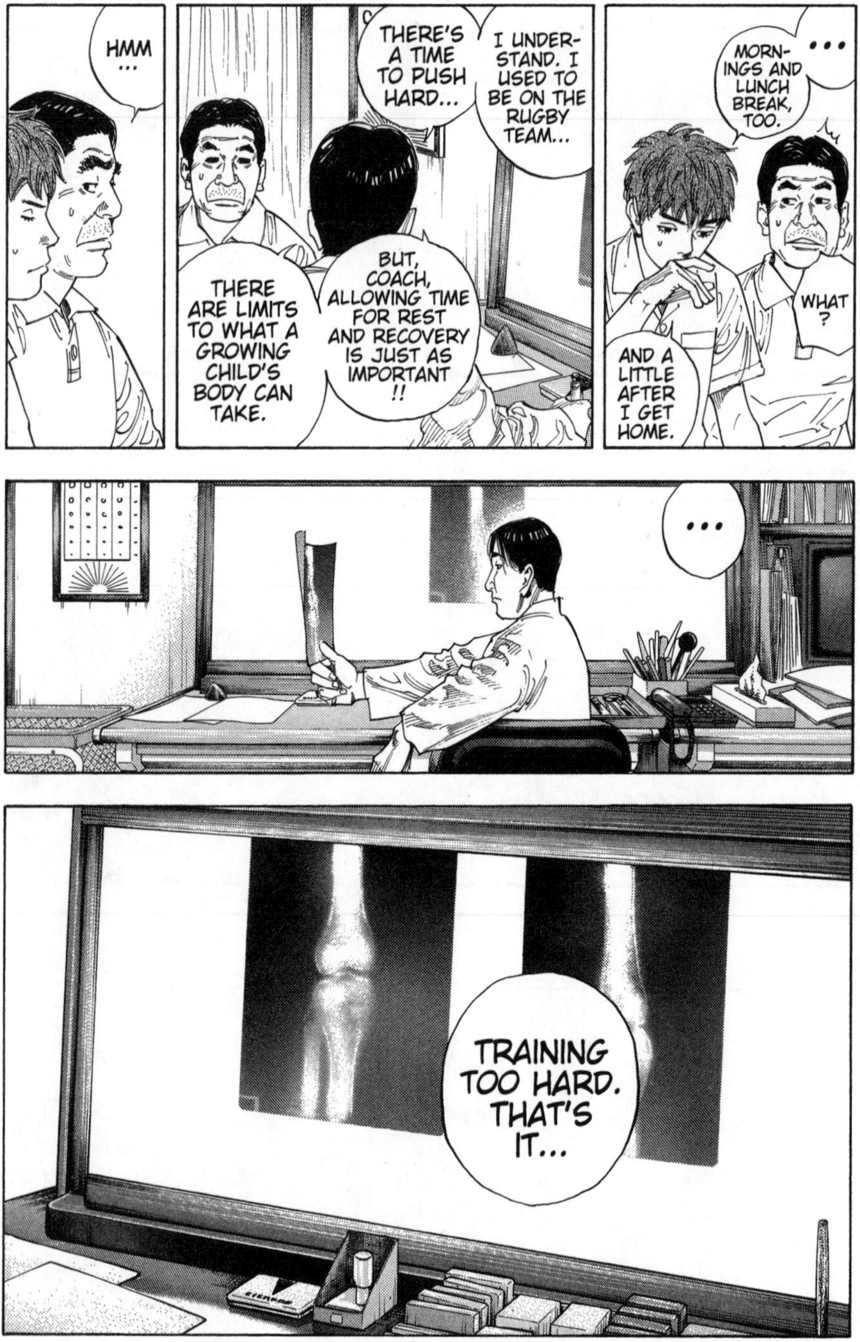
...
MORNINGS AND LUNCH BREAK, TOO.
WHAT?
AND A LITTLE AFTER I GET HOME.
I UNDERSTAND. I USED TO BE ON THE RUGBY TEAM...
THERE'S A TIME TO PUSH HARD...
BUT, COACH, ALLOWING TIME FOR REST AND RECOVERY IS JUST AS IMPORTANT!!
THERE ARE LIMITS TO WHAT A GROWING CHILD'S BODY CAN TAKE.
HMM...
...
TRAINING TOO HARD. THAT'S IT...

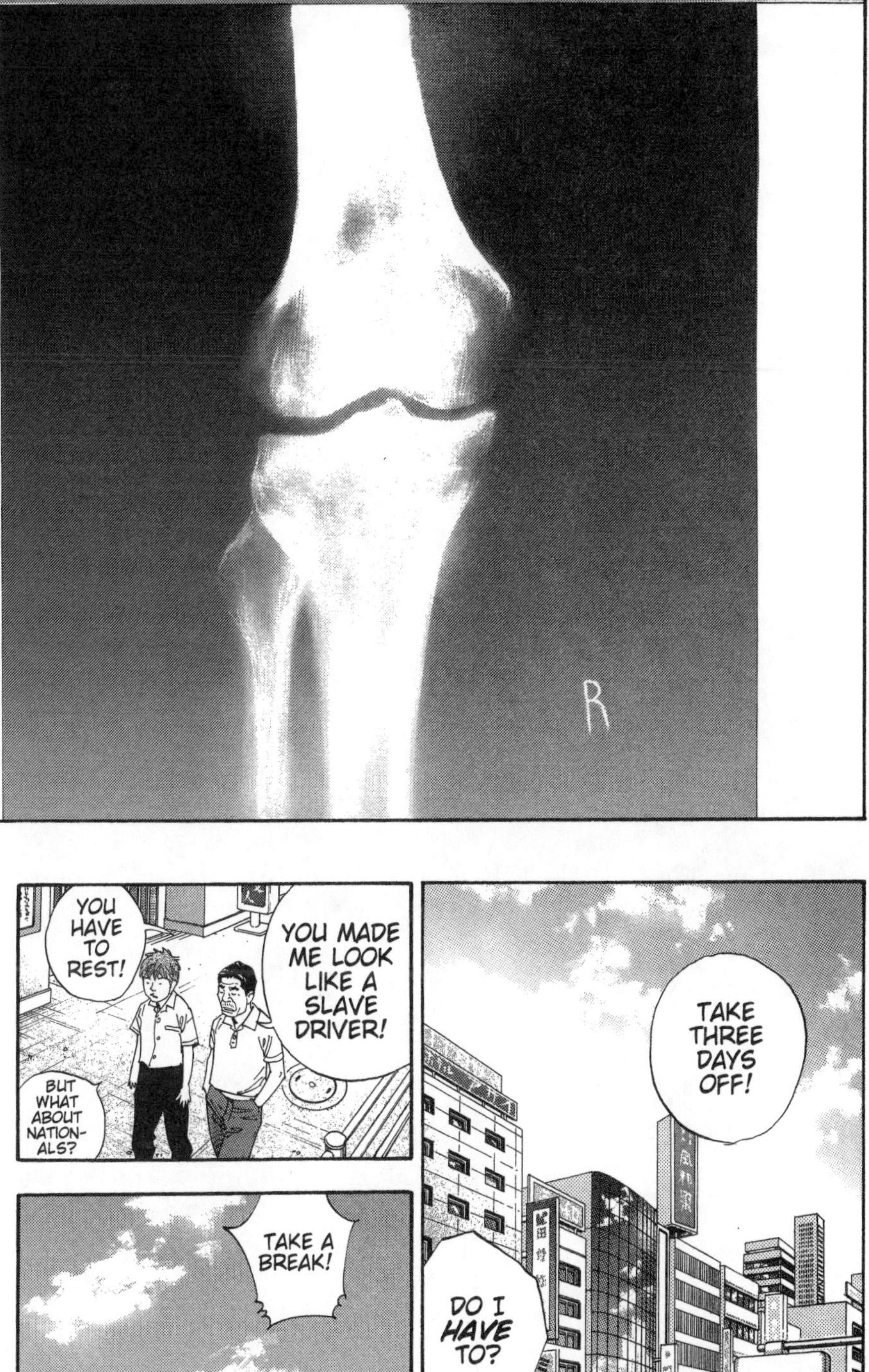
R
TAKE THREE DAYS OFF!
DO I *HAVE* TO?
YOU MADE ME LOOK LIKE A SLAVE DRIVER!
YOU HAVE TO REST!
BUT WHAT ABOUT NATION-ALS?
TAKE A BREAK!

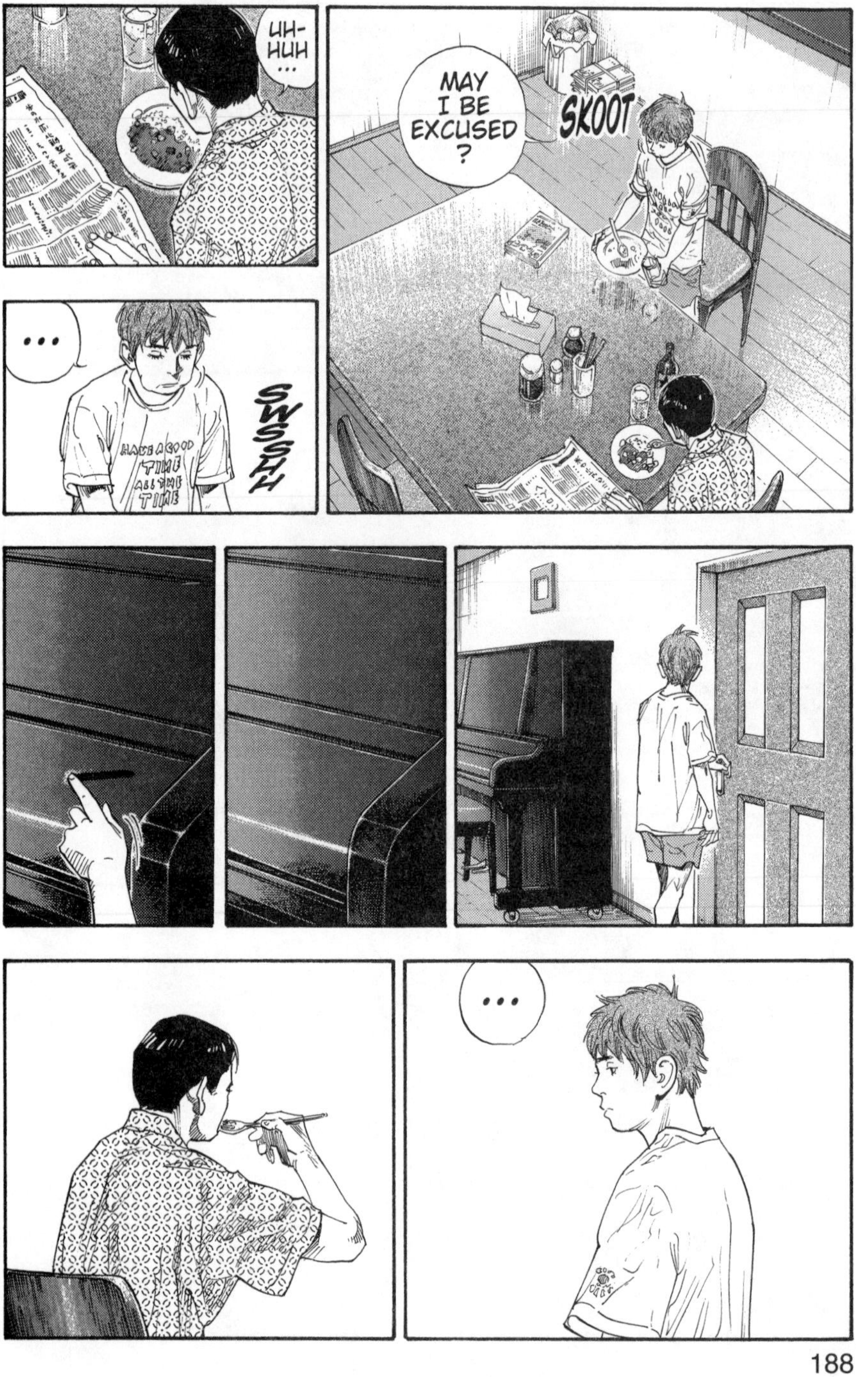
MAY I BE EXCUSED?
SKOOT
UH-HUH...
...
HAVE A GOOD TIME ALL THE TIME
SWSSHH
...

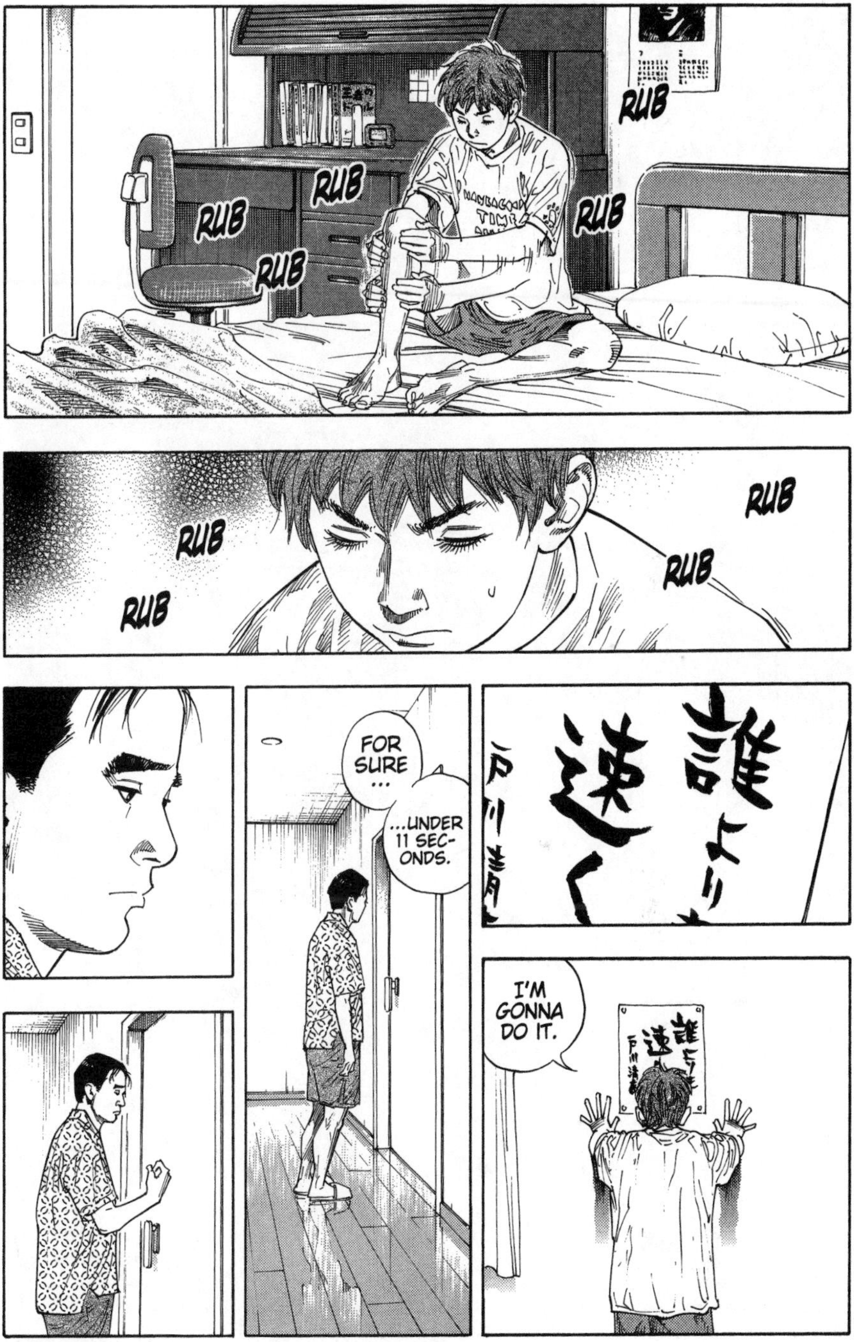
RUB
RUB
RUB
RUB
RUB
RUB
RUB
RUB
RUB
誰より速く
戸川清
I'M GONNA DO IT.
FOR SURE...
...UNDER 11 SECONDS.

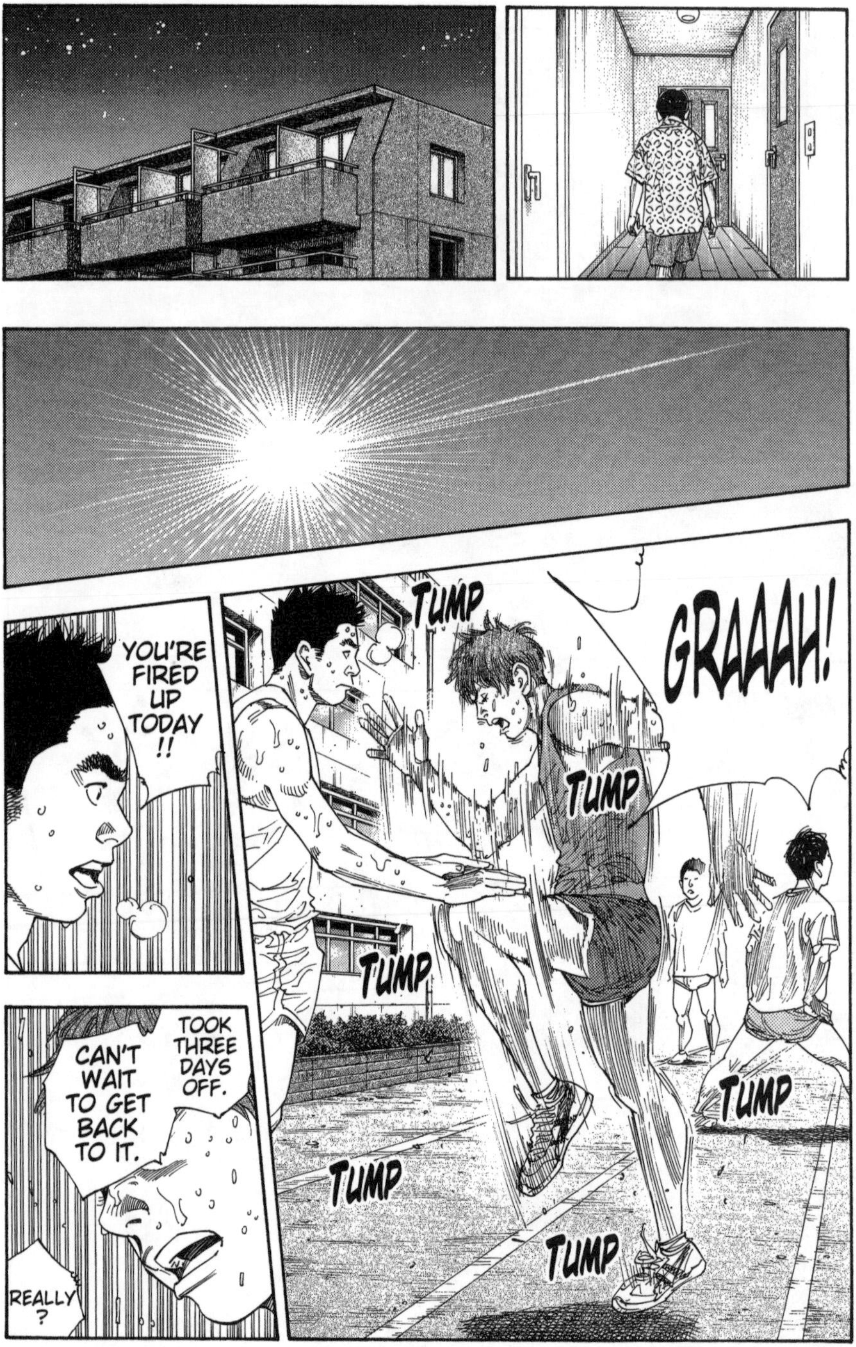
GRAAAH!
TUMP
TUMP
TUMP
TUMP
TUMP
TUMP
YOU'RE FIRED UP TODAY !!
TOOK THREE DAYS OFF.
CAN'T WAIT TO GET BACK TO IT.
REALLY ?

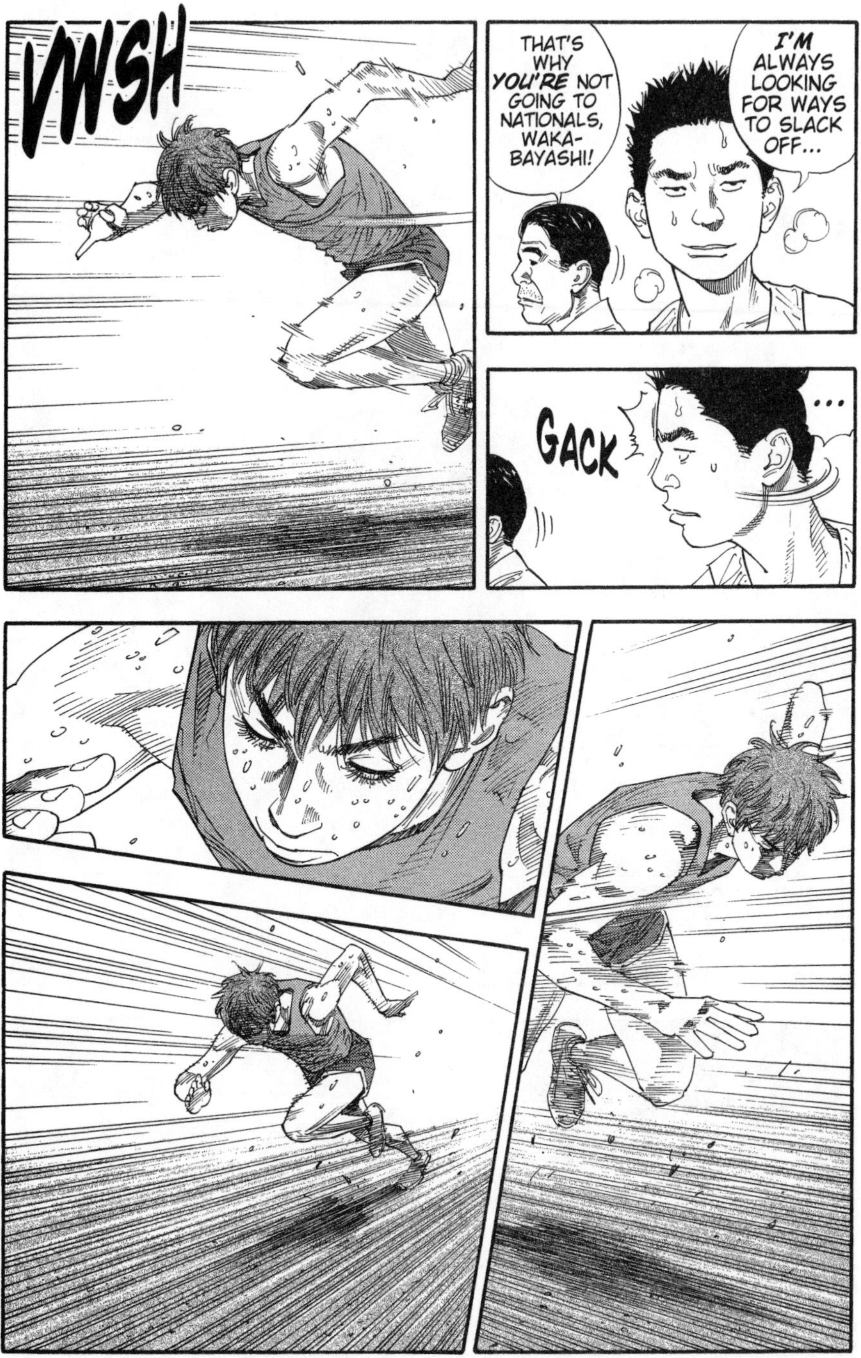
I'M ALWAYS LOOKING FOR WAYS TO SLACK OFF...
THAT'S WHY YOU'RE NOT GOING TO NATIONALS, WAKA-BAYASHI!
...
GACK
VWSH

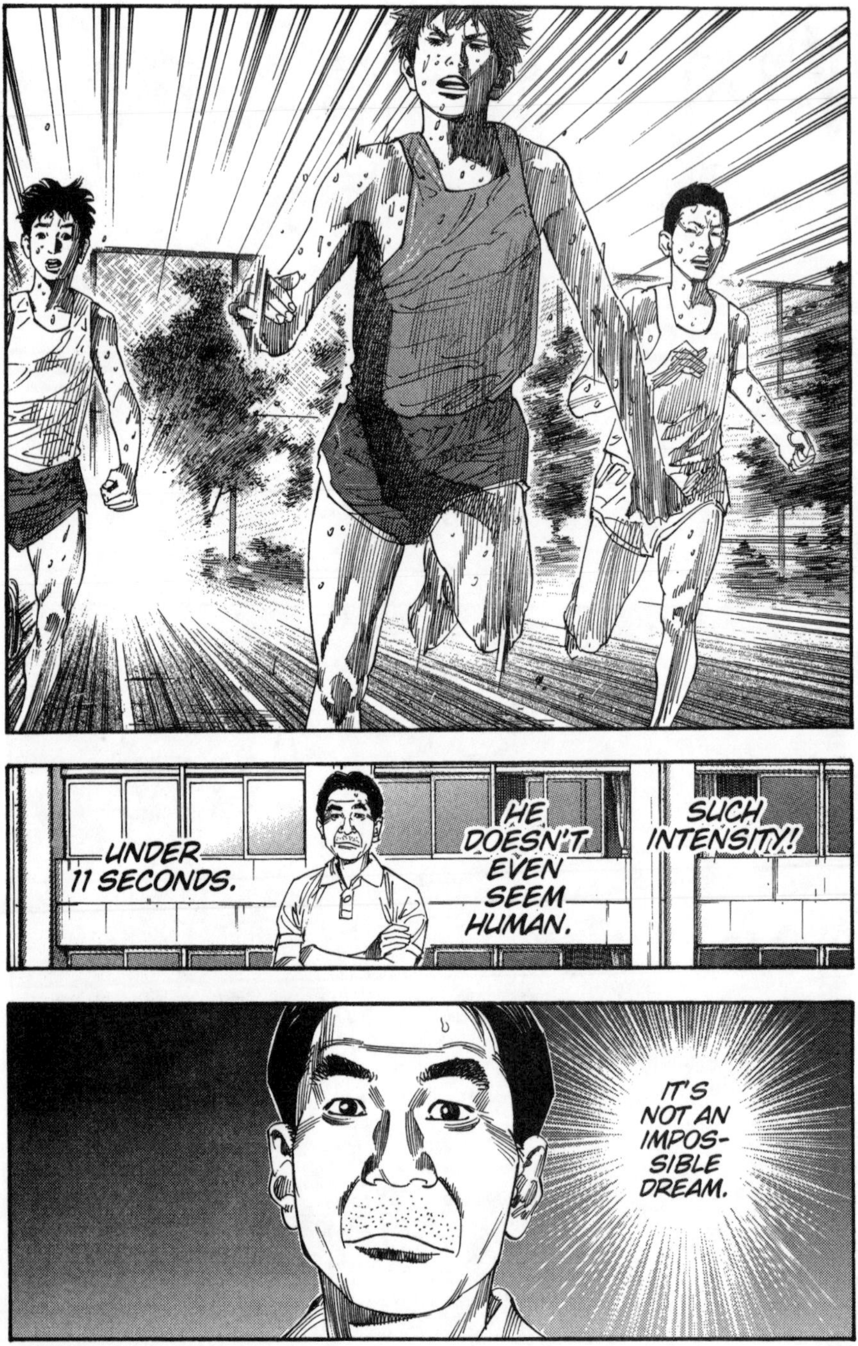
SUCH INTENSITY!
HE DOESN'T EVEN SEEM HUMAN.
UNDER 11 SECONDS.
IT'S NOT AN IMPOS-SIBLE DREAM.

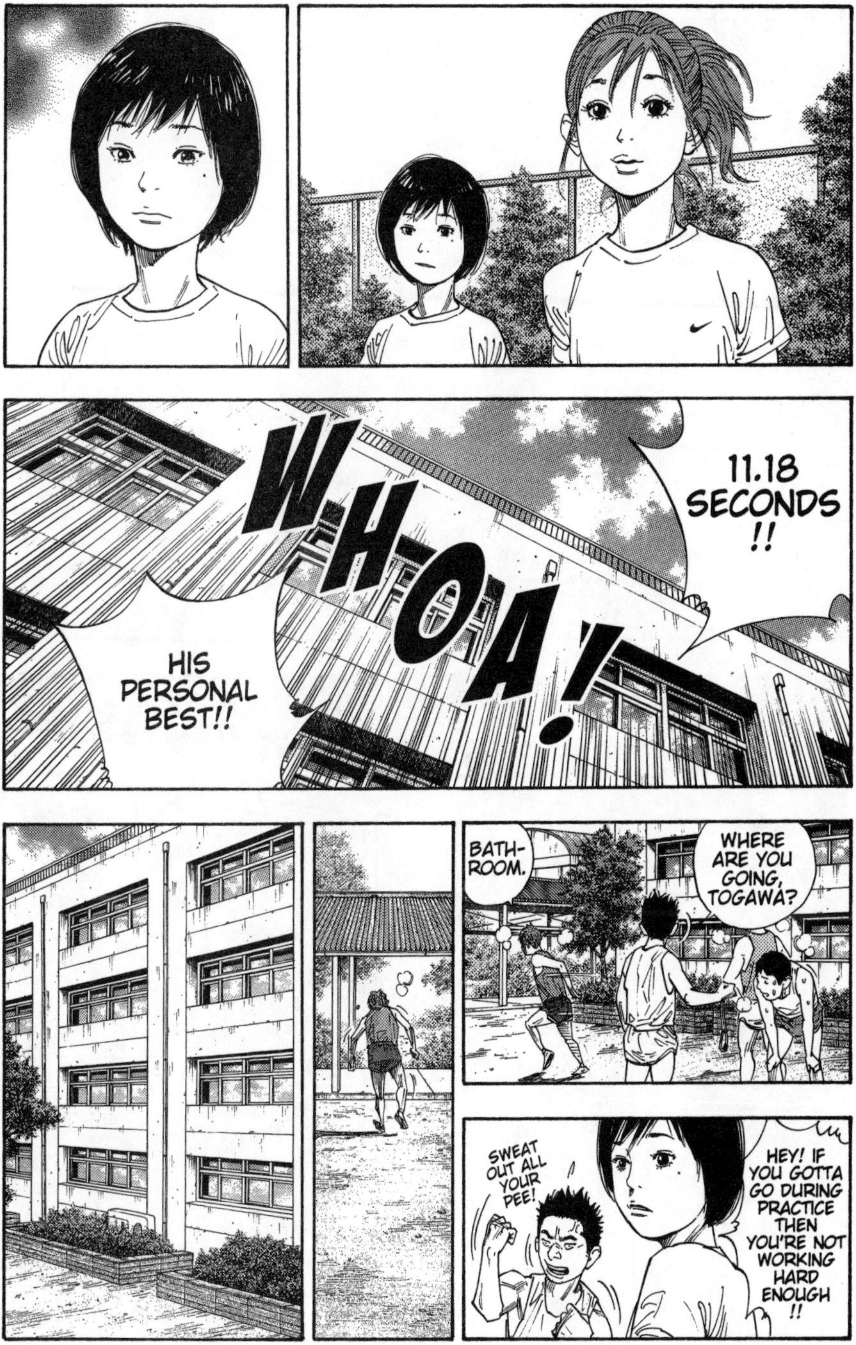
11.18 SECONDS !!
WHOA!
HIS PERSONAL BEST!!
WHERE ARE YOU GOING, TOGAWA?
BATH-ROOM.
HEY! IF YOU GOTTA GO DURING PRACTICE THEN YOU'RE NOT WORKING HARD ENOUGH !!
SWEAT OUT ALL YOUR PEE!

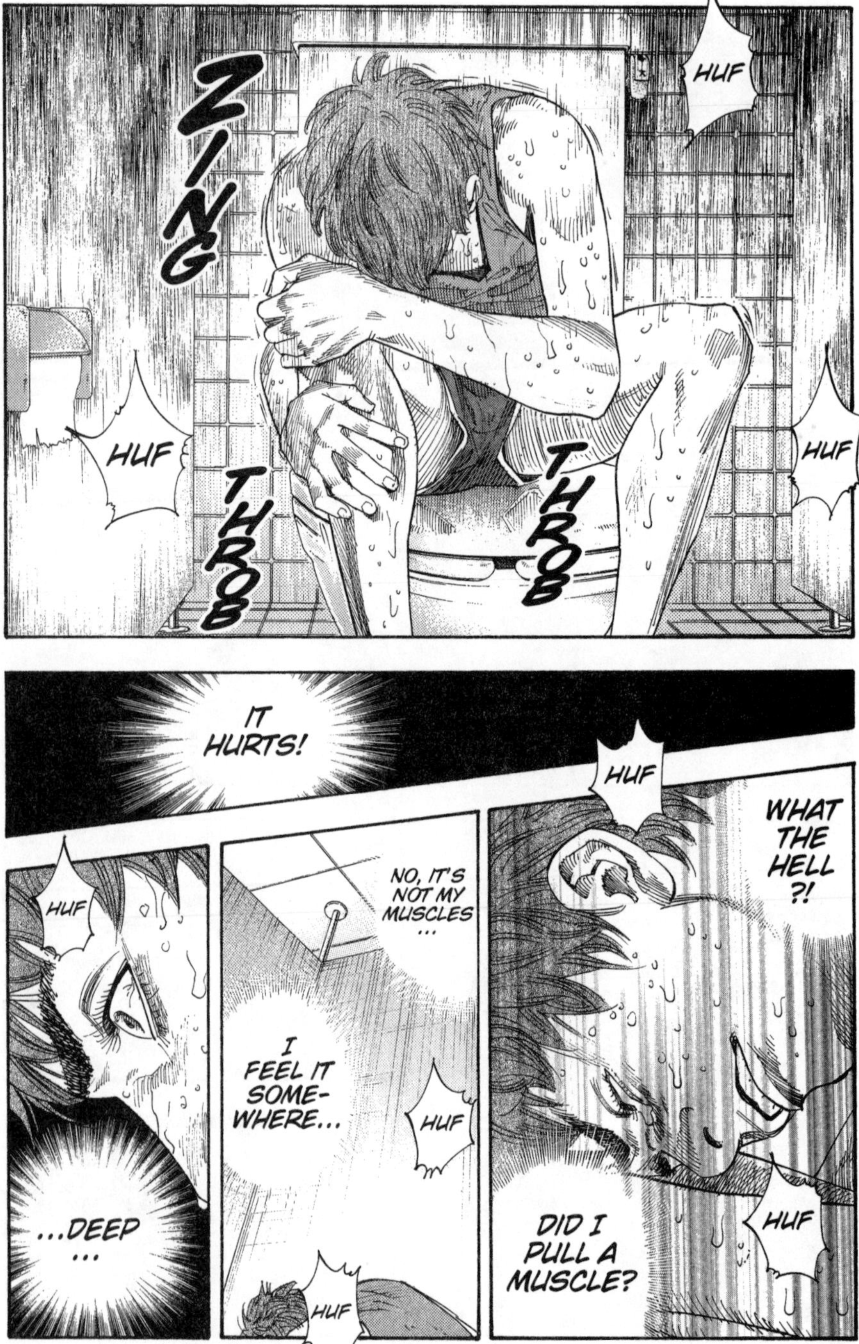
HUF
ZING
HUF
THROB
THROB
HUF
IT HURTS!
HUF
WHAT THE HELL ?!
DID I PULL A MUSCLE?
HUF
NO, IT'S NOT MY MUSCLES ...
I FEEL IT SOME-WHERE...
HUF
HUF
HUF
...DEEP ...

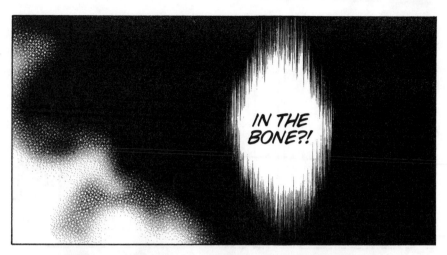

IN THE BONE?!

NO! DOC SAID THAT WASN'T IT.

I'VE COME SO FAR. I CAN'T STOP NOW.

SWSSHH

SKRK

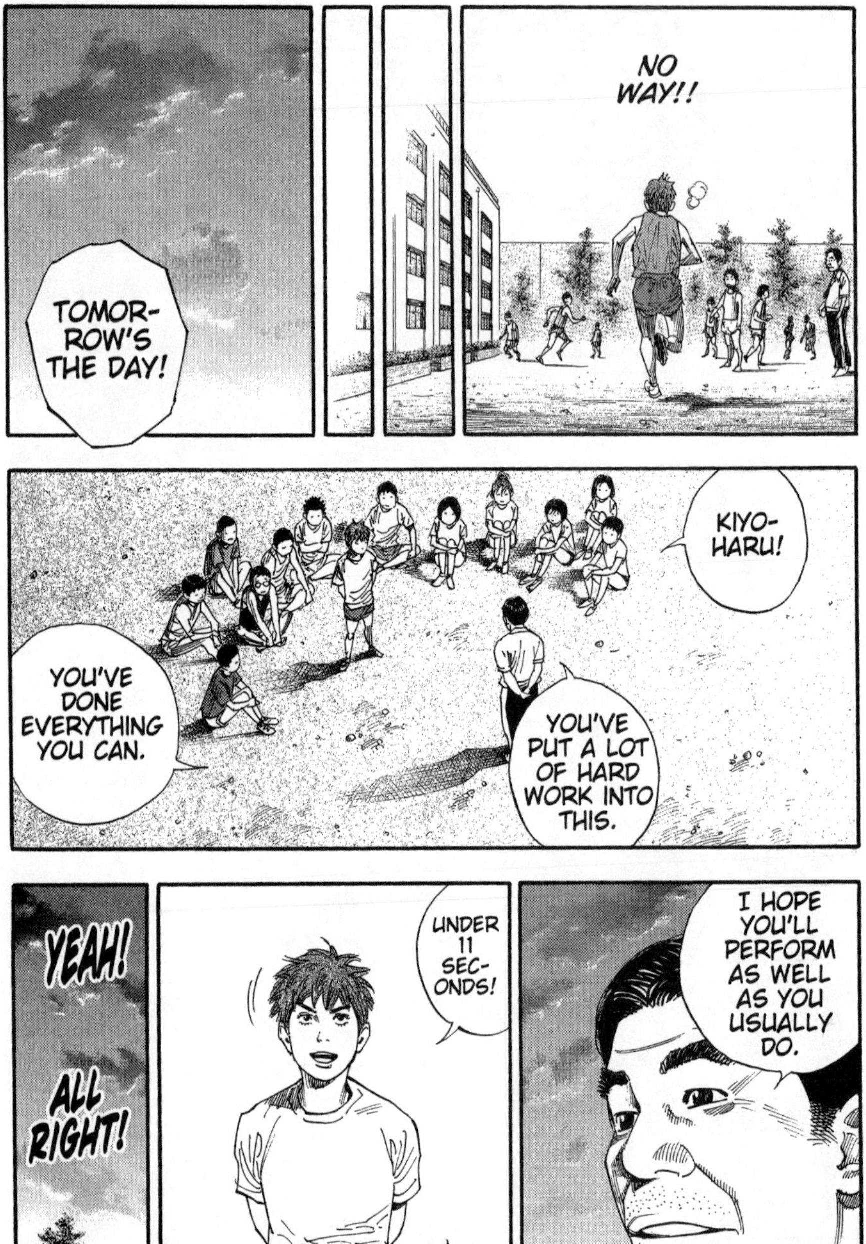
NO WAY!!
TOMOR-ROW'S THE DAY!
KIYO-HARU!
YOU'VE PUT A LOT OF HARD WORK INTO THIS.
YOU'VE DONE EVERYTHING YOU CAN.
I HOPE YOU'LL PERFORM AS WELL AS YOU USUALLY DO.
UNDER 11 SEC-ONDS!
YEAH!
ALL RIGHT!

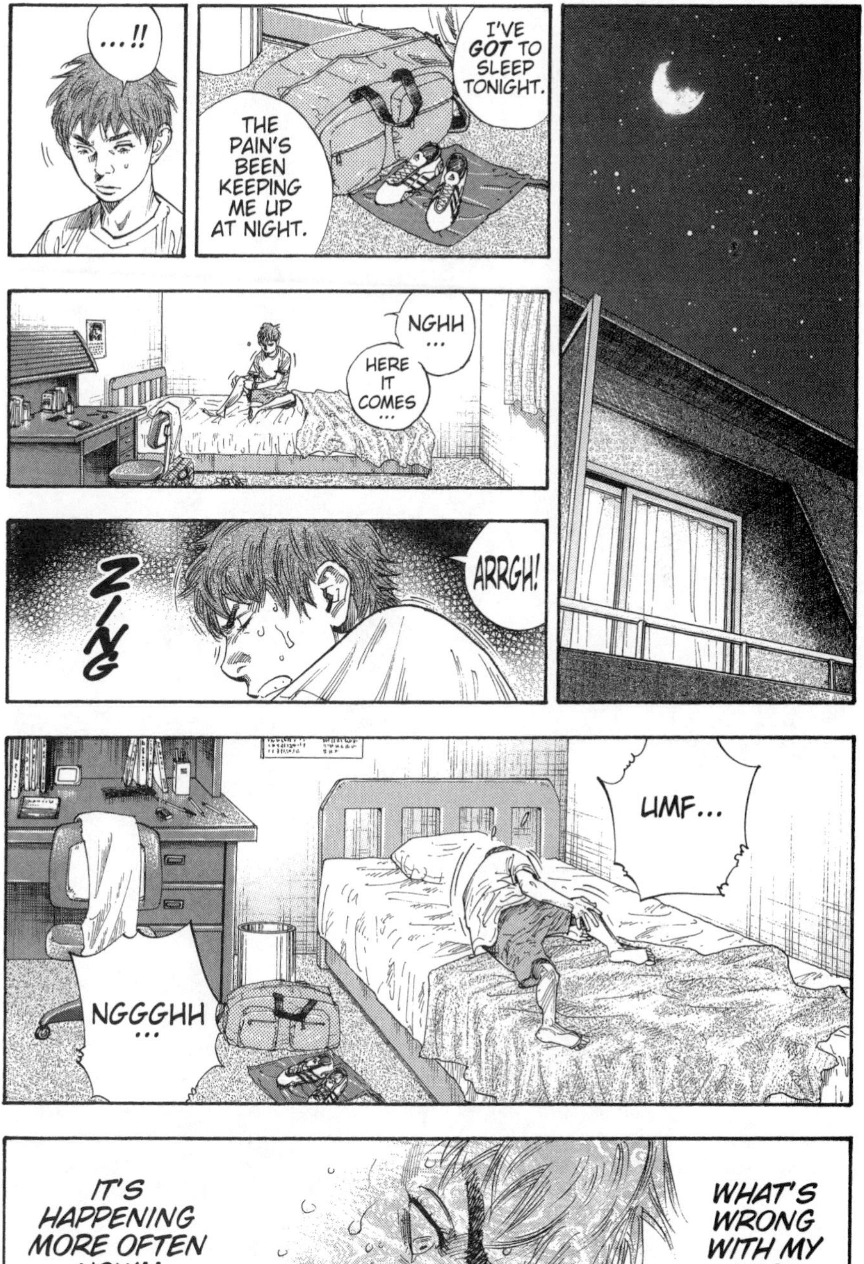
I'VE GOT TO SLEEP TONIGHT.
THE PAIN'S BEEN KEEPING ME UP AT NIGHT.
...!!
NGHH...
HERE IT COMES...
ARRGH!
ZING
UMF...
NGGGHH...
WHAT'S WRONG WITH MY LEG?
IT'S HAPPENING MORE OFTEN NOW!!

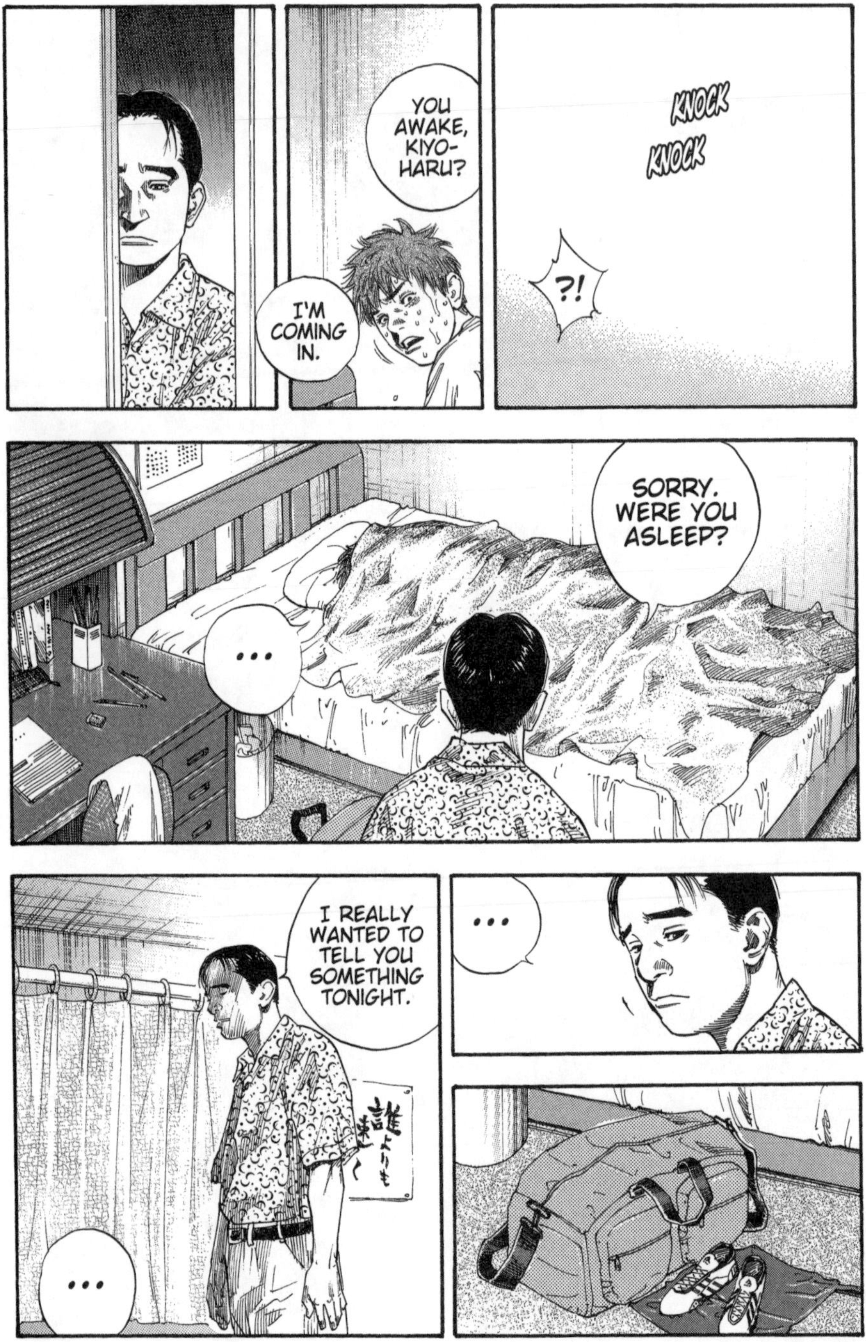
KNOCK
KNOCK
?!
YOU AWAKE, KIYO-HARU?
I'M COMING IN.
SORRY. WERE YOU ASLEEP?
...
...
I REALLY WANTED TO TELL YOU SOMETHING TONIGHT.
誰よりも速く
...

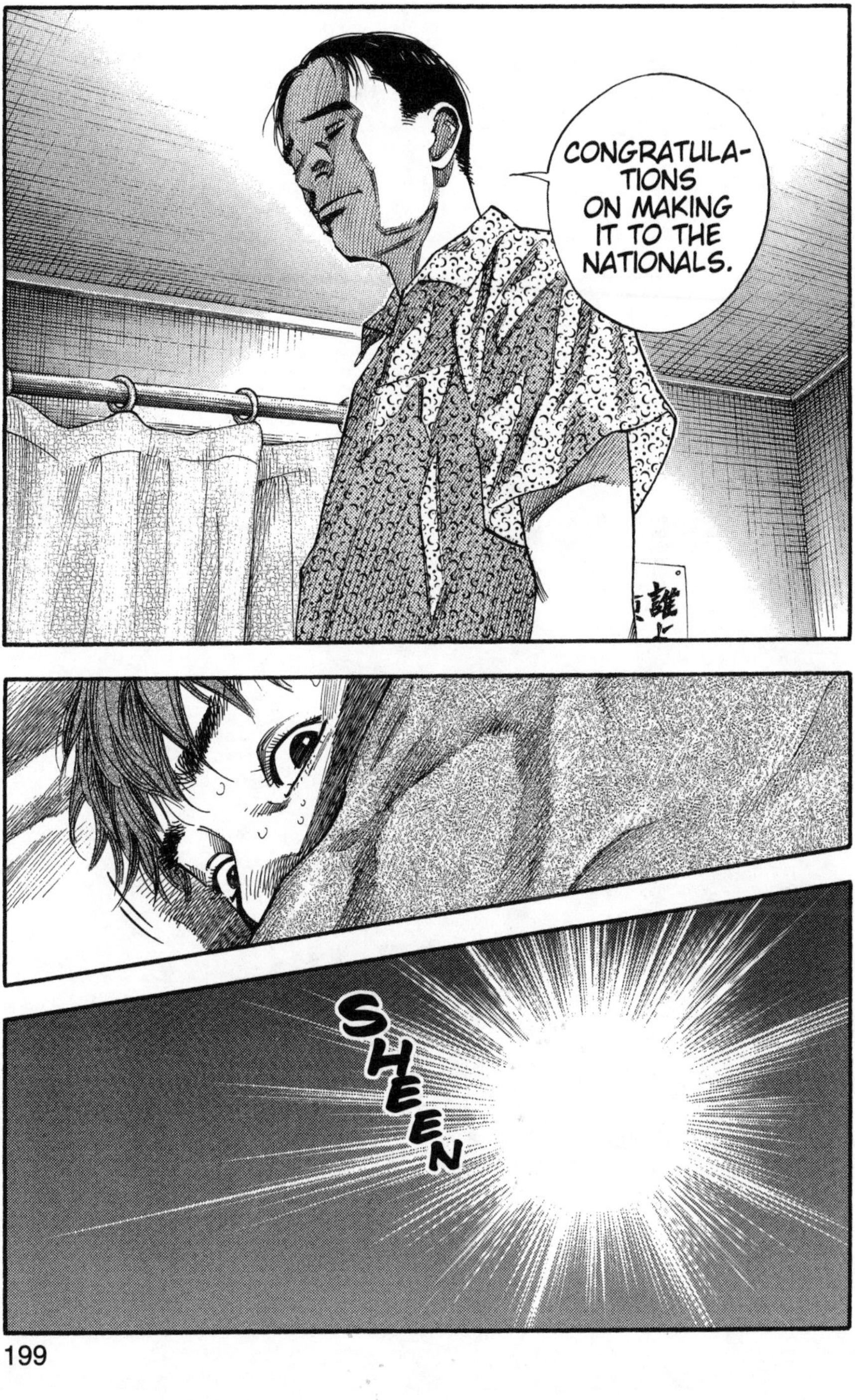
CONGRATULA-TIONS ON MAKING IT TO THE NATIONALS.
SHEEN

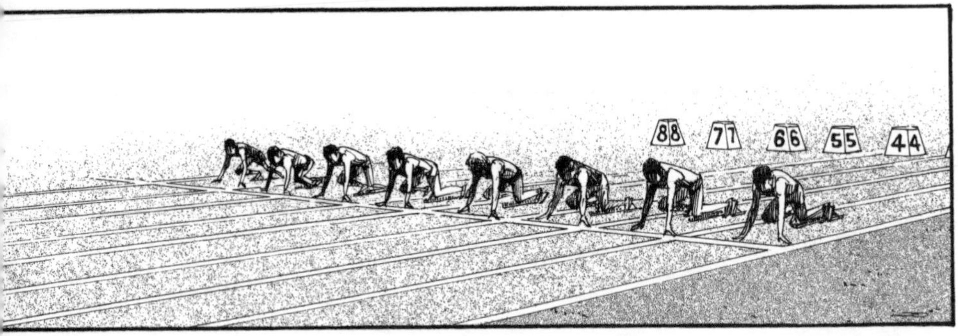
88
77
66
55
44

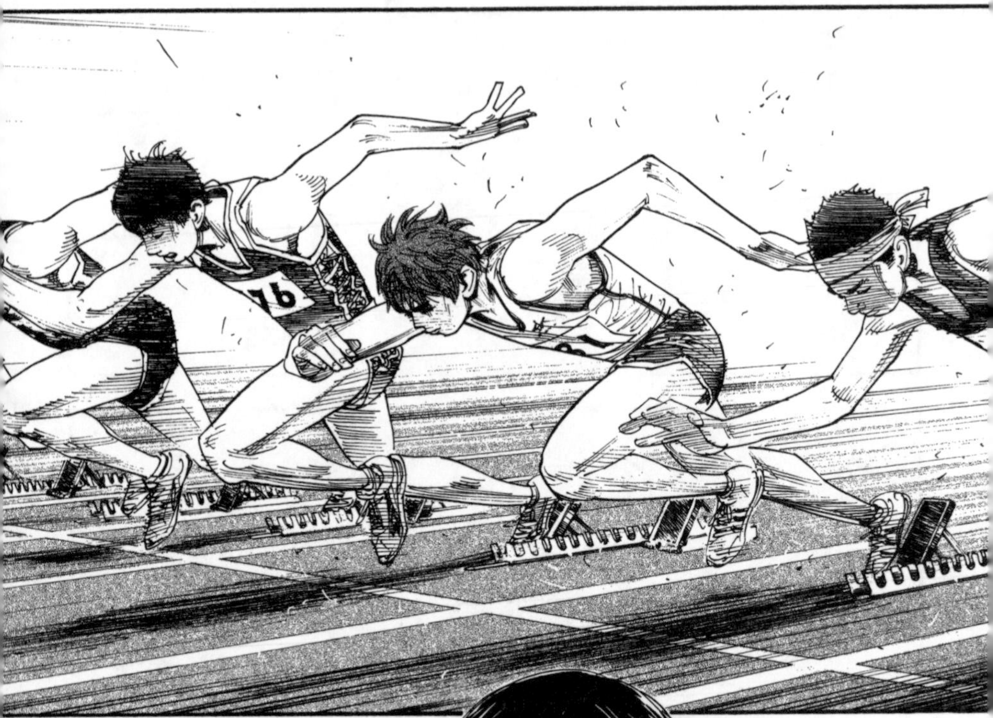
76

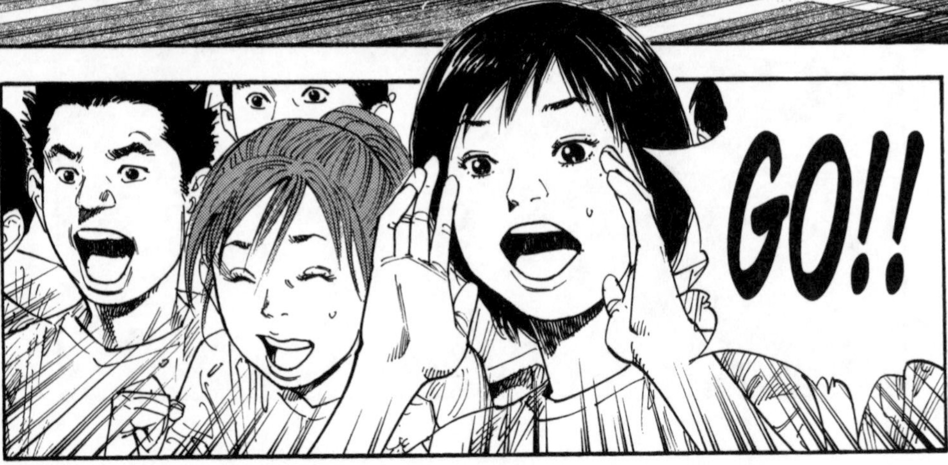
GO!!

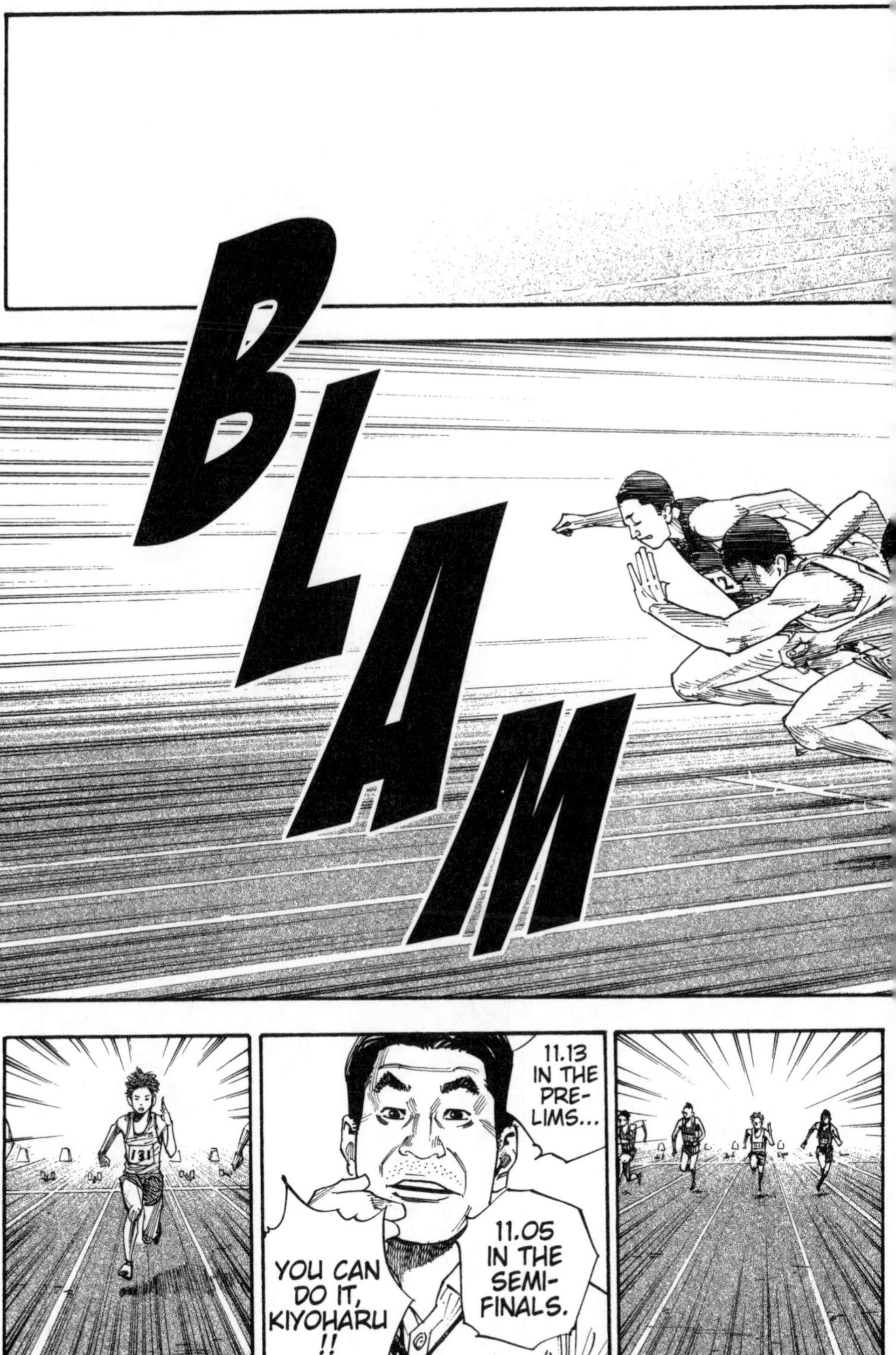
BLAM
11.13 IN THE PRE-LIMS...
11.05 IN THE SEMI-FINALS.
YOU CAN DO IT, KIYOHARU!!

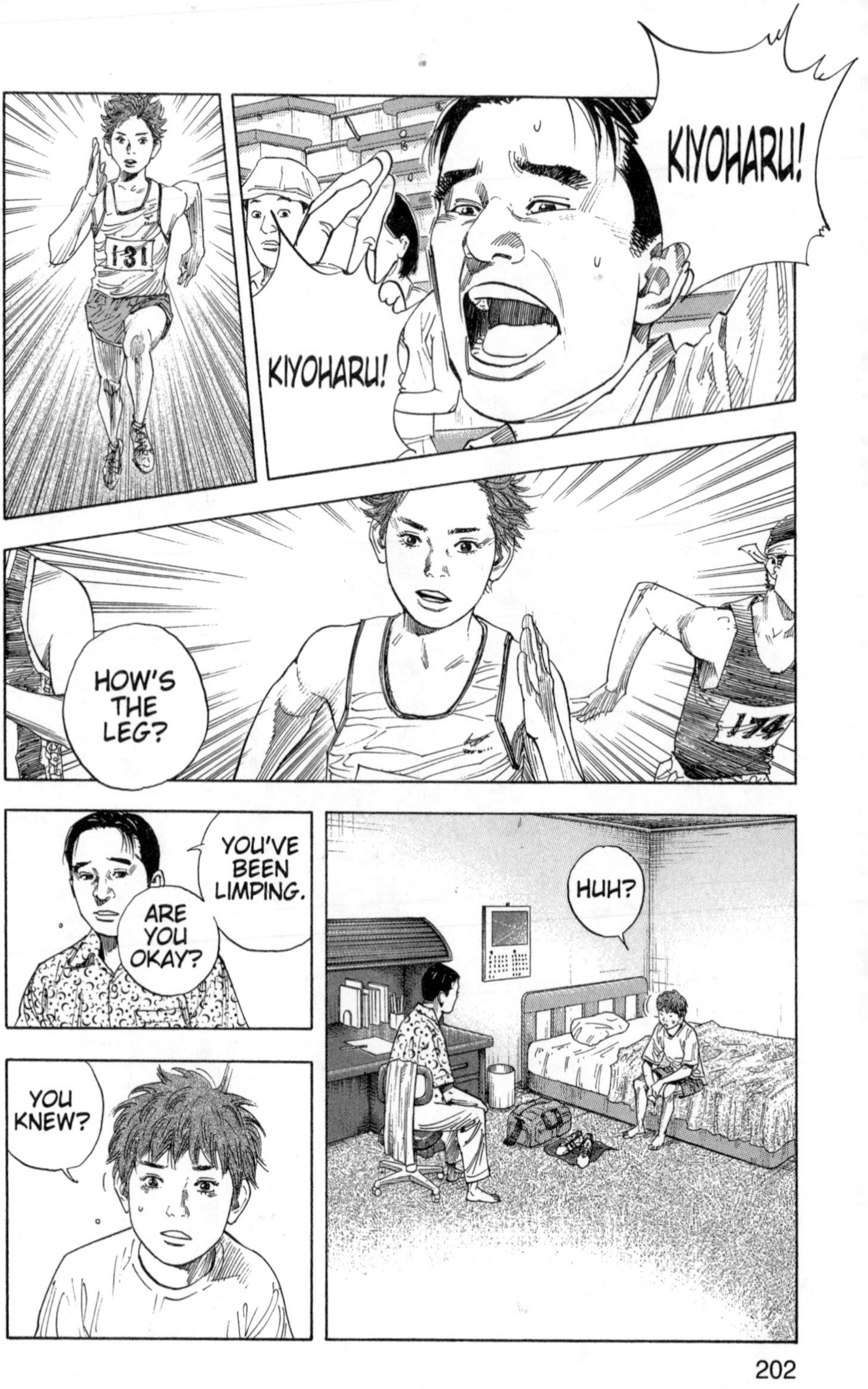
KIYOHARU!
KIYOHARU!
HOW'S THE LEG?
HUH?
YOU'VE BEEN LIMPING.
ARE YOU OKAY?
YOU KNEW?

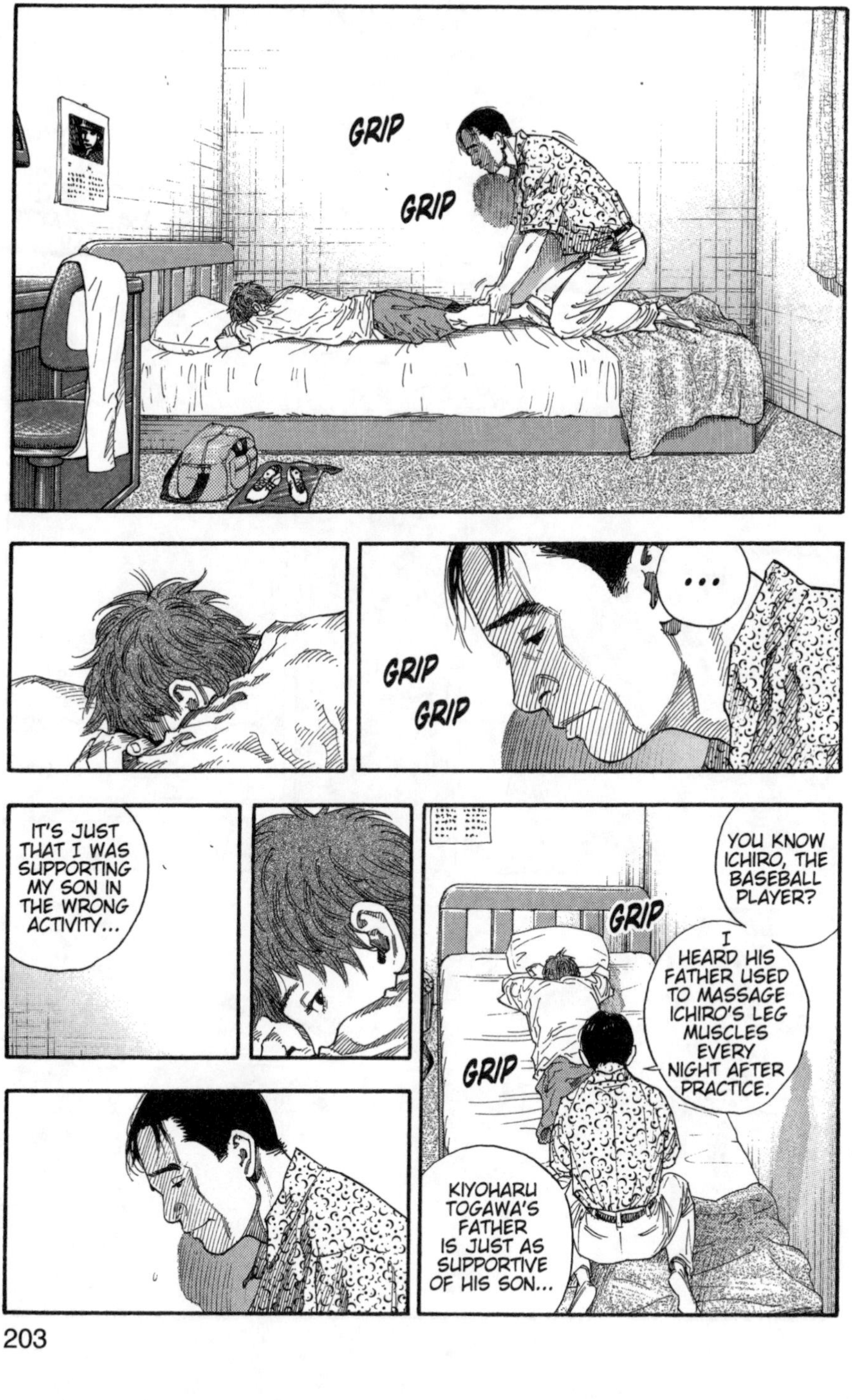
GRIP
GRIP
...
GRIP
GRIP
YOU KNOW ICHIRO, THE BASEBALL PLAYER?
GRIP
I HEARD HIS FATHER USED TO MASSAGE ICHIRO'S LEG MUSCLES EVERY NIGHT AFTER PRACTICE.
GRIP
KIYOHARU TOGAWA'S FATHER IS JUST AS SUPPORTIVE OF HIS SON...
IT'S JUST THAT I WAS SUPPORTING MY SON IN THE WRONG ACTIVITY...

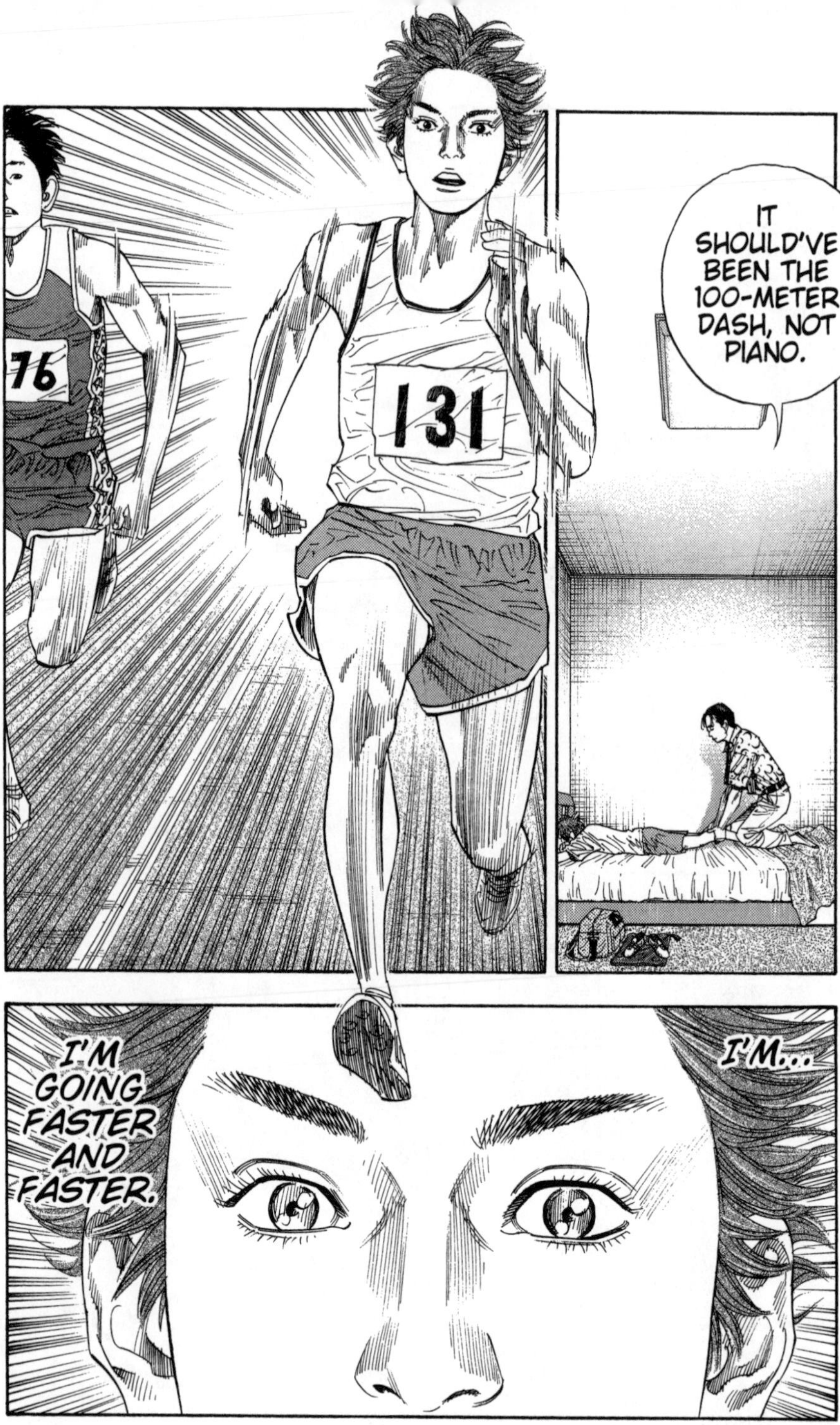
IT SHOULD'VE BEEN THE 100-METER DASH, NOT PIANO.
131
76
I'M...
I'M GOING FASTER AND FASTER.

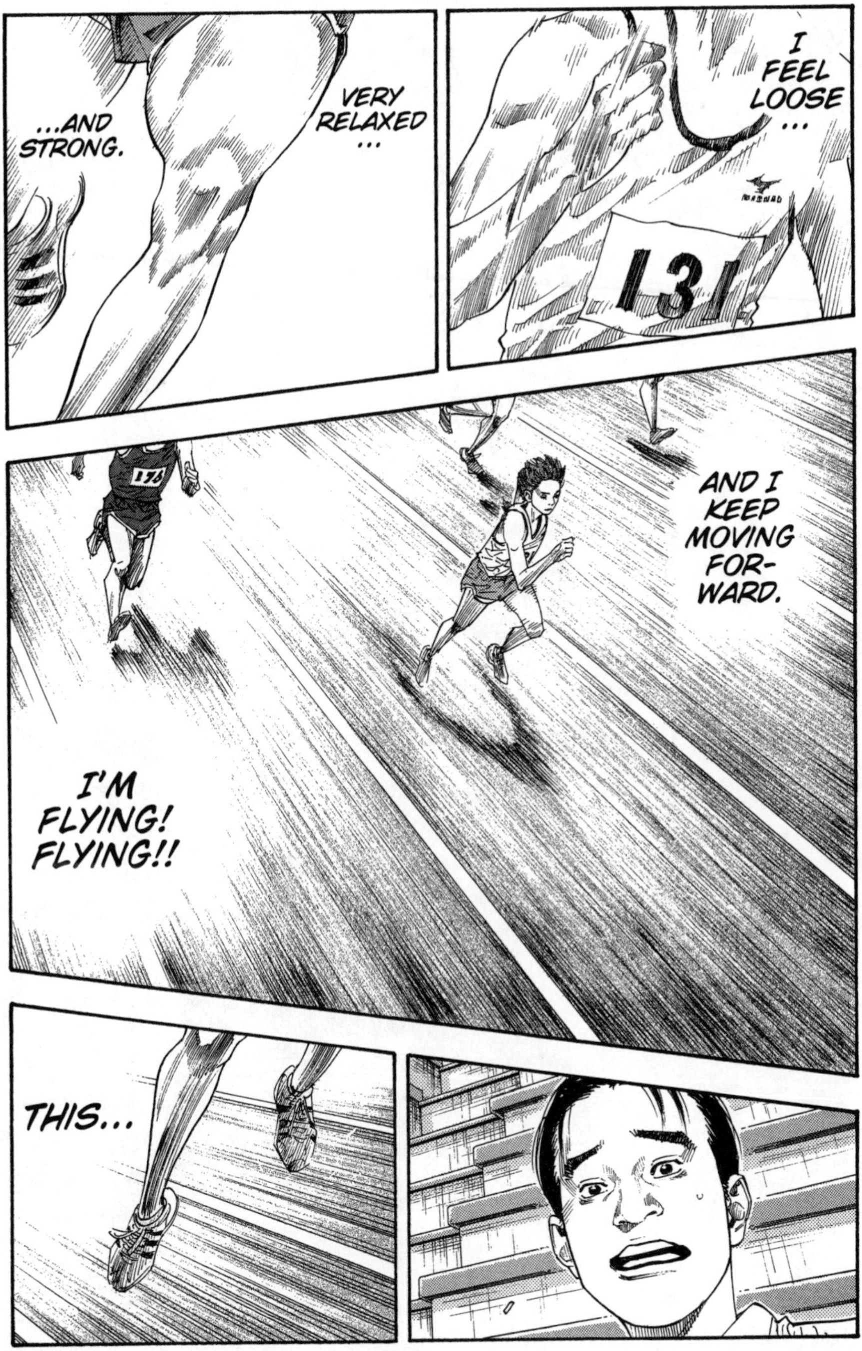
I FEEL LOOSE...
VERY RELAXED...
...AND STRONG.
AND I KEEP MOVING FOR-WARD.
I'M FLYING! FLYING!!
THIS...

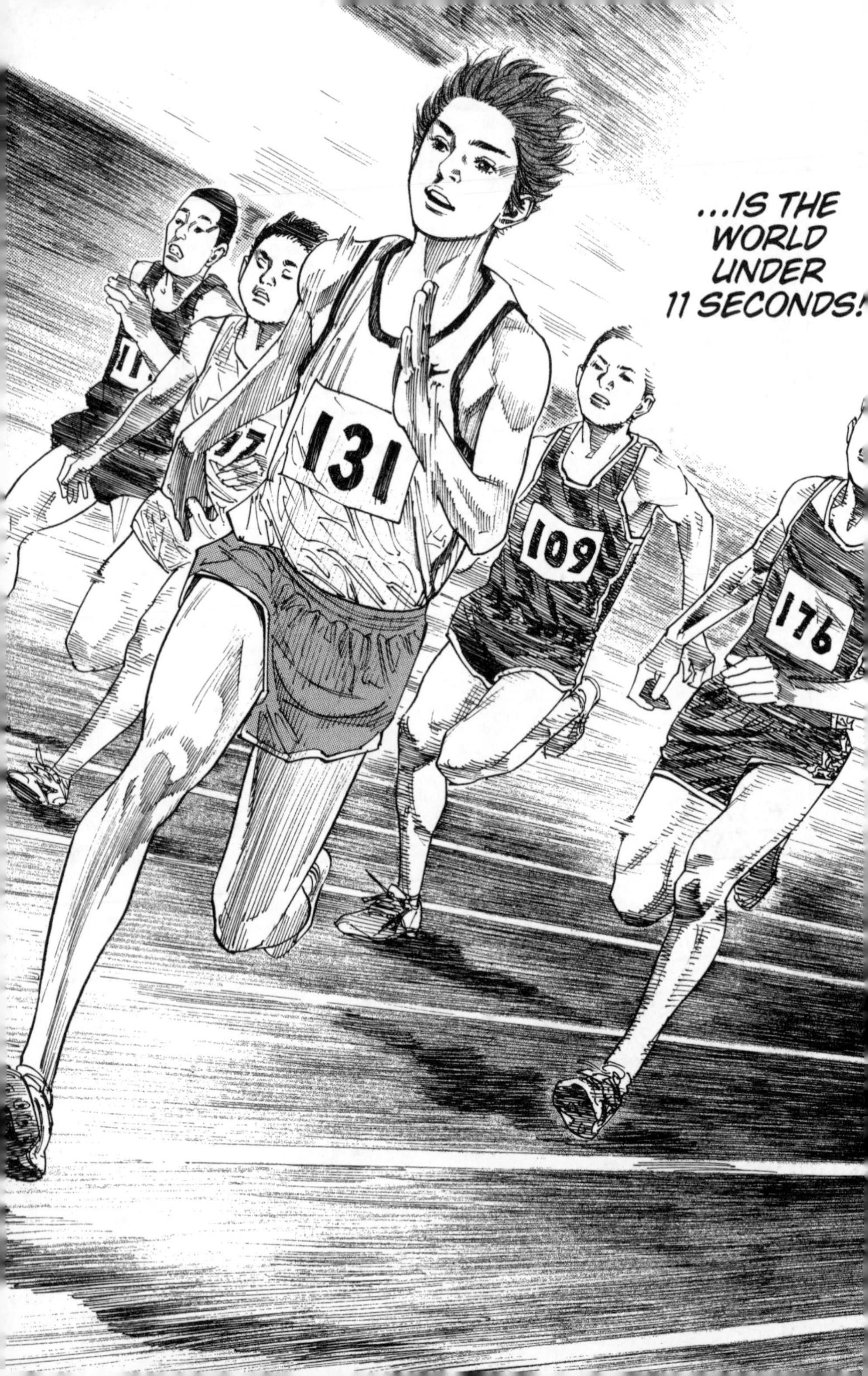
...IS THE WORLD UNDER 11 SECONDS!
131
109
176

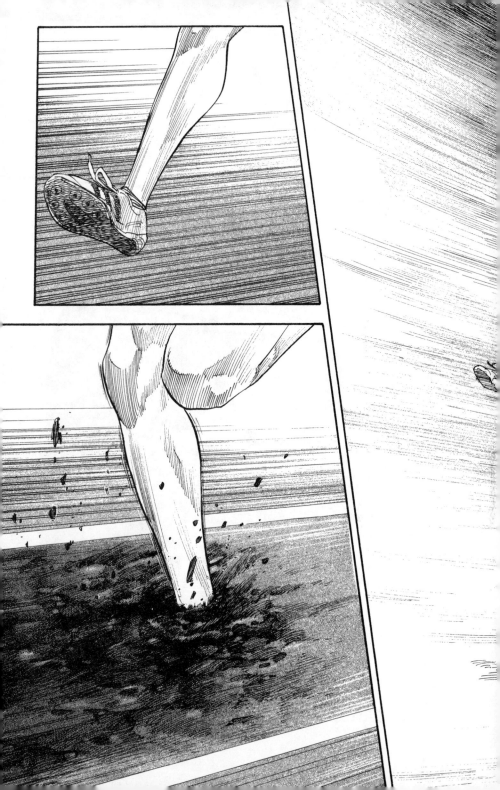

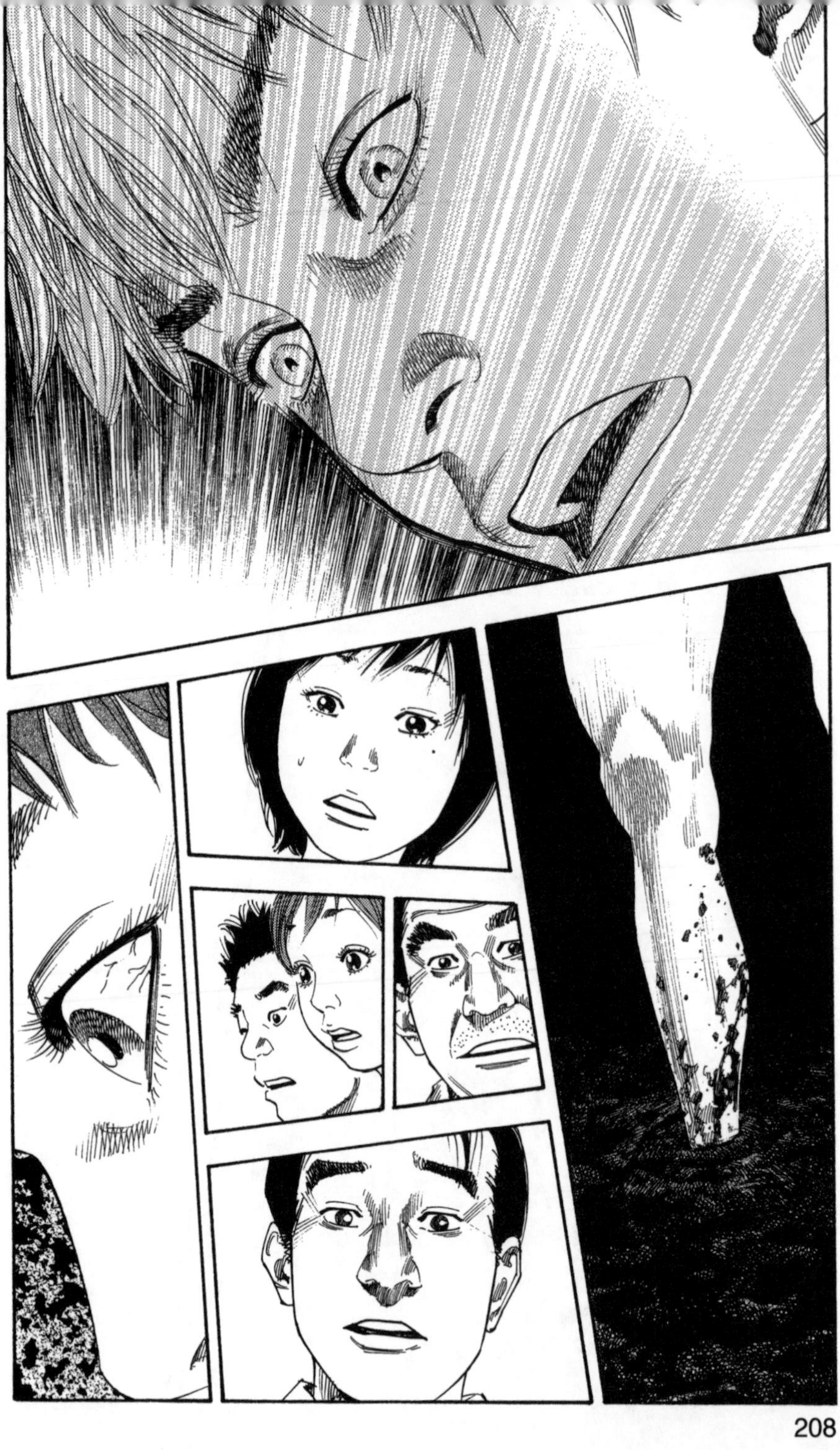

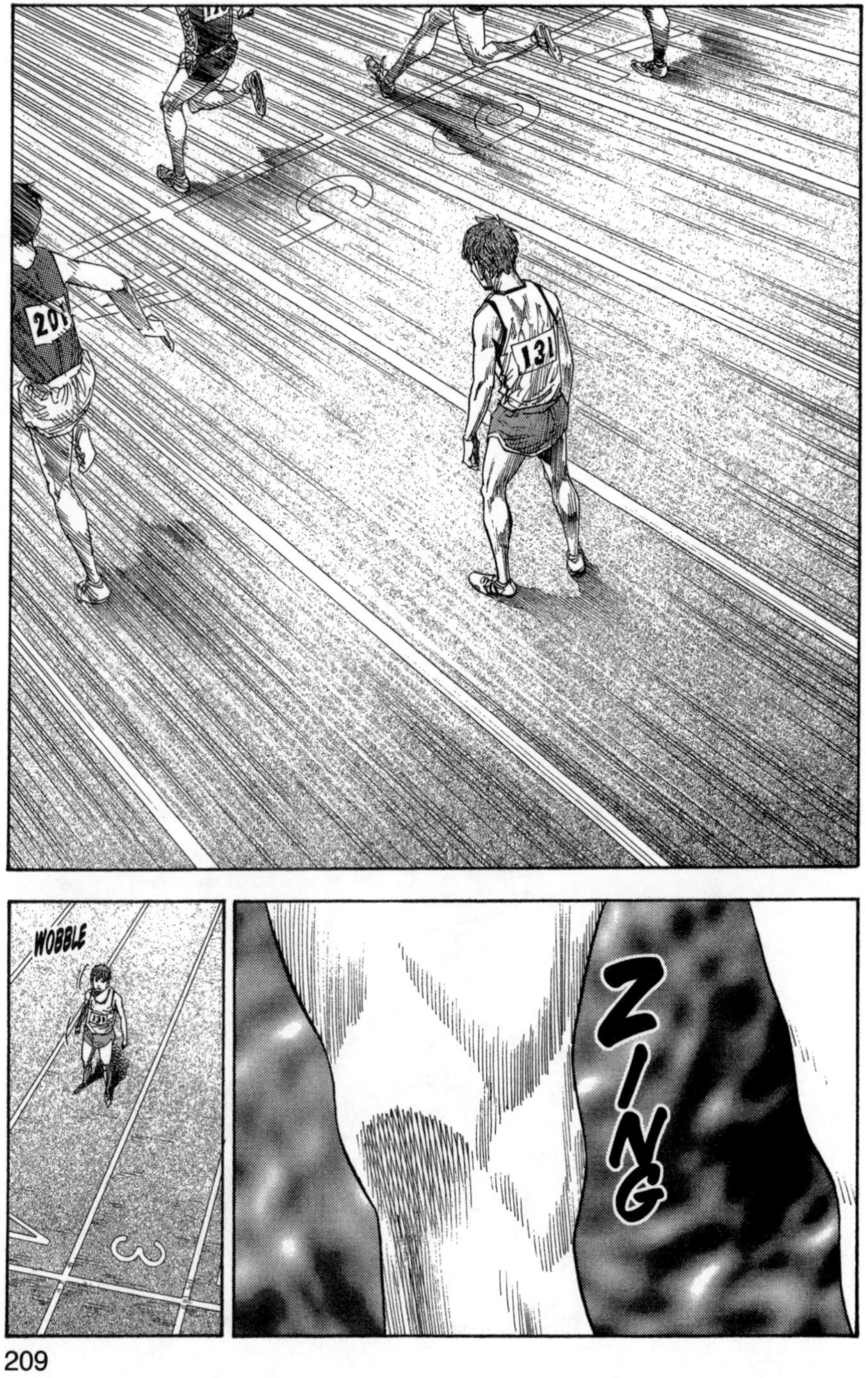
ZING
WOBBLE

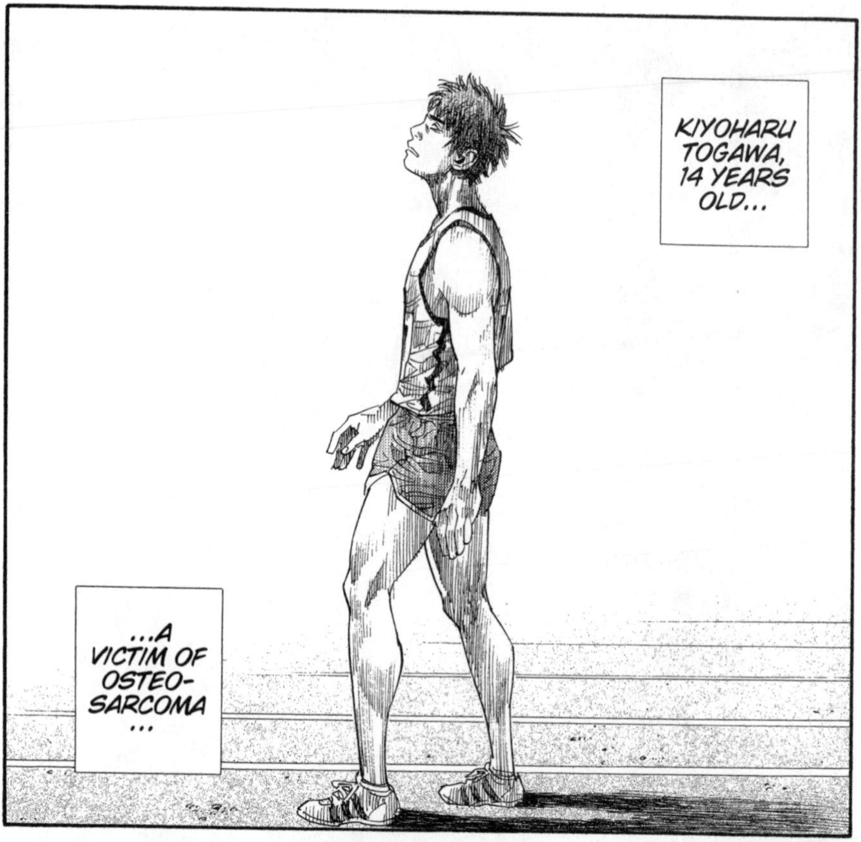
KIYOHARU TOGAWA, 14 YEARS OLD...
...A VICTIM OF OSTEO-SARCOMA...

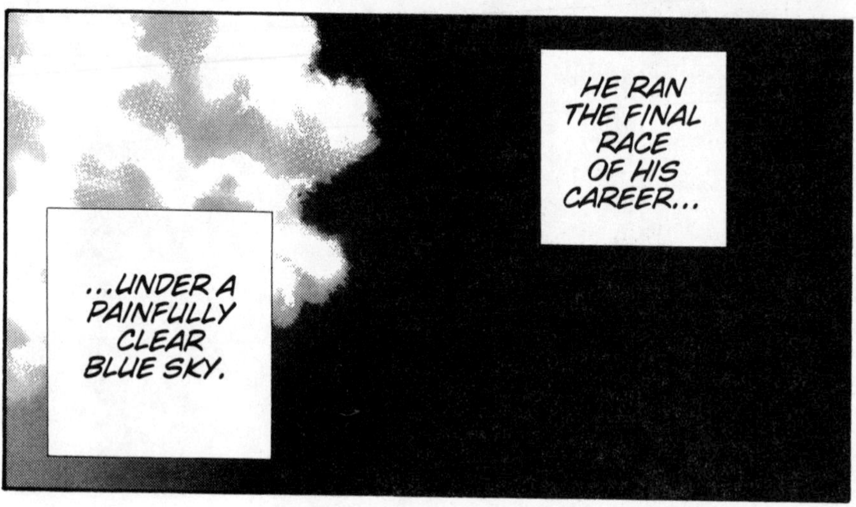
HE RAN THE FINAL RACE OF HIS CAREER...
...UNDER A PAINFULLY CLEAR BLUE SKY.

Editorial Notes

This series follows Western name order convention, with given name followed by surname. For example, with Tomomi Nomiya, Tomomi is the first name and Nomiya is the last name. In addition, because the editor felt information about any given character's relationship to another can be gleaned from dialogue and other narrative clues, honorifics such as *-san* and *-kun* have been dropped. On occasion, however, an honorific has been retained for added effect.

Signs and other background text have been left in the original Japanese to retain the integrity of Inoue's artwork. This series takes place in Japan, so it makes sense that store signs and other background material are in Japanese. Translations will be provided in footnotes placed in between panels when such information is necessary to drive the narrative flow and when it is not graphically intrusive. Otherwise, translations will appear here in the Editorial Notes.

Page 27, panel 4: *Kochikame* is an abbreviated way of referring to Osamu Akimoto's *Kochira Katsushi-ku Kameari Koen Mae Hashutsujo,* the longest continuously running manga series of all time. *Kochikame* began its run in *Weekly Shonen Jump* in 1976 and is currently "only" up to volume 160.

Page 27, panel 4: *Jojo's* is an abbreviated reference to a popular manga series by Hirohiko Araki called *Jojo's Bizarre Adventure*. Another long-running series that started in *Weekly Shonen Jump,* *Jojo's* is currently up to part 7, volume 15, but the sum of all its parts totals a whopping 95 volumes. Inoue pokes a little fun at the astounding longevity of *Jojo's* and *Kochikame* by exaggerating the length of each series.

Page 39: In a moment of self-referential fun, Inoue depicts the TV show that Kanta and his friend are watching as none other than *Slam Dunk,* the anime adaptation of Inoue's other basketball manga series. *Slam Dunk* is now available in English from VIZ Media.

Page 157: Sports festivals, or *undokai,* are annual events held by schools in Japan where students compete in numerous athletic activities such as running races. Some schools, as shown here with Kiyoharu's elementary school, feature races in which the parents also participate.

Real Vol. 2
VIZ Signature Edition

Story & Art by
Takehiko Inoue

Translation/John Werry
Touch-up & Lettering/Steve Dutro
Cover & Graphic Design/Yukiko Kamematsu Whitley
Editor/Andy Nakatani

Editor in Chief, Books/Alvin Lu
Editor in Chief, Magazines/Marc Weidenbaum
VP, Publishing Licensing/Rika Inouye
VP, Sales & Product Marketing/Gonzalo Ferreyra
VP, Creative/Linda Espinosa
Publisher/Hyoe Narita

Published by VIZ Media, LLC
P.O. Box 77010
San Francisco, CA 94107

10 9 8 7 6 5 4 3 2 1
First printing, October 2008

www.viz.com store.viz.com

CAT EYED BOY

IN THE SHADOWS, WHERE NO MAN OR DEMON DARES GO, LIVES A HALF-HUMAN, HALF-MONSTER CHILD. LIKE A SUPERNATURAL VIGILANTE, CAT EYED BOY PROTECTS THE INNOCENT AND PUNISHES THE WICKED.

CAN ANYONE—OR ANYTHING—ESCAPE HIS JUDGMENT?

story and art by
KAZUO UMEZU
CAT EYED BOY
volume one

Find out in the *Cat Eyed Boy* manga from KAZUO UMEZU, creator of *The Drifting Classroom* and *Orochi: Blood.*

Buy the two-volume series today!

story and art by
KAZUO UMEZU
CAT EYED BOY
volume two

VIZ Signature

On sale at store.viz.com
Also available at your local bookstore and comic store.

RATED T+ FOR OLDER TEEN ratings.viz.com

VIZ MEDIA www.viz.com